THE JESUS PUZZLE

From reviews of Earl Doherty's second book, *Challenging the Verdict:
A Cross-Examination of Lee Strobel's 'The Case for Christ'*

"Well-intentioned people like Lee Strobel and his 'expert witnesses' in *The
Case for Christ* have been inspired to speak half-truths, misrepresentations,
and plain absurdities in defense of Christian doctrine. Earl Doherty confutes
Strobel and his theologians point for point so thoroughly and convincingly
that one is left wondering, how did I not see that before? Christian
apologetics' faith-based thought processes contrast with Doherty's reasoned
refutation and clearly reveal how intellectual integrity is sacrificed at
religion's altar of 'believe at any price'."

> LEE SALISBURY, a former evangelical church pastor 1978-1988;
> writer and speaker for atheist groups and publications from 1992.

"In his systematic refutation of Strobel's book, Earl Doherty takes on not only
Strobel but the many prominent apologists Strobel interviews and quotes
throughout the book….Doherty performs a great service by taking on the new
generation of slingers of the same old hash. His book is a great tool. When
someone says, 'Here, read Strobel, and your skeptical questions will all be
answered!' we may hand them Doherty's counterblast….Doherty's chief goal
is not to argue the Christ Myth theory, but neither does he soft-pedal it, since it
often simply pops up as the glowing alternative once one sees the preposterous
nature of the apologists' arguments."

> ROBERT PRICE, Fellow of the Jesus Seminar and author of
> *Deconstructing Jesus* and *The Incredible Shrinking Son of Man*; from
> a review appearing in Free Inquiry magazine, Summer 2002.

AGE OF REASON PUBLICATIONS

Dedicated to attaining an Age of Reason in the application
of rational thought to society's laws, ethics and beliefs,
and to entering upon an age of reason in our individual lives.

<www.AgeOfReason.org>

THE JESUS PUZZLE

Did Christianity Begin with a Mythical Christ?

Earl Doherty

Age of Reason Publications

Ottawa Canada

Published in 2005 by Age of Reason Publications
PO Box 49059, 110 Place d'Orleans
Ottawa, ON K1C 7E4
Canada.
www.AgeOfReason.org

Fourth Printing: January 2005
Fifth Printing: September 2006
Sixth Printing: October 2007
ISBN 0-9689259-1-X

Previously published by Canadian Humanist Publications
ISBN 0-9686014-0-5
First Printing October, 1999
Second Printing (with revisions) September, 2000
Third Printing June, 2001

Canadian Cataloguing in Publication Data

Doherty, Earl, 1941-
The Jesus puzzle : did Christianity begin with a mythical Christ?
Earl Doherty. – 4th print.

Includes bibliographic references and index.
ISBN: 0-9689259-1-X

1. Jesus Christ—Historicity. I. Title

BT303.2.D64 2005   232.9'08   C2005-900091-0

Cover created by Richard Young
Text designed by Greg Singer

Printed and bound in Canada

To the memory of
Trevor Banks
who supported me all the way
but didn't quite make it
to the finish line

iv

CONTENTS

About Translations

There are many available translations of the New Testament. In this book, I have not followed any single one, since all of them will occasionally betray Gospel preconceptions in their translation of the epistles, and because parts of a given translation are, in my view, more accurate and effective than other parts. I have sometimes combined the features of more than one translation in a given quotation, and may occasionally include an element of my own, usually in the direction of rendering the original Greek more literally, for clarity's sake and to eliminate preconceptions. For most biblical quotations I have indicated the translation(s) used, including my own.

Abbreviations of translations: NEB (New English Bible); NASB (New American Standard Bible); NIV (New International Version); RSV (Revised Standard Version); NAB (New American Bible); KJV (King James Version). I have drawn most often on the NEB, with its modern, informal style which can bring out clarity of meaning.

Glossary and Abbreviations

Most explanatory information is provided in the text and Notes.

Apocrypha = ("hidden") writings not regarded as sacred, excluded from the canon of scripture. Many are included in bibles after the canonical texts.

Christology = study or teaching about the nature of Jesus / Christ

Diaspora = Jewish communities spread throughout the Roman Empire and beyond, as a collective entity, in both a cultural and geographical sense

Exegete / exegesis = one who interprets the meaning of a biblical text / the process of doing so

Kerygma = "proclamation" about Jesus by the early Christian apostles

Parousia = the "presence": meaning arrival in glory of Christ at the End-time

Redaction = editing of a document or source according to the editor's interests

Soteriology = theories/teaching about redemption, as bestowed by a savior god

New Testament references: eg, Galatians 3:23-25 = chapter 3, verses 23 to 25. Abbreviations of document title are used only within brackets. (See Index for abbreviations of each of the New Testament documents.)

f = 'and following': means an unspecified number of pages after the one stated; p. = page; n. = Note; ch. = chapter; *c* = circa (around, referring to a date); ie = that is; eg = for example. In the Index only: c. = century; d. = died.

op.cit. = In bracketed references to published works, this signifies 'the book title by this author stated in the last reference to that author.'

Brackets: In a quotation, round brackets signify paraphrase or clarification, square brackets signify the present writer's comments.

End-notes are numbered consecutively throughout the book.

THE TWELVE PIECES OF THE JESUS PUZZLE

This list is a summary overview only and does not follow the layout of the book

---

[1] Jesus of Nazareth and the Gospel story cannot be found in Christian writings earlier than the Gospels, the first of which (Mark) was composed only in the late first century.

[2] There is no non-Christian record of Jesus before the second century. References in Flavius Josephus (end of first century) can be dismissed as later Christian insertions.

[3] The early epistles, such as Paul and Hebrews, speak of their Christ Jesus as a spiritual, heavenly being revealed by God through scripture, and do not equate him with a recent historical man. Paul is part of a new "salvation" movement acting on revelation from the Spirit.

[4] Paul and other early writers place the death and resurrection of their Christ in the supernatural/mythical world, and derive their information about these events, as well as other features of their heavenly Christ, from scripture.

[5] The ancients viewed the universe as multi-layered: matter below, spirit above. The higher world was regarded as the superior, genuine reality, containing spiritual processes and heavenly counterparts to earthly things. Paul's Christ operates within this system.

[6] The pagan "mystery cults" of the period worshiped savior deities who had performed salvific acts which took place in the supernatural/mythical world, not on earth or in history. Paul's Christ shares many features with these deities.

[7] The prominent philosophical-religious concept of the age was the intermediary Son, a spiritual channel between the ultimate transcendent God and humanity. Such intermediary concepts as the Greek Logos and Jewish Wisdom were models for Paul's heavenly Christ.

[8] All the Gospels derive their basic story of Jesus of Nazareth from one source: whoever wrote the Gospel of Mark. The Acts of the Apostles, as an account of the beginnings of the Christian apostolic movement, is a second century piece of myth-making.

[9] The Gospels are not historical accounts, but constructed through a process of "midrash," a Jewish method of reworking old biblical passages and tales to reflect new beliefs. The story of Jesus' trial and crucifixion is a pastiche of verses from scripture.

[10] "Q", a lost sayings collection extracted from Matthew and Luke, made no reference to a death and resurrection and can be shown to have had no Jesus at its roots: roots which were ultimately non-Jewish. The Q community preached the kingdom of God, and its traditions were eventually assigned to an invented founder who was linked to the heavenly Jesus of Paul in the Gospel of Mark.

[11] The initial variety of sects and beliefs about a spiritual Christ shows that the movement began as a multiplicity of largely independent and spontaneous developments based on the religious trends and philosophy of the time, not as a response to a single individual.

[12] Well into the second century, many Christian documents lack or reject the notion of a human man as an element of their faith. Only gradually did the Jesus of Nazareth portrayed in the Gospels come to be accepted as historical.

INTRODUCTION

Once upon a time, someone wrote a story about a man who was God.

We don't know who that someone was, or where he wrote his story. We are not even sure when he wrote it, but we do know that several decades had passed since the supposed events he told of. Later generations gave this storyteller the name of "Mark," but if that was his real name, it was only by coincidence.

Other writers followed after, and they enlarged on the first man's tale. They borrowed much of what he had written, reworked it in their own particular ways and put in some additional material. By the time another half century had passed, almost everyone who followed the religion of these storytellers accepted their work as an account of actual historical events and a real historical man. And so did the people who came afterwards, for close to two thousand years.

About two centuries ago, these "Gospels" began to be subjected to some searching examination. Not only were they found to contradict one another on important matters, it was eventually realized that they had been conceived and put together in ways, and with motivations, which suggested that they were not reliable historical accounts. Their fantastic and uncritical dimensions, such as the miracles and the involvement of God and the supernatural, placed them outside the genre of history writing as we know it. That process of scholarly examination has continued to this day, with results that have undermined the very foundations of the Christian faith.

Recently, a scholar began his book about the Jesus of history, the actual man and his career that were supposed to lie behind those non-historical accounts, with this sentence:

"On a spring morning in about the year 30 CE,[1] three men were executed by the Roman authorities in Judea. . . ." (E. P. Sanders, *The Historical Figure of Jesus*, p.1)

But is even this statement to be questioned? Is even this piece of "irreducible data" a part of the tale written by the storyteller who penned the first Gospel? Did that third man crucified by the Romans on a hill in Judea, beside the two highway brigands, have any historical existence at all?

The story told in the Gospel of Mark first begins to surface toward the end of the first century CE. Yet the curious fact is that when we search for that story in all the non-Gospel documents written before that time, it is nowhere to be found. It is missing even from certain documents produced after that period, some extending into the latter half of the second century.

If we had to rely on the letters of the earliest Christians, such as Paul and those who wrote most of the other New Testament epistles, we would be hard pressed to find anything resembling the details of the Gospel story. If we did not read Gospel associations into what Paul and the others say about their Christ Jesus, we could not even tell that this figure, the object of their worship, was a man who had recently lived in Palestine and had been executed by the Roman authorities with the help of a hostile Jewish establishment.

Could this be because they are not in fact speaking of any such figure? Could it be that if we remove those Gospel-colored glasses when reading the early Christian writers, we would find that all of them, Paul especially, have been telling us in plain and unmistakable terms exactly what the earliest Christians *did* believe in, and what the Christ they all worshiped really was?

Gaining an understandable picture of the early Christian movement, to which Paul's writings are the most important surviving witness, requires that we delve into some of the thinking of the age among both Jews and gentiles: the philosophy, views of the universe and kinds of myths those people believed in. Christianity, like all other human expression, was a product of its time and did not arise in isolation from the thought world around it. Christianity was also by nature a sect, in that it adopted and advocated new ideas which brought it into conflict with the milieu it grew out of. Thus its development must be understood in the context of how sects behave and interact with the world around them.

As part of this picture of the times, we will need to be aware of the crossover influence which took place between Judaism and the Greco-Roman society it lived in. Even as it struggled to stave off integration, Jewish culture, especially in the Diaspora (those Jewish enclaves distributed throughout the Roman empire), absorbed a great deal from its wider environment. Nor was the process a one-way street. Jewish monotheism and ethics were embraced by great numbers of gentiles who joined Jewish synagogues and sects in varying degrees of conversion. One of the features of Christianity was the formation of gentile groups who adopted Jewish ideas and practices, eventually considering themselves the new inheritors of the Jewish God's promise. These mutual crossover influences gave rise to a new faith which was a hybrid of both cultures, and a product which would shape the future of the Western world.

And yet to use the word "Christianity" or a phrase like "the Christian movement" is fundamentally misleading. It implies that the phenomenon being studied was a single entity, something unified, that it began in a particular location out of an identifiable set of circumstances and events. It also implies—so Christian tradition has it—that it was all set in motion by a specific historical figure, Jesus the Christ, and by the actions of those who responded to him. But such a picture evolved only later. In reality, "Christianity" in its beginnings was much more diffuse. It was made up of several unrelated strands of activity within the religious philosophy and culture of the time, strands which lacked any common point or figure of origin. Only through a unique set of circumstances did all of those strands come together to produce the picture of Christian origins which the world has envisioned for so long.

The focal point of that coming together was the first Gospel, the Gospel of Mark, which created the figure of Jesus of Nazareth and made him the personification of all the preceding strands. Once that turn in the road was taken (my estimation is that it took place some time around the years 85 to 90—for which I will be providing arguments), the picture thus created gradually impacted on the different expressions of the movement until eventually all those who styled themselves believers in the Christ thought that their faith had begun with an actual man who had lived at a recent time in history and had given rise to all the varied beliefs and practices they shared.

This book will continue to use the words "Christian" and "Christianity," but in that initial period before the Gospels bestowed a new meaning on them, such terms will refer to the wide variety of groups, Jewish and gentile, that believed in a Christ or Son of God who was a divine Savior, but who was not yet regarded as having been on earth.

Two Traditions

With this overview in mind, the basic pieces of the Jesus Puzzle can be laid out. The Gospel story is an amalgamation of two principal and separate elements, the wedding, if you like, of two different parents. This was a 'couple' who had never associated, who may not even have known of each other's existence until those unique circumstances arose which led "Mark" to bring them together in his Gospel.

The first parent was a Jewish preaching movement centered in Galilee, although it seems to have extended beyond that region. (Galilee is an area of Palestine located about 75 miles north of Jerusalem, flanking the western shore of the Sea of Galilee.) The itinerant prophets of this new 'counter-culture' announced the coming of the kingdom of God and anticipated the arrival of a heavenly figure called the Son of Man who would judge the world. They taught a new ethic and advocated a new society, they claimed the performance of miracles, and they aroused the hostility of the religious establishment.

Some of this movement's traditions[2] came from different sources, so that it comprised multiple strands of its own. No Jesus, divine or human, was originally present on the scene, although later in its development one segment of this kingdom sect invented for itself a founder figure who fed into the creation of the Gospel Jesus. Before his entry into Mark's Gospel, however, this founder was linked to no death and resurrection, no events in Jerusalem. To apply a term used in modern scholarship, this side of the puzzle, this half of the composite picture of Christianity, will be called the "Galilean Tradition."

The second parent was not so localized. Even though this side of the puzzle will be referred to by another term in scholarly usage, the "Jerusalem Tradition," and even though Jerusalem was an important center for this half of the Christian picture, in reality it too was comprised of many strands. It came to life in numerous places across the eastern half of the Roman empire, expressing a great variety of ideas. It too was a preaching movement, built on a Jewish base but combining Jewish and pagan traditions. It was conducted by apostles who might roam far afield to deliver their message and establish communities of believers.

That message was about a heavenly Son of God who was both an intermediary between God and the world, and a Savior figure. He was variously called Jesus, or Yeshua (meaning "Yahweh Saves" in Hebrew), the Christ (Greek for the Hebrew "Mashiach," or Messiah, meaning "Anointed One"), and the Son. Some looked upon this new

Son of God as a Revealer who bestowed saving knowledge of God, others as one who had undergone a sacrificial death and a resurrection. All manner of apostles like Paul were going about preaching this divine being and often not agreeing among themselves about him; indeed, they could be at each others' throats, as certain passages in Paul's letters reveal.

This Son and Savior was not identified with a recent human man or placed in an earthly setting, much less given a ministry of teaching and miracle-working in Galilee. Instead, he was a heavenly deity who had done his redeeming work in the supernatural dimension. He bore strong resemblance to two important expressions of the time. One was a philosophical idea that can be called "the intermediary Son," a spiritual channel between God and humanity; this was the dominant philosophical-religious concept of the Hellenistic[3] age. The second resemblance was to a wide range of pagan savior gods found in the Greco-Roman "mystery cults," the predominant form of popular religion in this period, going back to ancient roots. Like Paul's Christ, these savior gods were thought of as having performed acts in the supernatural world, acts which brought sanctity and salvation to their believers. Such cults had mythical stories and ritual practices very much like those of the Christian movement.

Like the people who preached the kingdom of God in Galilee, the apostles who spread their faith in a redeeming Son of God, and the communities across the empire which formed in response to them, envisioned an imminent end or transformation of the world. It would come with the arrival of the Son from heaven. Such groups were thus sectarian in nature, and they too aroused hostility on the part of society around them. Even more so than the Galilean movement, partly because it was so widely diffused, the Son of God faith was uncoordinated, with no central governing authority or set of doctrines.

Divisions of the Book

Because these two sides of Christianity originally had nothing to do with one another, they must be examined separately. This book falls into three divisions. The first two deal with the two Traditions, the third with their artificial union in the Gospels and how that amalgamation changed the course of Christian and world history.

The first division will examine the so-called Jerusalem Tradition. (This term is used in scholarship because the Gospel picture has created the belief that the death and resurrection of Christ which Paul preached was an earthly one, located in Jerusalem.) The record of this Son of God movement lies in the New Testament epistles and other early Christian letters and documents. In the Christian canon—the collection of writings chosen by the Church as authoritative and divinely inspired—the epistles have been appended to the four Gospels and the Acts of the Apostles as though they all relate to the same Jesus figure, as though they follow on the Gospels and Acts in some natural sequence. But this "New Testament"[4] was put together only in the latter part of the second century. The majority of the epistles, which came from all over the Christian world, were written earlier than the Gospels, and demonstrate no knowledge of those Gospels or their content. Nor do virtually all of those which were written later.

Thus, the first division of the Jesus Puzzle will examine Paul's Son of God movement, what its ideas were and where they came from, as revealed by the documents themselves and the wider picture of the times. And it will survey in some detail the silences in those documents about anything to do with the Gospel Jesus and his story.

The second division of the Jesus Puzzle will examine the Galilean Tradition. This kingdom of God movement in Galilee produced all the traditions which ended up in the Gospels as part of the ministry of the fictional Jesus: about conflict with the establishment, healings and miracles, a new ethic for the kingdom, about the imminent end of the world and the arrival of the Son of Man. The evidence for this Galilean side of the puzzle lies mostly in the Gospels themselves, specifically the three Synoptics,[5] Mark, Matthew and Luke. The focus will be on an ancient document which has not come down to us but which modern scholars have reconstructed out of certain common parts of Matthew and Luke. They have called it "Q" (for the German *Quelle*, meaning "source"). It is from this otherwise lost collection of sayings and anecdotes, together with a recently rediscovered document outside the New Testament—another collection of sayings attributed to Jesus called the Gospel of Thomas—that modern critical scholars have put together their picture of a "genuine Jesus," a picture I will argue is unfounded.

Out of the Galilean Tradition grew the Gospel of Mark. Its picture of the ministry of Jesus is based on the preaching movement represented by Q (even though Mark did not have a copy of the Q document used by Matthew and Luke). But in a bold, innovative stroke, the evangelist incorporated into his Gospel the idea of the heavenly Savior who died and rose from death in the thought of Paul. This dimension of the story Mark placed in Jerusalem.

At that point, the book will digress to look at the non-Christian witness to Jesus, as found—or not found—in the Jewish and pagan writings of the period, with a special detailed look at the Jewish historian Flavius Josephus.

From there, the third and final division of the book, "A Composite Christianity," will examine how the Gospel of Mark was constructed, how it was followed and enlarged upon by other Gospels, and how the new ideas they all contained gradually spread until Mark's central character of Jesus of Nazareth came to be regarded as the historical originator of the entire movement.

Symbolic Originators

While many factors went into the creation of the Gospel Jesus, one general principle lies at the basis of its understanding. The Gospel picture centers on its main character, Jesus of Nazareth. It is he who pronounces the new teachings, he who performs the miracles. It is he who engages in controversy with the religious establishment which does not approve of the things he is saying and doing. To judge by orthodox tradition, it was Jesus himself who was the source of all the new ideas and reforms which swept the religious scene at that time, in Palestine and beyond. It was he who had unleashed a new anticipation of God's kingdom on earth. This view continues to enjoy support from many modern scholars, though the most liberal among them have considerably whittled down the catalogue of actual sayings and deeds they are willing to attribute to him.

But there is another way of viewing this picture, and of understanding how the artificial figure of Jesus emerged in the first place. It is a natural human tendency to explain the development of progressive ideas, new technologies, better social and political systems, as the product of exceptional individuals, idealized forerunners, sometimes even as proceeding from divinities. The reality is typically otherwise. Society as a whole or a group within it produces the innovation or the swing in a new direction. There may be a trend 'in the air,' a set of subtle processes taking place over time. Eventually, these developments become attached in the popular or sectarian mind to a famous figure in their past, or embodied in an entirely fictitious personality. History is full of invented founders for religious, social and national movements, such as Taoism's Lao-Tse, Lycurgus of Sparta, or William Tell at the time of the founding of the Swiss Confederation. It is now generally recognized that these people, and others like them, never lived. A famous figure whose existence has recently been questioned is the Chinese philosopher, Confucius.[6]

This means that much of what has been attributed to Jesus, the pieces that went into the Gospel picture, are really descriptive of the communities which lay at the roots of those Gospels. These things represent the experiences of their leaders and preachers, of the foot soldiers who carried on the sect's activities. It is the sectarian community itself that is in conflict with the establishment around it.

The idea of the imminent arrival of God's kingdom was one of the driving forces of the age; groups like the one which produced the Q document had formed to preach it. It was their prophets who performed 'miracles,' a phenomenon that was an expected and indispensable sign of the coming of the kingdom. The new movement as a whole, in its various manifestations, produced the innovative ethics, drawing in some cases on precedents and outside sources. Indeed, the urge to such reform, in an attempt to correct the injustices of the age, was one of the main impulses to this activity in the first place.

Much of the human Jesus, the catalogue of what he says and does, is simply the epitomizing of all these trends and personalities. At the same time, because the tendency to impute ideas and practices to an imagined, idealized individual took place, in the case of both Traditions, within a sectarian milieu, other factors were impelling the creation of Jesus. The demands of sectarian life and its struggles with the outside world make the acquiring of such an innovator and founder, especially one of heroic or divine proportions, something of immense advantage. The sayings and deeds attributed to this founder become more authoritative; they may gain more respect from the establishment. The members of the sect are inspired to greater fervor and willingness to follow their leaders. This development of a glorified or fictitious founder figure is a relatively common occurrence among sects and religions throughout history and around the world, and we will look at some of the factors in the behavior of sects which would have contributed to the emergence of a founder figure for the Q community and a Jesus of Nazareth for Mark's Gospel.

And to those who might wish to claim, as modern trends of thinking increasingly do, that at the base of some of these processes a real human man did exist, even if he was not or never claimed to be the Son of God, I simply say: wait until all the pieces of the puzzle have been examined. You will find that they cannot be assembled in such a fashion.

I : THE JERUSALEM TRADITION

Modern scholars have begun to recognize the great divide between the world of the Gospels and the world of the epistles. They now postulate that what happened in response to Jesus' ministry in Galilee remained separate from what happened in response to his death in Jerusalem, since the two "Traditions" seem to have nothing in common. The documents which supposedly record Jesus' preaching career in the towns and countryside of his home province—the Q document imbedded in Matthew and Luke, and the Gospel of Thomas—say nothing about him going to Jerusalem or about anything that happened to him when he got there. There is no reference to a death and resurrection, nor is the Jesus figure found in the Q document given a role as a Savior. On the other side of the divide, the message or "kerygma" (the proclamation) of apostles like Paul who went about the empire preaching a Son of God, has nothing to say about a ministry in Galilee. The epistles attribute no teachings, no miracles, no appointment of apostles, no biographical details to the Christ Jesus they talk about. They focus entirely on the believer's relationship to the heavenly Son and on his redeeming sacrificial death and resurrection. The latter are never placed in an historical earthly setting.

One final step needs to be taken. Those two sides of the great divide must be severed completely, and regarded as artificially joined for the first time in the Gospel of Mark. That new picture of Christian origins is reflected in the threefold division of the Jesus Puzzle.

This first division, the Jerusalem Tradition, will take a close look at the world of the epistles, bringing in other documents from the early Christian record which are a part of that world as well. Part One, "Preaching a Divine Son" (Chapters 1 to 5), will lay out the general features of the Son of God faith: how apostles like Paul described their Christ Jesus and his role in salvation, what they taught about ethics and the coming end of the world, how the apostolic movement itself functioned. The background history and spirit of the times which gave rise to the new faith will begin to emerge.

An integral part of this picture of the movement will be a demonstration of what it does *not* contain. Since the elements of the Galilean Tradition later assigned to an earthly Jesus, his teachings, miracle working and apocalyptic prophecy, have been misleadingly combined in the Gospels with Paul's Son of God, it needs to be shown that the preaching of the Son as found in the epistles does not contain these things. The silence on the general ministry of Jesus and on Jesus as the source of the movement's teachings will be considered at various points in Part One, while the silence on the details of the Gospel story of Jesus' life and death, or indeed on *any* biographical details about a human Jesus, will be presented in Part Two, "A Life in Eclipse."

Part Three, "The Gospel of the Son," delves into the sources of Paul's view of the heavenly Christ. Chapter 8 will open the pages of the Jewish scriptures, those sacred writings more or less equivalent to the Christian Old Testament, to reveal where Paul got his ideas about crucifixion and resurrection, along with much else. Chapter 9 uncovers the pervasive "intermediary Son" concept in the thinking of the time, the idea of a spiritual emanation of God that served as a channel of contact between Deity and humanity, which philosophers made so much effort to understand.

Part Four, "A World of Myth and Savior Gods," enters the multi-layered universe of the ancients. Chapters 10 and 11 will examine their view that a vast unseen dimension lay above the earth, where all sorts of supernatural proceedings took place among gods and spirits. Here lay the processes of salvation, the activities of the Greco-Roman savior gods. Here is where Paul and the early Christians placed their Christ Jesus and his redeeming acts. In Chapter 12, these insights will be applied in a perusal of three very revealing New Testament passages.

Finally, with the workings of the Son of God movement laid out, Chapter 13 will make a broad survey of the early Christian landscape and offer a new nativity scene for Christianity's birth. The varied expressions of the Jerusalem Tradition found across the empire will reveal the extent of Christian diversity and the lack of a common founder and point of origin.

Part One
PREACHING A DIVINE SON

1

A Heavenly Christ

The New Testament epistles are often described as "occasional writings." That is, each one was written on a particular occasion to deal with a specific situation faced by the writer. Some of these writers, such as Paul, would not have penned their epistles themselves; they dictated them to a scribal companion or professional.

Such a letter might be dashed off overnight, so to speak, with little review or polishing before it was sent on its way; in some cases, a certain amount of care might be taken. On the other hand, a few of the New Testament epistles, such as the epistle to the Hebrews, are clearly not spur-of-the moment affairs, but carefully constructed little treatises. In the Pauline corpus, I would suggest that Romans and Ephesians fall into such a category, possibly others. Finally, the odd epistle, notably 1 John, shows revision over time, a 'layering' of later parts and insertions over earlier ones.

What could we reasonably expect to find in such a motley collection of writings?

First and foremost, these writers are, within the situations their epistles address, discussing their faith, one that centers on the figure they worship. They may not be setting out to present a comprehensive statement of that faith and that figure—although it might be argued that Hebrews does, and to a certain extent Romans. Nevertheless, we should reasonably expect that from this collection of early Christian correspondence (to which one could add Revelation) basic defining doctrines and a background picture of the Christian movement, even if only piecemeal, would emerge.

Yet what, in fact, does emerge?

On the one hand, important fundamentals of doctrine and background, which almost two millennia of Christian tradition would lead us to expect, are entirely missing. Those anxious to protect that tradition lay emphasis on the "occasional" aspect of the writings, as though this should excuse them from containing any of this basic information. On the other hand, the epistle writers seem to be saying things about doctrine and background which present quite a different picture than the one tradition has given us.

Paul began his known career as a persecutor of the Son of God faith, acting on behalf of the Jewish authorities. "How savagely I persecuted the church of God," he tells the Galatians (1:13). Following his conversion, an event about which he reveals very little except that it was a call "by God," he became part of that faith. After a time, he made contact in Jerusalem with a group of "brothers" and apostles which included certain men named Peter and James, "who were apostles before me" (1:17). In 1 Corinthians 15:11-12, he says that "this is what we all proclaim . . . that Christ was raised from the dead." All are part of the same 'Jerusalem Tradition,' proclaiming salvation through belief in a dying and resurrected Christ, a divinity who is not identified with a recent historical man.

But although this Jerusalem sect around Peter and James was an important force in the Son of God faith, and had considerable influence which extended at least into Syria, it was by no means a central authority for all apostles working in the field, or for all the many Christian communities which dotted the eastern empire in the time of Paul. Nor, as indicated earlier, is Jerusalem to be considered as the sole point of origin for the movement. ⟨-⟩° oᒪⁱſ

It also needs to be stressed that the nature of the divine Son being preached could be quite different from one apostle or group to another, from one document to another. While Paul and the Jerusalem sect offered a Son and Christ who had died for sin and risen from death, some of Paul's rivals in the field rejected a dying and rising Christ. They proclaimed a Christ who was a Revealer Son, an imparter of wisdom and knowledge about God, a different means to salvation. Such a clash we see in Paul's defense of "God's wisdom" (meaning his own) in 1 Corinthians 1 and 2. And there were other variations. Here, for the most part, we will focus on the sacrificial Son found in Paul and most other New Testament epistles, with a glance at the non-sacrificial versions as we go along. It was the Son and Christ Paul preached which eventually defined the theology of Christianity as we know it.

The Documentary Record

In that portion of the New Testament following the Gospels and the Acts of the Apostles, there are 22 documents. Most of them were not written by the authors whose names they bear. Among the 13 epistles assigned to Paul, scholarly study and computer analysis have judged only seven as genuine: Romans, 1 and 2 Corinthians, Galatians, Philippians, 1 Thessalonians, and Philemon.[7] (2 Corinthians is an editing together of at least two separate letters, and 1 Corinthians may also contain splicing and editing.) Colossians, Ephesians and 2 Thessalonians were likely written within a decade or two after Paul's death (presumably in the 60s) by followers or members of his congregations. Their authors used Paul's name in order to give their letters greater authority. The three Pastoral epistles (1 & 2 Timothy and Titus) are also in Paul's name, but they present a picture of a later period and are assigned to the early second century, usually 110-130.

The epistle to the Hebrews is anonymous. Of those under the names of Peter, James, John and Jude, none today are judged to be authentic. That is, they were not written by those legendary followers of Jesus. These epistles too may originally have been anonymous, or had their original ascriptions dropped; new names were added, possibly at the time the epistles were collected and a canon was being formed (see Chapter 24). The term for this custom of adopting the name of a famous figure of the past to give one's writing greater authority is "pseudonymous."

Dating many of these documents is notoriously difficult, and wide leeways are allowed. Traditional scholarship has tended to date Hebrews and James early—possibly before the Jewish War of 66-70. 1 Peter and the three Johns come perhaps in the 80s or 90s. 2 Peter tends to be dated late, 100-120; this requires Jude to be earlier, since some of its passages have been inserted into 2 Peter. Finally, Revelation, written by a prophet named John who is no longer identified with the Gospel apostle of that name, is placed most often in the mid 90s. Taken as a whole, then, most of the epistolary corpus predates the Gospels; virtually all of it predates the wider dissemination of those Gospels.

As we go along, some early Christian writings that did not end up in the New Testament will be brought in: the epistle 1 Clement, the letters of Ignatius, the "church manual" called the Didache (DID-a-kee), the Shepherd of Hermas, and the epistles of Barnabas and Polycarp, as well as some Jewish and Greco-Roman documents which cast light on the picture. Details and dates of these will be discussed at such times.

All the documents of the New Testament, as well as almost all the non-canonical ones of the first two centuries, were written in Greek, the international language of the time.

A Missing Equation

So let's begin. From the record of what the New Testament epistles do *not* say, we will look at a puzzle piece I call "The Missing Equation."

Those 22 documents in the latter part of the New Testament contain roughly 80,000 words. They are the product of about a dozen different writers, Paul being the most prominent. In them, one encounters over 500 references to the object of all these writers' faith: "Jesus" or "Christ" or a combination of these names, or "the Son," plus a few to "the Lord" meaning Christ.

Even if these writings are "occasional"—and some of them are more than that—is it feasible that in all this discussion and defense of their faith, nowhere would anyone, by choice, accident or necessity, happen to use words which would identify the divine Son and Christ they are all talking about with his recent incarnation: whether this be the man Jesus of Nazareth known to us from the Gospels, born of Mary and died under Pilate, or some other "genuine Jesus" unearthed by modern critical scholarship? As astonishing as such a silence may seem, an equation such as "Jesus of Nazareth was the Son of God and Messiah" is missing from all the early Christian correspondence. The Jesus of the epistles is not spoken of as a man who had recently lived.

There are two passages in the epistles which present apparent exceptions to what has just been said, plus a third which could be claimed to fall into such a category, and I will deal with them immediately so as not to compromise the argument.

One is 1 Thessalonians 2:15-16. After a statement that the Thessalonian Christians have been mistreated by their fellow countrymen just as the Christians in Judea have been persecuted by their fellow Jews, we read this additional comment about those Jews:

". . . [15]who killed the Lord Jesus and the prophets and drove us out, the Jews who are heedless of God's will and enemies of their fellow-men, [16]hindering us from preaching to the gentiles to lead them to salvation. All this time they have been making up the full measure of their guilt, and now retribution has overtaken them for good and all." [NEB]

That last sentence is an obvious allusion to the destruction of Jerusalem, which happened after Paul's death and many years after 1 Thessalonians was written. The sentiments in those two verses are also very uncharacteristic of Paul's feelings towards his fellow Jews as expressed elsewhere in his letters. For those reasons, many scholars have judged these verses to be an interpolation, something inserted into the text at a later date. This, by the way, is the only passage in the entire corpus of New Testament epistles which assigns the Jews any responsibility in the death of the Christ figure.

The second "apparent exception" is found in 1 Timothy 6:13, a passing reference to Christ making a confession before Pontius Pilate. While not so clear-cut a case, some commentators find that this reference does not fit well into its surrounding context, and so one can ask whether it was part of the original letter. In any case, since this epistle comes from the early decades of the second century, the reference to Pilate, if authentic, could reflect the newly-developing view that Jesus had lived at Pilate's time and was executed by the Roman governor. (For a full discussion of the authenticity of the 1 Thessalonians and 1 Timothy passages, see Appendix 1.)

The third passage mentioned above is the sole Gospel-like scene to be found in all of Paul's letters: 1 Corinthians 11:23-26. Here Paul attributes words to Jesus at what he calls "the Lord's Supper," words identifying the bread and wine of the thanksgiving meal with Jesus' body and blood. But is Paul recounting an historical event here? There are several arguments to be made that this is not the case, that Paul is instead describing something which lay in the realm of myth, just as the cult of the savior god Mithras had a myth about the establishment of its own sacred meal. In fact, the opening phrase of the passage points to Paul's reception of this information through revelation, not through an account of others who were supposedly participants at such an event. This is an important passage, and it will be discussed in fuller detail later. For now, it does not have to be regarded as a necessary reference to an historical Jesus who had lived on earth in Paul's own lifetime.

Thus, we are left with an entire corpus of early Christian correspondence which gives us no indication that the divine Christ these writers look to for salvation is to be identified with the man Jesus of Nazareth whom the Gospels place in the early first century—or, indeed, with any man in their recent past.

It is important to realize that the many references in the epistles to the "death" or "rising" of Christ are not, in themselves, references to physical events on earth or in history. They, along with a handful of 'human' sounding terms, are part of the *myth* of the Son; they relate to the activities of this divinity *in the supernatural realm*. For all its jarring incongruity with our modern outlook, not to mention centuries of tradition about a Gospel Jesus, this is a view that would have been perfectly at home in the philosophical and mythical thinking of the time. It was, in fact, a view shared by a whole range of pagan salvation cults, each of which had its own savior god who had performed deeds in the mythical world. Like Paul's Christ, savior gods such as Attis and Osiris had been killed; like Paul's Christ, Osiris had been buried (after being dismembered); like Christ on the third day, Adonis and Dionysos had been resurrected from death. All these things were not regarded as historical; they had taken place in the world of myth and higher reality.

A Starting Point in Heaven

To get a clearer focus on the Missing Equation, let's look at a passage from Acts, a document which many scholars now date to the second century and no longer regard as historically reliable (see Chapter 24). In Acts 2:22-36, the author puts a speech into the mouth of Peter. Here Peter says: "Men of Israel, hear me. I speak of Jesus of Nazareth, a man singled out by God and made known to you through miracles, portents and signs. . . ." He goes on to tell about this Jesus, concluding with these words: "God has made this Jesus, whom you crucified, both Lord and Christ."

This would surely be the most natural and inevitable way Christian discussion and preaching would proceed. The movement had supposedly begun as a response to a human man. This man had had such a profound effect on people that they forsook everything in life to preach him; for this man's sake they had abandoned, even betrayed, much that was held sacred in their Jewish heritage. He should have lain at the forefront of their minds. And so Acts would seem to indicate. In speech after speech, the Christian apostles *start* with the man Jesus and make certain factual statements and faith declarations about him.

But what do we find in the letters of Paul and other early writers? They start with the *divine* Christ, the figure of the Son in heaven, and make their faith statements about him. And there is no equation with an historical man, a human teacher who had recently lived. Paul believes *in* the Son of God, not that anyone *was* the Son of God.

Here is Paul stating a capsule summary of the gospel of salvation he preached to the Corinthians:

> ". . . that Christ died for our sins, according to the scriptures; that he was buried; that he was raised on the third day, according to the scriptures." [1 Corinthians 15:3-4, NIV]

Isn't there something missing here? If Paul tramps into town and begins to preach in the marketplace or the local synagogue, would his listeners, from this, have known that the Christ he is speaking of was a man who had undergone this death and resurrection only a couple of decades ago, on a hill and from a tomb just outside Jerusalem? Would not an essential part of his gospel be the identity of the human incarnation of this Son of God and Christ—or even the fact of the incarnation itself?

But perhaps Paul left out such preliminaries when quoting his capsule gospel. What of his 'definition' of Father and Son in 1 Corinthians 8:6?

> "For us there is one God, the Father, from whom all being comes . . . and there is one Lord, Jesus Christ, through whom all things came to be and we through him." [NEB]

This is language very reminiscent of Greek philosophy. But it would seem that a fundamental description of the Son is not to include the fact that he was incarnated in the person of a human Jesus, the man through whom information about the Son was presumably derived. Such an idea Paul does not mention—either here or anywhere else.

Throughout his letters, Paul has much to say about faith. Faith in Jesus as the avenue to eternal life. Faith that God has raised Jesus from the dead. (Even Jesus' death, to judge by some passages, seems to be a matter of faith.) Faith that God has revealed his great mystery about Christ to apostles like himself. But he leaves out what is surely the most important faith of all, the one that comes first, without which none of the others come into play. Paul ignores the requirement that one must have faith that the man Jesus had been the incarnation of the divine, redeeming Son he is preaching.

Some of the epistles contain descriptions of the Son which are quite fantastic. Here is part of the one in Colossians 1:15-20:

> "He is the image of the invisible God; his is the primacy over all created things. In him everything in heaven and on earth was created . . . In him, the complete being of God, by God's own

choice, came to dwell. Through him God chose to reconcile the whole universe to himself . . ." [NEB]

Heady stuff, and very closely related to wider philosophical trends of thinking. Christ is not only the reflection of God, he is the agent through whom all the heavens and the earth have been created. He holds the entire universe together! Yet the writer fails to mention anywhere in his letter that this colossal power had been on earth in the person of Jesus of Nazareth. Would not such a bizarre elevation of a crucified criminal to so cosmic a level of divinity be an important point in his faith declaration? Why is no justification or defense ever offered by any epistle writer for such an unprecedented leap?

The author of the epistle to the Hebrews also waxes dramatic about the Son (1:2-3):

". . . whom he (God) has made heir to the whole universe, and through whom he has created all orders of existence: the Son who is the effulgence of God's splendor and the stamp of God's very being, who sustains the universe by his word of power."

Though this author devotes a dozen chapters to detailing the Son's redeeming activities in a heavenly sanctuary, he never identifies him with the man Jesus of Nazareth or any other human being. Though he can quote the Son's words in scripture, the "voice" through which God has spoken in the present age, he never gives his readers a single saying attributed to the Galilean preacher in the Gospels.

These and similar passages in the epistles illustrate the orientation of early Christian thinking. They start with the divine Christ and detail his activities. They do not start with the human man and identify their divine Christ with him, which is the approach we find in Acts.

Starring Jesus in a Mythological Drama

This preliminary dip into the early Christian view of the Son presents a picture which scholars have long found perplexing. The epistles cast Jesus in an exclusively mythological[8] and spiritual role, while ignoring the fact or identity of his supposed incarnation, the man whose career on earth presumably started it all. Here is how one scholar has put it (Herman Ridderbos, *Paul and Jesus*, p.3):

"No one who examines the Gospels, and then reads the epistles of Paul can escape the impression that he is moving in two entirely different spheres. . . . When Paul writes of Jesus as the Christ, historical and human traits appear to be obscure, and Christ appears to have significance only as a transcendent divine being."

But the question which mainstream New Testament scholarship has never asked is in fact the most natural one of all: suppose Paul made no such leap? If all we find in Paul's presentation of Christ is this transcendent divine being, whose activities are never linked to history or an earthly location, is there any justification for assuming that Paul's Christ arose out of Jesus of Nazareth, out of the human figure who appears for the first time only in Gospels that were written some time after Paul?

Those who derive their view of Jesus from the Gospels might be startled to realize the highly elevated nature of the Jesus preached by early Christians. He is a part of the very Godhead itself. His nature is integral with that of the Father. And he has been given all the titles previously reserved in Jewish thought for God alone.

This Jesus is pre-existent: that is, he existed before all time with the Father, before the very creation of the world. Indeed, it is through him that the world has been created, and he is the energy force through which the workings of the universe are maintained. In addition, he serves as God's redeeming agent in the divine salvation plan for humankind, reconciling an estranged universe to God (Colossians 1:20). He is the unifying force of the entire cosmos (Ephesians 1:10). He has subjugated the demon spirits who pervade the world and harass humanity, and he has been given lordship over all earthly and supernatural powers.

This supposed elevation of a human man is quite staggering. To the extent that they are familiar with them, Christians have had almost 2000 years to get used to such lofty ideas. But we lose sight of the fact that if the orthodox picture is true, someone or some group one day decided to apply all these ideas to a human being for the first time and actually went out and preached them.

Is it possible to conceive of circumstances in which followers of such a man, a humble preacher whose deeds—critical scholars are now agreed—could not possibly have matched those of the Gospel story, would have elevated him to such a cosmic level? Though men, such as the Roman emperors, could be called divine and "sons of God," Jesus' degree of elevation would have been virtually unprecedented in the entire history of religion.[9]

It is especially inconceivable among Jews. The Jewish mind had an obsession against associating anything human with God. He could not be represented by even the suggestion of a human image. Jews in their thousands had bared their necks before Pilate's swords simply to protest against the carrying of Roman military standards bearing human images into the city of Jerusalem. The idea that a man was a literal part of God would have been met by almost any Jew with horror and apoplexy.[10]

Yet we are to believe not only that Jews were led to identify a crucified criminal with the ancient God of Abraham, but that they went about the empire and practically overnight converted huge numbers of other Jews to the same outrageous—and thoroughly blasphemous— proposition. Within a handful of years of Jesus' supposed death, we know of Christian communities in many major cities of the empire, all presumably having accepted that a man they had never met, crucified as a political rebel on a hill outside Jerusalem, had risen from the dead and was in fact the Son of God and redeemer of the world.

Since many of the Christian communities Paul worked in existed before he got there, and since his letters do not support the picture Acts paints of extensive missionary activity on the part of the Jerusalem group around Peter and James, history does not record who performed this astounding feat.

Moreover, it was apparently done without any need for justification. There is not a murmur in any Pauline letter, nor in any other epistle, about a Christian need to defend such an outlandish doctrine. No one seems to challenge Christian preaching on these grounds, for the point is never addressed. Even in 1 Corinthians 1:18-24, where Paul defends the "wisdom of God" (the message he is preaching) against the "wisdom of the world," he fails to provide any defense for the elevation of Jesus of Nazareth to divinity. He can admit that to the Greeks and Jews the doctrine of the cross—that is, the idea of a crucified Messiah—is "folly" and "a stumbling block." But this has nothing to do with turning a man into God, a piece of folly he never discusses or defends, and a stumbling block no traditional Jew could have circumvented. That his opponents, and the Jewish establishment in general, would not challenge him on this fundamental Christian position, forcing him to provide some justification, is inconceivable.

Scholars have traditionally postulated this rapid application to Jesus of all the going philosophical and mythological concepts of the day. But they are unsure who did it, or why. It was hardly the product of that circle of simple fishermen whom the Gospels place around Jesus, men who would probably have been barely able to read much less understand philosophical concepts like the Greek Logos or Jewish personified Wisdom (to be examined in Chapter 9) and decide that the teaching Master they followed had been the very embodiment of these concepts.

More recent scholars, such as Burton Mack,[11] have suggested that gentile circles in places like Antioch were responsible over time for applying current philosophical interpretations about the workings of Deity to Jesus of Nazareth, and that Paul was converted to one of these "Christ cults." But this scenario runs into problems. Such groups, being distant from the places of Jesus' ministry and forming after his death, would have had no contact with the man himself. One has to wonder how anyone, gentile or Jew, would have been impelled to create such a cosmic product out of someone they had never laid eyes on. There is no question that what was allegedly made of Jesus owes much to Hellenistic (Greek) ideas, but these ideas not even gentiles had ever applied to an historical person. Thus we can judge that the leap would have been, in its own way, as unprecedented and shocking for them as it would have been for mainstream Jews.

Moreover, such a proposal founders on a very important consideration. To judge by the chronology he outlines in Galatians 1 and 2, Paul's conversion had to have taken place somewhere between 32 and 36, only a few years after Jesus' presumed death. Since Paul did not invent the Christ cult (he persecuted such groups, and there are pre-Pauline elements in his letters which are the product of others), it existed at that time. And because the evidence in Paul clearly implies that the Jerusalem group thought as he did on the question of Jesus' divinity—suggestions to the contrary notwithstanding[12]—it must have been thriving even in Jerusalem. Who, then, in the very heart of Israel, had turned Jesus into a cosmic deity and attached Hellenistic mythologies to him almost as soon as he was laid in his grave? Did Paul, a Jew born and bred, as he tells us, simply swallow the whole blasphemous proposition without a murmur of indigestion? Did he and so many other Jews allow gentiles—wherever they may have been—to persuade them to betray the most cherished principles of their Jewish heritage and turn a man into God?

Moreover, the question still needs to be answered: Why? What would have led Paul, or gentiles off in northern Syria, to take a simple preacher whom they knew only by report, and turn him into a cosmic deity—no matter what their diet of Hellenistic ideas? The appeal could not have been in his message and charisma as a teacher, since they immediately stripped off this skin and discarded it. If Paul had no interest in the teacher and his teachings, no interest in the miracle worker or apocalyptic prophet, of what use was this Jesus to him as a candidate for divine redeemer? Both Mack and Robert Funk speak of the Pauline cult's point of departure as the fact of Jesus' "noble death," but noble deaths are common enough in history, including Jewish history, and never before or since have they led to divinization on so exalted a scale. The simple fact of a reputed noble death would hardly have persuaded an educated, observant Jew such as Paul claimed to be, to contravene the most sacred precepts of his heritage and associate this particular man, one he had never met, with God.[13]

There is no denying that the earliest Christian record shows us a Jesus who is presented exclusively in mythological, transcendent terms, with no reference to any human career or earthly teachings and deeds (a silence we'll now start to investigate in detail). But if a group is going to elevate its teacher to divinity and apply every philosophical concept of the day to him, why would it at the same time strip away everything to do with the human life he had lived, the life which supposedly had engendered their response to him in the first place? Why would it create mythological statements, hymns and creeds about him which contained not a single reference to an earthly career?

If, as the scholars claim, the mythological overlay—the divinity, the pre-existence, the unifying force to a sundered universe, the redemptive significance—is an "interpretation" of Jesus of Nazareth, how are we to understand it as such when the object of the interpretation is never mentioned? Since the epistle writers themselves give us no hint that they are "interpreting" a human man, are not scholars guilty of 'reading into' the documents things they wish to see there, rather than what the documents actually say?

Would it not make better sense to view that earliest record as representing a belief in a spiritual entity who is a *version* of the prevailing myths and thought patterns of the day, something upon which an historical garment was eventually hung?

2

A Conspiracy of Silence

If we had no other documentary record than the New Testament epistles, we would probably regard the Son of God preached by apostles like Paul as a divine being like all the other gods of the day, or indeed of any day: confined to the supernatural dimension and communicating with believers and spokespersons through inspiration, visions and other spiritual manifestations. This is the way gods have been perceived to interact with the world from time immemorial. Paul's Christ would have been no different, and no more difficult to comprehend.

But if, on the basis of the later Gospel record, it is claimed that Paul and his colleagues are speaking of a human man who was recently on earth and set the new faith in motion, how is one to account for their silence on such a man and his career? We might, in tongue-in-cheek fashion, suggest that this silence is so profound that it could only be explained as a deliberate, universal conspiracy. But conspiracy or not, we need to become aware of the dimensions of that silence.

The Argument From Silence

What conclusions can be drawn from silence? Is the so-called "argument from silence" valid? It depends on a number of factors. We have to ask ourselves, how compelling to the writer should the subject have been? Does what he is saying invite a natural, perhaps inevitable reference to the subject, whether in passing or as an integral part of his argument? If, for example, a Christian writer is urging a certain course of action upon his readers, and the founder of the movement was known to have taught that very thing, this should almost guarantee that the writer would quote the founder or mention that he had so taught, in order to lend weight and persuasion to his argument. In other words, the more we have reason to expect that something would be mentioned and yet it is not, the more we are entitled to conclude from the silence that the subject is not known to the writer.

If that unexpected silence extends to many different writers and many documents, indeed to all writers and documents available from that period, if it extends to a multitude of elements on the subject, the greater becomes the evidential force of that silence. If the silence covers virtually every single element, the conclusions to be drawn become compelling.

Let's take an analogy. If a deceased man's descendant claims that the man once won a lottery, yet there is no contemporary record of such a win, no entry of a large sum in his bank statements, no mention of it in his diaries and letters or the letters of his siblings, no memory of a spending spree, if on his deathbed he told someone he never got a break in his life, and so on, we would have good reason to use the argument from silence to say that the claim is probably false, that he had never in fact won a lottery.

But what if we could go further and see that the way the writers speak of certain things virtually *excludes* any room or role for the subject in question? In that case, logic would compel us to postulate that the subject, in these writers' minds and experience, could not have existed.

If the early Christian record presents us with such a picture, such a compelling and inexplicable void on the Gospel Jesus, how likely is the possibility that such a man as the Gospels tell of, even reduced to human fundamentals, could really have lived?

The Christian movement began with Jesus the teacher. Or so modern scholars now tell us. Even though there are no early surviving documents which provide this information, an "authentic" Jesus, they claim, can be excavated from the later evidence. That evidence will be looked at in due course. Here we need to examine the evidence we *do* have from the early period, and see if it is possible to reconcile it with such a claim.

The reasons scholars have put forward to explain the silence on the part of Paul about the human Jesus are several: he felt no interest in the man and his career, he had no use for any aspect of Jesus' earthly life in his cosmic theology about the risen Christ, he was in competition with the Jerusalem apostles and so chose to downplay the advantages they enjoyed as followers of Jesus on earth, and so on. Regardless of the credibility of such explanations—and they will be considered as we go along—we can list other factors which should have been in play to counter this deliberate ignoring of the human man by such as Paul.

One is that he could never have gotten away with it in his missionary activities. If Paul were preaching a man who was God, his listeners and converts would demand to know about the life of this man, his sayings and deeds. Whether he liked it or not, Paul would have had to make an effort to learn a certain amount of information about Jesus' life. It would become one of the subjects of discussion between himself and his congregations, details of which would certainly surface in his letters. None do. (See Appendix 2 for an imaginary conversation between Paul and a group of new converts, which illustrates the impossibility that Paul could have ignored the earthly life of Jesus in his preaching mission.)

Nor is there much opportunity in evidence for him to have acquired details about Jesus' life, for in Galatians 1 and 2 Paul tells us that over the course of 17 years following his conversion, he bothered to go up to Jerusalem exactly once, for a two-week visit. All he did at that time, so he says (1:18), was "get to know Peter" and see James. Did they give him a quick course in their memories of Jesus' life and ministry? Paul gives no hint of such a thing, and no details are ever relayed to his readers.

I have already touched on the need Paul would face to defend the Christian elevation of a mortal to divinity, especially in the face of Jewish sensibilities. No defense is ever offered. With gentile listeners, the situation would have been rather different. The elevation of a human being to such cosmic status would, in the Greco-Roman world, also have been unprecedented and require defending, but not because pagans would have been offended. Quite the contrary. They had a longstanding fascination for the heroic figure known as the "divine man," an outstanding ruler or famous philosopher, etc., whose career demonstrated superior wisdom, superhuman qualities (including miracle-working) and a kinship with the gods. The Gospel Jesus of Nazareth would have fitted this category perfectly. In any mission to the gentiles, the human Jesus and his exploits would have been a tremendous asset. This makes Paul's total silence on the career of Jesus, his miracles and innovative teachings, quite inexplicable.

Christianity was also in competition with the Greco-Roman mystery cults. Most of the latter's savior gods (Osiris, Isis, Attis, Mithras, etc.) bestowed benefits similar to those enjoyed by devotees of Christ. A very important benefit was protection against the hostile demon spirits that were believed by Jew and pagan alike to pervade the world's very atmosphere, harassing and crippling people's lives.

Yet the writers of Colossians and Ephesians, who have a special interest in these matters, fail to point out that, unlike the other savior deities, Christ had been incarnated in flesh and blood. He had experienced and countered such demonic forces first hand, on earth. He had demonstrated his power over the spirits through his miracles, exorcising them from sick people. This is one of the purposes such miracles serve in the Gospels. In his ministry, the Gospels portray Jesus (along with quite different character traits) as showing compassion, tolerance, generosity, all those things men and women thirsted for in confronting a hostile, uncaring world. It is simply unthinkable that, if these traditions existed, Paul or anyone else would have ignored or lost interest in all those advantages provided by the life of the human Jesus when presenting to their listeners, gentile or Jew, the Christian agent of salvation.[14]

And yet every aspect of that life, for the circles Paul moved in, seems to have gone into total eclipse.

Searching for the Jewish Rabbi

Just how dark is that shadow? Let's see if we can uncover any glimmer of light.

What did Jesus teach? The Jesus Seminar[15] has rejected as inauthentic some three quarters of the sayings attributed to him in the Gospels. Even the famous "love your neighbor" commandment which Christian history has always regarded as the centerpiece of Jesus' teachings—even if he is consciously quoting the biblical book of Leviticus—has been judged "gray" (not too likely). What do the New Testament epistles have to say?

Throughout this book, in the course of examining the silence in the epistles on the life and teachings of Jesus, we will look at all of the Gospel elements, without discrimination. This will include those which critical scholarship has cast doubt on, or even totally rejected—such as the apocalyptic sayings or the existence of Judas. Those who consider elements like these to be unhistorical may not regard the silence about them in the epistle writers to be compelling evidence that no Jesus existed. But if *none* of the sayings and deeds of Jesus found in the Gospels are attributed to him in the epistles and other early documents, this will indicate that (a) the Gospels cannot be accepted as providing any reliable historical data, and thus (b) the fundamental basis for the historicity of Jesus—namely the Gospels, since he appears nowhere else in the surviving early record—has been seriously undermined.

If, in addition, no earthly teachings and no biographical details of any kind are to be found, we are entitled to take this as strong evidence that the epistle writers know of no such things, and that the faith movement they represent is not based on the career of a human man.

On the other hand, the vast majority of Christians still believe that most of the Gospel picture *is* reliable, including the fact that Jesus taught about love. If he did, we face a perplexing situation in regard to passages like James 2:8: "If you are observing the sovereign law laid down in scripture, 'Love your neighbor as yourself,' that is good." Here the writer draws no attention to Jesus' emphasis on this commandment. Twice does Paul express himself exactly as Jesus is reported to have done, and speaks of the whole Law being "summed up" in the two-edged rule of loving God and loving one's neighbor (Romans 13:9 and Galatians 5:14). But Paul seems to have no idea that he is imitating any preaching of Jesus. In fact, in 1 Thessalonians 4:9 he says to his readers: "You are taught *by God* to love one another."

"Blessed are the poor in spirit, for theirs is the kingdom of heaven." These memorable lines open Jesus' most famous sermon, as presented in the Gospel of Matthew. Yet the writer of James can say, without any attribution to Jesus: "Listen, my friends. Has not God chosen those who are poor in the eyes of the world to be rich in faith and inherit the kingdom?" One would think that he would wish to use Jesus' own words (ones the Jesus Seminar has judged are probably authentic) to press his argument more forcefully upon his listeners.

No less famous is Jesus' dictum to "love your enemies." "Turn the other cheek," says Matthew 5:39. These are sayings the Seminar has judged most likely to be authentic. Yet 1 Peter (3:9) can urge its readers: "Do not repay wrong with wrong, or abuse with abuse; rather, retaliate with blessing." How could this writer fail to draw on Jesus' own teaching here—or be ignorant of it?

Paul in Romans 4:13 says, "Let us cease judging one another." 1 John 3:22 declares, "We can approach God and obtain from him whatever we ask." "Humble yourselves before God and he will exalt you," advises James 4:10. Here are ringing echoes of Jesus' Gospel teachings, yet not one of these writers points to Jesus as the source of these things. Such examples could be multiplied by the dozen.

How have scholars dealt with all this silence in the epistles on the teaching Jesus? Commentaries are filled with perplexed observations like that of Helmut Koester in *Ancient Christian Gospels* (p.68): "It is surprising that there is no appeal [in 1 Timothy] to the authority of

Jesus." Graham Stanton (*Gospel Truth*, p.130-1) talks of "allusions" to Jesus' teachings in Paul, but admits that in these "it is difficult to be certain that the phrase or sentence comes from Jesus, rather than from a Jewish or Greek source. . . . Paul's failure to refer more frequently and at greater length to the actions and the teaching of Jesus is baffling. . . . In a number of places in his writings Paul fails to refer to a saying of Jesus at the very point where he might well have clinched his argument by doing so."

Even formal compendiums of ethical maxims which bear a strong resemblance to Jesus' Gospel teachings, such as the "Two Ways" instructions found in the Didache and the epistle of Barnabas, or the directives in Romans 12 and 13, are never identified as having come from Jesus. The inevitable conclusion must be that such ethics came from other sources, or were part of the general stock of ethical material of the times, and were only later attached to an historical Jesus.

Paul's letters contain debates about the necessity to apply Jewish practice to the new Christian sects. Were the strict dietary regulations urged by the Pharisees, with their obsessive concerns over the purity of certain foods, still to apply? This was a burning issue in the new faith movement. Paul in Romans 14:14 declares: "I am fully convinced, as one who is in the Lord Jesus, that nothing is unclean in itself" [NIV]. If ever there were a moment amid an emotional argument when one would expect Paul to seize on Jesus' own declared position for support, this is it. His silence can only indicate that he is truly ignorant of such traditions as those found in Mark 7 where Jesus accuses the Pharisees of hypocrisy and tells the people: "Nothing that goes into a man from outside can defile him." The evangelist drives home the point by concluding, "Thus he declared all foods clean."

Paul's ignorance is shared by the writer of 1 Timothy who similarly fails to draw on any support from Jesus when he asserts, in a discussion about foods, that "everything that God created is good." The second century epistle of Barnabas devotes an entire chapter to an attempt to discredit the Jewish dietary restrictions, yet not even here does a Christian writer who knows his traditional scriptures inside and out refer to Jesus' own Gospel words on the subject.

The question about foods was only one part of that central dispute which in the time of Paul threatened to tear the fledgling movement apart. As a sect within Judaism, was the observance of the Mosaic Law (those commandments contained in the Pentateuch, the first five books of the Hebrew bible) in all its details to be required of Christianity,

especially of its gentile converts who could be less than enthusiastic—
if they were male—about such necessities as circumcision? Paul knew
that the success of the new movement in the gentile world hinged on
this question, and here he drew his line in the sand. The Jewish/Mosaic
Law, he declared, had been superseded.

And what had Jesus to say on this crucial issue? The question is
never raised by Paul or his opponents. The decree placed in Jesus'
mouth in Matthew 5:18 and Luke 16:17, that not a dot or stroke of the
Law can lose its force, comes from Q. This would have destroyed
Paul's position, yet no one mentions it.

But regardless of whether or not Jesus actually said something on
an important issue like the continued applicability of the Law, it can
confidently be stated that it would not have taken long for one side or
the other in the debate to say that he *did*. If the founder of the
movement had been a dynamic and respected teacher, and disputes like
this later arose, it is inevitable that pronouncements on such subjects
would be invented and placed in his mouth. (This is exactly what we
find in abundance once the Gospel Jesus entered the picture.) Yet the
New Testament epistles offer no hint of such a thing.

Words of the Lord

All this silence does not prevent scholars from declaring that they
can detect "echoes" of Jesus' teachings in Paul—even if he never
attributes such things to a teaching Jesus. However, Paul four times
speaks of information he has received "from the Lord."

1 Thessalonians 4:16-17 is an apocalyptic oracle about what will
happen to living and dead Christians at the time of the Lord's coming,
expected soon. It has no parallel in the Gospels. 1 Corinthians 7:10-11
and 9:14 are presented by Paul as 'rulings' from the Lord about
community practice, the first that husbands and wives must not
divorce, the second that apostles proclaiming the gospel should be
financially supported. Both have parallels in the Gospels, but the
wordings are dissimilar.

Is Paul offering these things as pronouncements of the earthly Jesus,
words he has received from others who heard Jesus' own instructions?
There are those who think not.

Many scholars identify these passages as reflecting a phenomenon
common to the early Christian preaching movement. Prophets like Paul
were inspired through visions, through interpreting glossolalia
(speaking in tongues), through a study of scripture. They made

pronouncements which came, as they saw it, directly from the spiritual Christ in heaven. Paul is passing on to his readers directives and promises which he has received through inspiration.[16] (Whether this is to be regarded as the source of the fourth passage in this category, Paul's 'report' of Jesus' words at the "Lord's Supper" in 1 Corinthians 11:23f, will be examined in Chapter 4.)

Paul's own language points to a heavenly source for his "words of the Lord." Consider what he says a few verses after his directive against divorce, in 1 Corinthians 7:25:

> "About virgins (ie, celibacy) I do not have a command of the Lord, but I give my own opinion as one who by the Lord's mercy is trustworthy."

The first-person phrasing indicates a general category of things Paul is accustomed to possessing for himself, not as part of a wider community knowledge or inheritance from tradition. In offering his own opinion, its value is based entirely on his sense of personal worth and reliability in the eyes of God.

Paul has no sense of Jesus as a recent ethical teacher. Rather, Christ is a divine presence in Christian communities, bestowing revelation and guidance, a channel to God and to knowledge of spiritual truths. Christ has taken up residence in Christian believers themselves. It is the voice of this spiritual Son which Christians hear, not the passed-on words of a former teacher. And as we shall see, his very words can be read in scripture, God's way of revealing new truths to humanity.

All this is Paul's world. God and the heavenly Christ have been working through the Holy Spirit on men such as himself, and on believers who respond to them in faith. The next chapter will look at how Paul and the other writers describe this action of the Spirit, and how they have learned about the Son. But first we will turn to a background piece of the puzzle, for a view of the times out of which such a phenomenon arose.

3

A Thirst For the Irrational

In 334 BCE, when Alexander the Great led his army of Macedonians out of Greece and into Asia, he faced the ancient empire of the Persians and an even more ancient Oriental world with deep social and religious roots. Ten years later, when he reached Babylon after a path of conquest which swung as far east as India, the Persian empire lay in ruins and that ancient world was already being inundated by Greeks: Greek cities, Greek ideas, Greek culture. The new ruling class formed a veneer which never fully integrated with the native populations, but the mix inevitably produced a new culture. Predominantly Greek, infused with the old still-vital bloods, the eastern Mediterranean world embarked on the Hellenistic age. Its spirit lasted even into the era of imperial Rome, whose own culture continued to borrow heavily from the Greek east.

Alexander's grand vision of a new unified world of East and West was stillborn, for in 323, at the age of 33, he died of fever in Babylon after a drinking party. His generals fought for the spoils and the sprawling, short-lived empire broke up. The more easterly regions were almost immediately lost, but the rest solidified into three and eventually four kingdoms. War between them was prevalent. Old social cohesions crumbled in the new political situation. The Oriental temple-state form of nationalism gave way to one modeled on the Greek city-state, but without its former universal (male) democracy. Vast numbers of people felt lost and disenfranchised. Many had been displaced, and there was nothing familiar to return to. That ancient world was now bewilderingly multi-cultural. The individual was on his or her own.

Transcending the World

Formerly, religion had been tied to the state, an expression of the state's interests. People took part in it as members of a larger whole. But in the Hellenistic age, the focus of religion changed to one of personal concerns. When the world around them is unsettled and fragmented, people feel a greater thirst for understanding that world and how to cope with it. But even more so, how to transcend it.

Instead of the pursuit of philosophy for the sake of pure truth and to further the health of the state, as Plato and Aristotle had largely indulged in it, philosophical movements were now designed to help individuals find a place in a troubled world and give them peace of mind. The most important were the Stoics, Epicureans and Platonists. These and other systems had as a central concern the nature of deity (or lack of such) and how one should relate to it, together with the question of proper and beneficial moral behavior. Only in Stoicism was there any focus on taking an active part in public life; otherwise, the principal goal was to achieve freedom and self-sufficiency from the world.

Such doctrines were preached by wandering philosophers. They were a kind of "popular clergy," offering spiritual comfort—though usually demanding a fee. Some had an immense influence on a wide audience, as for example the Stoic philosopher Epictetus, who taught that the universe is governed by a benevolent and wise Providence, and that all men are brothers (in the sexist language of the time).

But philosophical advice was not the only thing people had recourse to. Healing gods, astrologers, magicians with their potions and spells, helped cope with evil forces in the world, and not only human ones. The conviction that unseen spirits and forces of fate were also working against them added to men's and women's distress. Demons were regarded as filling the very atmosphere of the earth and were thought to cause most misfortunes, from personal accidents and sickness to natural disasters. They even tempted the believer away from his faith.

Like the savior gods of the mystery cults, Christ Jesus offered deliverance from these evil forces, for the sacrificed god of the Christians was said to have placed all the supernatural powers of the universe under his subjection.

Some of the new Greek philosophical systems would have nothing to do with such superstitions. Stoicism and Epicureanism began as essentially rationalist philosophies. They aimed at living life according to Nature or to some rational principle by which the observable world could be understood or at least coped with. Views of Deity were fitted into this "natural" outlook. But during the first century BCE there developed a fundamental shift, and it coincided with the revival of Platonism which had lain, to a certain extent, in eclipse for a couple of centuries. In this new outlook, says John Dillon (*The Middle Platonists*, p.192), "the supreme object of human life is Likeness to

God, not Conformity with Nature." Middle Platonism, which soon came to dominate philosophical thinking in the period of early Christianity, was fundamentally religious and even mystical. A. J. Festugière (*Personal Religion Among the Greeks*, p.51) describes it as embodying a desire to escape: "Ah! To leave this earth, to fly to heaven, to be like unto the Gods and partake of their bliss."

This was the great religious yearning of the age: to undergo transformation, to transport oneself into a new world, an immortal life, union with the divine in a metamorphosed universe. The buzzword was "salvation." The ways to achieve it became the central concern of a proliferation of schools and cults, both Hellenistic and Jewish.

Higher and Lower Worlds

It is largely to Plato (who absorbed earlier ideas from Pythagoras and the mystery religion known as Orphism) and to the stream of later "Platonic" thinking which he set in motion, that we owe this sense of alienation from the world and the urge to move beyond it. In Platonism, there was a clear separation between the higher world (above the earth) of spiritual ultimate realities, where things were perfect and unchanging, and the earthly world of matter and the senses of which humans were a part. As an imperfect reflection of the upper one, comprised of things that were changing and perishable, this lower world was decidedly inferior. Human beings possessed a portion of the higher reality in that part of themselves called the "soul." It had existed before birth and been a part of the spiritual world. Now it was trapped in bodies of matter, but ultimately it would achieve release and reunite with the divine. The soul was immortal. Through the soul, the human being was destined to merge into some larger life.

Thus Christian ideas could show a respectable lineage for their division between the soul and the body, between the lower world and the higher, between this world and the future one—none of which was based on any observable evidence. By the time we get to Paul, Greek rationalism as embodied most fully in the Stoics is being openly maligned. It is "the wisdom of the world" which God has revealed (through apostles like Paul) to be foolishness.

Nor was human reason any longer the way to achieve the new wisdom. This too was a folly and even amenable to evil influence. The need for salvation could not be based on something as mundane as the power of the human mind to reason. In a sense, people looked for salvation from the limitations and weaknesses of being human, of living in an all-too-human world. The means to that salvation must therefore lie outside themselves, it had to be part of the thing being aimed at. Knowledge of salvation and the ways to achieve it could only come from God, through faith that he was providing these things.

People became convinced that they were receiving direct revelation from the Deity, through visions and ascents to heaven in dreams, through inspired understanding of sacred writings, through personal calls to preach. God was working in the world, and one need only attune oneself to him. The certainty that could not come from human reason came instead through faith.

Christianity and other Jewish apocalyptic sects, more mainstream Jewish proselytizing activities, various pagan salvation cults, all had their apostles tramping the byways of the empire, offering brands of redemption and future exaltation for the individual believer. By the middle decades of the first century, the world, in the phrase of John Dillon (*The Middle Platonists*, p.396), was "a seething mass of sects and salvation cults," operating amid a broader milieu of ethical and philosophical schools only a little less emotionally conducted. Stepping onto that stage is the first witness to the Christian movement, one who left us with the earliest surviving record of belief in a new Savior and system of salvation: the wandering apostle Paul.

The Spirit of God

When Paul steps onto that stage, where is he coming from? Has he been inspired by the career of the man he supposedly preaches? Does he see himself as carrying on Jesus' work? Is he part of a movement which traces its doctrines and authority back to the Son on earth?

There is no sign of such a thing, in Paul or any other epistle writer. Instead, Paul is driven by inspiration, and that inspiration comes through the Spirit of God. He tells us this over and over.

> "It is all God's doing. God has set his seal on us by sending the Spirit." [2 Corinthians 1:22, NEB]

> "We speak of these gifts of God in words found for us not by our human wisdom but by the Spirit." [1 Corinthians 2:13, NEB]

> "Did the word of God originate with you? Are you the only people to whom it came? If anyone claims to be inspired or a prophet, let him recognize that what I write has the Lord's authority." [1 Corinthians 14:36-37, NEB]

Elsewhere, the same sentiments can be noted. The writer of 1 Peter 1:12 tells his readers: "Preachers brought you the gospel in the power of the Holy Spirit sent from heaven."

This is a preaching movement begun and inspired by God, by revelation through the Spirit. There is not a word spent on any role for a human Jesus, on a beginning in the career of a recent historical man.

2 Corinthians 5:5 should astound us: "God has shaped us for life immortal, and as a guarantee of this he has sent the Spirit." How could Paul not have said that to give us life everlasting, God had sent Jesus? God, through the avenue of the Spirit, is the sole agent in all that has transpired, the sole source. It is he who has bestowed grace, his are the gifts. Romans 1:2 speaks of the "gospel of God," 3:24 of "God's act of redemption." It is God "who began the good work" in Philippians 1:6. Hebrews 13:7 refers to the apostles "who first spoke God's message to you."

So many writers pointedly ignore the centrality of Jesus' own role and actions. As late as 1 Timothy, the writer speaks of "the gospel which tells of the glory of God who is blessed." Such silences resound throughout the early Christian correspondence. They have a cumulative impact which cannot be dismissed.

Revealing the Secret of God's Son

And what is it that the Spirit of God, through revelation, has imparted to men like Paul? In a passing description of his conversion experience, Paul tells the Galatians:

"God chose to reveal his Son in me [to me and through me: NEB], in order that I might preach him among the gentiles." [1:16]

Paul is claiming that *he* is the medium of God's revelation; through him the world is learning about the Son, the newly-disclosed means of salvation for Jew and gentile alike.

The centerpiece of God's revelation is Christ himself: the existence of the Son and the role he has played in God's plan for salvation. Such things are not based on historical record, or on the interpretation of a recent man. They are part of a divine mystery, a secret hidden with God which has now been revealed.

In defending Christian doctrine in the opening chapters of 1 Corinthians, Paul says: "We speak of God's secret wisdom, a wisdom that has been hidden and that God designed for our glory before time began." When was that secret revealed? Through what agency?

In Romans 16:25, Paul proclaims his gospel

". . . about Jesus Christ, according to the revelation of the mystery kept in silence for long ages but now revealed, and made known through prophetic writings at the command of God . . ." [my trans.]

God's secret has lain unknown throughout the long ages of history. It has been disclosed for the first time through Paul's gospel, the source of which lies in scripture. In Colossians 2:2, pseudo-Paul speaks of the Laodiceans learning "the mystery of God, namely Christ, in whom are hidden all the treasures of wisdom and knowledge."

Earlier in that letter (1:26), the writer declares that the mystery "kept hidden for ages and generations is now disclosed . . . (that) Christ is in you, the hope of your glory." A passage in Ephesians (3:5) contains all the elements of the new drama: "The mystery about Christ (with its equal benefit to the gentiles) which in former generations was not made known to the human race, is now revealed to dedicated apostles and prophets through the Spirit."

No room has been made in any of these passages for Jesus' life and work in the process of revelation. All is from the Spirit sent to "dedicated" apostles like Paul, a secret revealed after being hidden throughout history with God in heaven. In the latter two passages above from Colossians and Ephesians, the "secret" has a narrower definition (Christ in you, the gentiles as sharers of the promise), and there are those who might argue that Jesus himself may not have been regarded as having taught these particular points. But is writer after writer going to speak of anything to do with the revelation of God's secrets surrounding Christ and never express the thought that the Son on earth was the first and primary revealer of such things?

Look at Titus 1:3, speaking as Paul.

"Yes, it is eternal life that God, who cannot lie, promised long ages ago, and now in his good time he has openly declared himself in the proclamation which was entrusted to me by God our Savior."

There is not a crack in this facade where Jesus could gain a foothold. In the past lie God's promises of eternal life, and his first action on those promises is the present revelation to apostles like Paul who have gone out to deliver the message. Jesus' own proclamation of eternal life, or whatever he may have proclaimed, has evaporated into the wind. Here is a prime example of the very exclusion of a human, historical Jesus.

The Language of Revelation

Christ has been revealed in the present time. The verbs used to describe this event express the language of disclosure, of revelation. No one says that Christ "came to earth" or "lived a life." Translators will sometimes convey the sense of incarnation, by reading into these words the Gospel idea of Jesus' life on earth, but such meanings are unnecessary.

The NEB gives an acceptable translation of 1 Peter 1:20:

"He (Christ) was predestined (or chosen) before the foundation of the world, and in this last period of time he was made manifest (or was revealed) for your sake."

To manifest or reveal is the predominant meaning of the Greek verb *"phaneroō."* It means "to bring to light, display, make known," to make evident to the senses or to mental perception things previously hidden or unknown. In a religious context it refers to a god (or God) giving evidence of his presence, or providing knowledge about himself (see 2 Corinthians 2:14) as in a religious experience. Occasionally it will refer to a dramatic appearance, as in a post-resurrection manifestation of Jesus (in the interpolated ending to the Gospel of Mark, 16:12) or his coming at the End-time (Col. 3:4, 1 Pet. 5:4). It would be difficult to make this verb encompass the idea of incarnation and living a life.

The image in passages like that of 1 Peter is one of God revealing Christ to the world in these last times. This fits everything which Paul says on the subject as well, though Paul prefers *apokaluptō* (to uncover, reveal, as in "apocalyptic"). This verb, too, can hardly apply to an incarnation.

The writer of Hebrews also uses *phaneroō* in speaking of what has happened in the present time (9:26). "But now, at the completion of the ages . . . he (Christ) has been manifested." Again, there is no reason why this verb cannot be taken in its basic meaning: Christ has been brought to light; God has revealed knowledge about him.

In Romans 3:21, Paul speaks of God's justice as being "brought to light," using *phaneroō*. He goes on to say that God has "displayed" or "set forth publicly" Christ and his atoning act. Finally, the Pastoral epistles use the word *epiphaneia*, "appearance," which in Hellenistic literature refers to the manifestation of a god's presence, with no sense of incarnation.

That a whole range of Christian writers would consistently use this sort of language to speak of Christ's coming in the present time, with never a more explicit reference to a life on earth, is curious to say the least. The two passages in the epistles which seem to constitute a direct reference to human characteristics of Christ (Romans 1:3 and Galatians 4:4) will be dealt with in detail later.

But Paul, inspired by God's revelation, has discovered more than the existence of the Son. He and the circles he moves in have learned, as part of God's newly-disclosed secret, that this Son had undergone a sacrifice—in the higher spiritual realm—and that certain benefits are now available to the believer. God, through Jesus' sacrificial act, has stored up the means of redemption in a heavenly bank account, as it were, and that account is now open for withdrawals. Such funds are available through faith and the rite of baptism. The nature of Jesus' sacrifice and the rising from death which followed it will be examined in Part Four, together with the mythical realm where it all took place.

But now we return to the picture of the apostolic movement which was preaching these things.

4

Apostles and Ministries

If Jesus had conducted a ministry within living memory, within Paul's own lifetime, remembrance of that ministry would surely have loomed large in Christian awareness. In the rough and tumble world of religious proselytizing, the appeal to Jesus' own words and actions, the urge to claim a direct link back to Jesus himself in order to confer authority and reliability on each apostle's preaching of the Christ, would have been an inevitable mark of the early missionary movement. There would also have been an appeal to the apostles who had been chosen by Jesus and heard the words he spoke. If too much time had passed, that appeal would have been to those whom such followers had themselves appointed and given the proper doctrine.

As Christianity approached the second century of its existence, these ideas start to appear in the wider written record and are known as "apostolic tradition."

Fishers of Men

Yet the surprising fact is that such a picture is completely missing in all the non-Gospel evidence of the first century. That evidence contains a void on the very concept of followers of an earthly Jesus.

If an earthly Jesus had chosen personal followers—referred to in the Gospels and Acts as "disciples"—one would not know it from Paul or other early writers. The word "disciple(s)" never appears in the New Testament documents outside the Gospels and Acts, even though many of these supposed followers of Jesus would still have been alive at the time of Paul, brimming with memories and stories of their experiences with the Master himself. On such things the epistles are silent.

By contrast, the word "apostle" means "messenger," and the epistles are saturated with the idea. It refers to those who are "sent out" to deliver a preaching message, usually by God. This was an age when many believed they were being called by some deity or other to go out into the world and offer a message of salvation. In the Gospels, the term refers to those chosen and sent out by Jesus, and it became narrowly applied to the group known as the Twelve, although these could also be referred to, in their attendance on Jesus during his ministry, as the "twelve disciples." Strictly speaking, when these "disciples" went out to preach, both during and after Jesus' life, they became "apostles." (See Matthew 10:1-2.)

Yet Paul gives us no hint that this selection of disciples and apostles by Jesus was a factor in the world in which he moved. In 1 Corinthians 12:28, he says that in the church, *God* had appointed apostles, prophets and teachers. In Galatians 1 and 2, he calls the Jerusalem group "those who were apostles before me," with no suggestion that there was any difference in the quality or nature of their respective apostleships. In 2:8 he declares that God has made Peter an apostle to the Jews just as he made Paul an apostle to the gentiles.[17] (Every apostle regarded himself as "called," and any who had been followers of Jesus could not fail to have regarded themselves as being called by him.)

But the most important dispute Paul has to deal with is the threat to his very legitimacy. As Galatians and the Corinthian letters show, Paul and his gospel are being challenged by others. His competence, his authority, his reliability are being denigrated by rivals. And what is Paul's standard for legitimacy? In 1 Corinthians 9:1 he asks plaintively, "Am I not an apostle? Did I not see Jesus our Lord?" Paul's claim that he too has "seen the Lord" implies that his type of seeing—which no one would dispute was entirely visionary—is the same as that of the apostles to whom he is comparing himself. Otherwise, his appeal to his own vision of the Lord as placing himself legitimately within their ranks would be meaningless. But those other apostles include Peter and the Jerusalem group. Thus the conclusion must be that these men too knew the Lord *only* by this kind of "seeing," namely a visionary one.

In a highly emotional defense of his apostleship in 2 Corinthians 10-12, Paul compares himself to unnamed rivals who are competing for the Corinthians' affections:

"Someone is convinced, is he, that he belongs to Christ? Let him think again, and reflect that we belong to Christ as much as he does." [NEB]

The issue of a connection to an earthly Jesus is nowhere in sight. Nor does it surface in arguments like the following (2 Cor. 12:11-12):

"In no respect did I fall short of these superlative apostles, even if I am a nobody. The marks of the true apostle were there, in the work I

(did among you, which called for such constant fortitude, and was attended by signs, marvels and miracles." [NEB]

"Are they servants of Christ?" Paul asks in 11:23. So is he, he declares, and goes on to list the sufferings and setbacks he has endured in the service of the gospel. Paul appeals only to the strength and reliability of his own revelations. He has been in direct contact with heaven. He is an apostle who owes his gospel directly to God, he says,[18] not to some other men who taught him the results of their own revelations (Galatians 1:11-12).

The picture we get from Paul is of a sprawling, uncoordinated movement of wandering apostles going about preaching a divine Son. Rivals accuse one another of not carrying the proper doctrine, of not being qualified, but no one appeals to Jesus as an authority, no one traces anything through channels leading back to him. This is a level playing field.

Where has that "proper doctrine" come from? In 2 Corinthians 11:4, Paul defends himself against those apostles who have made inroads into his congregation in Corinth:

> "If someone comes who proclaims another Jesus, not the Jesus whom we proclaimed, or if you then receive a spirit different from the Spirit already given to you, or a gospel different from the gospel you have already accepted, you manage to put up with that." [NEB]

The teaching of these rivals, as well as his own, is not derived from a human Jesus. It is the product of perceived revelation. It comes through the "Spirit" which everyone claims to have received from God. The spirit his rivals have received Paul declares to be different and inferior to his own. In fact, their preaching of "another Jesus" is so incompatible with his that he can condemn them as "sham apostles, crooked in all their practices, masquerading as apostles of Christ . . . (who) will meet the end their deeds deserve." [11:13-15, NEB]

Such language should tell us that these apostles are not the group in Jerusalem around Peter and James. Not only would Paul have been unlikely to speak of the Jerusalem apostles as basing their view of Jesus on the Spirit (they would do so instead according to their *memories* of him), Paul could never have spoken of them with such vilification and absolute rejection. Elsewhere, his dealings with Peter and the others are at least courteous, if at times uneasy, and throughout his career he is engaged in making a financial collection from his gentile communities on behalf of the church in Jerusalem.

Of his rivals in Corinth, Paul is forced to allow, grudgingly, that they are, by some objective standard which the Corinthians accept, "servants of Christ." All this supports a picture of early Christianity as a varied, amorphous movement of groups and individuals, inspired by revelation, owing no allegiance to a central authority, having no unified point of origin or set of doctrines. Each apostle proclaimed his own version of the spiritual Christ to the hearts and minds of anyone who would listen.[19]

"The Twelve"

Paul applies the term "apostle" to a wide range of Christian missionaries, from himself and Barnabas and assorted other colleagues, to rivals he viciously condemns. As noted above, it is only with the Gospels, written a half century or more after Jesus' supposed death, that we find the term narrowed to a select group of men personally chosen by Jesus. Some scholars, such as Rudolf Bultmann (*Theology of the New Testament* I, p.37), have rejected outright the historicity of the Twelve as an inner circle accompanying Jesus in his ministry.

Does Paul give us any evidence of the "twelve" apostles as the Gospels present them? The term appears once in his letters, when he lists those who had visions of the Christ (1 Corinthians 15:5-7):

". . . he was seen by Cephas, and afterward by the Twelve . . . then he was seen by James and afterward by all the apostles."

From this, one might conclude that Peter (Cephas) is not a member of "the Twelve" and that the group known as "the apostles" is larger than the Twelve and may not include them. What this body actually constituted in Paul's time remains a mystery. Paul's account in Galatians of his first visit to Jerusalem following his conversion makes no mention of them as a group, and the only names of apostles from Jerusalem which he records anywhere in his letters are Peter, John and James, the latter being the head of the Jerusalem church, not the James of the twelve in Gospel tradition.[20]

Apostolic Tradition

When it finally developed in the second century, the concept of apostolic tradition served important needs for the growing Christian movement. After the Gospel Jesus of Nazareth came to be regarded as an historical figure, Christian congregations felt the need for a pipeline back to him, a guarantee that the doctrines they held were correct and had been instituted by Jesus himself. The point of contact at the other end of that pipeline became a select group of followers Jesus had called to be witnesses to his teachings, death and resurrection. Many were based on legendary apostles of the early period. A reliable conduit to those original witnesses had to be formed, a supposedly unbroken chain of teaching and authority extending from the earliest apostles to the later church. When records of bishops and other appointees were found not to exist, they were simply constructed. Every Christian group, orthodox or heretical, eventually had its own chain going back to one of those original apostles, usually regarded as the founder of its own community and serving as a guarantor of its doctrinal "correctness."

That this "apostolic tradition" was missing earlier can be seen from several documents. Chapter 11 of the Didache contains instructions to the community on how to judge the legitimacy of wandering apostles, both in their teaching and their charismatic activities. Yet no part of this judgment is based upon the principle of apostolic tradition; there is no question of tracing authority or correctness back to Jesus or even to earlier apostles. In Hebrews 13:7, the author tells his readers: "Remember your leaders, those who first spoke God's message to you." Not only are those leaders not located in a line going back to the earliest apostles, the message is not from Jesus, but from God.

But the truly arresting silence is found in 1 John 4:1.

"Do not trust any and every spirit (ie, prophetic utterance), my friends; test the spirits, to see whether they are from God, for among those who have gone out into the world there are many prophets falsely inspired." [NEB]

What is the test which determines whether a Christian apostle is speaking truth? This epistle was written probably in the last decade of the first century. One would think that by this time such Christians would possess a body of material regarded as proceeding from Jesus himself, transmitted to them over the decades through a channel of authorized apostles and leaders. But such an idea is nowhere to be found in the Johannine epistles. There is not even the barest concept of a teaching passed on between generations, arising out of an apostolic past. Instead, as in Paul, true doctrine comes directly through revelation from God, inspired by the Holy Spirit, though some "spirits" are false and come from the devil. (Here they are labeled the "Antichrist," the first appearance of this term in Christian documents.)

For I Received What I Passed On To You

Does Paul never refer to apostolic tradition? The Greek verb "*paralambanō*" is used in three key passages in his letters. It means to "receive," to "take over" something passed on to oneself, usually relating to information or instruction. However, it was a verb also used in the Greek mysteries and in religious experiences generally, to refer to the reception of a revelation from a god. Paul himself applies it in both ways in a crucial passage in Galatians 1:11-12:

> "For I neither received it [ie, the gospel Paul preaches] from (any) man, nor was I taught it, but [understood: I received it] through a revelation of Jesus Christ." [NASB]

In this one sentence, Paul uses *paralambanō* in both meanings: receiving something from other men, and receiving something by revelation. (In the second thought, the verb is understood, but it cannot be anything other than the "received" verb used earlier; the "taught" verb would be in contradiction to the idea of revelation.)

Here Paul makes a clear and passionate statement that the gospel he preaches about the Christ has come to him through personal revelation, not through human channels, not from other apostles. The details of that gospel are not spelled out here, but from what he has said in the preceding verses, and from common sense, Paul must be referring to his central message about the Christ, his fundamental doctrine.

As such, Galatians 1:11-12 must determine how we read the statement he makes in 1 Corinthians 15:3-4:

> "For I delivered to you . . . what I also received, that Christ died for our sins according to the scriptures; and that he was buried; and that he was raised on the third day, according to the scriptures." [NASB]

Here we have a statement of Paul's basic gospel. In Galatians 1:11-12 he has declared that he received his gospel from no man, but through revelation. Unless we accept that he is blatantly contradicting himself, logic dictates that Paul's "received" in 1 Corinthians 15:3 must mean "received through revelation."

A corollary. If Christ dying for sin and rising from death is a revealed gospel, then it would seem that both the death and resurrection are articles of faith, not of historical witness. Paul is not likely to declare that he knows of these things through revelation if they are common knowledge through passed-on oral tradition. And where has Paul derived his information about Christ's death and resurrection? He tells us twice in 1 Corinthians 15:3-4: "according to the scriptures." While scholars have always taken this to mean "in fulfilment of the scriptures"—though this is an idea Paul nowhere discusses—the Greek preposition *kata* can also render the meaning of the phrase "as we learn from the scriptures."[21]

If the "receiving" of Paul's gospel is through revelation, this enables us to interpret the third important passage in which he uses the same verb. This is crucial to the argument of the myth theory, and is that third "apparent exception" to my Missing Equation I spoke of in Chapter 1, the passage that seems to be the sole Gospel-like scene in all of Paul's letters.

1 Corinthians 11:23-26 begins:

> "For I received (the verb *paralambanō*) from the Lord that which I passed on to you, that the Lord Jesus, on the night he was delivered up, took bread, and when he had given thanks, broke it and said: 'This is my body, which is for you . . .' " [my trans.]

Since *paralambanō* has meant 'received through revelation' in other places, and since Paul speaks generally about his doctrine as coming through this channel—and since the words plainly say so—we ought to read this passage as meaning that Paul has received this information through a direct revelation from the Lord Jesus himself.

But here too, if he means that this information came to him through revelation, he is unlikely to be referring to an historical event. In the Corinthians' eyes, it would be ridiculous for Paul to say he got it from the Lord if the Supper and the words spoken there were an historical incident well-known to Christians. Most scholars, however, still insist on viewing this as passed-on tradition, presumably from apostles like Peter who were at the supposed event.[22]

If Paul knows of this "Supper" not through human reportage but by personal revelation, this removes the whole scene from any necessity of having taken place in history. It can be assigned to the realm of myth, where similar scenes in the mystery cults were located. We will revisit 1 Corinthians 11:23f and look at some of its other features when examining ancient myth and the mysteries in Part Four.

Paul's Ministry of Glory

When Paul speaks of his work as an apostle, there is no sense that he regards himself as building on the work of Jesus. It is Paul who has received from God "the ministry of reconciliation" (2 Cor. 5:18-19); it is he whom God has qualified "to dispense his new covenant" (2 Cor. 3:5). Paul's disregard for Jesus' own ministry of reconciliation or dispensation of the new covenant is astonishing. The parallel to Moses' splendor in the giving of the old covenant is not Jesus' recent ministry, it is the splendor of Paul's ministry through the Spirit (2 Cor. 3:7-11).

The role of Jesus on earth seems to have been forgotten. "It is all God's doing," Paul tells the Corinthians, "he has set his seal upon us" (2 Cor. 1:21-22). It is "by God's own act" (Gal. 4:7) that the gentiles are heirs to the promise. No act of Jesus is in evidence. "All that may be known of God by men . . . God himself has disclosed to them," Paul states in Romans 1:19. But what had Jesus been doing on earth if not disclosing God? Had not God's attributes been visible in him?

Nor does Jesus play a role in the response of the believer. It is God who calls the Corinthians "to share in the life of his Son" (1 Cor. 1:9), God who "appeals" to them through Paul (2 Cor. 5:20). The Christians of Thessalonica have been "called to holiness" not by Jesus but by God (1 Thess. 4:8), and if they flout Paul's rules, they flout God, "who bestows on (them) his Holy Spirit."

The void Paul reveals on the ministry of Jesus is nowhere so evident as in Romans 10. Here he is discussing the 'guilt' of the Jews for not responding to the message about the Christ, even though they had every opportunity to do so. But what did that opportunity encompass? Paul speaks only of those apostles like himself who had been sent out to deliver the message (10:13-21). Where is the opportunity the Jews had enjoyed when they heard it from the person of Jesus himself? For at least some of them had been witnesses to his earthly ministry. How could Paul fail to highlight his countrymen's spurning of the Son of God in the flesh?

In this passage, Paul contrasts the Jews with the gentiles who have accepted the gospel message. But he passes up the obvious point of contrast: that whereas the Jews had rejected the message even though delivered by Jesus himself, the gentiles had accepted it second-hand.

Paul goes on in Romans 11 to reveal another remarkable silence. As part of his criticism of the Jews' failure to respond to men like himself, he refers to Elijah's words in 1 Kings: "Lord, they have killed thy prophets." This idea that the Jewish establishment had a long habit of killing prophets sent from God was popular among Jewish sectarian circles, although it was founded on little historical basis. But it is a telling silence that Paul does not add to this supposed record the ultimate atrocity of the killing of the Son of God himself.

5

Apocalyptic Expectations

Paul and other Christian apostles are not only preaching salvation through the Son. They are forecasting an imminent and dramatic overthrow of the present world.

In 1 Thessalonians 4:15-17, Paul informs his readers:

"For this we tell you as the Lord's word: we who are left alive until the Lord comes shall not forestall those who have died; because at the word of command, at the sound of the archangel's voice and God's trumpet-call, the Lord himself will descend from heaven; first the Christian dead will rise, then we who are left alive shall join them, caught up in clouds to meet the Lord in the air. Thus we shall always be with the Lord." [NEB]

A few verses later, Paul warns: "For you know very well that the day of the Lord comes like a thief in the night." This is very similar to Jesus' saying in Matthew 24:42 and Luke 12:39, where he warns of the unpredictable arrival of the Son of Man, yet Paul shows no sign that he is aware of any such saying by Jesus. Several other epistle writers make predictions about the coming End, about troubled times and the arrival of a heavenly judge, but none point to Jesus' Gospel predictions about the Day of the Lord and his own arrival at the End-time. No one mentions any element of the Gospel picture of Jesus (Mark 13 and parallels) as a prophet of an apocalyptic transformation of the world.

The Day of the Lord

The Day of the Lord. The determining mythic belief of much of Jewish society. It colored the entire post-Exilic period until the destruction of Jerusalem and the Jewish state in two cataclysmic revolts against Rome: 66-70 CE and 132-135 CE. Thereafter, the Jewish people were truly dispersed for almost two millennia.

Through centuries of foreign subjugation—abated for one century under the Maccabean kings—from the Babylonian conquest in the 6th century BCE which sent much of the population into exile, through successive overlords Persian, Macedonian and Roman, the Jews built a unique future myth for themselves.

This myth said that God would one day rescue the Jews from their distress and humiliation, establish a new covenant with his chosen people, and raise them to their destined rule over the nations of the earth. One line of thought said that God would accomplish all this through a Messiah (Anointed One), a conqueror and righteous ruler who would be descended from the great king of Israel's past, David.

Prophets at the time of the Exile had begun the trend by promising a restoration at God's hand from the ravages of the Babylonians. But although many eventually returned from Babylon to set up a new state when Cyrus the Persian overthrew the Babylonian empire, Israel remained under foreign yoke and hardly enjoyed a restoration on the scale that Ezekiel, Jeremiah and (Second) Isaiah had confidently promised. And so, their prophecies, supplemented by those of other prophets, came to be seen as speaking of a time yet to come, and the tale grew with the telling. Disasters for their enemies, miracles and a resurrection for the pious, a remaking of the whole earth, such things became the popularly-held scenario of the eagerly awaited day when God or his Messiah would arrive to judge the world and establish his kingdom. God's kingdom became the beacon that lighted the future toward which so many turned their gaze.

But it was all contingent on one thing: the achievement of Israel's purity through a faithful observance of God's Law. This outlook was one of the driving forces in the study and refinement of the Mosaic laws, in a quest to discover just exactly what it was that God wanted of his people. The problem was that this achievement of national purity lay nowhere in sight, as the Hellenistic age progressed and Greek culture made substantial inroads into Jewish society, especially at the level of the ruling class. As time went on, therefore, many despaired and a new idea entered the picture. Only a righteous elect would be saved, while all the rest, Jew and gentile alike, were to be consigned to some cataclysmic judgment of fire. This expectation of a violent transformation of the world is generally called "apocalypticism."[23]

To these nationalistic yearnings we need to add broader social ones. The poor, the socially disadvantaged, the oppressed, also looked for some kind of upheaval in which justice would be dispensed and the lot of rich and poor reversed. War, disease, taxation and superstition took their toll on people's spirits until only the direct intervention of God was seen to promise a way out of the world's misery. It was an emotionally unsettled era. In Roman times, Zealot leaders and would-be Messiahs regularly arose to lead great numbers of the common people into excited demonstrations and riots. They were usually slaughtered by the Roman military authorities.

Such conditions and expectations led to the formation of special interest and sectarian groups within Jewish society, until eventually the 'mainstream' class surrounding the Temple cult was fringed by numerous sects going off at countless tangents of religious philosophy and apocalyptic hopes. They included reform movements, some of whom rejected the Temple cult; baptist sects advocating repentance, using ritual washings; esoteric groups based on their own interpretations of scripture, many imbued with ideas from Hellenistic theology, philosophy and magic. Much of this sectarian activity went on outside Palestine, where Greek influences were especially strong.

Among a profusion of Jewish apocalyptic sects was the movement we now call Christianity. It was neither uniform in origin or in beliefs, unless it be in its focus on a divine Christ. For something had happened to the human figure, the Anointed One of God, descendant of David, who would arise to establish God's kingdom on earth. In the minds of some he had been transformed into a divinity, part of God himself, and he would arrive from heaven at the climax of history.

The Coming of the Lord

At the end of 1 Corinthians, Paul makes an urgent plea in Aramaic: *Marana tha*—Come, O Lord! John the prophet, at the end of his sanguinary prophecy of the world's destruction and renewal, the Book of Revelation, makes a similar entreaty: "Come, Lord Jesus!" In between, epistle writers from Paul on make frequent reference to the arrival of the Son at the End-time. But is this a *second* coming? Consider the flavor of these passages:

> Philippians 1:6: "The One (ie, God) who started the good work in you will bring it to completion by the Day of Christ Jesus."
> Philippians 3:20: "We are citizens of heaven, and from heaven we expect our deliverer to come, the Lord Jesus Christ."
> 2 Thessalonians 1:7: "(God will send relief to us) when our Lord Jesus Christ is revealed from heaven with his mighty angels in blazing fire."
> 1 Peter 1:7: ". . . so that your faith may prove itself worthy when Jesus Christ is revealed."

If readers can free themselves from Gospel preconceptions, they should find that these and other references of the same nature convey the distinct impression that this will be the Lord Jesus' first and only coming to earth, that this longing to see Christ has in no way been previously fulfilled. We keep waiting for the sense of "return" or the simple use of a word like "again." We wait for these writers to clarify, to acknowledge, that Jesus had already been on earth, had begun the work he would complete at the Parousia (his "coming" at the End-time); that men and women had formerly witnessed their deliverance in the event of Jesus' death and resurrection; that he had been "revealed" (one of Paul's favorite words in speaking of the Parousia) to the sight of all in his incarnated life as Jesus of Nazareth. But never an echo of such ideas do we hear in the background of these passages.

Perhaps the most telling reference of them all is Hebrews 10:37:

"For soon, very soon (in the words of scripture) 'he who is to come will come and will not delay.' "

This is from Habakkuk 2:3 (LXX[24]). The prophet was referring to God himself, but by the Christian period this was one of those many biblical passages reinterpreted as referring to the Messiah. Indeed, the Greek participle *erchomenos*, which the Septuagint (LXX) employs, became a virtual title, used with a masculine article, "*the* Coming One," and referred to the expected savior figure who would arrive at the End-time. Hebrews is clearly using it as a reference to Christ.

But stop and think a moment. The writer is affirming his belief that "the Coming One will come, and soon," for so the prophet has promised. Is he referring to the Gospel Jesus and his supposed Second Coming in glory? It is certainly the coming in glory at the End-time that he has in mind, but how can it be a *second* coming, for the writer has made no room for a previous one. If the prophet has prophesied Christ's coming, was this not earlier fulfilled in his incarnation, when he came to earth as Jesus of Nazareth? This is how Christians later interpreted all those prophetic passages about the Messiah: they referred to his life on earth. Even if the writer of Hebrews wishes to apply Habakkuk's words to the Parousia instead, he needs at least to show some awareness of Jesus' earlier coming, in order to avoid confusion. His silence indicates that for him Christ's coming is still to be, that he has no concept of the Son of God already having been here. As 10:37 expresses itself, the scriptural promise of Christ's arrival has not yet been fulfilled.[25]

Despite the picture provided by the Gospels that it is Jesus who will arrive at the End-time to judge the world and establish God's rule, early Christian documents are far from unanimous that it is the Son who is destined to perform this task. James, for example, speaks of the Parousia of the Lord (5:7) where he clearly means God himself, and 1 John, though the meaning is sometimes debated, also envisions the arrival of God, not Jesus (2:28-3:2). The same is true of the Didache 16, "The Lord will come," which quotes Zechariah 14:5, referring to God.

The Son of Man

No picture of Jesus coming at the Parousia should be able to ignore his End-time identity as the Son of Man. The Son of Man saturates the Gospels. Yet this dramatic apocalyptic figure, with whom Jesus identifies himself in all his predictions, who announces himself before the High Priest, this favorite self-designation of Jesus even in regard to his activities on earth, is in fact studiously ignored by Paul and every other writer of the New Testament letters.

The Son of Man was born in the fevered mind of the author of the Book of Daniel. This was probably written during the crisis surrounding the Maccabean revolt (c168 BCE), when the Jews successfully resisted the desecration of the Temple by the current Greek overlord, Antiochus IV. The author purports to be Daniel, a wise Jew living at the time of the Babylonian Exile. (This makes his 'predictions' about the intervening four centuries quite accurate!) Daniel undergoes visions of the far future—the time of the writer—in which the Jews are foretold as finally overthrowing all foreign oppressors and receiving dominion over the earth from God. The latter event is symbolized by the vision scene in 7:13-14 in which "one like a son of man" approaches the divine throne and is granted "sovereignty and glory and kingly power . . . so that all people and nations of every language should serve him." This is said to be a sovereignty "which shall never pass away."

Whether this "one like a son of man" is regarded by the author as an angel, or a son-like divine figure, or simply as a metaphor, is something still under debate, but he is described by the angel interpreting the vision (7:27) as representing the "saints of the Most High," namely, the righteous elect of Israel. As such, he is their *paradigm* (see Part Four).

In the latter half of the first century CE, the Danielic Son of Man surfaces in a cluster of Jewish and Christian writings (4 Ezra, 1 Enoch,

Revelation, Q and the Gospels), variously interpreted. He has now become an entity in his own right, an apocalyptic figure from heaven who will be involved in the imminent End-time, usually as a judge— God's agent, Messiah-like, perhaps even divine. Only in the Gospels and the latest layer of Q is he identified with an historical Jesus.

That the Son of Man was not a figure in early Christian expectation—let alone identified with a human Jesus—is virtually certain from the complete silence about him in all the epistles. Paul in particular is preoccupied with the imminent End. It seems inconceivable that if the Gospel picture were correct, Paul would either be unaware of Jesus' declared role as the Son of Man, or choose to ignore it.

The Change of the Ages

Given the early Christian view of the imminent transformation of the world and the establishment of God's kingdom, an apostle like Paul should have looked back to the life and ministry of Jesus as a milestone, a crucial point in the ongoing pattern of salvation history which was to culminate in the Day of the Lord.

The Jewish conception of history and time was fairly simple. The period stretching back through known history was the "old age," an age of sin and evil and darkness, when God had permitted Satan to rule, when the righteous were persecuted and divine justice was delayed. The "new age" would begin with the arrival of some heavenly figure or messianic agent of God, who would direct the overthrow of Israel's enemies and the forces of evil generally. This would be preceded by a build-up period in which woes and natural disasters would be visited upon the earth, to test the faithful. In some pictures, an archetypal evil figure, sometimes Satan himself, sometimes his lieutenant, would direct all this final mayhem, but he would ultimately be overthrown and the kingdom would dawn. Later, in Christian thinking, this figure would be known as the Antichrist. Still, the pattern of salvation history, stretching in a line from past through to future, fell into two sections: the old age and the new. Scholars refer to this pattern as "two-age dualism."

In the orthodox picture of Christian origins, however, a radically new dimension has been added. The Messiah had come, but not the kingdom with him. Christ had died and been resurrected, but still the new age had not dawned. That was to be delayed until his return, this time in glory and as judge at the Parousia. Between the two comings of

Christ, as brief a period as that might be, the gospel message had to be carried to as many as possible and the world had to be made ready.

If this was indeed the scenario faced by the first few generations of Christian preachers and believers, we would expect to find two things. First, a significant recasting of the two-age pattern. The coming of Jesus would have been seen as a pivotal point in the ongoing scheme of redemption history. Second, that very failure of expectation would have required explanation. No one could have anticipated—and no one did—that the arrival of the Messiah would *not* be accompanied by the establishment of the kingdom. We would expect to find some kind of apologetic industry arising within the Christian movement to explain this disappointing turn of events.

But do we find either of these two features in the epistles?

We have seen several passages in the Pauline letters which speak of the long-hidden divine "mysteries" which God has now revealed to "apostles and prophets." There was no sign of Jesus' ministry there, no mention of a distinctive stage between the primal event of God's promise and the present missionary movement heralding the new age.

But the revealing passages are those in which Paul expresses his apocalyptic expectations. The first one to look at is Romans 8:22-3:

> "Up to now, we know, the whole created universe groans in all its parts as if in the pangs of childbirth. Not only so, but even we, to whom the Spirit is given as firstfruits of the harvest to come, are groaning inwardly while we wait for God to make us his sons and set our whole body free." [NEB]

Here Paul's orientation is squarely on the future. The whole universe is groaning, waiting. Where is the sense of past fulfilment in the life and career of Jesus? Were some of the world's pains not assuaged by his coming? "Up to now," says Paul, has the universe labored to give birth, leaving no room for the dramatic pivot point of Christ's own birth and acts of salvation. Moreover, when Paul does refer to present or immediately past events, what are they? Only the giving of the Spirit, the revelation by God which has enlisted men like Paul to preach Christ and his coming. We have here no basic deviation from the traditional two-age picture.

Go on to Romans 13:11-12:

> "Remember how critical the moment is . . . for salvation is nearer to us now than it was when we first believed. It is far on in the night; day is near."

Was there no dawn at the incarnation of the Son of God? Had Jesus' recent presence on earth failed to dispel any of night's darkness? Even salvation itself is something which lies entirely in the future, and its only point of reference in the past is not Christ's act of redemption itself, but the moment when Christians first believed.

This is not a post-messianic world, it is not post-Jesus. To the extent that Paul envisions any pivot point in the past, it is the time of revelation, the giving of the Spirit, the arrival of faith when God disclosed Christ and people responded to the carriers of that revelation. Paul looks backward only to the unveiling of the mystery about the Son.

"Upon us the fulfilment of the ages has come!"

So Paul declares in 1 Corinthians 10:11, pointing to the Parousia which he believes is very near. But how can Paul avoid addressing the inevitable question: why had the actual coming of the Messiah not produced the turn of the ages? For this had been the expectation of centuries.

Christ "foretold" in the prophets. The day of salvation revealed in the scriptures. But was it the life of Christ that had been foretold? The Son's historical act of redemption, located in Paul's recent past? Not according to 2 Corinthians 6:2 (here literally):

"God says: 'At the acceptable time I gave heed to you; on the day of deliverance I came to your aid.' Behold, now is the acceptable time, now the day of salvation."

Paul's quote is Isaiah 49:8. It is one thing for Paul to ignore Jesus' career and claim the ministry of the new covenant glory for himself. It is quite another for Paul to claim that the prophetic words of scripture foretell not Jesus' life as "the acceptable time," not Jesus' acts of sacrifice and resurrection as "the day of salvation," but Paul's own activities and his preaching of the Christian message!

Luke at least could recognize the monumental inappropriateness of this (if he had even read Paul) for in 4:19 of his Gospel, he has Jesus in a Nazareth synagogue read a similar passage from Isaiah (61:1-2) and declare to the startled assembly that it is he to whom this sacred prophecy refers.

Part Two
A LIFE IN ECLIPSE

6

From Bethlehem to Jerusalem

If the voice of Jesus in the early Christian correspondence is silent on everything from ethical teachings to apocalyptic predictions, if his calling of apostles during an earthly ministry is nowhere in evidence in the early apostolic movement, what about the physical details of his birth, ministry and passion? Is the life portrayed in the Gospels that is supposed to have been lived in the time of two Herods and Pontius Pilate anywhere in evidence in the New Testament epistles?

Many of the elements in the Gospel story have been rejected by modern critical scholarship as unhistorical. But our purpose is to examine all of them, and to show that the Gospels are unreliable as an historical record, or as providing any basis for supporting the historicity of Jesus. This survey will also demonstrate that Christian documents outside the Gospels, even at the end of the first century and beyond, show no evidence that *any* traditions about an earthly life and ministry of Jesus were in circulation. Even in regard to Jesus' death and resurrection, to which many of those documents refer, there is no earthly setting provided for such events.

We will look at the epistolary silence on the Gospel story in two chapters, the first from the Nativity to the Last Supper, the second the passion scene of trial and crucifixion.

A Mortal Son of Mary

Around the year 107 Ignatius, bishop of Antioch, was escorted by Roman soldiers to the capital of the empire where he was condemned to die a martyr's death in the brutal arena. On the way, he wrote letters to various Christian churches in Asia Minor. In several of them he spoke out stridently on the subject of heresy. Those who held doctrines at variance with his own were labeled "mad dogs" and "beasts in the form of men."

Just what was this heresy? To the Christian community at Tralles, Ignatius wrote:

> "Close your ears, then, if anyone preaches to you without speaking of Jesus Christ. Christ was of David's line. He was the son of Mary, who was really born, ate and drank, was really persecuted under Pontius Pilate, was really crucified. . . . He was also truly raised from the dead." (Epistle to the Trallians 9:1f)

From the sound of it, Ignatius is arguing for a belief in the actual historicity of these events: that Jesus had been the son of a woman named Mary, that he had suffered and died under Pontius Pilate, the infamous Roman governor of Judea at the time of Herod Antipas. This is the Jesus Christ whom those he rails against seem not to be preaching. (See Appendix 3 on the question of docetism.)

Ignatius in the first decade of the second century believes in a Jesus born of Mary, baptized by John, executed by Pilate in the days of Herod. He does not seem to be familiar with a written Gospel, for he does not point to one to support his claims. Does anyone before him, outside the early Gospel writers, possess this biographical data about Jesus? To judge by all the surviving Christian correspondence, the answer is no. (The one reference in the epistles to Pilate, in 1 Timothy 6:13, if authentic, probably comes slightly later than Ignatius: see Appendix 1.)

Non-Gospel Christian writings before Ignatius have nothing to say about Mary; her name is never mentioned. Nor does Joseph, Jesus' reputed father, ever appear. The author of 1 Peter fails to offer Mary as a model in 3:1-6 where he is advising women to be chaste, submissive in their behavior, and reverent like those "who fixed their hopes on (God)." Instead, he offers the Old Testament figure of Sarah.

As for the Nativity stories in Matthew and Luke, images of the birth of Jesus bombard us at every Christmas, but nowhere in the first century are such images discernible. Shepherds, angels, magi, mangers or overbooked inns are never mentioned; nor is the city of Bethlehem or the great census under Augustus. No star lights up the night sky at Jesus' birth in either Christian or pagan writings. No association with the cruel Herod and his slaughter of innocent children, an event unrecorded by historians of the time, is ever made.

And what of Revelation 12? Amid the great portents of the End-time drawn by the prophet John is the vision of the "woman robed with the sun," the woman who, threatened by a great dragon, gives birth to "a male child destined to rule all nations with an iron rod." Later Christians took this as a reference to Mary and the infant Jesus, but the writer of Revelation makes no attempt to integrate his vision (whose fulfilment lies in the future) into any traditions about Jesus' birth and parentage. Immediately after the birth, the child is "snatched up to God and his throne," and the mother flees into the wilderness. There is not so much as a nod to Jesus' entire life. No connection is made between this male child and the sacrificed Lamb who is another of John's heavenly apocalyptic figures.

In fact, the scene has nothing to do with Mary and Jesus. It relates to Jewish apocalyptic mythology (borrowing motifs from Hellenistic myths of Leto and Apollo) about the miraculous birth of the Messiah, who simply waits in heaven for the End-time. But John's silence indicates that he knows nothing about traditions familiar to us from the Gospels, nothing about Mary or a human birth of Jesus. If he had, they would inevitably have influenced his crafting of characters which his readers would have assumed bore an obvious relationship to them.

Brother of the Lord

Did Jesus have a brother? Mark gives him four, and in Galatians 1:19 we read the words: "James, the brother of the Lord." It may well be this very phrase which led later Christians to make James the Just, head of the Jerusalem church until his martyrdom around 62 CE, a sibling of Jesus himself. But does Paul's reference to James mean this?

The term "brother" (*adelphos*) appears throughout Paul's letters, and was a common designation Christians gave to each other. In 1 Corinthians 1:1 Sosthenes is called *adelphos*, as is Timothy in Colossians 1:1. Neither one of them, nor the more than 500 "brothers" who received a vision of the spiritual Christ in Corinthians 15:6, are to be considered siblings of Jesus. "Brothers in the Lord" (*adelphōn en kuriō*) appears in Philippians 1:14 (the NEB translates it "our fellow-Christians"). This is a strong indicator of what the phrase applied to James must have meant. James was the head of a community in Jerusalem which bore witness to the spiritual Christ, and this group seems to have called itself "brethren of/in the Lord." The pre-eminent position of James as head of this group could have resulted in a special designation for him as *the* brother of the Lord.[26] Note, too, that such designations are always "of the Lord," never "of Jesus." We might also note that the term "*adelphos*" was common in Greek circles to refer to the initiates who belonged to the mystery cults.

But there is a further indication that early Christians knew of no sibling relationship between James and Jesus. The New Testament epistle of James opens this way: "James, a servant of God and of the Lord Jesus Christ . . ."

Few believe that James the Just actually wrote this letter, but if a later Christian is writing in his name, or even if only adding this ascription, common sense suggests that he would have identified James as the *brother* of the Lord Jesus if he had in fact been so, not simply as his servant. A similar void is left by the writer of the epistle of Jude. (Few likewise ascribe this letter to the actual Jude, whoever he was.) It opens: "Jude, a servant of Jesus Christ, and a brother of James . . ."

Now if James had been Jesus' sibling, and Jude is James' brother, this would make Jude the brother of Jesus, and he appears as such in Mark 6. So now we have two Christian letters ascribed to supposed blood brothers of Jesus, yet neither one of them makes such an identification. Attempted explanations for this silence are unconvincing.[27] They ignore the overriding fact that in the highly contentious atmosphere of most Christian correspondence, the advantage of drawing on a kinship to Jesus to make the letter's position and the writer's authority more forceful would hardly be passed up.

The Waters of the Jordan

The Gospels inaugurate Jesus' preaching career with a dramatic scene amid the waters of the Jordan, as Jesus is baptized by John the Baptist. Jesus immerses himself in the waters of the river, to emerge with the dove and God's voice descending upon him from heaven. Even if the Holy Spirit and the divine words were a later elaboration, they indicate that the incident of Jesus' baptism, were it an historical event, would very soon have been invested with mythic significance.

One would never know it from Paul. For Paul, baptism is the prime sacrament of Christian ritual, through which the convert dies to his old, sinful life and rises to a new one. In Romans 6:1-11 he breaks down the baptismal ritual into its mystical component parts. Yet never do any of those parts relate to the scene of Jesus' own baptism. The descent of the dove into Jesus would have provided the perfect parallel to Paul's belief that at baptism the Holy Spirit descended into the believer. The voice of God welcoming Jesus as his Beloved Son could have served to symbolize Paul's contention (as in Romans 8:14-17) that believers have been adopted as sons of God. Yet from first century writers like Paul we would never even know that Jesus had been baptized.

And where is the Baptist? In Christian mythology there is hardly a more commanding figure short of Jesus himself. The forerunner, the herald in camelskin coat, the scourge of the unrepentant, the voice crying aloud in the wilderness. Until the Gospels appear, John is truly lost in the wilderness, for no Christian writer refers to him. Even as late as the end of the first century, the writer of 1 Clement, an epistle sent from the church at Rome to the church at Corinth, is silent on John when he says (17:1): "Let us take pattern by those who went about in sheepskins and goatskins heralding the Messiah's coming; that is to say, Elijah, Elisha and Ezekiel among the prophets, and other famous names besides." Those other famous names he goes on to enumerate are all from the Old Testament.

Ironically, the one surviving writer of the first century (outside the Gospels) who does refer to John the Baptist is a non-Christian: the Jewish historian Josephus (*Antiquities of the Jews*, 18.5.2). However, he fails to make any link between John and Jesus or the Christian movement. (See chapter 21).

There was a common Jewish belief that the coming of the Messiah would be preceded by the appearance of the ancient prophet Elijah, to herald his advent. If first century Christian preachers were at all concerned with justifying their claim that Jesus was the Messiah, John the Baptist would have been very useful as an Elijah-type figure to fulfill this expectation.

Signs and Wonders

The occurrence of miracles and wondrous events was an indispensable sign of the imminence of the Kingdom. Anyone who claimed that the Day of the Lord was at hand had to produce signs and wonders to prove it. All awaited the events spoken of in prophets like Isaiah:

"Then the eyes of the blind shall be opened,
And the ears of the deaf unstopped;
Then shall the lame man leap like a hart,
And the tongue of the dumb sing for joy." (35:5f)

"But thy dead live, their bodies shall rise again.
They that sleep in the earth will awake and shout for joy." (26:19)

Modern scholars tend to relegate the Gospel accounts of Jesus' miracles to exaggeration, hallucination or later tradition. But such traditions should not have been long in developing if Jesus was declared to be the Messiah soon after his death.

In that case, it seems strange that Paul, in urging his readers to be confident that the advent of Jesus and the kingdom lay just around the corner (eg, Romans 8:19, 13:12), would never point to traditions about miracles by Jesus as the very fulfilment of the wonders that were expected at such a time. In 1 Corinthians 1:22 he scoffs at the Jews who always call for miracles to prove Christian claims, but here he should have the perfect answer for such calls: the signs which Jesus himself had provided.

The epistle to the Hebrews 2:3-4 speaks of the occasion when the "announcement of salvation" was delivered. To this announcement God is said to have added his own testimony, through signs and miracles and the distribution of gifts of the Holy Spirit. Yet if this were a reference to an earthly ministry of Jesus, it would have been more natural to point to Jesus' own signs and miracles, rather than to some perceived testimony by God.

The Gospels tell us how the sick pressed to touch the hem of Jesus' garment; how they stood in the byways and called out to him as he passed, crying for deliverance from their afflictions. Jesus had shown mercy to them all, even if those who wish to bring the Gospel accounts down to earth suggest that many of these healings were psychological. But their presence in the Gospels (and in Q) shows that such things would have been expected of him, that as a preacher of the kingdom the dimension of miracle worker would inevitably have been attached to Jesus' activities. Thus, traditions about healings and other signs and wonders should almost immediately have developed.[28]

Yet one would never know it from James 5:15:

> "Is one of you ill? The prayer offered in faith will save the sick man, the Lord [meaning God] will raise him from his bed, and any sins he may have committed will be forgiven."

It is probably safe to say that the writer would not have passed up appealing to the fact that Jesus himself had done these very things, had he possessed any such traditions. Mark 2:1-12 presents us with a miracle scene in which Jesus does both. To the paralytic he says: "Take up thy bed and walk," and at the same time he pronounces the man's sins forgiven. The writer of James has clearly never heard of it.

Nor has the writer of the epistle 1 Clement. In chapter 59 'Clement' delivers a long prayer to God, apparently in the liturgy of the Roman church. Here is one part of it:

"Grant us, O Lord, we beseech thee, thy help and protection. Do thou deliver the afflicted, pity the lowly, raise the fallen, reveal thyself to the needy, heal the sick, and bring home thy wandering people. Feed thou the hungry, ransom the captive, support the weak, comfort the faint-hearted." [trans. M. Staniforth, *Early Christian Writings*]

The Gospels tell us that Jesus did these very things, from healing the sick to feeding the hungry. In God's own name, as he walked the sands of Galilee and Judea, he pitied, he supported, he comforted, he revealed God. Yet Clement and his community show no knowledge of such activities.

Claims that Jesus had raised people from the dead are today not taken seriously by liberal scholars or the general public, but the Gospels show that the first century mind had no trouble accepting such feats. If Jesus had performed healings which tradition later turned into raisings from the dead, and the Gospels are regarded as evidence of such traditions, it is perplexing that no epistle writer shows any knowledge of them. (Once again, Q shows that raisings from the dead would have been imputed to a Jesus as early as the time of Paul.)

Paul's ignorance of such things is illustrated in passages like 1 Corinthians 15:12f. Here he addresses those in Corinth who question whether human beings can be resurrected from death:

"How can some of you say there is no resurrection from the dead?"

Yet would Paul not have had the perfect rejoinder, proof that humans *can* come back from the dead? He could point to traditions about the revival of Jairus' daughter (Mk. 5:21-43), about the astounding emergence of Lazarus from his tomb (John 11:1-44). Lazarus might still have to die again, but an eternal resurrection would surely be seen as prefigured by the temporary ones granted by Jesus on earth, and it is impossible to think that Paul would not have appealed to them in his argument.

Nor is it likely he would have passed up an appeal to Jesus' own promises on the matter. Luke offers this saying: "You will be repaid on the day when good men rise from the dead" (14:14). The Gospel of John is pervaded by Jesus' promise that "he who believes in me will have life everlasting." Had such promises, such traditions about Jesus' miracles, been circulating in the Christian communities of Paul's time, there would have been no need for his plaintive inquiry: "How can some of you say there is no resurrection of the dead?"

Four decades later, neither Lazarus nor Jesus' promises have yet surfaced. 1 Clement (24, 26) offers examples *in nature* of "the process of resurrection," and God's promises that the holy and faithful shall be raised are all from the Old Testament.

Unto the Holy City

Since no direct mention is made in the New Testament epistles to Jesus conducting an earthly ministry, it should come as no surprise that a reference to Galilee nowhere appears. At the end of his ministry, the Gospels have Jesus journey to Jerusalem where he is to meet his fate. Does anyone else in the first century ever place Jesus in the holy city?

The simple answer is no. Paul never locates Jesus anywhere, and for all his talk about the death and resurrection, no historical data about these events appears in his letters. Hebrews 13:11-13 says that Jesus "suffered outside the gate," but no city is mentioned, and the idea is determined by scripture. For this writer, Jesus' experience in the realm of myth (see Part Four) must be portrayed as paralleling the sacrifice of animals which took place "outside the camp," referring to the Israelite camp at Sinai. The sacrificial cult described in Exodus is the model to which Jesus is compared throughout the epistle.

An earlier passage in Hebrews (7:1-3) also indicates that the writer possesses no concept of Jesus ever having been in or near Jerusalem. Jesus in his role as heavenly High Priest finds his archetype, his scriptural precedent, in Melchizedek. This figure was "king of Salem [ie, Jerusalem] and priest of God Most High," as mentioned in Genesis 14:18-20. In comparing Melchizedek to Jesus, the writer is anxious to draw every parallel he can between the two figures. Yet he fails to make what should have been an obvious comparison: that Melchizedek had officiated in the very same city where Jesus later performed his own act as High Priest—the sacrifice of himself.

We can still shiver at the Gospel scene where Jesus makes his entry into the city, sitting humbly upon a donkey, hailed by excited crowds waving palms of peace and hope and singing from the Psalms. How the whole city would have been set abuzz by the dramatic confrontation in the Temple, when Jesus single-handedly—and with no response from the authorities[29]—drove out the traders and the animal-sellers. Such things are the stuff of which legends are quickly made, tales that grow in the telling. But this cannot be judged by the first century epistles because these incidents are never mentioned. (Nor are they mentioned by any historian of the time, including Josephus.)

The Last Supper

Next to the crucifixion, the Gospel scene most immortalized in almost 20 centuries of Christian art is undoubtedly that of Jesus sitting at a table with his twelve apostles gathered about him, partaking of a Supper which was to be both a last and a first. It was the last communal meal he would enjoy with his followers. But it would be the first sacramental meal in a perpetual celebration of his death, embodying a theology of atonement and salvation founded on Jesus' sacrifice. It was, in Jesus' own words, the establishment of a new covenant.

In the epistle to the Hebrews 9:19-20, we read:

"For when, as the Law directed, Moses had recited all the commandments to the people, he took the blood of the calves, with water, scarlet wool, and marjoram, and sprinkled the law-book itself and all the people, saying, 'This is the blood of the covenant which God has enjoined upon you.' " [NEB]

At the core of this writer's theology lies the new covenant established by Christ's sacrifice, a sacrifice which takes place in heaven. His interpretative technique revolves around the drawing of parallels between his own community's ritual and theology, and the embodiment or prototype of these things found in the scriptures. Yet the prime scriptural event which had established the old covenant, the blood sacrifice of animals conducted by Moses and the words spoken over this ritual (Exodus 24:8), is presented without a glance toward Jesus' own establishment of the new covenant, in the words Jesus is reported to have spoken over the bread and wine at the Last Supper.

The parallel between the old and the new, the very striking similarity between the words spoken by Moses in Exodus and the words spoken by the Gospel Jesus at the sacramental meal which established the celebration of his sacrifice, should have been so compelling that the author could not have avoided calling attention to it. The only conclusion to draw is that he knew of no such event, and no such words spoken by Jesus at a Last Supper.

Once again, the passage concerning Melchizedek in Hebrews 7:1-3 shows an ignorance on the part of the writer, this time about the Last

Supper. The passage from Genesis mentioned above (14:18-20) begins: "Then Melchizedek . . . brought food and wine." Despite his concern for parallels between the two figures, between his own brand of Christian theology and its embodiment in the sacred writings, the writer fails to point to this "food and wine" as a prefiguring of the bread and cup of the eucharistic sacrament established by Jesus.

The Christian document compiled toward the end of the first century, known as the Didache ("Teaching," later described as "of the Twelve Apostles") also contains a silence on Jesus' establishment of the Eucharist. In chapters 9-10, community prayers attached to a communal thanksgiving meal are quoted. Here the bread and the wine have no sacramental significance and there is no mention of Jesus' death, nor is he said to have instituted this ceremony. In fact, there is no reference to any aspect of Jesus' life and death in the Didache. Jesus' role in the theology of this community seems to be nothing more than a kind of conduit from God, as indicated by this passage, quoting a verse from the prayers:

> "At the Eucharist, offer the eucharistic prayer in this way. Begin with the chalice: 'We give thanks to thee, our Father, for the holy vine of thy servant David, which thou has made known to us through thy servant [or child] Jesus.' " [trans. Staniforth, *op.cit.*]

Since no mention is made of any of Jesus' teachings, with even the Lord's Prayer and the community's "gospel" attributed to God, we must assume that any "making known" by Jesus is through spiritual channels.[30]

The writer of the epistle 1 Clement can speak of his community's "eucharist to God" (ch.41) with no reference to a ritual meal based on Jesus' Last Supper.

This brings us to 1 Corinthians 11:23-26. Paul calls the meal "The Lord's Supper" (11:20), a term found nowhere else in the New Testament. In Chapter 4 we saw how the opening words of the verse imply knowledge of this scene through personal revelation, not historical tradition, and in Chapter 11, after examining the sacred meals of other savior god cults, we will judge it to be an origin myth of the same nature, probably created by Paul himself. In view of the universal silence in the rest of the early literature on anything resembling a Last Supper, Paul is even less likely to be referring to an historical event.[31]

7

The Passion Story

We continue our survey of the epistolary silence on the Gospel story and examine the trial, crucifixion and resurrection, followed by a look at one very revealing missing element.

Of Agony and Betrayal

"See to it that there is no one among you who forfeits the grace of God, no bitter, noxious weed growing up to poison the whole, no immoral person, no one worldly-minded like Esau. He sold his birthright for a single meal, and you know that although he wanted afterwards to claim the blessing, he was rejected." [Heb. 12:15-17, NEB]

Dante in his Inferno places Judas in the pit of Hell, locked in ice, gnawed on by Satan. The arch-betrayer who planted his deceitful kiss on Jesus' cheek and helped deliver him to death was to become a symbol in later Christian minds of all falsehearted and disbelieving Jewry. Judas inaugurated the Jew as demon, and an entire race suffered fiercely for it over two millennia. Yet before he appears to fill his treacherous role in Mark's passion story, no ghost of Judas haunts the Christian landscape. He is notably missing from the above passage in Hebrews, where the selling of the Lord himself for 30 pieces of silver by a man embittered, jealous and deceitful, would have been a far more apt symbol of the bitter, poisonous weed that arises unchecked within the community of the holy.

Nor would a reference to Judas have been out of place in Paul's own presentation of his "Lord's Supper." Here he is criticizing the Corinthians for their behavior at the communal meal. He speaks of rivalry and "divided groups," of those who "eat the bread and drink the cup of the Lord unworthily." If anyone had been guilty of such things, it was surely Judas at the very first Supper.

The writer of 1 Clement also deals with the theme of jealousy, but to his list of Old Testament figures who suffered at the hands of jealous men, he fails to add Jesus himself, betrayed by the perfidious apostle in his own company.

The Gospels give us other, less unforgivable moments of betrayal on the night of Jesus' arrest. The great triple denial of his Master by Peter himself, with the bitter remorse which followed as the cock crew, is nowhere referred to in the epistles. Paul can show outbursts of anger and disdain toward Peter and others of the Jerusalem group (as in Galatians 2), but never does he bring up a denial of the Lord by Peter to twist the knife. Earlier in the Gospel account, the favored three of Peter, James and John had slept through their Master's agony in the Gethsemane garden, a beautifully crafted and emotionally effective scene of Jesus kneeling before God in naked isolation, fearing the ordeal in store and wishing in some part of his humanity that it could be put aside. Paul never mentions it. Nor do any of the other epistle writers, who often deal with situations in which Christians are in danger of falling away from their resolve and devotion.

From Death to Life

For 2000 years the icon of the cross has towered over Western society. It has defined our philosophy, our ethics, our psychologies, our art. It has governed our spiritual beliefs and expectations. Scarcely anyone born in the western world over the last two millennia has not had the shadow of the crucifix fall on his or her life in one way or another. A man hanging from a piece of wood: the image is so familiar, so much a part of our world, adorning our walls and decorating our persons, that we have lost the gut-wrenching sense of just how gruesome it is, or the wonder that upon such an image so many have laid their hopes.

It would be strange indeed to find that the cross was not a universal motif in all Christian expression from the very birth of the faith. The cross and the resurrection: together they formed the twin pillars of Christian trust in salvation. Together they provided the explosive catalyst for the religious movement which turned a Jewish preacher into the Son of God and brought the message about him to the far corners of the earth. Or so we would be forgiven for thinking.

But the fact is that both the death of Jesus and his rising from the tomb are missing in significant pieces of Christian witness. Not, it is true, in Paul. There is no shortage of Christ crucified in everything Paul has to say about Jesus; and his resurrection from the dead forms the basis of the Pauline hope for immortality. Yet the point has been made that Paul nowhere places this death and resurrection in an historical earthly setting. Nor do any of the other epistle writers.

Outside the New Testament, several documents judged to be Christian show no sign of a Christ who died and was resurrected. We have already encountered one of these, the Didache. Others include the Shepherd of Hermas and the Odes of Solomon. (These and other documents will be looked at more closely in Chapter 13, which considers the great diversity that existed in earliest Christianity.)

Within the New Testament itself, one of the underlying sources of many of the sayings in both Matthew and Luke, the Q document which forms the basis of the Galilean Tradition, can be shown to contain no concept of a Jesus who suffered and died, let alone one who was resurrected. A non-canonical document related to early Q, the Gospel of Thomas, also presents a collection of sayings attributed to Jesus which shows no awareness that this Jesus had undergone death. For all its focus on "eternal life," the epistle 1 John has nothing to say about the resurrection, and even the specific concept of the cross is missing. In the latest layer of this epistle, allusions to the idea of sacrificial propitiation creep in, and 3:16 declares that "Christ laid down his life for us," but that is the closest one gets to Calvary. The earlier layers display the idea that eternal life is gained through knowledge of the Son, the original Johannine idea, not by any atoning death.

The epistle of James is judged to be Christian on the basis of its sole reference in 2:1 to "the Lord Jesus Christ, who reigns in glory," and because so many of its moral maxims bear strong resemblance to the teachings of Jesus in the Gospels, even though they are never attributed to him. But the death and the resurrection of James' shadowy Christ are missing. And not because there was no occasion to bring them up. In 1:21 the writer urges his readers to "accept the message implanted (in you) which can bring you salvation." It is the reception of an ethical message which "saves your souls," not Jesus' atoning sacrifice or his rising from death. About these things James has nothing to say.

When in 5:10 the author advocates "patience under ill-treatment," does he offer the obvious example of Jesus in his passion? No, he says: "Take the prophets of old who spoke in the name of the Lord." In 5:6 he condemns the rich and powerful of this world and their injustices toward the poor and the disadvantaged: "You have condemned the innocent (man) and murdered him; he offers no resistance." No parallel to Jesus' own experience seems to have crossed the writer's mind here.

The Didache, as noted earlier, has nothing to say about a death and resurrection for Jesus (who appears only in its eucharistic prayers). The epistle to the Hebrews, while focusing on Jesus' sacrifice, places it in the heavenly realm, with no mention of Calvary. The name Calvary appears not once in the New Testament epistles. Hebrews also turns a blind eye on the Easter miracle; 13:20 has a passing reference to God 'leading up' Jesus after death, but this hardly conveys the drama of the empty tomb or the post-resurrection appearances. In 7:16 the author extols Jesus as one who owes his priesthood "to the power of a life that cannot be destroyed." Is this founded on Jesus' conquest of death through his resurrection? No such idea is hinted at. Instead, the remark is based on a scriptural passage, Psalm 110:4 with its comparison to Melchizedek, declaring: "Thou art a priest forever."

A Trial and Crucifixion Scene

The Gospel details of Jesus' trial and crucifixion are imbedded in our cultural heritage, from Pilate to the crown of thorns, from the raising up of the cross between two thieves to the gambling of the soldiers for Jesus' clothes, from the darkness over the land at his death to Josephus of Arimathea laying Jesus in his own tomb. Yet none of these details surface in the wider Christian picture before the second century. "We preach Christ crucified," says Paul. But he does not tell us where or when, or that Roman or Jew was involved. None of the great cast of characters which passes through the various stages of the Gospel trial and crucifixion are ever mentioned in his letters. Paul does not even tell us that Jesus was *tried*!

No one quotes any words of Jesus at the crucifixion. Ephesians 4:32 urges that Christians "forgive one another as God in Christ forgave you." The writer is apparently unaware of the moving words which Luke gives us (23:34), spoken by Jesus as he hung on the cross, words which would have provided a noble example to follow:

"Father, forgive them, for they know not what they do."

The writer of 1 Clement (53:4), after a long dissertation on forgiveness, searches for words to sum up his point. They are not the words of Jesus on the cross, but the plea of Moses to God that he forgive the disobedient Israelites.

If Jesus on his cross *did* speak such words of forgiveness, Christians failed to heed them. For almost 2000 years the Jews have endured vilification, hatred and outright slaughter as "killers of Christ." The author of the Gospel of Matthew dramatizes their frenzied cry at Jesus' trial, words which drew down upon themselves the wrath of the ages: "Crucify him! His blood be upon us and upon our children!" Would the Jews take any consolation in realizing that no one before the Gospels shows any conception that they had been involved in Christ's death? It is worth repeating here that 1 Thessalonians 2:15-16, where Paul seems to condemn the Jews "who killed the Lord Jesus," is widely judged to be a later insertion (see Appendix 1).

As discussed earlier, Paul has given himself the ideal opening to mention the Jews' killing of Jesus in Romans 11 when he is discussing the guilt of the Jews in regard to their lack of faith. He refers to Elijah's words in 1 Kings: "Lord, they have killed thy prophets." This guilt apparently does not include the killing of the Son of God himself, for Paul makes no mention of such an event.

If Paul and his contemporaries attribute no guilt to the Jews in the death of Jesus, how do they view the Romans? In Mark's Gospel tale, Judas may be the villain from within, and the Sanhedrin the Jewish religious authority which wanted Jesus eliminated, but Pilate was the figurehead of imperial justice who carried out the execution. All the Gospels, for tendentious reasons, render Pontius Pilate a complex character and largely whitewash him of responsibility for a death other forces made inevitable. But can we imagine that this man, had he enjoyed any role in the death of Jesus, would immediately sink from Christian consciousness for some three-quarters of a century? What of Pilate's struggle to free a man he believed was innocent, his dramatic gesture when he washed his hands of Jesus' blood? What of his offer to release Jesus, only to be refused by a crowd who demanded Barabbas instead?[32] Could these dramatic elements have proven of no interest to the first three generations of Christians who based their faith on the event of Jesus' execution?

It would be some 80 years before Pilate first came to light in the letters of Ignatius. It may have been around the same time that the sole reference to Pilate in the New Testament epistles was penned, in 1 Timothy 6:13. Even here, there are indications that this may be a later insertion (see Appendix 1).

A figure like Pilate seems far from Paul's mind when he says in Romans 13:3-4:

> "Rulers hold no terrors for them who do right . . . (the ruler) is the minister of God for your own good."

Can Paul have any knowledge of Jesus' historical trial and crucifixion and still express such sentiments? Pilate, whether he believed in Jesus' innocence or not, delivered this righteous man to scourging and unjust execution. If the story of such a fate suffered by Jesus of Nazareth were present in every Christian's mind, Paul's praise of the authorities as God's agents for the good of all, and from whom the innocent have nothing to fear, would ring hollow indeed.

In fact, all the early writers lack the essential atmosphere of the Gospel presentation of Jesus' death: that this was the unjust execution of an innocent man, beset by betrayal and false accusations and a pitiless establishment. Instead, Paul in Romans 8:32 extols the magnanimity of God who "did not spare his own Son but surrendered him for us all." And for the writer of Ephesians (5:2) it is Christ himself who in love "gave himself up on your behalf as an offering and a sacrifice whose fragrance is pleasing to God." Wherever Paul and others in the first century envisioned this sacrifice as having taken place, it seems light-years from the dread hill of Golgotha, from the scourges and the plaited thorns, the jeering soldiers and taunting crowds, where God expresses his dark wrath in earthquake, blackened heavens and a rending of the veil to his own holy sanctuary.

And On the Third Day

All the Gospels conclude with the climactic story of the empty tomb and, except for Mark (in its original version), an account of various appearances by the risen Jesus to his disciples. Acts has him continue to appear on earth for 40 days. How do the first century letter writers view the tradition of the Easter miracle?

Most early Christian thinking seems to have envisioned Jesus as ascending to heaven immediately after his death. The epistle writers show no concept of a bodily resurrection after three days, or of a period during which the risen Christ made appearances to human beings on earth. Such a blind spot would be hard to conceive, if we accepted the orthodox picture of a Christian movement which began in response to a perceived return of Jesus from the grave.

Yet that blindness seems clear in passages like the following:

"In the [flesh] he was put to death; in the spirit he was brought to life. . . . (Baptism) brings salvation through the resurrection of Jesus Christ who entered heaven after receiving the submission of angelic authorities and powers, and is now at the right hand of God." [NEB]

Here the writer of 1 Peter (3:18-22) can mention something which took place in the spirit realm in the course of Christ's ascension to heaven, but he has nothing to say about Jesus' bodily appearances on earth. (The meaning of "in flesh" will be examined in Part Four.)

Or Ephesians 1:20:

". . .which (God) exerted in Christ, when he raised him from the dead, when he enthroned him at his right hand in the heavenly realms." [NEB]

There is even less room for a resurrection to earth in Hebrews 10:12: "Christ offered for all time one sacrifice for sins, and took his seat at the right hand of God." In 13:20, the writer has God "lead up" Jesus from the dead. Both verses illustrate Hebrews' lack of any concept of bodily resurrection.

Then He Appeared To

Does Paul have any idea of a bodily return of Jesus to earth? Does his concept of the resurrection progress beyond the documents just examined?

In 1 Corinthians 15:5-8, after a capsule summary of the gospel he preaches, Paul goes on to list a series of "appearances" by Christ to various people in Jerusalem. The nature of those appearances cannot be squared with the Gospel picture.

Paul nowhere shows any knowledge of the story of the empty tomb. He makes no mention of the women who first discover it, nor of details matching any of the appearance stories of the Gospels. On the other hand, the appearances to James and to "over 500 of the brothers at once" seem to be unknown to the evangelists.

Throughout this description, Paul uses the word *ōphthē* (was seen): Jesus was seen by so-and-so. There is no evidence that he means anything more than a simple vision, and this is borne out when Paul lists his own "seeing" with the rest. He makes no distinction between them. Since his own experience of the risen Christ—even as described in Acts—is a vision from heaven of the disembodied, spiritual Christ, it would seem that they have all experienced the same thing. Modern liberal scholars, such as the Jesus Seminar,[33] have recently come to acknowledge that all these appearances are in the nature of 'visions,' and even this may be too strong a word.[34]

We also have to take into account something which Paul says a few verses later (15:12-16).

"[12]But if it is preached that Christ has been raised from the dead, how can some of you say that there is no resurrection of the dead? [13]If there is no resurrection of the dead, then not even Christ has been raised. [14]And if Christ has not been raised, then our preaching is vain, your faith also is vain. [15]Moreover, we are even found to be false witnesses of God, because we witnessed against God that he raised Christ, whom he did not raise if in fact the dead are not raised. [16]For if the dead are not raised, not even Christ has been raised." [NASB/NIV]

There are some powerful implications to be drawn from this passage. Paul expresses himself as though the raising of Christ from the dead is a matter of faith, not of historical record as evidenced by eyewitness to a physical, risen Jesus at Easter. He is so adamant about the necessity to believe that the dead will be raised, that he is prepared to state—and he repeats it four times—that if they are not, then Christ himself "has not been raised." If men he knew had witnessed the actual return of Jesus from the grave, it is unlikely he would have thought to make even a rhetorical denial of it.

Moreover, the verb for "witness" (*martureō*) is often used in the sense of witnessing to, of declaring one's belief in, an item of faith, not of factual record (though it can mean the latter in some contexts). Compare Romans 10:9: "If . . . (you have) in your heart the faith that God raised (Jesus) from the dead, then you will find salvation." There, too, Paul seems to be implying that the raising of Jesus is a matter of faith. In 1 Thessalonians 4:14, where Paul says that "we believe Jesus died and rose again," even Jesus' *death* seems to be a matter of faith.

Such a meaning of "witness" in the 1 Corinthians passage above (verse 15) is strongly supported by what follows this verb: *kata tou theou*, or "against God." Translators often seem uncertain of the exact import of this phrase, but Bauer's Lexicon declares it as meaning "give testimony *in contradiction to God.*" The idea that Paul is trying to get across here is that if in fact God did *not* raise Jesus from death (which would have to be the conclusion, he says, if all of the dead are not raised) then, rhetorically speaking, Paul and other apostles have been contradicting God and lying about Jesus' resurrection.

Paul is saying that knowledge about Jesus' raising has come from God, and that his own preaching testimony, true or false, relates to information which has come from God—in other words, through revelation. Not history, not apostolic tradition about recent events on earth. In all this discussion about the actuality of Christ's resurrection,

Paul's standard is one of faith, faith based on God's testimony—meaning, in scripture. Historical human witness plays no part.

As will be seen in Part Four, the events of Christ's death and resurrection took place in the supernatural realm of myth, and thus there is no temporal link between such events and the "appearances" in 1 Corinthians 15:5-8. Paul is in the same position as the other early Christian writers. He possesses no concept of an interval between the resurrection and ascension to heaven, no idea that Christ had spent time on earth during such an interval, and no details about anything Jesus might have done or said at such a time. The graphic scenes which Gospels like John give us, with the unbelieving Thomas placing his fingers against Jesus' pierced hands and sides, are utterly unknown to Paul. A "doubting Thomas" would have been an invaluable asset in his arguments against the doubting Corinthians.

In the Footsteps of Jesus

From Bethlehem to Calvary, there is a resounding void on the places and details of Jesus' life and death which resonates throughout the entire record of early Christian correspondence. And yet there is one striking and pervasive silence which seems paramount. It can be summed up in one question: Where are the holy places?

In all the Christian writers of the first century, in all the devotion they display about Christ and the new faith, not one of them expresses a desire to see the birthplace of Jesus, to visit Nazareth his home town. No one talks about having been to the sites of his preaching, the upper room where he held his Last Supper, the hill on which he was crucified, or the tomb where he was buried and rose from the dead. Not only is there no evidence that anyone showed an interest in visiting such places, they go completely unmentioned. The words Bethlehem, Nazareth and Galilee never appear in the epistles, and the word Jerusalem is never used in connection with Jesus.

Most astonishing of all, there is not a hint of pilgrimage to Calvary itself, where humanity's salvation was presumably consummated. How could such a place not have become the center of Christian devotion, how could it not have been turned into a shrine? Each year at Passover we would expect to find Christians observing their own celebration on the hill outside Jerusalem, performing a rite every Easter Sunday at the site of the nearby tomb. Christian sermonizing and theological meditation could hardly fail to be built around the *places* of salvation, not just the abstract events.

Do Christians avoid frequenting such places out of fear? Acts, possibly preserving a kernel of historical reality, portrays the apostles as preaching fearlessly in the Temple in the earliest days, despite arrest and persecution, and the persecution has in any case been much exaggerated for the early decades. Even such a threat, however, should not and would not have prevented clandestine visits by Christians, and there should have been many other places of Jesus' career where visitation would have involved no danger. In any case, there would have been no danger in *mentioning* them in their own correspondence.

How could Paul have been immune to the lure of such places? In Philippians 3:10, he says:

"All I care for is to know Christ, to experience the power of his resurrection, to share in his sufferings . . ."

And yet, does he care enough to visit the hill of Calvary upon his conversion, to experience those sufferings the more vividly, to feel beneath his feet the sacred ground that bore the blood of his slain Lord? Does he stand before the empty tomb, the better to bring home to himself the power of Jesus' resurrection, to feel the conviction that his own resurrection is guaranteed? This is a man whose letters reveal someone full of insecurities and self-doubts, possessed by his own demons, highly emotional, a man driven to preach else he would go mad, as he tells us in 1 Corinthians 9:16. Would he not have derived great consolation from visiting the Gethsemane garden, where Jesus was reported to have passed through similar horrors and self-doubts? Would his sacramental convictions about the Lord's Supper, which he is anxious to impart to the Corinthians (11:23f), not have been heightened by a visit to the upper room in Jerusalem, to absorb the ambience of that hallowed place and occasion?

This type of consideration supplies yet another reason to regard as unacceptable the standard rationalization that Paul was uninterested in the earthly life of Jesus. (Even if that life was not the Gospel life, it is difficult to imagine an early Christian movement following a human teacher and yet knowing no biographical details of his career, real or invented.) Moreover, when Paul undertook to carry his mission to the gentiles, surely he would have wanted—and needed—to go armed with the data of that life, with memories of the places Jesus had frequented, ready to answer the inevitable questions his new audiences would ask in their eagerness to hear all the details about the man who was the Son of God and Savior of the world.

Instead, what did he do? By his own account in Galatians, he waited three years following his conversion before making a short visit to Jerusalem,

". . . to get to know Cephas. I stayed with him for fifteen days, without seeing any of the other apostles except James, the brother of the Lord."

Nor was he to return there for another fourteen years. Did Paul learn all the data of Jesus' life on that one occasion? Did he visit the holy places? Not having felt the urge to do so for three years, his silence on such things may not be surprising. But if he did make his own pilgrimage to Calvary and the empty tomb, can we believe he would not have shared those experiences—and they would have been intensely emotional ones—with his readers? If not here, then at least at *some* point in his many letters?

But it is not only the places of Jesus' life and death that are missing in the early record. What about the relics? Jesus' clothes, the things he used in his everyday life, the things he touched? Why would such items not have remained behind, to be collected and prized, clamored for, to be seen and touched by the faithful themselves? Would not an apostle like Paul be anxious to carry such a memento of the man he preached? Would not a rivalry develop between apostles, between Christian communities (as it did later) to gain such mementos and relics for worship and as status symbols? If the Gospel account had any basis, we would expect to find mention of all sorts of relics, genuine or otherwise: cups from the Last Supper, nails bearing Jesus' flesh, thorns from the bloody crown, the centurion's spear, pieces of cloth from the garments gambled over by the soldiers at the foot of the cross—indeed, just as we find a host of relics all through the Middle Ages that were claimed to be these very things.

Why is it only in the fourth century that pieces of the "true cross" begin to surface? Why is it left to Constantine to set up the first shrine on the supposed mount of Jesus' death, and to begin the mania for pilgrimage to the holy sites that has persisted to this day? Why would someone in the first hundred years of the movement not have similarly sought to tread the same ground that the Son of God himself had so recently walked on? The total absence of such things in the first hundred years of Christian correspondence is perhaps the single strongest argument for regarding the entire Gospel account of Jesus' life and death as nothing but literary fabrication.

Of critical scholarship which has begun to admit that much of the Gospel story—and virtually all of the passion account—is indeed fabrication,[35] we might ask: if not the Gospel story, why not some other? Why not places and relics relating to Jesus' *actual* experiences? Could Paul and the Jerusalem Tradition have believed in and preached an historical man who had undergone death and resurrection, without these events being attached to *some* location? If a "genuine Jesus" had lived and preached and died under any circumstances at all, would the memory of the places associated with his career have been completely lost, would they have been of no interest to Christians? If it is said that in fact nothing of Jesus' life was known by early Christianity—a fallback position that is increasingly being suggested—what created the vitality which launched the movement in the first place, what kept it alive in such a vacuum? At the very least, the need for a story about the man they all preached would soon have generated a legendary or fictitious biography, and thus we are led back once again to a Gospel-like situation, to a quandary of silence over the places and relics of such a career. In any case, that the Jerusalem Tradition could have begun based on an historical man's death and imagined rising, with yet nothing of historical circumstance known about those events, is a proposition which does not logically commend itself.

Part Three
THE GOSPEL OF THE SON

8

The Word of God in the Holy Book

A Time of Faith

As outlined in Part One, several passages in the New Testament epistles declare that Christ and his activities are God's secrets, things hidden for long ages (Romans 16:25, Col. 1:26, 2:2, Eph. 3:5, Titus 1:3). Only now are they being made known to inspired apostles like Paul through revelation and the Spirit. The events of the present time are not the life and acts of Jesus on earth, but the actions of God, the arrival of faith, the sending of the spirit of the Son.

If this is an age when faith has arrived, upon what is that faith based? If God is revealing Christ, whence came the content of the revelation? Paul and other prophets did not simply hear voices, telling them about the new spiritual Son. They say they have received their inspiration through God's Holy Spirit, but upon what is that Spirit acting? Undergoing a mystical experience or having a conviction that God has granted a revelation may be a psychological event, but it happens in response to the study or meditation which the mystic has applied to his subject. That subject, in the case of Paul or any other Jewish prophet, was the ancient body of Jewish scripture.

Revealed Through the Sacred Writings

One of the impediments to an acceptance of the myth theory is the apparent incredibility of the proposition that the story of Jesus of Nazareth could have arisen with no historical basis whatsoever. But we have to realize how much the educated ancient Jew lived within his holy books, as did many of those gentiles who attached themselves to Judaism. The Jewish scriptures offered a universe in themselves, in which the avid scholar and prophet could move and breathe. He governed his life by the writings. Like the Jewish philosopher Philo of Alexandria (in Egypt), he could construct whole philosophies from elements of scripture, aided at times by mystical experiences. Ancient philosophy as a whole, its view of the universe and of God, was the product of intellectual contemplation. Modern principles of scientific observation and experiment were virtually unknown. True reality lay outside the observable world; ultimate truths were reached through the rejection of the world and the abandonment of the body. God was believed to communicate first through his scriptures, second—for those fortunate enough to be blessed with such things—through visionary revelation.

The bible was God's revelation of himself and his workings. The most important aspect of those workings was the divine plan for salvation. God's plan had to reside in scripture, for that was how he communicated with the world. All it needed was the right key, the right inspiration through the Spirit to unlock that coded information. Thus the writings of the prophets were regarded not as meant for their own time, not as relating to conditions they themselves had lived through (which, of course, in all cases they were), but as prophecies of the future. Inevitably, that future was taken to be the period of those who were studying these writings. God's prophetic message was meant for themselves. Paul's conviction that the Spirit was guiding him as he sought meaning from the sacred texts guaranteed that he would get the message he was looking for.

For several centuries, Judaism had asked the question: How was God to save his people? Who would be the agents involved? In many people's minds, that agent would be an Anointed king, the Messiah, a descendant of David. The Greek word for "Anointed One" is Christ. It is not a proper name, but a designation, a title. Strictly speaking, the Christian icon should be referred to not as Jesus Christ, but as Jesus *the* Christ. Jews regarded the information about this anticipated Messiah as having been embodied in prophetic and other writings, and the number of passages taken to refer to him grew in proportion to the number of those who searched for such things.

For most Jews, the Messiah would be a human figure, though one destined to be exalted by God. For others, however, the agent of salvation became more spiritual. The "one like a son of man" in Daniel 7 offered itself as a divine, or semi-divine savior figure. In the latter first century, such an End-time agent of God surfaces in Q and the

Book of Revelation, and eventually in all the canonical Gospels. Among Jewish sects he puts in an appearance in the documents 4 Ezra and 1 Enoch, showing that even purely Jewish groups had begun to envision a Messiah figure who was more than human, someone waiting in heaven for the great day to arrive when he would bring about God's salvation of the righteous.[36]

It is only a small step further to regard Christianity, in its earliest form, not as a response to a human man, but as a religious and philosophical expression of the same nature. These varied circles of belief encompassed an unknown number of uncoordinated Jewish and gentile groups in Palestine and throughout the empire. (In Chapter 13 we will examine the wide diversity in that early movement of "Christ belief.") They offered a spiritual Savior, a fully divine Son of God. Some of the same scriptural passages which more 'mainstream' Jews were interpreting as referring to a future human Messiah were seen as pointing to a spiritual Christ, a Son of God waiting in heaven for the End-time when he would appear on earth.

To this heavenly Christ, some of these circles—though not all, as we shall see—gave the name "Jesus" (Joshua/Yeshua), the name of the deliverer under Moses who conquered the Promised Land. The name means "Yahweh Saves" and makes an ideal and natural name for a savior deity. Some of these circles—though again not all—envisioned this Christ as having undergone self-sacrifice in the supernatural world, the same realm where the activities of all the other savior gods of the era had taken place. That this Son and Christ had died by crucifixion (some refer to it only as "hanging"), that he had risen from death, could be found in the sacred scriptures.

A Gospel From Scripture

In a few passages, Paul tells us quite clearly that he has derived his information and gospel about the Christ from the scriptures. In 1 Corinthians 15:3-4, the fact that "Christ died for our sins," that "he was raised on the third day," is "according to the scriptures." The latter phrase, as pointed out earlier, can have the meaning of 'as we learn from the scriptures.' In Romans 16:25, Paul proclaims his gospel "about Jesus Christ, according to the revelation of the mystery kept in silence for long ages but now revealed, and made known through prophetic writings at the command of God. . . ." Here the words plainly say that Christ is a mystery that has been hidden for a long time, but is now revealed by God through scripture.

Although it is often pointed out that mainstream Jews of the time drew no doctrine of a sacrificed Messiah from their sacred writings, it does not follow that *no one* did. For Paul's gospel that "Christ died for our sins according to the scriptures," we need look no further than Isaiah 53 to see the probable passages Paul is speaking of.

> "[4]He bears our sins, and is pained for us. . . . [5]But he was wounded on account of our sins, bruised because of our iniquities. . . . [6]All we as sheep have gone astray, everyone has gone astray in his way, and the Lord [delivered him up] for our sins. . . . [12]because his soul was delivered up to death . . . and he bore the sins of many and was delivered because of their iniquities." [from the trans. by L. Brenton of the Septuagint (Greek) passage]

Although the writer of Second Isaiah (Isa. 40-55) in this so-called Suffering Servant Song was speaking of a contemporary prophet—perhaps even of himself, though some suggest that this passage is by others, after he suffered death—for early Christians Isaiah 52:13-53:12 was a loaded passage. It became a source for all sorts of theology and information, first about the spiritual Christ, then for the fabricated passion story of the Gospels. Paul hardly needed more than this one passage, saturated with the concept of God delivering up[37] the "Servant" (Greek *pais*, also translatable as child or son), to come up with his gospel of 1 Corinthians 15:3. The rising on the third day of the next verse is more than likely dependent on Hosea 6:2: "After two days he will heal us, on the third day he will restore us." The story of Jonah also speaks of a rescue from the fish's belly after three days and three nights.

As for the manner of Christ's death? The "wounded" of Isaiah 53:5 above is sometimes translated "pierced." Psalm 119:120 (in the Septuagint) contains the phrase "penetrate my flesh with thy fear." The verb in some contexts means "fasten with nails." Psalm 22:16, another piece of writing heavily mined for Gospel passion details, says "they have pierced my hands and my feet." Zechariah 12:10 (speaking of a person in his own time) links the piercing with a "son":

> "They shall look on . . . him whom they have pierced . . . and shall wail over him as over an only child, and shall grieve for him bitterly as for a first-born son." [NEB]

The Gospel of John 19:37 calls attention to this verse of Zechariah as a text in scripture which Christ has fulfilled. What lies behind

John's statement, however, is that verses like Zechariah 12:10 are the *source* for the 'fact' that Jesus had been crucified.

One of the features of scriptural study in this period was the practice of taking individual passages and verses, bits and pieces from here and there, and weaving them into a larger whole. Such a sum was much greater than its parts. This is one of the key procedures of "midrash," a Jewish method of interpreting the sacred writings. (There will be much to say about midrash when looking at how the Gospels were constructed.) This bringing together of widely separate scriptural references and deriving meanings and scenarios from their combination was the secret to creating the early Christian message. Scripture did not contain any full-blown crucified Messiah, but it did contain all the necessary ingredients. Jewish midrash was the process by which the Christian recipe was put together and baked into the doctrine of the divine Son who had been sacrificed for salvation.

Preaching a Gospel from Scripture

A spiritual, crucified Messiah and Son of God based on readings out of scripture? Some find it hard to believe that this concept could have excited anyone without some relation to an historical event, that it could have been spread across the empire by apostles like Paul unless linked to a flesh and blood person and historical words and deeds.

But how did pagan proselytizers spread the cults of Attis or Mithras, or any of the other savior gods of the mystery religions? *They* had no link to an historical event lying in the background of their mythic story of the god. Philo of Alexandria formulated his "myth" of the universe and its working, salvific parts, entirely by applying Platonic philosophy to the Jewish scriptures. He may not have come up with a sacrificial Son, but his concept of an intermediary entity that was the "first-born of God," was a general counterpart, if along more abstract lines, to Paul's dying-for-sin Christ.

Those who have difficulty conceiving of a faith movement not linked to an historical man and his words and deeds are nevertheless confronted with an early record which completely ignores that historical man and his deeds, and fails to attribute any teachings to him. Whereas one can hardly turn a page of the epistles without encountering an appeal to scripture as the basis on which the writer is making his statements. Amid all the philosophical and religious influences operating during the period of incipient Christianity, it is not difficult to envision certain scriptural investigators constructing their own mythical savior deity from the sacred writings, trying to formulate a "truth" and a "salvation" along Jewish cultural lines.

God's Gospel of the Son

At the very beginning of the collection of New Testament epistles, in the opening verses of Romans, lies a statement which many declare requires us to go no further. Even if Paul were never to breathe another word about Jesus of Nazareth, they say, in verse 3 lies something which unmistakably points to the concept of an historical man in Paul's view of the Christ. And yet, the situation is quite the opposite. This illuminating statement has stood at the head of the Pauline corpus for almost two millennia, and should long ago have revealed both the true beginnings of Christianity and the role scripture played in them, as well as the absence of any historical Jesus in Paul's mind.

> "[1]Paul, a servant of Jesus Christ, called to be an apostle, set apart for the gospel of God, [2]which he promised (or, announced) beforehand through his prophets in the holy scriptures, [3]the gospel concerning his Son, who . . ." [RSV]

And he goes on to itemize two elements of that gospel about the Son, as will be seen in a moment. But consider what Paul is saying in these verses and ask yourself: Is there something wrong with this picture?

The gospel is God's gospel, received through revelation. Not from other men, not from Jesus himself through channels of apostolic transmission. This gospel God had promised beforehand, or announced it [NEB]: both are valid translations of the Greek *proepangelō*. (The root of the verb is the same as the word for "angel," God's announcer and messenger.) This gospel had been announced in scripture, in the holy writings of the prophets. This is the source of Paul's gospel about the Son. It was all there ahead of time, encoded by God into the writings, awaiting Paul's discovery. God in scripture had looked ahead—*not to Jesus, but to the gospel that told of him.*

How can Paul present things in this bizarre way? He is telling the Roman Christians that scripture contains the forecast of his own gospel, not the forecast of Jesus and his life. But if God had encoded into scripture information about Jesus that would form part of Paul's gospel, then God would have been first and foremost foretelling Jesus. We would expect Paul to say that God had announced information beforehand about *Jesus*, not about his own gospel.

As Paul presents it, scripture was not the prophecy of Jesus' life and activities. It was the prophecy of the gospel which told of those activities.

In this picture, no life of Jesus has intervened between the writing of scripture and the revelation of the gospel to Paul. Wherever or whenever the activities of the Son had taken place, they had not been located in history between the two events.

This is perfectly consistent with the manner of presentation we see throughout the epistles, especially in connection with the revelation of God's "mystery." The secret of Christ has been hidden for long ages, and the first bringing to light of that secret, the first action on God's age-old promises, has taken place not in a life of Jesus in the recent past, but in the inspirations and activities of missionary prophets like Paul.

We are led to conclude that, in Paul's past, there was no historical Jesus. Rather, the activities of the Son about which God's gospel in scripture told, as interpreted by Paul, had taken place in the spiritual realm and were accessible only through revelation.

But let's go on. In Romans 1:3-4, following on the last quote above, Paul gives us two items of this gospel about the Son, encoded by God into scripture:

> "[3] . . . who arose from the seed of David according to the flesh, [4] and was designated Son of God in power according to the spirit of holiness (or, the holy spirit) after his resurrection from the dead, Jesus Christ our Lord."

This part of the sentence is frustratingly obscure, as reflected by the many different translations to be found of its various elements. (The above translation of verses 3 and 4 is partly my own, in an attempt to lean toward the literal Greek.) Here Paul offers two elements about the Son. One is *kata sarka*, literally "according to the flesh," a vague and particularly cryptic phrase that is used throughout early Christian literature in a variety of subtle ways, often with unclear meaning. The other is *kata pneuma*, literally "according to the spirit." Whether the latter is a reference to the Holy Spirit is also uncertain. Perhaps Paul is using *kata* to refer to something like "in the sphere of the flesh" and "in the sphere of the spirit." This is a suggestion put forward by C. K. Barrett.[38] Such a translation is, in fact, quite useful and possibly accurate. But let's look at *kata sarka* first.

". . . who arose from the seed of David, according to the flesh [or, in the sphere of the flesh] . . ."

Is this a piece of historical information? If so, it is the only one Paul ever gives us, for no other feature of Jesus' human incarnation appears in his letters. But the fact that it is linked with the "according to the spirit" element which, as we shall see, is entirely a heavenly event derived from scripture, suggests that the reference to David's seed is not an earthly, biographical feature Paul is offering.

In fact, it follows, grammatically and conceptually, out of what Paul has just said: it is an element of the gospel about God's Son which has been announced in scripture. Paul has told us clearly and unequivocally that this is where he has obtained this piece of information. In verses 1-2, he has focused on the message to be found in the sacred writings. Why would he suddenly step outside that focus and interject a biographical element about Jesus derived from historical knowledge— then return to scripture for his second element?

Paul did not need to appeal to history here, for scripture was full of predictions that the Messiah would be descended from David. In reading these, Paul would have applied them to his own version of the Christ, the Christ who was a spiritual entity, not a human one.

Was it possible for the divine Son who operated entirely in the spiritual realm to be "of David's seed/stock," and in a way that was "in the sphere of the flesh"? I will suggest (in Part Four) that the answer is yes, and that Christ's "arising from David" is a characteristic of Christ *in the spirit world*, a mythological feature.

But let's continue with the second element of Paul's gospel about the Son in Romans 1:3-4, as derived from scripture:

". . . and was designated Son of God in power, according to the spirit [or, in the sphere of the spirit], by his resurrection out of the dead."

This is clearly an entirely spiritual event, taking place in heaven after Christ's death and resurrection (which were themselves spiritual events). And where did Paul get his information about this particular heavenly scene?

That last quotation above contains two relevant features: Christ's designation as Son of God and the phrase "in power." Where in the sacred writings could Paul have found an important passage which contained those two elements side by side, and which could be regarded as applying to the Messiah?

Psalm 2 is a royal coronation hymn. God is represented as welcoming and anointing his king, and the writer warns the foreign nations to beware of their plots and ambitions. In verses 7-8 God declares, and both Jews and Christians took these words as directed to the Christ, the Messiah:

"I will tell of the decree of the Lord:
He said to me, 'You are my son, today I have begotten you.
Ask of me, and I will give you the nations as your inheritance,
and the ends of the earth as your possession . . .' " [RSV/NEB]

This passage is a prime candidate for the source of Paul's second gospel element: Jesus is proclaimed God's Son by God himself. And he is invested with power, receiving the nations of the earth as his possession. (The original Psalm writer had Israel herself, through its king, in mind, though the sentiment was no doubt rhetorical.) The theme of Jesus as king runs like a thread throughout the entire history of Christian tradition, and it certainly was not based on Jesus' recorded life experiences.

The two elements, the one in the sphere of the "flesh" (which I will locate in the lowest heavenly sphere, associated with the material world), the other in the sphere of the "spirit" (the highest level of God, to where Jesus ascended after his "death"), go hand in hand. They are both a part of God's gospel about his Son, relating to the Son's activities in the spiritual realm, found in scripture. Paul is preaching a Jesus entirely derived from the Hebrew bible.

The analysis in this chapter has led to the conclusion that it is the sacred writings which have created the picture of the spiritual Christ and determined many of his features. This will be pursued further in later chapters. To those accustomed to the Gospel picture of a Jesus 'meek and mild,' imparting hope, healing and enlightened teachings in an earthly ministry, it may seem jarring to contemplate that Paul and his contemporaries could feel love and devotion to a figure who was based solely on the interpreted words of a book.

Yet these were the words of God. They told of a hidden realm whose existence was as real as the one men and women moved in every day. Jews believed that everything in this world was mirrored and predestined in heaven. Angels and spirits filled the layers of the heavens above them. The mystical dimension was real, a place and a state to be yearned for, to achieve through salvation. In the Platonically dominated outlook of the period, scripture was God's window onto that true, perfect reality, the higher realm of the spirit.

Perhaps it was not so strange, then, that Paul and a host of believers could love and commit themselves to a Christ no one had yet seen. Everyone around them was doing the same. Philosophers moved in purely mystical spheres. Isis, Mithras, all the savior gods, they had not come closer to earth than myth. God himself was entirely supernatural. He had never left heaven, yet countless generations of Jews had devoted their lives and destinies to him.

Why not to a Son of God?

9

The Intermediary Son

Paul may have found God's Son in the sacred writings of Israel, and we have touched on some of the influences which led Paul to look for him there. But two major factors in the environment of the time were influencing people like Paul, and fed into the creation of the spiritual Son and Christ. The first was a philosophical one and forms the subject of this chapter. The other was religious and mythical and will be the focus of Part Four.

Greek Philosophy and the Logos

The spiritual Son was born in a very broad cradle, and it was nowhere near Bethlehem. He was, in fact, the fundamental religious idea of the age, an idea which Christianity synthesized and presented to the future.

Judaism had a long history—though not as long as it believed—of understanding its God as the sole supreme being, enduring throughout the ages, more or less unchanging. But several centuries before Christianity, Greek thinkers had arrived at their own concept of monotheism. Because they perceived the universe as moving in obedience to a stable law, they postulated a single cosmic mind or governing force behind it. Strands of ideas before Plato became consolidated in Plato, and out of his school came later ideas which, if they did not all go back to the Master himself, were attributed to him and called "Platonism."

This Platonic conception of God was that he was an Absolute Being, a Unity, that he constituted pure mind and inhabited a world of pure spirit. He was not and never could be a part of the imperfect world of matter and the senses, nor could he make any personal contact with it. To humans who inhabited the material, changing world he was inaccessible and incapable of being understood. This is the meaning of the word "transcendent." God is a transcendent being, totally separated from the material universe.

By contrast, Stoicism offered an "immanent" God, because God was equivalent to Nature or the world itself, meaning the total universe. The reasoning or governing principle within the universe was thought of as the mind of God, and this the Stoics called the "Logos" (LAW-goss). Humans possessed this reason within themselves (the Stoic "soul") so that they shared in God's nature. They were an integral part of the cosmic world, in continuity with God.

For Stoicism's rival, Platonism, the governing force of the universe (God) was something which lay outside matter. God was the true reality while the visible world was only a distant, imperfect reflection of him. Thus the universe was "dualistic" (in two parts). But it was obvious that such a system by itself was too stark, too unsatisfying. A compromise was necessary, otherwise humanity could have no contact with God at all—something the religious mind will not countenance. For how was God to be revealed if he possessed no interface with the world of humans? How would humanity benefit from what God had to offer if there were no channel between them? How, indeed, had the world even come about if God was so remote?

Some intermediate force or being had to be postulated. The first task of this intermediary had been creation. In Platonism, the process of creation can be described by saying that the mind of God produced Ideas, and another aspect of this mind, God's creative energy (which Plato called the "Demiurge"), took these Ideas or Forms and fashioned copies of them out of matter, thus producing the material world perceived by the senses. All these elements in the mind of God, his Ideas, the creative forces, were seen as "intermediate" and came collectively to be referred to by the term Logos (literally, "Word").

The Platonic Logos was thus an emanation of God and his point of contact with the world. In addition to being the agent of creation, the Logos revealed God, his nature, the divine will and was the channel of divine aid to the world. The Logos was also the image of God according to which humans were created.

Platonists tended not to regard the Logos as a personal being, but more an abstract force. For some, however, the Logos could provide salvation. In a revealing little document called *Discourse to the Greeks*, erroneously ascribed to Justin Martyr, the writer speaks of the Logos as instructing and having "ceaseless care over us," making "human beings gods." Here the Logos has become a personal divinity, and while there is no hint of Christ or Christianity in this document, it is undeniably cut from the same intellectual cloth.

The impulse of the age was to bring the intermediary between God and the world closer to matter, make him more personal, more accessible on a human level. A strong monotheist like Philo—the most prominent philosopher of Hellenistic Judaism[39]—stopped short of making his Son and Logos a personal divine being. Instead, he envisioned Moses as a man into whom the power and qualities of the Logos had been infused. But other Jews did not feel the same rigid restrictions toward God, and could envision their Son as a personal divinity beside God in heaven. From the Logos of Greek and Philonic philosophy to Paul's Christ Jesus is scarcely a stone's throw.

Jewish Personified Wisdom

Hellenistic Jews like Philo adopted Logos ideas to create a melding of Hebrew and Greek. But more mainstream Judaism had its own intermediary figure going back centuries, certainly as old as Plato. For the Jews, God was never quite so inaccessible, but scribes of the period after the Exile presented God as making himself known and working in the world through a part of himself they called "Wisdom."[40]

This was no "Son" of God, however, for the figure of Wisdom was a female. (The grammatical gender of "wisdom" in Hebrew is feminine.) Wisdom took on a status and personality of her own. She developed her own "myths" about coming to earth, although there was never any thought of her being physically incarnated.

Here is what the Old Testament Book of Proverbs has to say about Wisdom (from 8:1-36):

> "By the gate, Wisdom calls aloud: 'Men, it is to you I call . . . I am Wisdom, I bestow shrewdness, and show the way to knowledge and prudence . . . The Lord created me the beginning of his works . . . when he set the heavens in their place I was there . . . I was at the Lord's side each day . . . Happy is the man who keeps to my ways."

There are two important aspects of Wisdom here. First, she is "pre-existent," that is, she was with God in heaven before the creation of the world. And she is associated with God in that work, serving as an instrument in the process of creation:

> "In wisdom the Lord founded the earth and by understanding he set the heavens in their place." (3:19)

These are two of the primary attributes given to the spiritual Christ in the thought of Paul, pre-existence and a role in creation.

Baruch 3:37 gives us a line which, even though originally intended as a reference to the Torah (the Jewish Law contained in the five biblical books of Moses, which mainstream rabbinic thought identified with Wisdom), may have had a profound influence on the future:

> "Thereupon wisdom appeared on earth and lived among men."

Was this one of the footsteps on the path that eventually brought to earth a different emanation of God—the Son? Perhaps the writer of the hymn to the Logos which was adapted as a Prologue to the final version of the Gospel of John turned it into a song of the incarnation: "So the Logos (Word) became flesh and dwelt among us." (Jn. 1:14)

In the "Wisdom of Solomon," perhaps the most important surviving piece of Hellenistic Jewish writing, we can see a clear and exotic blending of Wisdom with the Logos. This document was almost certainly written in Alexandria, probably in the early first century CE. Like the Logos, Wisdom is now the divine power active in the world, the spirit that pervades and governs all things. She, too, is pre-existent and an agent of creation. She is God's "throne-partner," a step away from Christ sitting at the right hand of God.

> ". . . she rises from the power of God, a pure effluence of the glory of the Almighty . . . She is the brightness that streams from everlasting light, the flawless mirror of the active power of God and the image of his goodness . . . She spans the world in power from end to end, and orders all things benignly." (7:22-30)

The Son as Wisdom and the Logos

The type of thinking in the Wisdom of Solomon pervades the New Testament epistles. Consider the opening verses about the nature of the Son in Hebrews, a document which comes either from Alexandria, or from some Palestinian circle with close ties to that city's philosophy.

> ". . . the Son who is the effulgence of God's splendor and the stamp of God's very being, who sustains the universe by his word of power."

The hymn in Colossians 1:15-20 is stamped with the same imagery:

> "He (God's Son) is the image of the invisible God; his is the primacy over all created things. In him everything in heaven and earth was created . . . And he exists before everything and all things are held together in him."

Paul himself tells us that Christ "is the power of God and the wisdom of God" (1 Corinthians 1:24) and "the very image of God" (2 Corinthians 4:4). In 1 Corinthians 8:6, he makes Christ the agent of creation, channeling the source of all things that resides in the Father:

"For us there is one God, the Father, from whom all being comes . . . and there is one Lord, Jesus Christ, through whom all things came to be and we through him." [NEB]

Paul and other early Christian writers are speaking of Christ in exactly the same language as we find in the broader philosophical world, both Greek and Jewish. Paul's idea of the spiritual Son has absorbed both the Logos and personified Wisdom. In reading scripture and imagining he is being inspired to a view of God's Son, Paul is drawing on the prominent ideas of his day and the deeper heritage which lay behind them.

Scholarship fully recognizes this, of course, but its answer is that all these current ideas were *applied* to Jesus, that those who came in contact with him, his apostles and other followers, were so overwhelmed by the force of Jesus' personality, by the things he had said and done, that immediately after his death and perceived resurrection they went out, gathered all this sophisticated mythological theory and heaped it upon the humble Jewish preacher they had followed. (They also must assume that in the process, those followers abandoned all former interest in the details of his life and teachings.)

The inherent fallacy in such a scenario is easy to see. In the above passages, early Christian writers are presenting the Son as "the image of the invisible God," etc. They are describing a divine figure in terms of divine attributes. No identification with a human man is ever made, no writer gives us even a hint that an "application" to an historical Jesus is anywhere in their minds. As suggested earlier, scholars are guilty of reading into the text things they find hard to believe are not there.[41]

A Channel Between God and the World

Paul's Christ, like Wisdom and the Logos, is God's channel in his dealings with the world. Paul has an expression to convey this idea.

In the letters of Paul and those who later wrote in his name, we find the phrase "in Christ Jesus" or "through Christ Jesus" over a hundred times. With Wisdom and the Logos in mind, we can see just what this phrase means.

In Romans 6:11 Paul says this (a literal translation):

> "Regard yourselves as dead to sin, but alive to God in Christ Jesus (*en Christō Iēsou*)."

Here Paul is using the idea of "in Christ" to represent a channel of contact with God; Christ is the means by which Christians are "alive" to God. This intermediary channel is a force in the present, something spiritual; it has no reference to a recent historical event or person. At the opening of 1 Corinthians, Paul says that the congregation at Corinth is "dedicated to God in Christ Jesus." Christ is the medium which links the believers of that city with God himself.

Look at Romans 8:39: "Nothing in all creation can separate us from the love of God in Christ Jesus our Lord." Here Christ is the spiritual force which embodies and conveys God's love. Like the Logos, though in a more personal sense, the intermediary Christ allows humanity to reach God and to receive benefits from him. It is often said that the idea of the Logos pervades Paul, but the word itself is missing.

Titus 3:4-6 tells us:

> "When the kindness and generosity of God our Savior dawned upon the world . . . he saved us through the water of rebirth and the renewing power of the Holy Spirit. For he sent down the Spirit upon us plentifully through Jesus Christ. . . ." [NEB]

The saving acts which have occurred in the present time are not the events of Jesus' death and resurrection. They are God's granting of the rite of baptism and the bestowing of the Spirit. Jesus is the channel along which this Spirit has flowed from God to the world.

Christ, then, operates entirely on a spiritual level. He is a communicating and sacramental power now present in the world, impregnating the hearts and minds of believers. These are highly mystical ideas, and there is no justification for scholarship's frequent attempt to see the Pauline phrase "in or through Christ" as a cryptic summary of Jesus' life on earth.

Sending the Spirit of Christ

God's Son is an entity that is only now being revealed to the world, but he is also a Son who has been "sent" into the world. Early Christians saw the spiritual Christ as having arrived in a real way, active and speaking through themselves. When Paul and other writers speak of the "Spirit" sent from God, they are usually referring to the traditional idea of the Holy Spirit, the power and presence of God acting within inspired teachers and apostles. Yet on occasion we see a more explicit identification of this Spirit with Christ himself (as in Philippians 1:19), so that Christ becomes a spirit force in his own right.

"God has sent the spirit of his Son into our hearts," says Galatians 4:6. 1 John 5:20 reads: "We know that the Son of God has come (literally, "*is come*"—in the present tense) and given us understanding to know him who is real." The Son is working among Christians at the present time, imparting knowledge of God.

In the same way, we can understand the "coming" in Ephesians 2:17: "And coming, he (Christ) announced the good news . . ." For what was the content of that news?

". . . peace to you who were far away and peace to those who were near, for through him we both alike have access in one spirit to the Father." [NEB/my trans.]

Instead of taking the opportunity to refer to some of Jesus' earthly teachings, the writer quotes scripture: Isaiah 57:19, which speaks of an end-time reconciliation between peoples. Even the preliminary words about preaching good news are based on Isaiah 52:7. This is the Christ who has "come" in the spirit and speaks to the world—a "speaking" found in scripture. The final phrase of the quote identifies him as a spiritual channel to the Father.

A Christ Who Inhabits the World of Scripture

This has led to an important insight into how the early Christians viewed Christ. Not only is the Son revealed in scripture, the Son *speaks* from scripture. Certain passages in the sacred writings were regarded as the voice of the Son, speaking directly to the world.

This is most evident in the epistle to the Hebrews. It begins with the statement (1:2) that "in this final age (God) has spoken to us through the Son." This, however, would seem to be something other than the teaching of Jesus of Nazareth, for not a single Gospel saying is offered through 13 chapters, not even a reference to the fact that Jesus had taught in an earthly ministry. Instead, when 'quoting' the voice of the Son to make his arguments, the author draws on passages from scripture that are identified as the Son's own words.

When seeking to illustrate (2:12) that the Son considers believers to be his brothers, he offers Psalm 22:22, "I will proclaim thy name to my brothers." More than one commentator has sought to explain why the writer would not have drawn on such sayings as are found in the Gospels, for example in Mark 3:35: "Whoever does the will of God is my brother."[42]

The scriptural 'sayings' are prefaced by a "he says"—in the present tense—showing that in the writer's mind, the Son is an entity who is known and communicates now and today, through the sacred writings, not through any past preaching career on earth.

An even more telling "voice of the Son" is presented in Hebrews 10:5, also prefaced by a "he says," but this will be left until we have examined the mythical realm where the Son lives and performs his act of redemption. The writer views scripture as presenting a picture of spiritual world realities, where the Son operates and speaks. This is the meaning of the epistle's opening statement, for God in this final age speaks to the world not through the teachings of an earthly Jesus but through a new reading of scripture, in which the voice of the Son is to be heard.

As late as the end of the century, the same phenomenon can be detected in the epistle 1 Clement. In chapter 22 'Clement' says:

"All these promises (by God) find their confirmation when we believe in Christ, for it is he himself who summons us through the Holy Spirit, with the words: 'Come, children, listen to me, and I will teach you the fear of the Lord.' "

Clement regards this quote from Psalm 34 as a personal summons from Christ, as though Christ himself is telling Christian readers that he will teach them the fear of the Lord. When he earlier (ch.16) describes Christ's sufferings, he quotes a passage from Psalm 22, again presenting it as the voice of Christ himself, telling of his experiences of suffering and rejection through the words of scripture.

These early writers provide us with an insight into the fundamental nature of early Christian thought. Christ was a spiritual figure, a present force who was accessible through the sacred writings. *Scripture was not the prophecy of the Christ event, but its embodiment.* The Son inhabited the spiritual world of the scriptures, God's window on the unseen true reality. To that unseen, mythical world we will now travel.

Part Four
A WORLD OF MYTH AND SAVIOR GODS

10

Who Crucified Jesus?

The pieces of the Jesus Puzzle in Part Three revealed how the New Testament epistles present Christ as a spiritual force in the present time, functioning as a channel between God and humanity. But there is another, even more important role being given to him, for in some unspecified time and place, Paul's Christ had performed a redemptive act. The saving benefits of that act are only now being revealed and made available.

In the epistles, Christ's act of salvation is not located in the present, or even in the recent past, and certainly not within the historical setting familiar to us from the Gospels. Christ had existed from before time began, and it was in a non-historical time and place, in a supernatural realm, that this Son of God had undergone a redeeming "blood" sacrifice.

To understand that setting, we need to look at the ancients' view of the universe and how it worked, the concept of myth, and the features of the pagan salvation cults known as the "mysteries." In these, a multitude of savior gods functioned much like Jesus and offered similar guarantees of happy afterlives and immortality.

Spiritual and Material Worlds

In Chapter 3, we dipped our feet into Platonic waters and saw how the universe was perceived as "dualistic," split into two main divisions of higher and lower, spiritual and material worlds. The upper world was the realm of God and supernatural forces, containing perfect and timeless realities; the lower world was the realm of humanity and matter, where things were changing and perishable, imperfect copies of those higher, genuine realities. This was pure Platonism. But the more popular view, a melting pot of more than one line of thought and many cultural and religious backgrounds, was a little less pristine and a lot more chaotic.

When the eye of many an ancient philosopher or even the average layperson looked skyward, it imagined it could see a populated spirit world where the bulk of the workings of the universe took place. Near the bottom of this multi-level system lay humanity's sphere, the material earth; only Sheol or Hades, the underworld, was lower. Various supernatural layers (usually seven, controlled by the seven astronomical bodies) extended upwards. They were filled with spiritual life forms, reaching to the highest heaven of pure spirit where the ultimate God dwelled in timeless perfection. The nature of this dualistic reality involved far-reaching parallels between the higher and lower realms, between spirit and matter.

Even before Plato, near-eastern mythology envisioned primal or archetypal forms existing in heaven, of which earthly things were counterparts. A sacred site such as the Jerusalem Temple was the earthly counterpart of a greater, more perfect heavenly Temple. Nations, rulers, groups on earth possessed a corresponding angelic or divine being who represented them, a superior counterpart in heaven, a champion. Evil nations possessed evil angels. That counterpart in heaven embodied the qualities which the people he represented claimed for themselves, or looked forward to achieving when the time of salvation arrived. Events expected to take place on earth had already been worked out in some fashion in archetypal processes in the heavenly realm, or in the mind of God. Figures to be revealed in the future already existed and were preparing themselves in heaven. And so on.

Paul and the earliest Christians thus lived at a time when the world of matter was viewed as only one dimension of reality, the observable half of a larger, integrated whole. The other—invisible—half was regarded as the "genuine" reality, accessible to the intellect. It was characteristic of mythological thinking that the heavenly counterpart was more real and permanent than the earthly one, and prior to it in order of being. (See John J. Collins, *The Apocalyptic Imagination*, p.150.) Such an outlook must be taken into account in any interpretation of the earliest Christian writings.

The World of Myth

When a culture is dominated by the sense that the world it inhabits is an outpost or antechamber of a more important world, a visible dimension beside or below a vast invisible dimension, it must envision a relationship as well as links between the two.

Myths represent the other end of the channel flowing between the spiritual world and the human one, by which the latter is sustained and vitalized, given meaning and purpose. Before Platonism, myths were generally set in a dim, distant past. This was, and continues to be, the approach of all pre-scientific societies around the world. And although by the period of early Christianity mythical thinking tended to be recast along more Platonic lines, this long tradition of primordial myth continued to flow as an undercurrent.

Anthropologists of religion such as Mircea Eliade[43] call this distant time of myth the "sacred past." This was a primordial time at the beginning of things when supernatural beings created the world and first performed acts and established institutions which set the patterns of behavior and belief that society now follows. Primordial time has established the model, the *paradigm*; present society embodies its copy, its repetition. Human beings have always needed to justify their beliefs and practices, even their sufferings, to invest them with greater-than-human significance, by anchoring them in some divine precedent, in a time and setting which bestows on them a venerable authority. This explains the fundamental appeal of religion: through myth the individual is invested with significance; he or she is rendered sacred by acknowledging a divine ancestry and entering into a new state of being—a rebirth into union with the supernatural paradigm.

A suitable past, therefore, has to be created, as do links with that past. This is the purpose of rituals and sacraments, essential companion pieces to myth. By performing a rite which "re-creates" the primordial event, society keeps it alive, makes it recur for itself. The vitality and benefits which the divine act had originally generated are regenerated in the present. Those participating in the rite can draw on that regenerated power. Primordial time, in the language of the anthropologists, is made into an "eternal now," always accessible and repeatable. An example is the Christian sacrament of the Eucharist. By staging the rite in the celebration of the Mass, the priest draws Christ into the proceedings, embodied in the priest's reenactment of Christ's original act. That act is kept alive, its benefits continually available to the devotees.

Ancient views of myth had, by the first century, been dramatically affected by Platonic philosophy. Even though processes continued to operate in a similar fashion, the time and place of mythical happenings had, in the minds of philosophers at least, been shifted from the distant primordial past to a higher world of spiritual realities. Instead of looking back to archaic beginnings, religious ritual could reach into that parallel, upper dimension and find its paradigms, its spiritual forces, right there. In this higher world, the myths of the mystery cults and of earliest Christianity were placed. Here the savior god Attis had been castrated, here Mithras had slain the bull, here Osiris had been dismembered. (For more sophisticated thinkers like the first century Plutarch and the fourth century Sallustius, such mythical stories were not literal, but merely symbolic of timeless spiritual processes which the human mind had difficulty grasping.)

In this upper world, too, Christ had been crucified at the hands of the demon spirits. Certain texts will be offered to support this. For Paul and his contemporaries, the sufferings which Christ underwent and the available benefits flowing from them are God's secrets. They are the "mysteries" of this higher sphere, taking place "before or beyond time" (the *pro chronōn aiōniōn* of 2 Timothy 1:9, a passage we'll look at later). Such mysteries have been revealed by God, through scripture and the Spirit.

Here, Christian myth was to some extent qualified by its Jewish heritage. Whatever the primitive Hebrew view of a "sacred past" may have been in the prehistoric period, it eventually moved into a more concrete setting. Primordial figures and processes became part of an archaic history, embodied in legends of human patriarchs who had enjoyed special contacts with the Deity. All of it became firmly anchored in an historical past which could be chronicled year by year. Neither Abraham nor Moses—who may or may not be based on actual historical figures—were located in a true sacred past or higher reality. The promises God made to them, the precedents they set (such as the practice of circumcision) were pinpointed in historical time. This heritage fed into Christian myth and modified the type of thinking Christianity had taken from the conceptual world of the Greeks.

Thus where the Greek myths were essentially timeless, unrelated to a chronicled past, Paul's myth of Christ had features which were derived from scripture, a scripture which presented an ongoing system of salvation history. The redemptive actions of the mythical Christ in the spiritual world had to be 'fitted into' this ongoing pattern.

For example, Christ had to be "of David's stock" (Romans 1:3), for the spiritual Son was now equated with the Messiah, and the clear testimony in scripture that the Messiah would be a descendant of David could neither be ignored nor abandoned. He thus was viewed as possessing a Davidic or Judaic nature.[44] (Even some of the pagan savior gods could be said to possess an ethnic lineage.) As an expression of the new covenant, Christ had also operated under the old Jewish Law with the purpose of abrogating it. The 'historicity' and human characteristics of scripture rubbed off on the picture of Christ presented by early Christian writers, such as the declaration that he was "born of woman" in Galatians 4:4, under the influence of Isaiah 7:14. All this made the evolution of the spiritual Christ into an historical figure much easier.

Rites, Sacraments and Paradigms

Just as today we perceive natural laws and forces working in nature and the universe, the ancients perceived spiritual forces operating between the natural world and the supernatural, between the present, earthly reality and the primordial past or higher divine reality. For Paul, the rite of baptism was a sacrament in this sense, something which drew on invisible spiritual forces operating between past and present, between heaven and earth. Baptism linked the Christian initiates with Christ in the spiritual realm. It made them part of a collective, mystical body: Christ as the Head, believers the limbs and organs. It also linked them with Christ's mythical act of death and resurrection, conferring a new birth upon them. Paul calls this effect "dying and rising to Christ." Drawing on the spiritual forces generated by Christ's redemptive act, the believer dies to his or her old life in sin and rises to a new one free of sin; and he or she inherits the promise of future resurrection. Such sacramental thinking was not derived from Judaism, but from Hellenistic religious thought, as expressed in the mysteries. (See F. W. Beare, *The First Epistle of Peter*, p.57.)

In describing the relationship between the upper and lower worlds, scholars (eg, Collins, *op.cit.*, p.150) speak of a "parallelism of action" between heavenly and earthly counterparts, a "structural homologue" (G. Theissen, *Sociology of Early Palestinian Christianity*, p.121). Actions by divine beings in the spiritual realm have their consequences for those on earth who are joined to them. This idea is the key to understanding the concept of salvation which early Christianity shared with the Greek cults. The absorption of the spiritual power generated by the deity and his acts is accomplished through a pattern of "likeness." Here is the way Paul puts it in Romans 6:5:

"For if we have become united with him in the likeness of his death, certainly we shall be also in the likeness of his resurrection." [NASB]

In other words, the spiritual force set up by the acts of the deity in the primordial past or higher reality impacts on the devotee in the present in a parallel process. Death creates a "death," resurrection creates a "resurrection." Whether in the primordial or higher world setting, the spiritual model, the paradigm, sets the pattern for the earthly copies. Christ's act of resurrection guarantees the resurrection of the convert who undergoes baptism; the rite is the means of harnessing that available spiritual force and making it flow to the believer.[45]

All this fits into that most fundamental of ancient concepts outlined earlier: the idea that earth was the mirror image of heaven, the product proceeding from the archetype, the visible material counterpart to the genuine spiritual reality above. Heavenly events determined earthly realities. It follows that in such a philosophical system, the determining acts of divine forces which conferred salvation would of necessity be located, not on earth, but in that higher realm. Everything Paul says places him in that sort of thought world.

The Rulers of This Age

Who does Paul identify as having slain Christ? That one reference to a human agency, namely "the Jews" in 1 Thessalonians 2:15-16, has been rejected by a good part of modern scholarship as an interpolation (see Appendix 1). For Paul's true outlook, let's look at 1 Corinthians 2:6-8:

"[6]And yet I do speak of a wisdom for those who are mature, not a wisdom of this passing age, nor of the rulers of this age who are passing away. [7]I speak of God's secret wisdom, a mystery that has been hidden and predestined by God for our glory before time began. [8]None of the rulers of this age understood it, for if they had, they would not have crucified the Lord of glory." [my trans.]

A great amount of scholarly ink has been spilled over the meaning of "the rulers of this age" (*tōn archontōn tou aiōnos toutou*, verses 6 and 8). In both pagan and Jewish parlance, the word *archontes* could be used to refer to earthly rulers and those in authority (as in Romans 13:3). But it is also, along with several others like it, a technical term for the spirit forces, the "powers and authorities" who rule the lowest level of the heavenly world and who exercise authority over the events and fate (usually cruel) of the earth, its nations and individuals. That invisible powers, mostly evil, were at work behind earthly phenomena was a widely held belief in Hellenistic times, including among Jews, and it was shared by Christianity.

There has not been a universal scholarly consensus on what Paul has in mind in 1 Corinthians 2:8, but many commentators[46] over the last century, some reluctantly, have decided that he is referring to the demon spirits. The term *aiōn*, age (or sometimes in the plural "ages") was in a religious and apocalyptic context a reference to the present age of the world, in the sense of all recorded history. The next, or "coming" age was the one after the Day of the Lord, when God's kingdom would be established. One of the governing ideas of the period was that the world to the present point had been under the control of the evil angels and spirit powers, and that the coming of the new age would see their long awaited overthrow.

Humanity was engaged in a war against the demons, and one of the strongest appeals of the Greek salvation cults was their promise of divine aid in this war, on a personal level. Thus, "rulers of this age" should not be seen as referring to the current secular authorities who happen to be in power in present political circumstances. Rather, Paul envisions that those in the present age who have controlled the earth and separated it from heaven, the evil angelic powers, are approaching their time of "passing away" (2:6) and that they did not understand God's purposes, namely their own destruction, when they inadvertently crucified "the Lord of glory."

Ephesians 3:9-10 echoes these hidden purposes of God, and declares that they have now been brought to light:

> ". . . the application of this mystery which has been hidden for long ages in God the creator of the universe, so that through the church the wisdom of God might be made known to the rulers and authorities in the heavens, in accordance with his eternal purpose which he carried out in Christ Jesus our Lord." [my trans.]

Here the rulers are identified as the ones in the heavens. We might note that the writer is consistent with general Pauline expression, in allotting the task of revealing God's long-hidden mystery to the "church," to men like himself, not to any recent historical Jesus. That last phrase refers to the workings of Christ in the higher spiritual world, his redeeming actions within God's eternal realm and time. In other words, the world of myth.

A prominent first century Christian idea was that Christ by his death had subjected all the spirit powers and authorities, both good and evil, to his control. In this light, Colossians 2:15 again places Jesus' crucifixion in a supernatural milieu, for it is difficult to see any historical scene on Calvary contained in this idea:

> "On the cross he discarded the cosmic powers and authorities like a garment; he made a public spectacle of them and led them as captives in his triumphal procession." (NEB)

Ephesians 6:12 also speaks of the fight which is not against human foes, but against the "cosmic powers, authorities and potentates of this dark world, the superhuman forces of evil in the heavens." These were thought of as having political organizations like rulers on earth. They were well placed and capable of executing a spiritual Christ who had descended from the higher divine realm into their territory, and we will look in a moment at a document which paints such a picture of the Son descending from heaven to be crucified by the evil angels.

S. G. F. Brandon (*History, Time and Deity*, p.167) is a scholar who unflinchingly faces the conclusion that although Paul's statement "may seem on cursory reading to refer to the Crucifixion as an historical event . . . the expression 'rulers of this age' does not mean the Roman and Jewish authorities. Instead, it denotes the daemonic powers who were believed to inhabit the planets (the celestial spheres) and control the destinies of men. . . . Paul attributes the Crucifixion not to Pontius Pilate and the Jewish leaders, but to these planetary powers."

However, Brandon (like everyone else) fails to address the question of how Paul could have spoken in such terms if he had the tradition of Jesus' recent death in Judea before his eyes, providing not so much as a hint of qualification to this supernatural picture. It will not do to suggest that since earthly rulers are considered to be controlled by heavenly ones, the latter are seen as operating "through" the former. Paul would not likely have presented things in this way without an explanation. And by the time we get to the Gospel picture which first makes a clear reference to earthly rulers in the death of Jesus, the heavenly dimension which is supposed to lie behind them disappears, or in the case of John retires into the distant, allusive background.

Descending Gods

The concept that a god, in order to perform a salvific act, had to approach or enter the "world of flesh" was arrived at by philosophical reasoning. In the higher celestial spheres where deity was perfect and unsullied by any contact with the world of matter, gods existed in their fully divine state. There they could not do something as human as to suffer. Pain, blood, death: these were the unfortunate features of the lower, baser levels of the universe.

To undergo such things, the god had to come down to humanity's territory. He had to take on material characteristics and capacities. If contact between flesh and divinity was to be made, the initiative lay with the god. Deity had to humble itself, compromise its spiritual purity. It had to descend. And descend it did, for the concept of the "descending redeemer" seems to have been a pervasive idea during this era, though the evidence for the pre-Christian period is patchy and much debated.

As noted earlier, the spiritual part of the universe was popularly seen as divided into several levels—usually seven. As a deity descended from the higher reaches of pure spirit, he passed through ever degenerating spheres of the heavens, and could take on an increasing likeness to lower, material forms as well as an ability to suffer fleshly fates, such as pain and death. The lowest level of the spirit realm was the air, or "firmament," between the earth and the moon. This was the domain of the demon spirits—in Jewish parlance, of Satan and his evil angels—and it was regarded as closely connected to the earthly sphere. The demonic spiritual powers belonged to the realm of flesh and were thought of as in some way corporeal, though they possessed 'heavenly' versions of earthly bodies.[47]

Thus it was wholly conceivable for Paul's Christ in that spiritual world to descend into the realm of the demon spirits. Here he would be in the sphere of flesh, which fits the early writers' almost universal use of such stereotyped phrases as "in flesh," "according to the flesh." (C. K. Barrett, as noted earlier, translates *kata sarka* in Romans 1:3 as "in the sphere of the flesh.") Here Christ could assume counterpart characteristics of the visible world, undergo suffering and death at the hands of the spirits as a blood sacrifice, and be raised by God back to the highest heaven. Even if it was all a part of God's "mystery," something that had taken place in God's eternal time, hidden for long generations and knowable to men like Paul only through divine revelation in scripture.

Such ideas were not restricted to Judaism and Christianity, although the few surviving writers who touch on the Greek mysteries and the activities of their deities tend to be sophisticated philosophers like Plutarch and Sallustius. These men saw the stories of the Greek salvation cults as "eternal meanings clothed in myths." They were allegorical interpretations only, even if the minds of 'ordinary men' might see them as more literal. (Some of those average devotees of the cults may also have retained a more traditional way of viewing the myths of the savior gods as belonging to a primordial past on earth.)

The fourth century philosopher Sallustius calls the story of Attis "an eternal cosmic process, not an isolated event of the past" (*On Gods and the World*, 9), which places his understanding in a timeless spiritual world. Similarly, his mentor, the emperor Julian "the Apostate," describes (in *Orations V*, 165) Attis' descent to the lowest spirit level prior to matter, undergoing his death by castration to give the visible world order and fruitfulness; but he regards this as a symbol of the annual cycle of agricultural rebirth, the generative power which descends into the earth from the upper regions of the stars.

Myths of the descent and ascent of deity are often interpreted (especially in Gnosticism and Neoplatonism) as symbolizing the ancient idea of the fall of the soul into matter, its suffering and death within that base, imperfect world, followed by a reascent into its proper abode and state, an exaltation. The myth of the redeeming god, the paradigm for the soul's descent and ascent, guarantees this destiny for the believer.

Clear echoes of such thinking are found in the epistles (eg, Romans 6:5, as quoted earlier). The Pauline corpus also contains examples of Christian cultic mythology, liturgical poems about the divine Christ which scholars call "christological hymns." These are generally regarded as pre-Pauline, though no one has any idea who wrote them. Consider the hymn in Philippians 2:6-11:

> "[6]For the divine nature was his from the first; yet he did not think to snatch at equality with God, [7]but made himself nothing, assuming the nature (or form) of a slave. Bearing the human likeness, [8]revealed in human shape, he humbled himself, and in obedience accepted even death—death on a cross. [9]Therefore God raised him to the heights and bestowed on him the name above all names, [10]that at the name of Jesus every knee should bow—in heaven, on earth, and in the depths—[11]and every tongue confess, 'Jesus Christ is Lord,' to the glory of God the Father." [NEB]

This is the early Christian epitome of the descending-ascending redeemer myth, and there is not a breath of identification with any Jesus of Nazareth. Three times does the hymn allude to the idea that this divinity took on a likeness to base, material form, but never does it say that he became an actual man, much less give him a life on earth. Instead, this deity descends to undergo death (some commentators feel that the phrase "death on a cross" is probably a Pauline addition, since it interrupts the pattern of the poetic lines) and is raised back to the highest heaven, where he is exalted.[48]

The shorter hymn in 1 Timothy 3:16 offers a similar descent-ascent pattern performed by a divine being:

> "He who was manifested in [flesh], vindicated in spirit, seen by angels; who was proclaimed among the nations, believed in throughout the world, glorified in high heaven." [NEB]

Once again there is no identification with a human man, and any suggestion of a ministry is pointedly lacking. This deity seems to have been seen only by angels and engaged in no proclaiming of his own. The "in flesh" of the first line (*en sarki*) can be translated "in the sphere of the flesh," as noted earlier. However, no Christian writer or hymnist expresses the view that the Christ myth is allegorical or symbolic. Paul seems to have very much believed in the divine Jesus' literal suffering at the hands of the demon spirits.

Both of these hymns, with their strange anomalies, have stood in the New Testament epistles for centuries, and much scholarly analysis has gone into them. They have resisted understanding because the wrong preconceptions have been brought to them. But without the Gospels and their historical Jesus in mind, they can be seen for what they are, reflections of ancient world mythic thinking the basis of which has long been abandoned. G. A. Wells, the most prominent proponent of the no-historical-Jesus theory in the latter 20th century,[49] has pronounced much of what is found in the epistles as "unintelligible" to modern readers. And correctly so. This is because we have lost sight of the context for Pauline belief, or have refused to apply it, blinded as we have been for 19 centuries by the artificial creation of the Gospels.

The Descent of the Son

In a Jewish/Christian piece of writing called the Ascension of Isaiah we can find corroboration for this picture of a divine Son who descends into the lower reaches of the heavens to be crucified by the demon spirits. This document falls into two sections which were originally independent. The second section, the Vision of Isaiah (chapters 6-11), underwent its own evolution before being combined with the first, and it contains a detailed picture of the descent-ascent motif we have been discussing.

This is a difficult document to analyze in any exact fashion, since the several surviving manuscripts differ considerably in wording, phrases and even whole sections. It has been subjected to much editing in a complicated and uncertain pattern of revision. But a couple of passages seem to indicate that in its earlier strata, the Vision speaks of a divine Son who operates entirely in the supernatural realm.

The community that wrote this, probably toward the end of the first century, lived in a world of apocalyptic expectation and revelation from the Holy Spirit (6:6f). Salvation is expected for the righteous elect, who will be exalted as a consequence of the death and exaltation of the Son (the *paradigm* effect). Isaiah is granted a vision in which he ascends through the seven layers of heaven and receives a view of God and his Beloved, also called the Chosen One and Christ. He learns that this Son is to descend to the lower world, where he will be killed and rise, rescuing the souls of the righteous dead from Sheol as he reascends to the highest heaven.

Here is the key passage. The seer and his angelic guide have reached the seventh heaven. There they see the Lord, the Christ, and the angel foretells this to Isaiah (9:13-17):

> "[13]The Lord will descend into the world in the last days, he who is to be called Christ after he has descended and become like you in form, and they will think that he is flesh and a man. [14]And the god of that world will stretch out his hand against the Son, and they will lay their hands upon him and hang him upon a tree, not knowing who he is. [15]And thus his descent, as you will see, will be concealed from the heavens, so that it will not be known who he is. [16]And when he has plundered the angel of death, he will rise on the third day and will remain in the world for 545 days. [17]And then many of the righteous will ascend with him."

This looks like a fleshing out of the implication behind Paul's reference to the crucifixion in 1 Corinthians 2:8. We have the descent of the Son through the layers of heaven, a taking on of the "likeness" of men. "They will think that he is flesh and a man" clearly implies that he is not. There is no suggestion of Jesus of Nazareth here. Nor is it likely to be a reference to docetism (Christ having an earthly body which only "seems" human: see Appendix 3), since the phrase looks to be related to the idea in verses 14 and 15 that his *identity* has been concealed. Nor is the Gospel trial and execution anywhere in sight in the reference to the hanging upon a tree. Rather, this hanging is something performed by "the god of that world," meaning Satan. Some manuscripts read: "*he* will hang him upon a tree." Though it is set "in the last days" (Jewish apocalyptic writers were not so Platonically strict), the entire thing has the ring of a mythological scene.

To undergo this fate, the Son will descend to the firmament where Satan and his evil angels dwell. At the beginning of his visionary ascent (7:9-12), Isaiah has passed through the firmament where he saw Satan and his warring angels. They are engaged in a struggle, his guide tells him, which "will last until the one comes whom you are to see, and he will destroy him." As in 1 Corinthians 2:8 and Colossians 2:15, one of the Son's principal tasks will be the conquest of the demon spirits.

Those who do the hanging will not know who this Son is. Once again, this would not seem to be a Gospel reference to Romans or Jews, but means the evil angels of the firmament, for verse 15 indicates that it is the layers of heaven where the concealment and the ignorance about the Son's identity lie. This ignorance on the part of the "god of that world" is similar to that of the "rulers of this age" who unwittingly crucify the Lord of Glory in 1 Corinthians 2:8.

Thus the crucifixion is something perpetrated by the supernatural powers and takes place in the spiritual world. In the opinion of M. Knibb, the translator and commentator on the Ascension of Isaiah in *The Old Testament Pseudepigrapha* (II, p.143f, from which the above translation is taken), the reference to rising on the third day and remaining for 545 days is a later addition to the text derived from gnostic sources which believed that Jesus remained on earth after his resurrection for 18 months (*op.cit.*, p.170, n.'v'). Other bits and pieces throughout the Vision are the reworkings of editors, so that it is difficult to uncover and differentiate the various strands. Knibb even voices the possibility (p.170, n.'g') that all entries of the names Jesus and Christ are later additions.

As part of Isaiah's vision (10:8-14), the Father gives instructions to the Son about his coming descent into the lower world and his reascent to the seventh heaven. There is nothing in this divine directive which speaks of an incarnation into flesh and earthly history, nothing of a ministry, nothing of a death at the hands of humans. There is not a whisper of any knowledge of the Gospels.

Chapter 11 inserts a primitive Gospel account into one manuscript line at some later time (see the discussion in Appendix 4). Had this earthly picture been in the mind of the writer of Chapters 9 and 10, it is difficult to believe that some elements of it would not have been reflected there. Outside of this one passage, the Son's activities seem to relate entirely to the spirit realm, layers of heaven extending through the firmament and including Sheol. God's instructions focus on how he is to proceed through these heavenly spheres, and on the task of destroying the power of Satan and the evil spirits and rescuing the souls of the righteous.

When Mark came to write his midrashic tale about a Jesus on earth, the war fought by heaven and the Son against the demons was translated into Jesus' war on earth against the new, humanized demons: the Jews. Just as the "rulers of this age," the evil spirits, were the murderers of Christ in the Pauline phase, the earthly Jews became the Christ-killers in the Gospel version. When Mark's symbolic character of Jesus of Nazareth became historical, that allegory, too, was turned into history.

11

The Mystery Cults

Tracing Jesus' Family Tree

There is no question that Pauline Christianity contains important elements which are deeply rooted in the Jewish scriptures and cultural heritage. At the same time, the nature of the salvation it offers, the sacramentalism involved, the features of its saving deity, are heavily dependent on Hellenistic precedents. But that is what religious syncretism is all about. Different beliefs and practices are combined to create something new, not with any overtly conscious intent, but because over time the human mind is continually generating fresh ideas out of what it assimilates from the past and the environment. This guarantees ongoing relevance, nourishment, and even healthy competition. Christianity was the great synthesizer of the ancient world's religious ideas, with mixed results for western society.

Paul's Christ Jesus bears too close a resemblance to the savior gods of the Greco-Roman mystery religions to allow it to be claimed that one has nothing to do with the other. There may be no evidence for an overt "borrowing" directly from the mysteries on the part of Paul (though we might advance an argument for one such case: see below). Yet it is undeniable that both phenomena are expressions of similar needs and impulses; both are branches of the same ancient world tree. The acts of Osiris, Attis, Isis and other savior deities who made salvation available to a host of initiates inhabited the same conceptual world as did Christianity's Christ.

Some scholars claim that "religions" is too strong a word for these organizations.[50] During the Empire it is true they were conducted almost like guilds, with rites that were to be kept secret (hence the term "mysteries") and membership that was in some ways select, if only because it could cost a hefty sum to go through all the stages of initiation. But some of these salvation "cults" (probably the better word) were widespread, and entailed well-developed philosophies and mythologies. Ethics was usually of minor concern. Their rites, which included various types of baptism, were looked upon as conferring rebirth on the initiate, protection in this world from harmful spirits and forces of fate, and the promise of some kind of afterlife. In the Greek way of seeing things, the latter did not involve bodily resurrection but only an immortality of the soul in blissful conditions. By the second century CE, the cult of Isis, the Egyptian goddess who contributed so much to the picture of the Christian Mary, was verging on a universal religion. Mithraism, though confined to men and strongest among the military orders, became a virtual state religion in the Roman empire during the century before Constantine converted to Christianity.

The word Paul uses for "supper" (*deipnon*) in his account of the "Lord's Supper" in 1 Corinthians 11 was commonly used for the cultic meal in the mysteries. Virtually all of them had one. Such a meal signified the union of the initiates with the god of the cult's worship, and a sharing in his nature and saving act—usually an overcoming of death in some way. The Sabazius cult observed a communal supper symbolizing the heavenly banquet of the blessed which the initiates could look forward to after death. The cult of Mithras had a myth which explained the origin of its sacred meal. After Mithras had slain the bull (the 'salvific act' in Mithraism), he and the sun god Helios sealed a covenant by dining together on loaves of bread—some say on the meat of the bull himself—and drinking from cups which contained water mixed with wine. The goddess Isis was looked upon as having personally established the mystery rites associated with her, rites which included a sacred meal.

The strong similarities between the mysteries and the Christian sacraments, especially the Eucharist, were explained by the second century Fathers of the Church as the work of the devil. He had plotted to weaken the faith of Christian believers by previously establishing false rites to resemble the Christian ones.[51] Whether in fact the mystery rites in the form the Fathers knew them had preceded Christianity is a matter of dispute, but men like Justin apparently thought so. This may well be what Paul is referring to when he speaks in 1 Corinthians 10:21 of "the table of demons."

The degree to which Paul could have been in contact with the mysteries, or the extent to which he might have absorbed their ideas, has been hotly debated for a century. Not only was he a Jew of the Diaspora who would have been exposed to cross-cultural influences, he is said to have been from Tarsus, which was the center of the Hellenistic Mithras cult from the end of the second century BCE.[52] It is undeniable that the Pauline "Lord's Supper" is alien to Jewish thought. Hyam Maccoby (*Paul and Hellenism*, p.99) points out that the content of the eucharistic rite in Christianity would have been repugnant—even idolatrous—to Jews, "since it involved the concept of eating the body and drinking the blood of a divine figure."

Thus the Eucharist as Paul presents it would have been virtually impossible in the primitive Palestinian church. On the other hand, his sacramental meal is strikingly similar to the idea of eating the flesh and drinking the blood of the mystery deities, a custom found in graphic form in the ancient cult of Dionysos and in more symbolic form in more contemporary cults, such as that of Attis. Paul has also interpreted the Lord's Supper in the manner of the mysteries, as a sacred communion of the participants with their Lord, a sharing in the benefits conferred by the deity, including immortality.

On the Night He Was Delivered Up

Is Paul's "Lord's Supper," then, influenced by or derived from the mysteries, and is it, like theirs, an entirely mythical event?

We saw in Chapter 4 that Paul's statement in 1 Corinthians 11:23, with which he introduces his account of the Lord's Supper, must be interpreted as referring to a personal revelation: "For I received from the Lord what I delivered to you . . ." It is thus quite possible that under the influence of examples like the Mithraic sacred meal, and through perceived inspiration, Paul has come up with an origin myth for the Christian communal meal which gives it the sacramental meaning and hallowed significance he wishes to impose on it, if only to get the Corinthians to better comport themselves at the table. As for the features of that mythical scene, ancient mythology is full of accounts of gods doing and saying things which have established some rite or practice now being followed. Paul declaring that a spiritual Christ had originated the meal, pronouncing its food and drink as representing his body and blood and directing Christians to make it a memorial to him, would not in itself have been out of the ordinary. But let's consider two other elements in the opening verse, as they are often translated:

> ". . . that the Lord Jesus, on the night he was betrayed (or, 'arrested'), took bread . . ."

The Greek verb for "betrayed" or "arrested" is *paradidomi*, which literally means to "hand over" or "deliver up." This is a term often used in the context of justice or martyrdom, and it means no more than to deliver up to custody or judgment—which could include execution. In the Gospel context it can take on a figurative meaning of arrest or betrayal (as in Mark 14:21), but in Paul there is no need to see it that way. He uses the same verb in Romans 8:32, "He (God) did not spare his own Son, but delivered him up for us all." Here it can hardly imply betrayal or arrest. In Ephesians 5:2 and 25 it is Christ who "gave himself up on your behalf." No thought of Judas or of an arrest on Passover eve would be present here.

As to the scene being set "at night," there is nothing to prevent mythical stories from being given such a setting, especially those involving death and sacrifice. If the Corinthian communal meal is observed after dark (Paul does not specify), the origin myth would likely be set at a corresponding time. Elsewhere, in 1 Corinthians 5:7, Paul links Christ's sacrifice with Passover. Its meal is celebrated after sunset. However, this association could simply be a symbolic one involving the identification of Christ with the idea of the Passover sacrifice, with no necessary link to a specific historical Passover.

The Origins of the Mysteries

The roots of the pagan mysteries are obscure. It is thought that the primitive common denominator behind these diverse cults was the yearly agricultural cycle, the dying and renewing of vegetation and food crops. People's experience of nature's round led to the concept that the gods who inhabited these plants or the earth they grew from regularly underwent a representative dying and rising themselves, or had once done so, perhaps even as a sacrifice to guarantee the annual return of fertility. Mythical stories grew up to embody such divine experiences.

But although the cycle of the seasons almost certainly played a formative part, scholars have recently been looking as well at male "rites of passage" in prehistoric societies. In these rites the tribe's youths were given sacred teachings and prepared by ordeals and secret ceremonies for a change of status and acceptance into adult life. Whatever the origins, it seems clear that the initiates in the mystery cults, through ceremonies and conformity to the group tenets, linked their destinies with that of the divinity being worshiped. They thereby guaranteed for themselves certain benefits in this life as well as some kind of happy immortality after death.

The most important and influential of the mysteries, going back at least to the 7th century BCE, were those celebrated at Eleusis, a town near Athens. The rites were based on the myth of Demeter, the agricultural (grain) goddess who rescued her daughter Kore (Persephone) from the god of the underworld, but only on condition that Kore spend part of the year in Hades, the other part above ground. This represented the yearly periods of crop fertility and infertility, and is a prime example of how story-myths are invented to explain natural processes. Through elaborate ceremonies which included fasting, ritual bathing, torchlight processions and the secret witnessing of sacred objects within the sanctuary, initiates could look forward to a blessed paradise after death. The myth and rites included the announcement of the birth of a divine child to Demeter, which may have symbolized the initiate's own rebirth. Eventually, people from all over the Mediterranean world participated in the Eleusinian mysteries, and even Roman emperors became initiates.

Other mysteries were also very ancient. The cult of the god Dionysos (Roman Bacchus, god of wine and of fertility generally) was originally conducted by women and involved notorious orgiastic rites. These included a cultic meal at which raw meat and wine were consumed—the body and blood (power) of the god. The myth of Dionysos tells of his murder and resurrection, and of his birth to a virgin goddess in a cave. Underlying the Dionysian myth was the concept that divine forces resided in both the natural world and humans, which gave promise of an afterlife.

Early on, the rites of Dionysos became linked with a broader expression of spirituality in Greek religious thought. If Christianity as a more all-inclusive "religion" than the mysteries had a precursor in the pagan world, it was in the movement known as Orphism. The Orphic mysteries were based on ancient poems which, put into writing around the 7th century BCE, were attributed to the legendary singer and poet Orpheus of pre-Trojan War days, who was regarded as a companion to the god Dionysos. At a more profound level than the other mysteries, Orphism sought to explain good and evil in human nature and to find ways of atoning for humanity's guilt. As E. R. Goodenough phrases it (*By Light, Light*, p.16) it gave the Greeks "a sense of sin." A virtuous, ascetic life liberated the soul and led to its eternal bliss on the far western Isles of the Blessed, while evil persons (and those uninitiated into the mysteries) faced a cruel punishment in the Underworld. Here was the Greek concept of Hell (Tartarus), probably pre-dating even the Jewish one, which the Jews in any case picked up from non-Jewish sources. Orphism also included the idea of reincarnation. Souls had to migrate a number of times before reaching their final reward or punishment, an idea probably of eastern origin. There was no resurrection of the body.

As a boy, so the myth went, the god Dionysos had been torn to pieces and eaten by the Titans (the Orphic "original sin"). The Titans were then destroyed by Zeus for their crime. But from their ashes rose the human race who thus possess divinity within themselves (the devoured Dionysos). This piece of divinity, the soul, is trapped in the prison of the body from which it seeks to escape. It longs to return to its heavenly home and its divine source, this being a later Dionysos who has since been resurrected by Zeus. The world and the flesh are thus devalued, and redemption from them becomes the goal of life. Though Christianity cannot be said to be "derived from" Orphism or any other mystery cult, the debt which it owes to the broader religious ideas of its era is plainly considerable.

Another prominent cult was that of the Great Mother Cybele from Asia Minor. She later acquired a lover, Attis, whom myth castrated to explain the practice of the priests of Cybele who in fits of ecstasy rendered themselves eunuchs. Much interpretation has gone into the public rites of Attis and Cybele, celebrated in a spring festival spread over many days. Reminiscent of the Christian Passion week, the death of Attis was mourned on one day, followed by an interim period of fasting and physical self-punishment. (Compare the Christian Lent.) Then came a ceremony which some used to interpret as symbolizing the resurrection of Attis; more recent opinion denies any concept of physical resurrection on the part of the god. Whatever the mythical details, later Christian commentators show that the rites did symbolize a sharing in some kind of triumph of the deity. The Christian Firmicus Maternus of the fourth century CE is much quoted for his preservation of the Attis cult's formula: "Be consoled, O initiates, for the god is delivered; therefore we too shall have deliverance from our troubles." This may or may not have referred to resurrection.

Other cultic gods and goddesses offered various rites of rebirth, future deliverance and union with the divine. The Persian light-god Mithras was originally regarded as a mediator between Ahura-Mazda (the Persian high god) and humanity, and he aided the ascent of the human soul to heaven after death. He was born on the 25th of December, had a miraculous birth out of a rock (some say in a cave) at which shepherds offered worship, and was to raise the dead and judge mankind at the end of the world. He did not undergo any suffering and death, and his salvific act involved the slaying of a bull, whose blood and marrow gave rise to the earth's bounty of food and drink. Mithraism, with its baptism and cultic meal, was a major competitor to Christianity among the mysteries during the second and third centuries CE.

Egypt supplied several cultic deities, all of them interrelated, like Serapis, Osiris and Isis. Isis controlled fate and all supernatural powers. Those initiated into her mysteries were guaranteed her protection both here on earth, where they underwent rebirth in her service, and when they descended into the blissful Elysian fields after death (so Apuleius tells us in his famous 'novel' *The Golden Ass*). Her links with the slain Osiris and his ancient cult of death and salvation are too complex to go into, but their child Horus provided a model for the infant Christ, especially in Christian art which copied the image of "Isis with Horus at her breast" and turned it into the Madonna and Child we still see today.

If we can remove the Gospel overlay from the epistles, the religion of Paul emerges as something closely related to the salvation cults of the time. Seen in such a light, Christianity is the great surviving mystery religion, with the exception that its theology was not kept secret, and the "mystery" revealed through its rites was God's.

The Role of the Mysteries

We know frustratingly little about the cults. The injunction to secrecy about the most sacred parts of the rites and their meanings was faithfully heeded through a thousand years of their existence, until they were washed away in the triumph of Christianity. We are left with only a few, suggestive comments by pagan writers, plus the odd revelation by pagans converted to Christianity which found its way into heresiologists like Maternus. Most of our sources come from the period of the second century CE or later.

Were the gods really thought of as undergoing resurrection from death? How did the initiate see him or herself as united with the divinity? What precisely was the nature of the salvation they offered? Clear answers cannot be given to such questions.

New Testament scholars concerned with minimizing the common ground between Christianity and the mysteries have tended to focus on the matter of resurrection, pointing out that actual physical rising of the pagan deities is (with the possible exception of Dionysos and Adonis) nowhere clearly presented. But this is to a great extent a straw man. The Greeks did not look for the survival of the body, an idea they found repugnant. It was the soul that was the recipient of everlasting life. We should not expect those who had such an outlook to invent gods who were resurrected in flesh in order to bestow the same fate on humans.

At a minimum, these deities were seen as having overcome the effects of death in some way, especially of death as a finality or as an eternal fate in some dreary underworld existence. Orphism and Platonic philosophy had set the goal as the soul's liberation from the flesh, not an eternal imprisonment within it such as Christianity was to envision. For the Greeks, the souls of the saved would enjoy eternal bliss in some divine sphere, and this was the fate which the activities of their savior gods and their own linking with those gods guaranteed.

Rites like those of Eleusis and the god Dionysos predate Christianity by many centuries, but when did the full-blown mysteries visible in the second century take shape? Although Mithras was an ancient Persian god, the form his cult took in Hellenistic times is a Greek version. Some scholars locate its inception in Asia Minor about 100 BCE (see Note 52), others as late as the latter first century CE. The cult of the Great Mother Cybele came to Rome around 200 BCE, but when was the figure of Attis added as her consort? Again, dates vary. But this is another straw man. Cults do not form overnight, nor do the ideas underlying their rites and myths spring fully into being at one moment. The basic concepts and practices of the mysteries were ancient. They undergirded much of the religious expression of the era. Both Christianity and the cults were an outgrowth of that soil, parallel expressions growing up side by side, with no doubt a fair degree of interaction over the centuries as both struggled to win hearts and minds with promises of eternal salvation.

We cannot say with any certainty that Paul and the early Christians formulated their doctrine with an eye on the mysteries, but one thing we can safely assume is that if they were in direct competition with salvation cults of this sort, they would not have refrained from calling attention to the most dramatic difference between themselves and their rivals: that the Christian savior god, unlike those of the mysteries, had been incarnated in flesh and had conducted an earthly ministry within living memory. (Their silence is in contrast to modern scholars who, when comparing Christianity to the mysteries, regularly point out this very difference.) It is hard to believe that Paul would have been able to discard Jesus' career as "of no interest," for his audiences would themselves have been making—and demanding—such comparisons.

12

Three Views Through the Window in Scripture

We will now focus on three passages in the epistles which tie together the picture of a Christ taken from scripture, and one who lives and operates in a realm outside the material, historical world.

Before Time Began

The Greco-Roman savior gods inhabited the mythical realm. Whether this realm was conceived of by the ordinary initiate as belonging to a primordial past on earth, or to a Platonic higher world, might be difficult to say. No doubt such concepts evolved over time. The Pauline Christ has been seen to bear strong resemblance to the pagan savior gods, and passages such as 1 Corinthians 2:8 and the Ascension of Isaiah 9 and 10 suggest that Christian thinking placed him in the spiritual parts of a layered universe, suffering and dying at the hands of evil spirits.

One passage in the epistles comes close to making that clear. We will use it to illustrate the two roles of the Son as noted at the beginning of Part Four, the two spheres of Christ's activities, present and past. 2 Timothy 1:9-10 contains, side by side, a reference to each of those "times." We'll work from the NEB translation, and place the reference to the "past" in italics:

> "[9]It is he [God] who brought us salvation . . . not from any merit of ours but of his own purpose and his own grace, *which was granted to us in Christ Jesus from all eternity* (*pro chronōn aiōniōn*), [10]but has now at length been brought fully into view by the appearance (on earth) of our Savior Jesus Christ. For he has broken the power of death and brought life and immortality to light through the gospel."

First of all, the NEB's gratuitous "on earth" does not appear in the Greek. Then note the phrase (verse 10) ". . . brought fully into view by the appearance of . . ." This is actually two revelation words, the verb *phaneroō* and the noun *epiphaneia*. The latter can signify the intervention or manifestation of a god, with no human incarnation involved. What the sentence is really saying, then, is that God's purpose and grace have been revealed by the revelation of the Savior Jesus Christ. No life on earth there.

Then consider what follows. The "he" of the last sentence refers to the Savior. But what has this Savior done? He has broken the power of death and brought life and immortality to light (yet another revelation word)—how?—*through the gospel*. The writer does not say that Christ at his "appearance" has overcome death and brought life through his own deeds, performed during his life on earth. Instead, these things were accomplished "through the gospel."

In the present time—"now"—what has happened is not the saving act itself, but the bringing of that act and its benefits to the light of human knowledge, through the preaching of the gospel. Nor can this mean the gospel preached by Jesus, for in verse 11 the writer goes on to define this gospel as the one assigned to Paul as "herald, apostle and preacher." We might also note that the whole of the above passage is introduced by the idea that "it is God who has brought us salvation." This manner of speaking seems out of place in a writer who should have possessed the image of Jesus coming to earth in the recent past to do just that.

The revelation to Paul represents Christ operating in the present time, through spiritual channels of inspiration. But where and when did his act of redemption take place? That act is pointed to in the italicized phrase of verse 9: "*which was granted to us in Christ Jesus from all eternity.*" Or, in a more literal rendering of the Greek *pro chronōn aiōniōn*, "before times eternal." This phrase has been much analyzed. It appears to refer to some kind of past time or state. Here we have an allusion to the "mystery," the secret which the Pauline writers are constantly referring to. Something that God has done, with Christ as the actual performer, has been hidden for long ages, unrevealed through countless generations.

We can bring in another reference to the same idea. Ephesians 3:9-11 says that the mystery hidden for ages in God has now "been made known through the church . . . according to his eternal purpose, which he accomplished (performed, carried out) in Christ Jesus." Again, the present is a time of revelation through apostles like Paul (the "church"), while Christ's act itself is something relating to the eternal.

Though all of this language may seem maddeningly obscure—and should alert us to the fact that we are dealing with ideas alien to us today—it seems clear that the performance of the act of Christ lies in some form of past. It has been unknown throughout the whole of history and is only now being disclosed to the world. The "achieving in Christ" of a passage like Ephesians 3:11 cannot be located in the present, if only because the present is always described as the time of "making known" or revealing. Through the proclamation of men like Paul, the veil over God's salvation accomplished through the Son is being pulled aside.

What do we see when that veil is removed? Let's focus on the *pro chronōn aiōniōn* of 2 Timothy 1:9.

The NEB translation, "from all eternity," is not literal and not particularly revealing. The NASB uses the same words, and the RSV's "ages ago" is woolly and noncommittal. The NIV gets closer: "before the beginning of time," since literally the Greek words (in order) are "before times eternal." A slightly different connotation is conveyed by the NAB and the venerable King James Version, with their "before the world began." But it would be better to keep some reference to the concept of time, and so the *Translator's New Testament* is preferable with its "before time began."

If the commentators are in agreement, it is that no one is really sure what the writer means by this phrase. *The Theological Dictionary of the New Testament*[53] wonders if it "can ever be answered with any certainty." If we drop the preposition, most scholars agree that "eternal times" refers to the full expanse of time that the world has passed through from creation to the present. While this is inconsistent with the modern meaning of the word "eternal," such a meaning is required by its use in Romans 16:25, that God's mystery about Christ has been kept silent "in times eternal." This must mean for as long as the world has existed.

Attaching the preposition *"pro"* lifts the meaning to a place which lies before or outside this span of total time through which the world has passed. Wherever that lies, it is essentially timeless, or at least it is time of a fundamentally different order. More than one commentator has noted that the adjective *aiōniois* by itself (ie, when not attached to *chronos*), can refer to a quality of being "eternal" which transcends time. The word is almost exclusively used in the New Testament of things relating to God.[54] As such, it conforms to the Platonic thought current at the time the epistles were written.

We thus arrive at a meaning for *pro chronōn aiōniōn* which places the idea of the redemptive act of Christ in a timeless sphere, the sphere of God. In other words, in the supernatural realm of myth, where all such divine activities were set. The early Christian writers are thinking very much along the lines of religious philosophers of the period. The redemptive work of God through Christ has been relegated by Paul and his kind to a dimension outside matter and beyond time. Humans have learned about it through God's revelation, a revelation imparted through the sacred writings and what was now being read into them.

This may not be something we in later ages can readily relate to; indeed, it may strike us as utter gibberish. But to delve into some of the philosophical thinking of the period is also an alien experience (one usually indulged in only by esoteric academia) and there is no good reason to claim that Christian thinking, especially by a mind of the caliber of Paul's, did not share in it. In fact, the Gospels might be regarded as a reaction against this type of thinking, literally a bringing down to earth of an outlook that the uneducated, broader masses could not so easily respond to or comprehend.

A Sacrifice in Heaven

No other New Testament document so clearly illustrates the higher and lower world thinking of Platonic philosophy as the epistle to the Hebrews. The writer places the sacrifice of Christ in heaven itself, in "the real sanctuary, the tent pitched by the Lord and not by man" (8:2). This tent of Christ's priesthood "is a greater and more perfect one, not made by men's hands, not part of the created world" (9:11). Christ's sacrifice is not spoken of in terms of a crucifixion on Calvary. Rather, it is the act of bringing his own "blood" into the heavenly sanctuary and there offering it to God. This act has "secured an eternal deliverance" (9:12) and established a new covenant. It is portrayed as a higher world counterpart to the action of the high priest on earth who, on the Day of Atonement, brings the blood of sacrificed animals into the earthly tabernacle, to obtain forgiveness for the people's sins.

Not only is Christ's sacrifice not located on Calvary, the writer never introduces into his Platonic comparison the fact that an important part of Jesus' act had taken place on earth. This is something which would have seriously compromised the purity of his upper-lower world comparison. He has said that Christ's sacrifice is "spiritual, eternal and unblemished" (9:14), and that this kind of superior (to the earthly) sacrifice is "required to cleanse heavenly things" (9:23). Yet this "shedding of blood," according to the Gospel picture, had taken place on earth. It was a blood that in Christ's human incarnation was the blood of matter. In that respect, it could not be spiritual, and the writer would merely be comparing an earthly thing with another earthly thing.

The author of Hebrews does nothing to address this anomaly. He shows no sign of being perturbed by any conflict in his theoretical universe. This, one is led to conclude, is because there was no historical Jesus, no sacrifice on an earthly Calvary, lurking in the background to disturb his finely drawn duality.

Some scholars have clearly recognized the nature of Hebrews' picture of Christ. "For the complete sacrifice has been offered in the realm of the spirit. . . . in the eternal order of things . . . it belonged essentially to the higher order of absolute reality" (James Moffat); Christ's ministry has been "exercised in a more perfect tabernacle and with a truer sacrifice" (Marcus Dods).[55] This does the mythicists' work for them, for such observations show that it is possible to recognize the mythical realm and to envision the sacrifice of Christ within it. On the other hand, such scholars invariably attempt to introduce an historical Jesus into the Platonic equation.[56]

The picture of the sacrifice in Hebrews shows that the concept of "blood" in regard to Christ can be applied in heaven. This is 'spiritual' blood. At one stroke we have eliminated the problem of those several passages throughout the epistles which speak of Christ as having blood and flesh, since these can be regarded as the spirit-world equivalents of earthly things. The same applies to the word "body" which appears in Hebrews 10:5. This is a very revealing passage:

> "That is why, at his coming into the world, he says:
> 'Sacrifice and offering thou didst not desire,
> But thou hast prepared a body for me.
> Whole-offerings and sin-offerings thou didst not delight in.
> Then I said: "Here am I: as it is written of me in the scroll,
> I have come, O God, to do thy will." ' " [NEB]

These verses of Psalm 40 (6 to 8) are introduced by a "he says" in the present tense. This is the Son speaking through scripture. But what about "his coming into the world"? This must also be in the same present time. While commentators have made attempts to relate this in some way to the incarnation,[57] the writer gives no hint of such a thing. Paul Ellingworth's suggestion (*Hebrews*, p.499) that the "he says" is "a timeless present [I would prefer "a mythical present"] referring to the permanent record of scripture," inadvertently gives us the answer. The passage has nothing to do with an historical context; rather, it presents a picture of spiritual world realities.

In that higher world revealed by scripture, Christ takes on a "body" for sacrifice, in order to do the will of God and supplant the old animal sacrifices that God no longer wants. Here we can see the type of source in scripture which could have given rise to the idea that the spiritual Son had taken on or entered "flesh," that he had undergone sacrifice. Since this was envisioned to have taken place within the lower celestial sphere, it placed him, as Hebrews puts it (2:9), "for a short while lower than the angels." (See Appendix 5 for an examination of one passage in Hebrews [8:4] which virtually tells us that Jesus had never been on earth.)

In this way, we can understand the concept of Christ being "in flesh" (*en sarki*, *kata sarka*, etc.) a stereotyped phrase which appears with surprising regularity in the epistles.[58] It signifies either that Christ took on the spiritual counterpart of flesh, its "likeness," when he descended to the lower celestial sphere (as in the Ascension of Isaiah 9 or the hymn of Philippians 2:6-11), or as Barrett has suggested, that he entered the "sphere of the flesh," which included the realm of the demon spirits in the firmament. On occasion, it may refer to Christ's 'visit' to that sphere, as in "the days of his flesh" in Hebrews 5:7.[59] In a more general way, the term may also entail the idea of Christ's activities being "in relation to the flesh," in their effect on the material world and humans.

The Greek salvation myths inhabit the same mythical world. They too can spin stories about their deities, born in caves, slain by other gods, sleeping and dining and speaking. None of these activities were regarded as taking place in history or on earth itself. The bull dispatched by Mithras was not historical; the blood it spilled which vitalized the earth was metaphysical. No one searched the soil of Asia Minor hoping to unearth the genitals severed from the Great Mother's consort Attis. (To which we can compare first-century Christianity's utter lack of interest in the places and relics of Jesus' activity.)

It may be difficult for the modern mind to grasp the type of mythical thinking which was a hallmark of the ancient world. Even so, we have the example of the mystery cults to demonstrate that, intelligible to us or not, such thinking existed. No matter how one defines the myths of the Greek savior gods, even if one might think to render them more intelligible by locating them in a primordial past, on a mythical earth rather than in the heavens—which the average devotee of the cults may have done—the mysteries provide us with a non-historical setting in which the early Christian Christ can readily be placed. (See Appendix 6 for a fuller discussion of the location of the cultic myths in the thinking of the period.)

Born of Woman

Finally, we return full circle to Paul himself, to the passage in his letters which, it could be said, most suggests that he has a human Jesus in mind. In this passage (Galatians 4:4-7) we can tie together all the observations made about the nature of the early Christian faith.

> "[4]Then in the fullness of time, God sent his own Son, born of (a) woman, [born] under the Law, [5]to purchase freedom for the subjects of the law, in order that we might attain the status of sons. [6]And because you are sons, God has sent into our hearts the Spirit of his Son, crying 'Father!' [7]You are therefore no longer a slave but a son, and if a son, then also by God's own act an heir." [NEB/my trans.]

First, let's look at the principal phrase, "God sent his own Son." As described earlier, this can be taken in the sense of the present-day revelation of Christ by God to apostles like Paul. It is a verb also used in the Old Testament in connection with the sending of spiritual beings such as angels, or Wisdom as in the Wisdom of Solomon 9:10. The basic form of the verb is regularly used to denote the sending of the Holy Spirit. And in verse 6 the same verb is used to say that "God has sent into our hearts the spirit of his Son." Both the sending in verse 4 and the sending in verse 6 seem to be taking place at the same time, namely in the Pauline present. This is the arrival of the spiritual Christ within the current phenomenon of divine revelation.

If Paul has the acts of an historical Jesus in mind when he speaks of freedom and attaining the status of sons (verse 5), why does he revert in verse 7 to calling such things the result of an act of God? In fact, in the Greek of verse 5, the subject of the verb "purchase freedom" (literally, redeem) remains God. In other words, Paul has introduced Jesus onto the present scene, but fails to let him do the redeeming while he is here. Paul continues his characteristic focus on God in subsequent verses.

The two qualifying phrases, "born of woman, born under the Law," are descriptive of the Son, but not necessarily tied to the present 'sending.' Edward D. Burton (*International Critical Commentary, Galatians*, p.216f) points out that the way the verb and participle tenses are used in the Greek, the birth and subjection to the Law are presented as simple facts, with no necessary temporal relation to the main verb "sent." In other words, the conditions of being "born of woman" and being "subject to the Law"—Burton's preferred translation—do not have to be seen as present occurrences. (Burton does not advocate that conclusion himself.) Paul has simply enumerated two of the features of the spiritual Christ which are relevant to the discussion.

Burton also notes that the word usually translated as "born" (*genomenon*) is not the most unambiguous verb that could have been used for this idea; the passive of *gennaō*, to give birth, would have been more straightforward. Instead, Paul uses the verb *ginomai*, which has a broader meaning of "to become, to come into existence." (Paul also uses the broader *ginomai* in Romans 1:3, where he says that the Son "arose from David's seed.") "Out of woman," of course, implies birth, but the point is, the broader concept lends itself to the atmosphere of myth.

Moreover, Paul's "born of woman" is not only something that was said of certain mythical savior gods, like Dionysos, it is a detail he could well have based not on history, but on his source for all that he says about the Son, the scriptures. The famous passage in Isaiah 7:14,

> "A young woman is with child, and she will bear a son, and call him Immanuel,"

was taken by Jew and early Christian alike to refer to the Messiah. (This is another passage which related to the prophet's own day, not the future.) Once again, a scriptural passage that could not be ignored was applied by early Christians to their heavenly Christ, in the sense of counterpart characteristics which he possessed in the higher world. National gods were often regarded as having the same lineage as the nation itself, which is one interpretation that could be given to Christ as "born" under the Law.

Not surprisingly, Paul fails to give us the name of this woman, and she is notably missing only a few verses later (4:24-31) when he gives his readers an elaborate allegory about sons and mothers in regard to the descendants of Abraham. One might ask why it is that Paul bothers to say that Christ was born of a woman, since this should be an obvious biological fact to his readers. His point may be that he wishes to stress the paradigmatic parallel between believers—who are themselves born of woman, as well as born under the law of the old covenant which Paul wants to abrogate—and Christ himself. Only through counterpart characteristics can paradigmatic effects exist. But such relationships by definition operate between higher and lower worlds, between the spiritual and the material. It follows, then, that Christ and his features must belong to the higher world, in order to be in appropriate counterpart to those of Paul's readers.

When any set of assumptions is firmly in place, the evidence is usually interpreted in accord with those assumptions. Yet it is clear that the New Testament epistles present the Christian reader and scholar with difficulties and anomalies at every turn. These have traditionally been ignored, glossed over, or subjected to unnatural interpretations and questionable reasoning in order to force them into the mold determined by the Gospels.

What is needed is a new paradigm, a new set of assumptions by which to judge the epistles (as well as the other non-canonical documents we have looked at), one capable of resolving all those contradictions and uncertainties. That paradigm should be determined by what we can see in the epistles themselves and how we can relate their content to what we know of the spirit and conditions of the time. When the new paradigm and the interpretations based upon it are revolutionary, at least by the standards of the old one, incredulity is to be expected. But dramatic reversal, even on the order of something like the Copernican revolution in astronomy, is not at all rare in the field of science and historical research. Dogma and received wisdom are regularly overturned in many areas. The investigation of Christian origins as an historical phenomenon enjoys no privileged exemption from such a fate.

If the elements of early Christianity as reflected in the epistles point to a faith movement which is based on an entirely spiritual deity, and this picture fits very well into the known religious thought of the time, then that is the path of investigation to follow. After the next chapter, which will apply the principles established in Parts Three and Four to the wider record of the Jerusalem Tradition, we will move to the other side of the Jesus Puzzle and discover whether support for this conclusion can be drawn from the second Tradition which fed into the foundations of Western culture.

13

A Riotous Diversity

The Birth of a Movement

Of all the puzzles in the New Testament record which scholarship has been forced to address, perhaps none has provoked a greater scramble for explanation than the amazing diversity of views about Jesus to be found in the surviving documents of the first hundred years. A survey of the record reveals notable differences in theology, ritual and expectation, between one writer and another, one Christian community and another. Within that diversity lies the key to understanding the true origins of Christianity.

Just as scholars such as Ridderbos have expressed astonishment at Jesus' presumed elevation to cosmic heights immediately after his death, many have also remarked on the seemingly rapid spread of the movement and the great multiplicity of forms it took in different centers. Of this, Wayne Meeks says (*The First Urban Christians*, p.5):

> "Christianity, even at the earliest moment we can get any clear picture of it, was already a complex movement taking form within several complex societies."

Ron Cameron ("The Gospel of Thomas and Christian Origins," in *The Future of Early Christianity*, p.381) summarizes Walter Bauer's thesis in the latter's now-classic *Orthodoxy and Heresy in Earliest Christianity* this way:

> "The beginnings of Christianity were exceptionally diverse, varied dramatically from region to region, and were dominated by individuals and groups whose practices and theology would be denounced as 'heretical'."

This diversity is characterized by scholars as different "responses" to the man Jesus of Nazareth, responses which at the same time managed to ignore most or all of the others and went off on distinct tangents. Even within the Gospels themselves, scholars have recognized that different elements seem to have an independent character of their own, containing little or no reflection of other elements.

Thus, Burton Mack, in his *Who Wrote the New Testament?* (1995), sees such things as representing "components" of Jesus' career which were separately preserved by groups of followers and believers who formed in various places in response to him. Each group focused on a specific aspect of that career: teachings of one sort, teachings of another sort, miracle traditions, apocalyptic expectations, and the most dramatic response of all, the message that he had brought salvation through his death on the cross and resurrection from the grave. Each of these groups supposedly produced and preserved their own specific records: miracle collections, prophetic sayings, a passion account, etc., and these later became available to the various evangelists.

This type of theory extrapolates backwards. It starts from the Gospels and assumes that all the different strands found within them can be traced back to a common source. But no concrete evidence exists for this postulated break-up of Jesus into his component parts, for this initial divergence of response to Jesus, followed decades later by a reverse convergence of those parts into the Gospels.

Rather, the separate strands which were later brought together to form the "Jesus tradition" of the Gospels are best seen as unrelated expressions within the broader social and religious milieu of the time, having nothing to do in their earliest stages with an historical Jesus, in some cases not even with a spiritual Jesus. Collections of wisdom teaching, aretalogies (lists of exploits and miracles attributed to famous men, or even to sectarian groups and their prophets), anonymous apocalypses, traditions of conflict with the establishment in the demand for reforms to social and religious practice: such things were the antecedents to the various Jesus strands and only at later stages did they become associated with such a figure, ultimately to end up in a composite Gospel. Some would have been linked to a Jesus only at the time of Gospel composition.

Add to this the wider record of contrasting and often incompatible views about the cultic Jesus, the different concepts of a divine figure in Paul, in Hebrews and other epistles, in secondary documents like the Odes of Solomon, none of which are associated with an historical Jesus of Nazareth, and we have a compelling picture of diversity which begs to be seen as having begun as diversity, not from some common starting point which immediately splintered in all directions.

Twin Traditions

The most recent scholarly tendency (as in John Dominic Crossan's 1998 *The Birth of Christianity*) has been to collapse the Gospel diversity into a fundamental division between two distinct responses to Jesus, namely the Galilean and Jerusalem Traditions we are surveying in this book. Yet even this simpler scenario fails to solve the basic problem. Once again, we are presented with multiple responses to Jesus which are separated by a wide gulf. The Galilean response preserves all the elements of a preaching ministry, even if that response is presumed to have enlarged on them and added things which Jesus had not actually said and done. This Tradition does not view him as the Messiah and shows no knowledge of the essential features of the other Tradition. That other, Jerusalem response shows no knowledge of the Galilean career and turns Jesus into a spiritual divinity in heaven, a part of God who closely resembles philosophical and religious expressions of the day.

But how did one man, operating in two different centers less than a hundred miles apart, give rise to two such divergent and incompatible responses? How did they flourish for so long in isolation from one another? Can we in fact reliably assign an historical Jesus even to the roots of the Galilean Tradition?

Even within the Jerusalem Tradition, within the Christ cult itself, there existed a widely diverse set of expressions, varied interpretations of a divine Son and what he had done, what he represented, what he offered. If the Christ cult began in Jerusalem as a response to the events of Jesus' death and perceived resurrection, giving rise to a missionary movement which spread outward from that place, how did such dramatic diversity develop, some of it very quickly? A survey of that diversity will lead to certain conclusions about the origins of Christianity that have already been intimated in previous chapters.

Hebrews in Egypt

Within the New Testament itself, we have examples of divergent variety. The picture of Christ in the epistle to the Hebrews is unlike any other. Scholars have often asked themselves what led its writer to think of portraying Jesus in this manner, as the heavenly High Priest whose blood sacrifice, offered in the heavenly sanctuary, is the higher world counterpart of the Day of Atonement sacrifice performed by the high priest in the sanctuary on earth. They ask what led this particular group of Christian believers to deviate so radically from what must have been the more standard Christian message about Jesus, the theological and historical picture they must have received through the apostolic channels by which they were converted.

But in the epistle itself, no sign of such a deviation can be detected. Such a question is never addressed. The writer and his community seem to move in their own world, a world exclusively dependent on scripture and its interpretation. Hebrews provides perhaps the best example in the New Testament of how belief in a divine Christ arose spontaneously out of currents and trends of the day, in independent expressions, each taking on its own characteristics as a result of the local conditions and people involved.

The epistle is what it is because certain sectarian minds formulated their own picture of spiritual realities. They searched scripture for information and insight about the Son of God, influenced by the wider religious and philosophical atmosphere of the first century—especially Alexandrian Platonism—and this is what they came up with. Their mediator between heaven and earth has been cast in the mold of the sacrificial cult of Sinai, as presented in the biblical book of Exodus. But they are not reinterpreting an apostolic message, nor are they giving their against-the-grain twist to the story of some recent man. No bow is made in the epistle to any wider Christian movement nor to any standard from which they are deviating. Hebrews, and the community it represents, is self-sufficient. It too, like all the other expressions of Christ belief of the day, from Paul to the Johannine community, professes its dependence upon, and defines its origins in, divine revelation and the sacred writings.

We see evidence of this picture in 2:3-4:

> "[3]What escape can there be for us if we ignore a salvation so great? For this salvation was first announced through the Lord; those who heard confirmed it to us, [4]with God adding his testimony by signs, by miracles, by various powerful deeds, and by distributing the gifts of the Holy Spirit at his own will." [based on the NEB][60]

Most commentators simply take this to be a reference to Jesus' preaching on earth. But there are too many problems with such an interpretation. Jesus would hardly have taught the unique christology contained in this epistle. In fact, the voice of Jesus teaching on earth is never heard in Hebrews; everything the Son "says" comes from scripture. Verse 4 refers to a validation of the "announcements" through signs and miracles. But these come from God. If this passage were describing Jesus' ministry, we should expect a reference to Jesus' own miracles which in the Gospels serve the very purpose of validating his teachings.[61]

What is being described is a revelatory experience undergone by the leaders of the community at some time in the past, an experience passed down to the present members of the group. The concluding phrase in the above quotation, "by distributing the gifts of the Holy Spirit," reinforces the idea inherent in the whole passage. This is a time and a process of salvation impelled by the activity of God's Spirit, not by the recent work of the Son on earth speaking and acting in his own person. Whether through visionary experiences or simply an inspired study of scripture, God is perceived as making his salvation known, and confirming it by certain wonderful happenings. The conviction of such revelation was the inaugurating event of this sect—or at least of its present beliefs and activities.

The Johannine Community

Another example of diversity within the New Testament is the Gospel of John. While its overall narrative structure is loosely the same as that of the Synoptics, the content of its teachings by Jesus is dramatically different. The great puzzle faced by Johannine scholars has always been to account for this. Did the unique christology of John arise independently of any contact with the Synoptics, or was it a later conscious supplanting of the earlier picture of Jesus by a newly-developed one in the Johannine community? If the latter, why? Why such a drastically different substitute?

Scholars have tended to approach the Johannine branch of the faith as though it were some ancient Shangri-la, a mountain fastness penetrated and converted by some mysterious apostle from Jerusalem, only to shut itself off from the wider world of the Christian movement and evolve in its own unique fashion. The view of Jesus contained in the Fourth Gospel is unlike any other in the New Testament. When the superficial overlay of the pattern of Jesus' ministry and passion is stripped away—something that was borrowed later from a Synoptic source—one finds a figure who bears little relationship to the Jesus of Mark and his redactors, or to the Jesus of Paul.

By any standard, the teachings of Jesus in the Fourth Gospel are bizarre. In fact, it might be said that there are *no* teachings of Jesus, unless it be the proclamation of himself, for he has nothing else to say. He is the Son, the light, life, the living bread, the living water. He has been sent from God, he is the one come down from heaven, he is the revealer of the Father, of the transcendent God whom "you do not know" (7:28). There are no ethics. To "love one another" is little more than an in-house rule, not a universal moral dictum; 13:35 shows that he is simply advocating love among his followers, who are part of an elect, so that "all will know that you are my disciples." In 12:48 he tells his listeners that judgment will be based on whether a man has accepted or rejected his words. In 6:29 he defines the "work that God requires." It is: "believe in the one whom he has sent." Have faith in Jesus, know the Father through him, and this in itself will guarantee that you will never die. Consume the Son as the bread of life, drink him as the living water and you will possess immortality.

Something is seriously awry here. The evangelist portrays Jesus as standing up in the marketplace or in a synagogue and simply declaring to all the world the most mystical, pretentious pronouncements about himself. "I am the light of the world." "I am the door of the sheepfold." "I am the resurrection and the life." Is it any wonder the Jews are portrayed as responding so negatively?

But the problem is solved if we regard these declarations as the theology of a previous phase of this community *about* the object of their worship: the mythical and mystical Son and Word, a purely spiritual entity, the mediatorial channel to God. It is only when they are placed in the mouth of a human Jesus walking through Palestine that they take on this air of unreality, this impression of megalomania. (This is, in fact, a strong indication that the writer of John did not intend his Gospel to be taken as history, but rather as allegory.)

Such teaching by the Johannine Jesus represents the earliest stratum of material in the Gospel of John. It represents a faith based on belief in God's revelation of knowledge about himself and the everlasting life he makes available through that knowledge. This knowledge and the salvation it bestows is imparted through the spiritual Son, an idea leading us once again to that fundamental philosophical concept of the age, that God reveals himself and dispenses salvation through an intermediary, an aspect of himself which is capable of having contact with the world. The Johannine Son and Christ is thus a *Revealer* Son, which is quite different from the Pauline version of a dying and rising sacrificial one.

And what of the crucifixion in John? It presents a monumental anomaly, for before the Johannine community encountered the Synoptic Christ, there was no suffering, sacrificial Savior in its library of ideas. When the Synoptics came along, their tale of an earthly ministry, death and resurrection was laid over the original Revealer material (which had possibly been in the form of a written document). Those 'teachings' were placed in the mouth of the new historical Jesus.

And yet, the evangelist doing the job would not allow the newcomer to interfere with the earlier tradition of salvation through faith in the Revealer Son. In John, Jesus does not redeem through his death and resurrection. There is not a whisper about atonement or any salvific consequence of Jesus' death. Jesus is not allowed to suffer— not even emotionally: there is no Gethsemane in John. The Eucharist must go as well, since it is based on a sacrificial concept. In John, Jesus' raising up on the cross is an "ascension," a glorification (12:23). It is the ultimate support for the proof of his claims, the ultimate miracle. Jesus is in control throughout the trial and crucifixion, bearing all in sublime detachment, fulfilling what must be "accomplished" by the will of his Father. The two strata of Revealer and Crucified One have simply not been integrated.

For a variety of reasons, the epistle 1 John must be dated earlier than the Gospel of John, with the possible exception of its very latest stratum of material. For 1 John is a layered document, reworked and added to over time.[62] Like Hebrews, 1 John gives evidence of the community's beginning in a revelatory event. Here are the first three verses of its so-called Prologue:

> "[1]It was there from the beginning; we have heard it, we have seen it with our own eyes; we looked upon it and felt it with our own hands; and it is of this we tell. Our theme is the word of life. [2]This life was made visible [manifested, *phaneroō*]; we have seen it and bear our testimony; we here declare to you the eternal life which dwelt with [literally, was with] the Father and was made visible to us. [3]What we have seen and heard we declare to you, so that you and we together may share in a common life, that life which we share with the Father and his Son Jesus Christ." [NEB]

Here we have the description of an event of revelation, or perhaps a longer process symbolized as a single event, a moment when certain people believed they were receiving evidence of God offering eternal life. These verses speak of that event, that life, in poetic terms—of seeing, hearing, touching it. Despite attempts by many commentators to make this passage a reference to Jesus' ministry, the pronouns are neuter, the tone is impersonal, the language that of revelation.

As the Prologue now stands, the offering of eternal life (verse 3) is said to be shared "with the Father and his Son, Jesus Christ." But there is reason to question whether any reference to the Son stood in the initial version of this passage. The key verse 2 talks of the eternal life as dwelling in the Father (we cannot presume to read this phrase according to later Johannine understanding) with no mention of the Son. Other parts of the epistle focus entirely on God. It is possible that the sect began with a characteristic Jewish focus on God alone, though with a type of doctrine and outlook reminiscent of groups like the Essenes. Only at a subsequent stage of this multi-layered document was the idea of the Son added (see Note 62), no doubt under the influence of prevailing 'intermediary Son' philosophy. This seems to have been especially strong in Syria, where the Johannine community was almost certainly located.

A Mystic Messiah

Almost a century ago, a lost document came to light that reveals yet another community which had a divine Son very unlike that of Paul and the Synoptics. This is the fascinating set of 42 little hymns, very like the Old Testament Psalms in character, though brighter, more lyrical and optimistic in tone, known as the Odes of Solomon. They were written, probably in the latter part of the first century, in the language of Syriac, which places them somewhere in Syria, perhaps in the region of Edessa. Their quiet ecstasy is the voice of the mystic, though it is impossible to say if the same person wrote them all.

The one New Testament document they resemble is the Gospel of John—or at least its underlying stratum relating to the spiritual Revealer Son. Common ideas and terms echo between both documents. The figure of the "Word" which permeates the Odes appears in the Gospel Prologue, though the latter is in a more advanced form, since the Odist never styles the Word as incarnated. The phrase "living water" flows repeatedly through the Odes to represent the gift of divine revelation and knowledge of God, but unlike John, it lacks a human personification. Images of light, rest, the door of salvation are common between the Odes and the Johannine documents. Perhaps both strands grew out of a common source, such as the Qumran Essenes, whose Dead Sea Scrolls also contain similar thought patterns.

The Odes never speak the name "Jesus," and the title "Messiah," which appears seven times, has a definite Jewish flavor. There is no reference to either the crucifixion or the resurrection, and the Son's role in salvation is not a sacrificial one. Consequently, there is no Atonement, no paradigmatic guarantee. Instead, salvation comes through knowledge of God, the revelation of his grace and truth, and belief in that revelation.[63]

The Odes focus on God, but this is a God with rich and active emanations. Knowledge of God comes through those intermediary forces, which the poet styles Word, Son, Messiah. While the poetry is often allusive and obscure, everything in it can be traced to scripture and traditional Jewish imagery, even if more imaginatively used than usual. Let's look at one passage, selected verses from the opening part of Ode 19 (trans. by R. Harris and A. Mingana):

1 A cup of milk was offered to me,
   and I drank it in the sweetness of the delight of the Lord.

2 The Son is the cup,
   and he who was milked is the Father;
   and he who milked him is the Holy Spirit. . . .

4 And the Holy Spirit opened her bosom,
   and mingled the milk of the two breasts of the Father . . .

5 And gave the mixture to the world without their knowing,
   And those who take (it) are in the fulness of the right hand.

6 The womb of the Virgin took (it)
   and she received conception and brought forth . . .

8 And she [labored] and brought forth a Son without . . . pain,
   For it did not happen without purpose . . .

Considering that in Ode 33, the "perfect Virgin" is clearly a reference to personified Wisdom announcing the sort of message one finds in Wisdom's mouth in Proverbs and Sirach 24, any suggestion that here in Ode 19 it constitutes a reference to Mary is misplaced. This passage is not about history, it is poetic allegory. The Odist is presenting a symbolic picture of the relationship between various aspects of the Godhead. He uses the metaphor of divine milk, with four divine personages involved in dispensing it to humanity: Father, Son, Holy Spirit, Wisdom (the Virgin). Wisdom in some ancient Jewish traditions is a kind of consort to the Father; Philo sometimes makes her mother to the Logos. These are poetic, allegorical ways of representing the workings of Deity. The end result is the translation of God's knowledge and peace, which itself bestows perfection and salvation (verse 5). The Gospel Son puts in no appearance here, nor does any idea of a salvation effected through his death and resurrection.

In this light, it might be claimed that the Odes of Solomon are not "Christian" at all, but a highly imaginative expression of one of those forms of Judaism which have moved beyond the 'mainstream.' But such a definition is only relevant in an orthodox context. In the picture of emergent Christianity portrayed thus far, the Odes are a piece in a multi-colored mosaic. They belong as much to "Christianity" as does the preaching kerygma of Paul, as does the heavenly High Priest of the epistle to the Hebrews.

In the formative period of the first century, when no historical Jesus had yet set foot on the scene, all were expressions of the new 'intermediary Son' philosophy, all conceived of different routes to salvation through him. As in most such uncoordinated movements, centripetal forces eventually pulled this diversity into a common central pool, and the strongest, most advantageous and most appealing elements established themselves as a new core, a new 'orthodoxy.' This later development then became the standard by which the earlier manifestations were evaluated, and the present was read into the past.

Other Sons and Christs

Another mystical Son is found in the longest and probably least known surviving Christian document before Justin, the Shepherd of Hermas. Though identified with the brother of Pius, bishop of Rome around 148 CE, this document was likely written before that time, probably in the late first century, which would fit its primitive theology and predominantly Jewish character.

For all its length, the names of Jesus and Christ are never used.[64] The writer refers to a "Son of God" who is a highly mystical figure devoid of human features. Salvation comes to those who are "called through the Son," but of a death and resurrection there is no sign. Sometimes the Son is equated with the Holy Spirit or the Jewish Law. He is part of the paraphernalia of heaven, the way Wisdom is portrayed in other circles of Jewish expression.

The central section of the Shepherd discusses a great list of moral rules, some resembling the teachings of the Gospels, but no attribution is made to Jesus. A passage in the Fifth Parable (6:3) has the Son "cleansing the sins of the people," but this *precedes* his "showing them the ways of life and giving them the Law," and it is never presented in terms of sacrifice or atonement.

In Chapter 10 we looked at the document known as the Ascension of Isaiah, which is a complex layering of elements Jewish and Christian. It contains a vision about a divine Son who will be dispatched by God to descend through the heavens, undergo "hanging upon a tree" by Satan, and rescue the souls of the righteous from Sheol. Except for a later inserted passage based on the Gospels (see Appendix 4) this Son functions as a heavenly paradigm who guarantees ascension to heaven for the elect who are associated with him.

The New Testament Book of Revelation, which most date to the 90s of the first century, offers essentially the same thing. The heavenly Christ who appears to John the prophet and writes letters to the seven churches is a visionary figure who communicates entirely through spiritual channels. He is said to have been "dead and came to life again" (2:8), but no earthly setting or circumstances are offered; no idea of a bodily resurrection is introduced. He is equated with the Danielic Son of Man in a way which indicates that the writer is drawing from the Old Testament Book of Daniel itself, not from any Gospel traditions about Jesus being associated with that figure.

This particular heavenly Christ, as a redemptive paradigm, has undergone sacrificial death, but it is not to bestow a universal redemption. The group who will be saved by "the Lamb who was slain" is an elect, while the rest of the earth has been consigned to a horrible judgment and calamitous fate. This 'salvation' of an elect group through the actions of a counterpart heavenly figure is probably the earliest expression of the higher/lower world paradigm principle. Here is another example within the New Testament itself of greatly differing ways of viewing the spiritual Christ and his role.

The Gnostic Savior

We might go further afield, into the obscure byways of the later first and second century religious movement known as Gnosticism. In ways still not fully uncovered, some forms of Gnosticism were related to Christianity. Some have a Christ figure who is an element of an immensely complex Godhead, a heavenly family of interacting divine aspects of God whose behavior caused the material world to be created by mistake, with divine 'splinters' falling into matter and being lodged in certain human beings. These are the 'gnostics' whose knowledge about their true selves will lead to a blessed return to their heavenly abode. Crossover influences led to strange linkages between the gnostic Christ and the Christian Jesus. Other forms of Gnosticism had no Christ or Jesus at all. But to suggest, as some have, that all of Gnosticism with its panoply of savior figures, such as Derdekeas (in The Paraphrase of Shem) or the Illuminator (in The Apocalypse of Adam), are ultimately derived from Jesus of Nazareth, is a more bizarre scenario than some of the pictures of the universe presented in the gnostic documents themselves.

The gnostic Savior figure is derived in part from a philosophical concept current in the early centuries of our era, which spoke of a "Primal Man" or "Heavenly Man." In the same way that the Logos was described as God's primary emanation, this myth said that God produced an Archetypal Man, the first (spiritual) being apart from himself, his direct image. (Sometimes God himself is the First Man and his image is the Son of Man.) This Archetypal Man in turn served as the model for the earthly man, who was made out of the dust of matter. Philo of Alexandria incorporated this Heavenly Man into his own picture of higher realities.[65]

There seems to have been a widely diffused myth (ultimately based on Persian ideas) of a Divine Man who existed with God in heaven, who descended—or fell—to the lower world, then re-ascended, eventually to rescue certain souls destined to be a saved race. The evidence for this so-called Descending-Ascending Redeemer is scanty and uncertain for the time before Christianity. Most of it comes from the second and third centuries CE in a range of gnostic documents as well as the Mandaean and Manichaean religions.[66] There are echoes of it in the Gospel of John. But such myths do not spring full-grown; they have antecedents. And gnostic writings like the Apocryphon of John and the Apocalypse of Adam are regarded by gnostic specialists today as being independent of Christianity and perhaps even a little *pre*-Christian. (See Charles W. Hedrick, *The Apocalypse of Adam*.)

Here, then, we have a heavenly being referred to as a "Man" descending the heavens to effect salvation, all independent of Christian thought or any link with a Jesus of Nazareth. In some sources that heavenly figure is spoken of as performing 'signs and wonders,' usually for the benefit of the evil spirit powers, and he is spoken of as being persecuted, even killed by them. (Eg, the Illuminator in the Apocalypse of Adam 76,9 - 77,18 and the Man of the Apocryphon of John 20,1-8; compare the Ascension of Isaiah.) That Man is regularly said to be of "human form." This does not refer to incarnation but to the image of God which in turn is translated into human copies on earth. The Apocalypse of Adam even speaks (78-82) of the Illuminator as being born from a virgin womb, by a desert, in a garden, dropped from heaven into the sea, borne by a bird onto a mountain, carried by dragons into a cave.

All these things are mythical and have nothing to do with an actual human being, much less the Gospel Jesus. But they are reflective of a pervasive form of esoteric mythology of the time, and the points of contact with Pauline Christianity are more than incidental: Paul's "born of woman" in Galatians 4:4; the term "*anthrōpos*" (man) as descriptive of Christ in Romans 5:15 and 1 Corinthians 15:21 and 47, with its dependent in 1 Timothy 2:5; Jesus crucified by the demon spirit "rulers of this age" in 1 Corinthians 2:8; but above all, the hymn in Philippians 2:6-11 (for text, see p.104) with its motifs of the divine image of God humbling himself, taking on a "likeness" to human form, descending and ascending, undergoing death and exaltation—and receiving the name "Jesus" (Savior) only at the time of his exaltation after death.

This pre-Pauline hymn imbedded in Paul's letter is a microcosm of all the mythology we have just outlined. It opens a window onto the cultic circles Paul was converted to, circles to which he eventually contributed his own ideas. They and he were not only feeding from the intermediary Son philosophy of Logos and personified Wisdom, they were moving in an atmosphere of ancient salvation mythology of descending, redemptive divine forces. They were putting their own twists on it all, deciding that their Redeemer had been crucified and had died for sin, ideas they derived from reading the Jewish scriptures. But all the basic ingredients of Christianity and its mythical Jesus were there in the atmosphere (quite literally) of the times. *And none of that mythological system had any reference to an historical person.*

This prolific variety illustrates the amazing fruitfulness of the Son and Savior ideas that were all the rage in the first century, and the freedom they gave to people like Paul and the Odist to populate heaven and formulate the workings of Deity upon the world.

A New Nativity Scene

A rich panoply of Son/Christ/Savior expression was rampant across the eastern half of the Roman empire by the late first century. Considering that Christian writers even in the early second century show no familiarity with the basics of the Gospel story, it seems ill-advised to trace all these ideas to an historical Jesus of Nazareth who died obscurely in Jerusalem and whose career on earth is not even preserved by those who allegedly turned him into the Son of God.

Indeed, within a handful of years of Jesus' supposed death, we know of Christian communities all over the eastern Mediterranean. As Ernst Haenchen has pointed out in his monumental study of Acts (*The Acts of the Apostles: A Commentary*, p.103, 298) the congregations at Damascus, Antioch, Ephesus and Rome were founded by unknown Christians, as were no doubt, countless other communities. Reading between the lines of the picture Acts presents concerning the spread of the faith, as well as between the lines of Paul's own letters, one perceives that Damascus in Syria already possessed a Christian community before Paul was even converted, and that both Antioch and Rome had congregations long before Paul got there.

Rome is a case of special interest. If Suetonius' reference to "Chrestus" refers to Christ, as many assume it does (see Chapter 20), Jews who professed the Christ faith were numerous and troublesome enough to be expelled from Rome by Claudius in the 40s, little more than a decade after the alleged crucifixion. Paul's letter to the Romans, probably written around 55, reveals a community that has "many years" behind it (15:23). In the orthodox picture of Christian beginnings, how could such a community have formed so soon? Who brought the kerygma there?[67]

The true answer may be indicated by the later churchman known as "Ambrosiaster," who remarked in his commentary on the epistle to the Romans that "One ought not to condemn the Romans, but to praise their faith; because without seeing any signs or miracles and without seeing any of the apostles, they nevertheless accepted faith in Christ, although according to a Jewish rite."[68]

Such a tradition points to something very revealing, and will bring us full circle to the conclusions arrived at in the first division of the Jesus Puzzle. Christ belief in Rome arose independently of any proselytizing movement from outside. It was not responding to an outlandish message about a crucified man executed as a subversive in Jerusalem. The multiplicity of early Christian expression does not need an explanation in the context of a single point of origin and an initially pristine doctrine about Jesus.

Rather, *Christianity was born in a thousand places*, in a host of different forms, growing out of the broad, fertile religious soil of the time. It sprang up in many independent circles and sects, both inside and outside Palestine, the product of many minds. All of it was the expression of the prevailing religious philosophy of divine intermediaries and the cravings of the age for "salvation."

Paul and the Jerusalem brotherhood were simply one strand of this Christ belief, though an important and eventually very influential one. The Pauline interpretation of the spiritual Christ caught on in many places, and later, in a myth-making process of its own, the Jerusalem circle with Paul as its satellite was adopted as the originating cell of the whole Christian movement.

But while Paul tramped the imperial roads, while Jews and gentiles in Rome were adopting faith in Christ "without seeing any of the apostles," no such unity or point of origin existed. At the same time, something was happening back in Galilee which was to have a profound effect on the later generations of those who were now responding to Paul and the forces of faith and philosophy in the capital of the empire. It was a preaching movement of a very different kind, a human response to a human situation, but its elements were destined to attach themselves to the spiritual Son and Savior whom Paul and his fellows had found in scripture and extracted from the mythological heavens around them.

II : THE GALILEAN TRADITION

Between Jerusalem and Galilee lies a distance of barely 75 miles, or 120 kilometers. Not far for an itinerant prophet and sage to travel, especially if accompanied by a group of his followers. The journey could be done comfortably in a few days. But in all the literature of the Jerusalem Tradition no record can be found of its Jesus figure making that short journey. Before the Gospels were adopted as history, no record exists that he was ever in the city of Jerusalem at all—or anywhere else on earth.

The second division of this book makes that journey of 75 miles, in the reverse direction. It will be traveling to Galilee to look at the record of a movement that was preaching the kingdom of God. An important part of this record lies in the ancient lost document now known as Q, which has been extracted by modern scholars from the Gospels of Matthew and Luke. At the time when the Q collection of sayings and anecdotes was incorporated by the two later evangelists into their reworking of Mark's Gospel, references to a figure who was represented as the originator of the sayings, as a miracle worker and apocalyptic prophet, could be found within that Q collection. Whether this figure was given the name Jesus is impossible to say. But Q itself had undergone an evolution. It can be shown to contain layers of different material which seem to have been added to the collection over time, and thus we can presume that the document went through a number of revisions. Working back through those revisions, identifying the nature and sources of Q's various components, and deciding whether in fact a Jesus figure under any name lay at the roots of Q's evolution, will be the principal task of this part of the Jesus Puzzle.

One thing is evident even before the excavation starts. A survey of Q as reconstructed by modern scholarship reveals no evidence that the 75 mile journey from Galilee to Jerusalem was ever made by the Q 'Jesus.' No mention of Jerusalem, no death and resurrection, no saving role for the teaching sage can be found in Q. More than that, some of the sayings strongly suggest, as in the epistles, that no room can be made for him in the early strata.

Part Five will begin in Chapter 14 by sorting out Q into its various layers of material and noting the great differences between them, along with the silence on anything to do with elements of the Jerusalem Tradition. Chapter 15 will shift the focus to the Gospel of Thomas, another collection of sayings attributed to Jesus which has no reference to a death and resurrection. Parts of Thomas have some connection to the earliest stratum of Q, and they will serve to help analyze Q itself. Chapter 16 will place the Q document in its social setting and uncover the possible sources of its early material. The question will also be asked: was a Jesus figure present in the earliest stages of the community's development?

Part Six will continue with the study of Q. Chapter 17 will suggest a different 'founder' for the Q preaching movement and make a case for regarding the presence of a Jesus in the final version of Q as the product of a late stage of revision. Chapter 18 will offer sectarian needs and impulses as the reasons for such an invention. Chapter 19 is the pivot point of the book, the fulcrum on which the entire history of Christianity swings. Here the Gospel of Mark will be presented as the ultimate evolution of the kingdom-preaching tradition, and the shadowy figure of Mark himself as the orchestrator of a master stroke: the integration of the newly-minted Q founder with the divine Son preached by Paul, creating a symbolic tale about a ministry in Galilee and a death and resurrection in Jerusalem. No piece of fiction before or since has had such an impact on world history.

With that climax attained, Part Seven will pause for a sideshow: a survey of the non-Christian record of the first and later centuries, both for its references and its silences concerning an historical Jesus. Pagans from Epictetus to Tacitus, Jews from Philo to the compilers of the Talmud will be surveyed in Chapter 20, while Chapter 21 will be devoted to a thorough examination of the two famous references to Jesus in the works of the Jewish historian Flavius Josephus. Here, in a much-tilled field, arguments old and new will be marshaled to call into serious question the reliability of those references.

Part Five

PREACHING THE KINGDOM OF GOD

14

Excavating the Roots of Q

Teacher of a radical new ethic. Miracle-worker and healer. Prophet of the kingdom. The story of the death and resurrection in the Gospels is preceded by the tale of a ministry, the career of a man who was all these things and more. Do the two belong together? Would a Galilean preacher of the kingdom go off to Jerusalem and get himself executed, only to be turned into the cosmic Son of God, creator and sustainer of the universe, redeemer of the world's sins, emerging alive from his grave and promising to come again at the end of the world to judge it in apocalyptic glory? How would such a progression, such an astonishing quantum leap, have taken place? Who would have done it? Who would have accepted it?

Do the two belong together?

Our study of the epistles and the kerygma of death and resurrection they represent has strongly suggested that the two do *not* belong together, for in that record there is no sign of the pre-passion ministry of the Gospels, no life on earth. If, when we move to the other side of the picture, we find a corresponding silence in the opposite direction, this will solidify the unbridgeable divide between the two Traditions.

However, the situation is not quite so straightforward when we try to identify and assemble the pieces of the Galilean side of the puzzle. We do not have as clear and concrete a record for the early kingdom movement as we do for the Son of God movement. No Paul of Tarsus left his name and writings to be examined first-hand. No collection of documents like the epistles which open windows onto the varied first century faith in a divine Son was brought together for the kingdom movement. With one exception—the Gospel of Thomas, recently unearthed from the sands of Egypt—the record from the Galilean side comes from the New Testament Gospels themselves and must be extracted from them through a process of excavation and distillation.

A cornerstone in the structure which modern majority scholarship has erected to explain the relationship between the canonical Gospels is the conclusion that Mark was the first one written, and that Matthew and Luke came later and independently created their own Gospels by copying and reworking Mark.

(Note that the names of the four Gospels are no longer considered to reflect the authors who actually wrote them. The assigning of the Gospels to legendary early figures of the Christian movement was a product of the later second century, and critical scholarship regards such traditions as inaccurate. However, the Gospels are still known by their traditional names. Such names are used to refer to the Gospels themselves or to their authors, whoever they may have been.)

In addition to their use of Mark, the Gospels of Matthew and Luke contain material not found in Mark, and much of this material is very similar, often almost identical in wording between the two. The best explanation for this commonality is that both drew on another source document which they integrated into their reworkings of Mark. This hypothetical document (no copy has survived) scholars call "Q", for the German *Quelle*, meaning "source." What it may have been called in the first century, or if it was referred to as a "gospel," is impossible to say. (The community which would have produced this document is called the "Q community," but again, this is a modern designation.)

Even though there is no independent evidence for Q (such as an identifying reference to it in the ancient record), majority scholarship's deduction that such a document did exist and was used by Matthew and Luke best accounts for that common material which they do not have from Mark. Some scholars have put forward other theories, such as that Luke copied material from Matthew which Matthew had himself created or derived from other sources. Such theories would deny that any Q document existed at all. However, the arguments in favor of the existence of Q are much stronger than those against it or in favor of some other explanation. The reader may consult Appendix 7 for a discussion of some of these arguments, along with those in favor of the priority of Mark. The existence of Q as the source of the common material in Matthew and Luke is assumed in this book.

The Q Document

The exact extent of Q is still a matter of debate, but its main content has been reasonably well established. For the most part, Q was made up of a collection of sayings, most of them apparently without any lead-in sentences or descriptive material that would place such sayings within a ministry of Jesus. We can assume this because in the vast majority of cases, Matthew and Luke use the sayings quite differently, placing them in different spots in their Gospel story and within different immediate contexts. In Q, such sayings were grouped into clusters of related subject matter. Sprinkled throughout the sayings were a few more extended pieces: a couple of miracle and controversy stories, the dialogue between Jesus and John, the Temptation of Jesus. There was no overall pattern that would reflect the course of Jesus' ministry or any other historical governing factor, with the exception that a description of John the Baptist's ministry comes first.

When Matthew and Luke share a saying or anecdote with a similar wording, it is likely they are drawing on the same written source, and such units can be confidently included within the Q document. Precisely identical wording is rare, but this can be put down to little changes made by one or both evangelists reflecting their own writing styles or fitting their individual editorial and theological agendas. These changes are often consistent with the changes apparent in their adaptations of Mark. When a wider discrepancy exists between sayings that seem similar, there may be some doubt whether they are to be included in Q. In this case, both evangelists may be drawing on some non-literary source, or perhaps two different literary versions.

What was the order of the sayings in the Q document? Assuming that Matthew and Luke used copies of Q which, if not identical, provided a generally common sequence and content, who better reflects the original Q order? Both present a different distribution of Q's pieces throughout their own Gospels. Since neither evangelist shows any compunction about rearranging some of their Markan material, one can conclude that both may have done the same with Q. Overall, however, scholars have judged that Luke better preserves the Q order, and so they list Q in the Lukan sequence, assigning it the chapter and verse numbers of the Lukan Gospel. Thus, Luke 3:7-9, the presumed first unit in the Q document, becomes Q 3:7-9. (Note that the reconstructed Q, therefore, does not use all possible numbers, but only those derived from Luke.) Those "pieces" or units of Q, depending on the scholar doing the breakdown, number anywhere from 60 to 100.

Layers Within Q

Once the elements comprising Q were identified and mapped out, it became evident that Q included different kinds of material. Two general types are obvious. The first is found in several clusters of sayings possessing a common atmosphere, style and purpose. They focus on ethics and discipleship and closely resemble the genre of Jewish (as well as non-Jewish) "wisdom" collections, such as the Old Testament Book of Proverbs. Wisdom collections were common in the ancient world. They offered sage advice on how to survive the vicissitudes of existence, be successful in life, and relate to divine forces in the universe. Such advice might be aimed at the governing class or the common person.

The wisdom sayings in Q, though somewhat different in character from the general type, include the famous Beatitudes, several pithy sayings and parables, along with some of the most prized of the Gospel ethics—none less so than the lines in Luke/Q 6:27-28:

> "Love your enemies, do good to those who hate you; bless those who curse you, pray for those who abuse you. To him who strikes you on the cheek, offer the other also; and from him who takes away your cloak do not withhold your coat as well." [RSV]

Scholars refer to this as the wisdom or "sapiential" layer of Q. The second type, again in clusters, stands side by side with the first, but the atmosphere and sentiments of these sayings are as different from the others as night and day.

> "Woe to you, Chorazin! Woe to you, Bethsaida! For if the mighty works done in you had been done in Tyre and Sidon, they would have repented long ago, sitting in sackcloth and ashes. . . . And you, Capernaum, will you be exalted to heaven? You shall be brought down to hell!" [Lk./Q 10:13-15, RSV]

Such sayings contain none of the wisdom quality, but instead are "prophetic" in nature, even apocalyptic. They condemn the outside world for its hostility and rejection, they look to a future upheaval and accounting. The figure of the Son of Man appears in several sayings, one who shall arrive at the End-time to judge the world. (This figure is derived from the apocalyptic scene in Daniel 7, as discussed in Chapter 5.) Here, too, we encounter John the Baptist, styled as a forerunner to the Q preachers, prophesying a great retribution at the hands of a coming one who will baptize with fire. He seems to be speaking of the

Son of Man and not a human Jesus. Also in this group are the two miracle stories in Q: the healing of the centurion's servant (Luke/Q 7:1-10), and the Beelzebub controversy (Luke/Q 11:14-20).

How are we to relate two such vastly different groups of sayings and anecdotes? Could they have come from the same man, or even the same community? The wisdom sayings are tolerant, often enlightened (whether or not they are always practicable). They possess insight and even touches of humor; they embrace a world one is attempting to peaceably change and find a place within. The prophetic material, on the other hand, is narrow-minded, fulminating, world-denying; its speakers look for no compromise with those who fail to heed them.

It seemed to modern liberal scholars that both types could not be assigned to a single source, that they may not even have been contemporary in time. Led by an influential Canadian scholar named John Kloppenborg (*The Formation of Q*, 1987), they identified the wisdom sayings in Q as a separate stratum of material and labeled it Q1. These were assigned to the earliest stage of the Q document and judged to be essentially the product of the "genuine" historical Jesus. The prophetic layer was labeled Q2 and assigned to a later stage when the original community preaching the kingdom began reacting to the failure of their message to win over wider segments of society. The sayings in Q2 were seen as unrelated to any sentiment expressed by the earlier, genuine Jesus and judged not to be his product. At some unknown time the Q2 sayings were added to the Q1 sayings, possibly with some reorganization and "redaction" (changes reflecting the interests of the editor) performed on the whole document.

This left a few elements in Q which appear to represent a further advance on both earlier stages, such as the Temptation Story (Q 4:1-13) or the saying about the Son who knows the Father (Q 10:22). These went into a Q3 layer which reflected a more advanced thinking about Jesus, showing stirrings of a biography or even giving him a touch of divinity. Again, further redaction was probably performed on the collection as a whole when these later insertions were made.[69]

A Resounding Silence

But another feature of Q emerged more clearly. Scholars had realized this for almost a century, reacting to it with more than a little disquiet. Nothing in the entire document spoke of Jesus' death and resurrection, nothing suggested a sacrificial or redemptive role for him. Why would the Q community have ignored the central message of

Christianity? Why would they have shown no interest in Jesus' acts of salvation? Surely they would not have been ignorant of what had happened to him when he made his fateful sojourn to Jerusalem.

We could enlarge on that mystery a little further. Did no sayings like those that were part of the passion story, the establishment of the Eucharist at a Last Supper, words from the cross: did none reach the community back in Galilee, to be added to the collection? Jesus' defiant Son of Man proclamation before the High Priest is not to be found in Q, nor anything from the "little apocalypse" delivered to Jesus' disciples in the Temple (as in Mark 13) about the coming misfortunes and the "abomination of desolation," nothing about the arrival of the Son of Man in glory. These and other sayings like them would have provided the prophetic stratum of the Q collection with a fitting climax. For it is a cold, hard fact that none of the elements of the Jerusalem phase of the Gospels appear in Q.

Another puzzling absence is that of the term "Christ"—the Messiah. The Gospels make the issue of the disciples' perception of Jesus a central part of his Galilean ministry. Jesus in Mark 8:28 asks his disciples: "Who do men say that I am?" And Peter replies: "You are the Messiah." Yet no suggestion that Jesus is the Christ, no reference to the concept itself, ever surfaces in Q.

A number of explanations have been put forward to deal with these omissions. As noted earlier, modern scholars such as Burton Mack and John Dominic Crossan create a great divide between Galilee and Jerusalem, as though the one world had no contact with or interest in the other. But there are too many anomalies created by such a scenario. Not only the Gospels, but the entire body of later Christian tradition portrays certain disciples who were involved in Jesus' Galilean ministry as accompanying him to Jerusalem. James the Just, the head of the Jerusalem church (to whom Paul witnesses), is supposed to be Jesus' own blood brother, so we can assume he would have maintained connections with the family and circle back home in Galilee.

If a group of Jesus' followers in Galilee had established a community there to preserve and propagate the Galilean teachings of Jesus (those presumably to be identified with Q1), such people could hardly have remained ignorant about what had subsequently happened to him in Jerusalem. They would hardly have remained impervious to the *input* from those in Jerusalem who responded to his death and perceived resurrection by establishing a whole other "tradition" about Jesus, one that regarded him not only as Messiah but as Son of God and Savior of the world. When that movement spread outward from Jerusalem, did it bypass Galilee? Did it leave that earlier response in some isolated, uncontaminated enclave, interested solely in Jesus' Galilean preaching? Would Jesus' Jerusalem followers and family members who had accompanied him from Galilee not have brought home the new message, the new Son and Savior response? Not to mention details about the trial and crucifixion, or sayings of Jesus associated with those events. How could such things not have found their way back to Galilee and into the Q collection?

It is sometimes claimed that the focus or interests in Q do not relate to such things, that the Q document had no 'room' for them. But it has already been shown that the apocalyptic element of the Jerusalem Tradition would have been very much at home in Q. One of the major motifs of the Q2 stratum is the killing of the prophets. Q 11:49-51 says:

"This is why the Wisdom of God said, 'I will send them prophets and messengers; and some of these they will persecute and kill;' so that this generation will have to answer for the blood of all the prophets shed since the foundation of the world; from the blood of Abel to the blood of Zechariah who perished between the altar and the sanctuary." [NEB]

Even if, as critical scholars like those of the Jesus Seminar now hold, such things are not to be attributed to an authentic Jesus, even if Jesus never spoke an apocalyptic word in his career in either Galilee or Jerusalem, this does not alter the fact that at the level of Q2 the community is very much interested in—even fixated upon—the idea of an establishment which kills those sent from God. Jesus could not fail to have been seen as just such a messenger, and Jesus had presumably been killed by the establishment. At the Q2 level at least, the death of Jesus, the killing of their own founder and the fountainhead of their teachings, would have been seen as the ultimate example of the alleged ancient phenomenon of the killing of the prophets sent from God. Yet this concept never appears in Q, and certainly not in the above passage of 11:49-51 where Jesus is not even included in the reference to those whom the Wisdom of God has sent.

One saying in Q is sometimes claimed to be an "allusion" to Jesus' death, Q14:27: "No one who does not carry his cross and come with me can be a disciple of mine." But this refers not to the cross of Jesus but to that of the prospective follower, and the saying seems to be simply a proverb about enduring hardship.[70]

It is virtually impossible that the Q community, over a period of a few decades, could have remained unaffected by what was being made of Jesus by a whole other apostolic movement proceeding out of Jerusalem. How could it have resisted the elevation of its own native son to the rank of divine Son of God and Savior? The subtle intimations of the Temptation Story and the saying about the 'Son who knows the Father' hardly fill that bill adequately, and still do not give a hint of death and resurrection, or of a redemptive role for Jesus.

By the same token, we might ask similar questions in the other direction. If Jesus, for reasons unknown (since the milieu of the city would not be the same as the one in Galilee), went off to Jerusalem, he was presumably accompanied by followers who had been with him in Galilee. It is reasonable to assume that some of them would have joined in the new response to him after his death. Certainly the Gospels portray it that way. But did those followers not have any influence on the new movement proceeding from Jerusalem? Did others who were involved in it refuse to hear anything about Jesus' Galilean teachings, about his healings and miracles, his conflicts with the establishment? We must assume so, since the surviving record of the Jerusalem movement, the letters of Paul and other New Testament epistles, show not a single element of the Galilean Tradition, no trace of the preaching, miracle-working prophet of the kingdom.

The suggestion has been made that the two Traditions do not belong together, and that we could clinch the argument if it could be shown that the ignorance on the part of the Jerusalem Tradition concerning anything to do with Jesus' ministry in Galilee also extended in the other direction. Thus far, the latter would seem to be the case. This silence will be compounded when we go on to examine Q in greater detail, but it is also compounded by evidence from another document, one that lies entirely outside the New Testament: the Gospel of Thomas.

15

The Gospel of Thomas

The complete Gospel of Thomas was part of a cache of manuscripts buried in a jar in Egypt in the fourth century and uncovered in 1945. That cache apparently belonged to a gnostic sect, and is known as the Nag Hammadi Codices. The Gospel of Thomas is a collection of 114 sayings attributed to Jesus, said to have been recorded by the apostle Thomas. Like Q, the Gospel of Thomas has no narrative element. Its sayings are listed in no particular order, or in some cases according to a catchword principle. One saying containing a certain word or phrase will be followed by another saying with a similar word or phrase. The document's overall organization is much more primitive than Q's, and most of the sayings are preceded by a simple "Jesus said" as in #54:

"Jesus said: 'Blessed are the poor, for yours is the kingdom of heaven.' "

Or #108:

"Jesus said: 'He who will drink from my mouth will become like me. I myself shall become he, and the things that are hidden will be revealed to him.' "

A few of the sayings have a little more elaborate set-up, such as the use of disciples to create a little dialogue with Jesus, as in #18:

"The disciples said to Jesus, 'Tell us how our end will be.' Jesus said: 'Have you discovered, then, the beginning, that you look for the end? For where the beginning is, there will the end be. Blessed is he who will take his place in the beginning; he will know the end and will not experience death.' "[71]

As in Q, different types of sayings are found in the Gospel of Thomas. About a third of its content closely parallels the sayings of Q1, often with similar wording. They too feature a wisdom-like ethical program based on the anticipation of God's kingdom, or on the view that such a kingdom has already arrived. Other sayings inhabit the same atmosphere but have no parallels in Q. There are a few allusions to an apocalyptic outlook, but no End-time Son of Man.

The remainder of the sayings in Thomas reflect a very different and more mystical philosophy. They have mild similarities to the movement known as Gnosticism, though some scholars balk at calling the Gospel of Thomas "gnostic." As in the second and third examples above, this mysticism relates to the acquiring of secret knowledge and states of being which confer immortality. Nothing of this latter nature is found in Q, or in the New Testament generally. It represents a line of thinking which developed independently of Christian "orthodoxy."

Thus we encounter a situation in the Gospel of Thomas much like that in Q, namely that two different types of material lie side by side. It seems probable that the 'mystical' stratum is a later overlay on the Q-like one, and few would suggest that its sayings are the product of Jesus. (Those judged "authentic" by the Jesus Seminar are from the stratum similar to Q1.) All, however, were eventually attributed equally to Jesus by the Thomas community. The recovered document, in Egyptian Coptic, was made in the fourth century, but is thought to be based on a Greek original that reached its present form some time in the first half of the second century, likely somewhere in Syria.[72]

Is Any of Thomas Genuine to Jesus?

What of the one-third of Thomas which is clearly related to the material in Matthew and Luke which comes from Q? Since the document was discovered, debate has centered on a key question. Did the compiler of Thomas—or of its early layer—simply pick and choose some of the sayings from the canonical Gospels, or was this material drawn from earlier, more primitive sources, perhaps oral tradition, thus constituting an independent witness to Jesus and his teachings?

The conclusion of scholars such as Stephen J. Patterson (*The Gospel of Thomas and Jesus*, 1992), H. Koester (*Trajectories Through Early Christianity*, p.130-32) and J. D. Crossan (*The Birth of Christianity*, p.116f), is that no part of Thomas is dependent on the Synoptic Gospels. Koester in *Ancient Christian Gospels* (p.95) is firm: "The materials which the Gospel of Thomas and Q share must belong to a very early stage of the transmission of Jesus' sayings. . . . Thus, the Gospel of Thomas is either dependent upon the earliest version of Q or, more likely, shares with the author of Q one or several very early collections of Jesus' sayings."

In other words, the relationship is a *literary* one. The close similarity of content between Q1 and the early layer of Thomas, often involving very similar wording, cannot have resulted from oral transmission, which is not capable of bringing about such a close correspondence. It must have occurred because Thomas copied from either a primitive Q (or possibly vice-versa) or from a source document on which Q1 was also based. Thus, it would seem that behind Q1 and the parallel early Thomas lies a single collection of sayings which is not derived from any written Gospel. Scholars of Q and Thomas like to date that collection, and with it the initial formulation of Q and Thomas, very early, perhaps to the 50s of the first century.

Like its counterpart in Q, the early layer of Thomas contains no mention of Jesus' death and resurrection, or of a theology of salvation based upon him. The later mystical layer of Thomas also has no reference to Jesus' death and resurrection, and thus no salvation by means of such events. There is a form of salvation in that following and understanding Jesus' teachings will lead to immortality (#1: one "shall not taste death") but this is not based on any action of Jesus. Even in the absence of a Jesus as their originator, such teachings would confer the same benefit.

Thus we find two quite different communities adopting and founding themselves on a tradition of teaching which is silent about the entire Jerusalem Tradition of Jesus' death and resurrection. Both evolve along their respective paths without integrating any such thing into their ongoing development.

Crossan has raised the question: if the earliest layers in the two documents, Q and Thomas, are based one on the other, or on an earlier written document, why do they not show traces of a common structure? Why is there not even an occasional shared order or parallel sequence within the material they possess in common? This, however, is not a major problem, for Q in its own evolution went through more than one major recasting as new material was added; so, for that matter, did Thomas. Such reorganization of old and new could well have wiped out any common sequence between them.

Does early Thomas belong to an "authentic" Jesus? That question will be answered in the next chapter in conjunction with a similar question about Q1. But here we can observe that the link with Jesus throughout the entire Gospel of Thomas is tenuous indeed. That slender "Jesus said" tacked on at the beginning of most of the sayings units, as well as the occasional longer introductory lines, could well be later appendages. The earliest phase of Thomas, including the original collection it may have been based upon, could have done without them. It is impossible to tell just when the attribution to Jesus was added, or whether it was before, during or after the overlay of mystical sayings. Certainly there is nothing to prevent such an attribution from being a second century product, added in response to the spread of a newly-developed historical Jesus.

When did the Thomas Community Form?

When the 'wisdom' sayings of Q1 and the Gospel of Thomas are compared, those in Thomas are usually found to be in a more primitive form. This does not necessarily indicate that the Thomas community is older or that it could not have based its sayings on an early Q document, since Q's versions of the sayings may have undergone alteration in their history, whereas Thomas may have more closely preserved the original forms. Thus a 'Thomas' community could have begun at roughly the same time as the Q one, in the mid-first century.

However, the association with an apostle by the name of Thomas cannot be supported at this early a date. It is only during the second century that we find signs of certain Christian communities in Syria tracing a foundational link back to such a figure. Thus the attribution of the entire document to "Thomas," as embodied in the Gospel's opening: "These are the secret sayings which the living Jesus spoke and which Didymos Judas Thomas wrote down," is almost certainly one of the last things added. It may well have come not long after the attribution of the sayings to an historical Jesus, if not at the same time.

Other elements of Thomas indicate that a second century redaction produced the version we see now. In saying #21, Mary asks Jesus a question. Her presence among the disciples, here and in the final saying #114, is a feature of several second-century gnostic "dialogue" Gospels. Saying #12, which has Jesus designating James the Just as the one who will take over leadership of the Christian community when he is gone, also indicates later thinking, for all the traditions which show an interest in tracing authority back to James appear to originate no earlier than the second century. The James witnessed by Paul in Galatians, the apparent head of a group of apostles in Jerusalem, seems to be involved in no missionary activity beyond his own home base, and in the earliest record no community outside Judea traces its origin and authority back to him.[73]

16

A Counter-Culture Movement in Galilee

If the set of sayings and teachings which lies at the roots of Q and the Gospel of Thomas was not the product of a man who went on to get himself executed in Jerusalem and give rise to a Son and Savior religion, what was it? If we can provide a satisfactory answer to that question, we have removed the second half of the Christian tradition from any necessary anchor in an historical Jesus.

The sayings in Q1 and early Thomas are not merely innovative ethical directives which one mind or group of minds just decided would be a good thing to implement. They were a response to a particular social and economic situation of the time. We can assume that the Q community was centered in Galilee by the references to the towns and cities of that region: Capernaum, Bethsaida, Chorazin. Since these places appear only in the Q2 layer, they are not part of the scene in Thomas, which in any case probably developed as a community somewhere further north.

Both documents speak of "the kingdom of God." As demonstrated in Chapter 5, this concept owed its roots to a longstanding expectation in Jewish circles that God would elevate the nation over its subjugators, effect judgment on the world and bring about a Utopian age. The Q community sees this arrival of the kingdom in apocalyptic terms: the heavenly Son of Man will arrive in a judgment of fire, and John the Baptist is claimed as a forerunner who preached his coming. The Gospel of Thomas expresses almost no apocalyptic expectation, and the Son of Man appears only in a saying (#86) which seems to have been simply a proverb about "man" in general.

Instead, Thomas is promoting new ways of viewing oneself and the world, new means to achieve a kind of inner kingdom and salvation through mystical knowledge. Yet both documents, on a wider scale, seem to be reacting against a society which has marginalized certain disadvantaged classes and created injustices so grievous that they can be remedied only by divine intervention or by withdrawal into a counter-culture.

Down and Out in Galilee

Consider the tone of many of the sayings of Q1. These may be cast in a wisdom style, but they are radically different in outlook from those found in either traditional Jewish or non-Jewish wisdom writings. The latter teach how to get along and be successful in the real world. In Q and Thomas, a reversal of normal class structure and fortune is in order. What is called for is the creation of a *new* world: "Blessed are the poor, for theirs is the kingdom of God." A parable about God's banquet in the kingdom, to which the rich have declined attendance, to be replaced by the poor of the streets and byways. To be a member of this movement and kingdom, one must hate one's father and mother, separate from one's family (since counter-cultures always involve splits with those who do not take part or who cannot sympathize). God will take care of his own; he takes care of the sparrow so he will certainly take care of us. And so on.

What, then, was the setting in which this original body of teachings arose, or were first applied? They seem to be the expression of a disadvantaged class, one that has removed itself—or been removed—from participation in society as a whole. It is made up of people who can only look to God and their own devices to survive. One might consider that throughout history, there have always been people and classes in such a situation, though not all of them have been part of a culture which has an active expectation of imminent intervention by God to set up a new world order. However, since we can locate the Q-Thomas expression somewhere in the mid-first century Palestine area, what can we identify about this particular movement?

John Dominic Crossan, in his 1998 book *The Birth of Christianity*, has formulated a very detailed and focused picture of the Q ethos. Some critics suggest that this picture has to some extent been created through a personal lens, namely the historical background of his native Ireland in its experience of a poor peasantry under the overlordship of English masters. Be that as it may, the type of picture he presents almost certainly agrees in quality with the situation on the Galilean scene.

That scene involved an increasing urbanization of the country under Roman rule. Herod Antipas, during the second and third decades of the first century, had rebuilt the city of Sepphoris and founded Tiberias within 20 miles of each other near the Sea of Galilee. This was to have devastating effects on the surrounding agrarian population. The new centers tended to drain the agricultural resources of the area, placing increased burdens of work and taxation on the rural peasantry. Urban elites gained ever greater ownership of the farming land, indenturing or dispossessing the peasants, often driving them to become beggars or bandits. (Crossan also sees artisans as a struggling group of formerly dispossessed peasants.) Exploitation accelerated and the gap between rich and poor widened.

Oppressed peasant classes rarely have the opportunity to revolt, and virtually never successfully. Their response is almost always one of attitude. They adopt highly critical stances against ordinary social conventions and political power structures. They refuse to cooperate any more than they have to with those in authority. They criticize wealth, the values of the cities and ruling circles, and the traditional religious institutions which are usually under the control of the rich establishment. A counter-culture movement with radical standards and expectations may develop, in which the newly disadvantaged can take part and take heart. There may be new religious and mythical dimensions to its outlook and expectations. If the dispossessed themselves lack the power to bring about change or restitution, a supernatural power may be regarded as being on their side and promising to effect the desired radical change and reversal. Utopias are envisioned and actively sought. The focus on evil in the world becomes less a concern with individual evil than with the evil arising from class inequalities. The prevailing outlook becomes a resistance movement against *systemic* evil.

In any Jewish (or Jewish-imitating) milieu, another factor will enter the picture. The best of the Hebrew biblical tradition, one expressed chiefly in the prophets, is the concept of the God of Israel as a God of justice and righteousness, one who champions the powerless, the vulnerable, the unfortunate. Social unrest and resistance may thus be grounded in the view that class inequalities and the suffering of the poor are contrary to God's will and that he will intervene before long to right all wrongs.

Thus Crossan sees a Galilee in the 20s of the first century pervaded by a peasant resistance movement brought about by the deleterious effects of increasing rural commercialization and fed by old biblical streams of religious idealism focused on social justice. This lower class resistance to Roman rule and its compromised Jewish aristocracy is witnessed by the many recorded disturbances in the supposed time of Jesus: prophets leading groups into the desert, to the banks of the Jordan, "usually unarmed, always slaughtered" (*op.cit.*, p.210). This social unrest eventually led to an explosion of banditry, political instability, finally to outright revolt culminating in the disastrous Jewish War of 66-70. In the Galilee of the 20s and 30s it created the so-called kingdom of God movement. For Crossan and others in the field, its driving force, its chief innovative wellspring, was Jesus of Nazareth.

The Q1 Sayings

Can we automatically assume that the bedrock layer of the two documents, the wisdom sayings of Q1 and their parallels in the Gospel of Thomas, are the product of a Jesus of Nazareth, or indeed of any single individual? Let's take a more detailed look at the Q1 sayings:

> "Blessed are the poor, for theirs is the Kingdom of God."
>
> "If you love only those who love you, what credit is that to you? . . . Treat others as you would like them to treat you."
>
> "Can one blind man be guide to another? Will they not both fall into the ditch?"
>
> "Do not carry purse or bag, and travel barefoot; exchange no greetings on the road."
>
> "Think of the ravens: they neither sow nor reap; they have no storehouse or barn; yet God feeds them. . . . Your father knows that you need these things."
>
> "Sell your possessions and give in charity. Store up your wealth in heaven where no thief can get it . . . for where your wealth is, there will be your heart as well."

This is a curious collection of sayings for a Jewish preacher, presumably within a community largely made up of Jews, or of gentiles who follow Jewish ways. In all of Q1 there is scarcely a Jewish idea to be found. N. T. Wright, in his *The New Testament and the People of God* (p.284-5), speaks of Jewish concerns in this period: "Far more important to the first-century Jew than questions of space, time and literal cosmology were the key issues of Temple, Land, and Torah, of race, economy and justice. When Israel's God acted, Jews would be restored to their ancestral rights and would practice their ancestral religion, with the rest of the world looking on in awe, and/or making pilgrimages to Zion, and/or being ground to powder under Jewish feet." But where are all—or any—of these Jewish preoccupations in Q1 or the parallel layer of Thomas? Where is the divine mandate, the will of the covenantal God of Judaism, the future role of the gentile, the restoration of Zion in a new Jerusalem?

Why do we find a complete void (beyond a passing reference to Solomon) on all things specifically Jewish? Would this Jesus never have expressed himself in Jewish terms, never given voice to the tradition of Yahwehan justice and righteousness, to the prophets as biblical precedent? Would he never give a hint of the traditional question (again going back into the prophets) of whether the people's sins and the need for repentance had anything to do with the present state of affairs? Would he never have allowed a flavor of prophetic or apocalyptic fervor to pass his lips? Why is it left to the Q2 generation to introduce such elements? Could it be that the bedrock layer of Q is not Jewish at all, but arises from a more cosmopolitan source, adopted and to some extent adapted, by a Jewish (or Jewish-imitating) community whose real character emerges in Q2?

A Cynic Precedent

If Q1 has no Jewish flavor, what flavor *does* it convey? Since the mid-1980s, certain scholars[74] have called attention to an intriguing and startling observation about the sayings in Q1. These "wisdom" aphorisms bear a strong resemblance to the spirit and style of a specific Hellenistic preaching movement of the time, that of the Cynics.

During the first century, wandering Cynic philosophers were tramping the cities and byways of the empire, urging people to adopt a lifestyle, an outlook on the world which was both religious and social. They claimed to be following the teaching and way of life of Diogenes of Sinope, the founder of the Cynic philosophy. They were gadflies, convinced that society was too authoritarian, too inegalitarian, too hypocritical. They were a kind of 'in your face' protester, motivated by the feeling that some divine power was directing them to shake up society.

Like Q, they too spoke of a benevolent God the Father. Epictetus, a Stoic philosopher who adopted Cynic traditions and preached to the poor and humble masses, was recorded to have said: "All men have always and everywhere a Father who cares for them." Dio of Prusa urged people to trust in providence, for "Consider the beasts yonder, and the birds, how much freer from trouble they live than man. . . ."

The Cynics, too, had their Beatitudes. Blessed is the person, said Epictetus, who enjoyed the proper relationship with the deity.

And what of Jesus' most distinctive teaching: Love your enemies, turn the other cheek? Seneca in the mid-first century reported this piece of counter-cultural Cynic philosophy: "Allow any man that desires to insult you and work you wrong; but if only virtue dwells in you, you will suffer nothing. If you wish to be happy, if you would wish in good faith to be a good man, let one person or another despise you." Epictetus reported favorably on the Cynic aspiration to brotherly love, remarking on their view that "when one is being flogged like an ass, he must love the men who flog him."

These are more than distant echoes of the Sermon on the Mount. They are teachings cut from the same cloth.

The Cynics and popular philosophy even possessed the concept of a kingdom of God, though with no apocalyptic associations. Rather, the phrase was a symbol for the stance toward the world which the Cynics were advocating. The one who ruled over his or her passions was a 'king' in a new domain, living in a different, natural order under special divine rule. This is the very atmosphere conveyed by the references to the kingdom in Q1.

When compared with Q's "rules of the road" (the Q preacher was an itinerant who went from village to village), the practice of Cynic preachers in their wanderings about the empire was almost identical. For both, the divine call necessitated a total break with family and possessions. As noted earlier, the saying in Q 14:27, that a disciple had to "take up his cross" and follow the Master, has been suggested as a Cynic-Stoic proverb, and Rudolf Bultmann thought it might have been used by the Jewish Zealots as well (see Note 70). It signified full submission to a calling of hardship and dedication.

Not only are the sentiments of Q1 similar to Cynic philosophy, the way some of them are presented fit the structure of the Cynic *chreia*. This was a little anecdote about a teacher, consisting of an objection and a response. A famous story about Diogenes took this chreic shape:

> "Diogenes was asked why he begged from a statue. He answered, 'So that I will get practice in being refused.' "

To which one could compare Q's *chreia*-like anecdote:

> "A man invited to follow Jesus said, 'Let me go and bury my father first.' But Jesus said: 'Leave the dead to bury their dead.' "

If taken out of context, Q1 could easily be mistaken for a Cynic product. The passing reference to Solomon and a few other tinges of Jewish provenance could be bits of overlay in the process of adaptation by the Q community.

Mistaken for a Cynic product. But would it be a mistake? We will look more closely at that question when examining Q2.

A Missing Jesus

Another major anomaly arises when we impute Q1 to an historical Jesus of Nazareth. Where, in fact, is this figure? If an historical Jesus was the driving, innovative force behind the movement, the originator of its sayings, the hero and leader of the Q community and presumably regarded as such by the Thomas community, why is his impact not stronger on the original stratum of material? Why *were* there no contexts preserved—or invented—for any of the sayings? Why would a certain degree of hero-worship not lead to incorporating his name, his personality and background, the circumstances of his ministry, into the preserved and transmitted traditions of the community, if only at the stage of writing it down? Why is it that commentators like Crossan must remark that the emphasis in the early Christian tradition is solely on Jesus' words and not on his person? 12-13-15 @ 0945

This void points to an initial *absence* of a figure with whom the sayings were subsequently associated. It points to a message and lifestyle not tied to any originating charismatic individual. If a human Jesus had been responsible for all this, it should have led to a fixation upon him which would surely have found its way immediately into the sayings and anecdotes of a preserved and transmitted tradition. In any case, the wide range of Q1's concerns, the telling and innovative nature of its observations, suggests that it was the product of a movement, not of a lone individual. It reflects the outlook of a group, a lifestyle followed by many. Its expression in finely-tuned aphorisms has the appearance of having been developed and honed over time. It hardly strikes one as the sudden invention of a single mind.

When one compares the Q1 sayings between Matthew and Luke, one finds that in each case the usage of that saying is placed in an entirely different context, with entirely different set-up lines. Take, for example, Luke/Q 17:5-6: "If you had faith no bigger than a mustard-seed, you could say to this sycamore tree, 'Be rooted up and replanted in the sea,' and it would obey you." Matthew, on the other hand, uses the same saying, with minor changes: "If you have faith no bigger than a mustard-seed, you will say to this mountain, 'Move from here to there,' and it will move." It seems unlikely that Q had presented this saying in any context involving Jesus, for Luke places it in Jesus' mouth in response to a request by the apostles to "increase our faith." This scene takes place during Jesus' long journey toward Jerusalem. Matthew gives the saying to Jesus as an explanation for the disciples' failure to cast a devil out of an epileptic boy. His scene occurs in Galilee immediately after the Transfiguration.

The same can be said for the Lord's Prayer. This is arguably the most important and enduring thing Jesus is ever recorded to have spoken. And yet not even this had come to Q attached to a specific setting in Jesus' career. Matthew includes it in the Sermon on the Mount, delivered to vast, attentive crowds. Luke offers it during the journey to Jerusalem, a private communication at the request of the disciples who ask, "Lord, teach us how to pray."

If either of these were an isolated case, one could argue that perhaps one or both of the evangelists had simply changed the context they found in Q, for their own purposes. But when the same diversity of context between Matthew and Luke is found in the case of every single saying in Q1, and in virtually all of those in Q2, we must assume that this is because Q, in these early strata, was simply a list of sayings, with no associations made to a Jesus or his ministry.

There is one exception in Q1. Although the surrounding context is different, within this complex of sayings an identical structure, along with the name "Jesus," appears in both Matthew and Luke (9:57-62):

> "As they were going along the road, a man said to him, 'I will follow you wherever you go.' And Jesus said to him, 'Foxes have holes, and birds of the air have nests, but the son of man has nowhere to lay his head.' To another he said, 'Follow me,' but he said, 'Lord, let me first go and bury my father.' But Jesus said to him, 'Leave the dead to bury their dead. . . .' Yet another said, 'I will follow you, sir, but first let me say goodbye to my family.' Jesus said to him, 'No one who puts his hand to the plow and then looks back is fit for the kingdom of God.' "

This is a set of three *chreiai*, remarks by an onlooker followed by responses from the teacher. Since the set appears in essentially the same way in both Matthew and Luke, we can assume they are copying it as it appeared in Q. Yet if one compares this set to the Gospel of Thomas, we find something very revealing. The only component of the complex to be found in the latter document is #86: "Jesus said: 'The foxes have their holes and the birds have their nests, but the son of man has no place to lay his head and rest.' " Here it is not connected to the other chreic anecdotes, which do not appear in Thomas at all. It is not even a *chreia*, since it lacks the lead-in remark.

It is a reasonable assumption that the Thomas version, being much simpler, is the earlier form, and that the complex of three *chreiai* in Q1 is artificially constructed. The root document, accordingly, would not have contained it. Just when this redacted version was inserted into Q is impossible to say. It would not necessarily have been done at the initial formation of Q1 itself; it could have happened at any time after.

Thus it is possible to maintain that in all likelihood, the name "Jesus" was entirely absent from the original Q1 layer.

Not only have we uncovered a silence in both Q and the Gospel of Thomas concerning anything to do with the Jerusalem Tradition's death and resurrection story, we find that at the bedrock layer of Q there is no sign of a Jesus figure at all. The material itself has a strikingly *non*-Jewish character, in fact a Hellenistic Cynic one. (The same statement can be made about Thomas, considering the possibility that the "Jesus said" introductions are a secondary overlay.) It would be ironic to think that the most important Gospel teachings of Jesus, the very ethical foundations of the Christian religion, were ultimately not the product of a Jewish way of thinking, but of a Greek philosophical movement.

A Fire in the Belly

What further insights can be drawn when we move on to Q2? The change in atmosphere is startling, to say the least.

"This is a wicked generation. It demands a sign, and the only sign that will be given to it is the sign of Jonah."

"Woe to you Pharisees. You are like graves over which men may walk without knowing it. . . . You build the tombs of the prophets whom your fathers murdered."

"Do you suppose I have come to establish peace on earth? No, I have come to bring division."

"There will be wailing and gnashing of teeth, when you see Abraham, Isaac and Jacob and all the prophets in the kingdom of God and yourselves thrown out."

"Hold yourselves ready, then, because the Son of Man is coming at the time you least expect him."

As noted earlier, it is difficult if not impossible to regard the same community, the same set of people—not to mention the same man—as having produced the two sets of sayings, one reflecting an enlightened lifestyle of tolerance, accommodation, mutual respect, trust in a benevolent God, etc., the other a fire-breathing, intolerant outburst of vindictiveness. How best, then, to explain the juxtaposition of the two groups of sayings in the same document?

The explanation that Q2 represents a later time, at which the same group of people are reacting to rejection and hostility, seems inadequate. First of all, it is not merely a case of a different personality and mode of expression. Q2 reflects an apocalyptically oriented mind or community, one which believes in the Son of Man. That type of orientation does not suddenly displace a previous stance of being without it. Furthermore, the message of Q1 is largely self-directed. It is a prescription for the members of a community to follow. It does not of itself seek large-scale conversion of others, especially the rich and powerful. Thus it would be difficult to envision the mindset of Q1 changing into the mindset of Q2 within essentially the same group of people, no matter what the perceived provocation.

The natural conclusion is that the two layers of Q proceed from two different sources. The original collection of sayings represented by Q1 appears to have been adopted by a Jewish (or imitation Jewish), apocalyptically-minded community which first began to preach a kingdom of God in Galilee, perhaps in response to conditions such as those Crossan describes. Somewhere in that formative period, if not at its very beginning, a certain group adopted a philosophy of behavior and an itinerant lifestyle which resembled that of the Cynics, as embodied in a collection of sayings and instructions. It is possible that these were regarded as a suitable ethic and mode of conduct for those who preached and awaited the arrival of God's kingdom, with its intervention of the Son of Man.

This collection came from a non-Jewish source, and perhaps in the adoption it underwent subtle changes. As the sayings found a new home in the Jewish prophetic milieu, they also attracted a new set of sayings—the prophetic expressions of Q2, which reflected the sentiments of the preaching community in reaction to the outside world. How long it took for this to occur is difficult to say. The exact form it assumed at any redactive stage is also impossible to tell, for further revisions still lay ahead. Those further revisions will be the subject of Part Six.

Does Q2 Know of a Founder Jesus?

So far we have called into question the idea that a single person lay at the inception of the Q1 sayings, whether a Jewish Jesus or any other. When Q2 is combined with Q1, does the picture of a Jesus emerge more clearly?

This is more difficult to determine, since after the initial stage of Q2's addition to Q1, it is not always possible to be sure when or where further revision has been made. Q scholars have established a Q3 level, but they do not always agree on exactly what this constitutes, how much revision of older material went on subsequent to Q2. (Kloppenborg sees only one or two units as belonging to Q3, Burton Mack some three or four sayings or complexes.) But the first thing to observe is that, like Q1, many of the sayings of the prophetic Q2 layer seem to have lacked contexts, any specific association with Jesus' ministry or mention of his name. Matthew and Luke incorporate each saying into their Gospels using different lead-in material and placing them at different points in their Gospel story. This leads to the conclusion that they have supplied their own contexts because none were present in Q itself.

For example, compare Luke 11:29 and Matthew 12:38-39:

Luke: "With the crowds swarming around him (Jesus) went on to say: 'This is a wicked generation. It demands a sign, and the only sign that will be given to it is the sign of Jonah.' " Matthew: "At this, some of the doctors of the law and the Pharisees said, 'Master, we should like you to show us a sign.' He answered: 'It is a wicked, godless generation that asks for a sign. . . .' "

Only the saying itself is common between the two. This leads to the conclusion that no context appeared in Q. (As was pointed out earlier in regard to the Q1 layer, one or two cases of this would not be conclusive; but if virtually every case exhibits the same phenomenon, one is permitted to draw a conclusion.) Different contexts, different set-up lines are supplied by each evangelist. If the saying in the quote above, about the generation that demands a sign, is taken by itself, one sees that there is no specific attribution to Jesus, and no setting as part of a story in which it is placed.

Another example. Luke/Q 22:28-30 says that the faithful followers of Jesus will "sit on thrones judging the twelve tribes of Israel." Apparently the apostles who received this assurance did not transmit it in the context in which they heard it. For it appears during the Last

Supper in Luke, but during Jesus' passage into Judea in Matthew. Both are anchored to preceding words which are quite different.

Narration or dialogue in Matthew and Luke involving apostles, Pharisees or onlookers who serve to keep a chain of sayings going as an unfolding scene, are never remotely similar between the two evangelists. This situation holds true for all sayings which can reliably be regarded as coming from either Q1 or Q2. Clearly, Q provided no narrative settings for any of these individual or clusters of sayings. The evangelists appear to have worked with skeletal raw material.

Yet why would such sayings, particularly those considered to be authentic, have been consistently transmitted and preserved with nothing to identify them with Jesus? Why would the Q compilers, especially at the earliest levels when they would have been closer to Jesus' memory, not have developed contexts which involved even his name?

We can only conclude that such sayings were spoken by the prophets of the Q community itself, and only later became attributed to an artificial founder figure. That figure does, in fact, appear in Q3, in the context of a few extended anecdotes, as we shall see in Part Six.

In addition to the lack of settings and identification with Jesus, there are several other indications that no Jesus lay in the background of the Q2 revision.

Luke/Q 16:16 says: "Until John, it was the law and the prophets; since then, there is the good news of the Kingdom of God, and everyone forces his way in." Matthew's version in 11:23 reads: "From the days of John the Baptist until now . . ." Q scholars regard Matthew as closer to the Q original, although both evangelists have adapted the saying to their own purposes and contexts. But consider what is missing. When the saying first originated, the community was looking back over its history. The implied time scale is much too great for it to be claimed as an authentic saying of Jesus, commenting on a year or two of his own ministry. This is Q's picture of the past, a past of years, perhaps decades.

Before the preaching of John the Baptist, now looked upon as a forerunner or mentor to the community's work, the study of scripture formed the prevailing activity and source of inspiration. But a new movement was perceived to have arisen at the time of John: the preaching of the coming kingdom of God, and it had inaugurated an era of contention. But why would Jesus himself not have been seen in this role? Surely the Q community would have regarded his ministry as the turning point from the old to the new. The saying would almost certainly have formed around *him*. At the very least, Jesus would have been linked with the Baptist as representing the time of change.

Q2's picture of its past lacks a Jesus at the critical point where he would be most expected to appear: at the movement's beginning.

Consider Luke/Q 11:49:

> "This is why the Wisdom of God said, 'I will send them prophets and messengers; and some of these they will persecute and kill,' so that the blood of all the prophets, shed from the foundation of the world, will have to be answered for by this generation. . . ."

It seems strange that such a saying would have been formulated with no mention of Jesus. Surely he, the Son of God, or at least the movement's founder and source of its teachings, was the most important of those whom Wisdom had sent. Moreover, as pointed out earlier, this saying reflects Q2's strong emotional focus on the great myth of the time among sectarian groups, that the Jewish leaders had a long history of killing God's prophets and messengers. Yet neither here nor anywhere else in Q is there even an allusion to the persecution and killing of the greatest of these: Jesus himself.

Consider the apocalyptic sayings about the Son of Man. Taken by itself, each of them refers to the Son of Man as an awaited figure who will arrive at the End-time. No identification of this figure is made with the Jesus who is supposedly the community's founder and originator of the sayings. (For example, Luke/Q 11:30: "For just as Jonah was a sign to the Ninevites, so will the Son of Man be to this generation.") If, from the time of the community's formation, the End-time Son of Man was identified with the founder, why does not a single one of these sayings make that identification clear? When a saying like this is eventually placed in Jesus' mouth (in the Q3 stage), he seems to be speaking of someone else, not of himself.

Finally, in the opening units of Q concerning John the Baptist's preaching about the coming retribution, there is no reference to Jesus. Instead, John makes this prediction (Lk./Q 3:16-17):

> "But there is one to come who is mightier than I. I am not fit to unfasten his shoes. He will baptize you with the Holy Spirit and with fire. His shovel is ready in his hand, to winnow his threshing-floor and gather the wheat into his granary; but he will burn the chaff on a fire that can never go out."

Is this a prediction of the enlightened teacher of Q1? Would the Q2 compilers have considered this an adequate representation of their founder and envoy of Wisdom? Or did this saying, when initially formulated, refer rather to John the Baptist's prophecy of the coming Son of Man, the apocalyptic judge who would baptize with fire and perform a ghastly separation of the wheat from the chaff? (The reference to "shoes" does not necessarily imply a human being. In fact, this particular image was a metaphor signifying a slave/master relationship and the vast gulf which existed between the two, and could easily be used in reference to a divine figure.)

This does not mean that John the Baptist would actually have preached the apocalyptic Son of Man, who seems to have been a figure restricted to documents written in the second half of the first century. (Some have suggested that John might have preached the coming of God himself on the Day of Lord in terms such as these.) Rather, this· appears to be the Q community bringing John into its own ranks and imputing to him what they themselves were preaching.

This saying indicates that at the time the material of Q2 was added to an earlier stage of the Q document, the community knew of no historical founding Jesus in its own background. Taken together with the other indicators discussed previously, we see at this juncture in Q's development a landscape devoid of any Jesus figure who had begun the movement, spoken the sayings, or symbolized those prophets sent from God whom an unreceptive world had rejected and murdered. (We will see at the beginning of Part Six just who might have been seen to fill that landscape.)

The Q2 community probably existed in the mid-first century, in the decade or two before the Jewish War, preaching its counter-cultural and apocalyptic message on the Galilean scene at the same time that Paul was tramping the byways of the empire bringing a Hellenistic-Jewish savior god to the gentiles. If the two had sat down together one evening to compare notes, they would have found that they had almost nothing in common.

But that was soon to change. Sometime after the Jewish War was over, Q3 would add an historical founder to its own past, and the Pauline heavenly Christ would put in a guest appearance in a midrashic creation symbolizing the community of Mark. All the details of how these two highly charged ingredients came together may never be known, but the resulting explosion is still being felt.

Part Six
AN EMERGING FOUNDER

17

Introducing Jesus to Q

Wisdom Working in the World

As we saw in Part Five, in the early strata of the Q document it is difficult to detect any clear sign of an individual, much less a Jesus of Nazareth, associated with the Q1 wisdom sayings. Even in the apocalyptic layer of Q2, reference to Jesus is missing in key places. If those early sets of sayings were not yet attributed to a founder Jesus, from what source did the Q community imagine they had come? A recognition of the Cynic philosophy as their ultimate provenance would hardly have been preserved in the community's traditions. They would very soon have been looked upon as possessing a more sanctified—and Jewish—origin.

Has Luke left us a clue as to that new concept of origin? Luke/Q 11:49 starts: "That is why the Wisdom of God said, 'I will send them prophets and messengers . . .' " Matthew renders the entire saying as the product of Jesus: "I send you prophets, sages and teachers . . ." Scholars judge the Lukan version to reflect the Q original, for there seems no reason why Luke would have identified the Wisdom of God as the source of the saying if Q had not already done so.

Could Wisdom herself have been regarded as the source of the community's pronouncements? Instead of "Jesus said," perhaps it was "Wisdom said." As seen in Chapter 9, Wisdom was the personified, communicating aspect of God, an entity who played an important part in Jewish thinking about God's relations with the world. She called people to knowledge of the Deity, his wishes and intentions. Perhaps the Q preachers regarded themselves as her spokespersons, her envoys. Q 7:35 says: "Wisdom is vindicated by all her children."

Perhaps when the initial collection of Cynic-like sayings was adopted by a new Jewish movement preaching the kingdom, they were presented as the voice of Wisdom. This was the common way of thinking within the genre of Jewish wisdom collections of the time, a genre with which the earliest layer of Q shares many characteristics. If Wisdom's words lay at the genesis of the community, why not Wisdom herself as the perceived 'founder'?

That little chink left open by Luke may reveal the entire early landscape of Q, a landscape empty of any Jesus figure at all, peopled by a preaching movement inspired from heaven and working under Wisdom's direction. As she had done throughout Israel's prophetic past, Wisdom—so Luke reveals in 11:49—has sent this culminating wave of messengers to proclaim God's salvation. As in the past, they have received hostility, rejection, even death.

If Wisdom stood as the figurehead of the preaching community for its first few decades, when did a founder Jesus enter the picture? For there does seem to have been a handful of passages in Q which contained him, where he is part of a common contextual element in Matthew and Luke: the Temptation story, the healing of the centurion's servant at Capernaum, the dialogue between Jesus and John, the Beelzebub controversy which involved a healing exorcism. Most Q scholars, from John Kloppenborg on, regard the Temptation story as the very latest addition to Q. Here Jesus seems to be pushed in the direction of divinity—depending on how we interpret the phrase "Son of God." The more advanced character of this episode establishes the principle of a Q3 stratum, though whether such a layer represents a body of material installed—or redacted—all at once or over time is difficult to say.

Because of the void on any Jesus figure in Q1 and Q2, I would suggest that Q3 represents a significant development in the thinking of the Q community: namely, the arrival of a perceived founder who took the place of Wisdom as the instigator of the movement and the originator of the sayings. What indicators can be found for such a proposal?

Preempting Wisdom

The two 'miracle' anecdotes could easily have begun life in the Q tradition as a record of wonder-working by the Q preachers. Some unnamed prophet may have performed a 'healing' on a centurion's servant/son, while the Beelzebub controversy is simply a group of sayings about the *practice* of exorcism and what this says about Satan's power and dominion. The involvement of a Jesus in these two scenes could well be a secondary redaction. In fact, the Beelzebub set is prefaced by a report of the drawing out of a devil from a dumb man, and here the difference in wording between the two evangelists makes it uncertain whether the name Jesus appeared in the Q original or not.

However, the most significant passage which marks the arrival of a Jesus in Q is the dialogue between Jesus and John: Luke/Q 7:18-35.

As we saw in the previous chapter, an earlier passage in Q involving John the Baptist seemed to indicate that the Q community knew of no Jesus figure in its past. Instead, John was made to prophesy the coming of the Son of Man, who would show no mercy and winnow the good from the bad (Lk./Q 3:16-17). But when the community reached the Q3 stage, John the Baptist was given a knowledge of Jesus and the two were brought together.

In Luke/Q 7:18-35, John in prison sends his disciples to ask Jesus if he is the expected "coming one." Jesus points to his miracles and tells those disciples to go back and give John the answer. He then declares to the people that John is more than a prophet, he is Jesus' own herald. Even so, says Jesus, the least in the kingdom will be greater than John. Jesus then offers a parable condemning the people of this generation for rejecting both John with his ascetic message and Jesus with his more liberal one. Yet both approaches are valid, Q suggests, showing that "Wisdom is vindicated by all her children."[75] (See note 75 for a full quotation of this passage.)

This extended scene is a composite one, a pastiche built up out of smaller, earlier units. It has been invented by a Q editor at a late stage of revision. This is indicated by a comparison with the Gospel of Thomas. There, saying #78 reads:

> "Jesus said, 'Why have you come out into the desert? To see a reed shaken by the wind? Or to see a man clothed in fine garments like your kings and great ones? Upon them are the fine garments and they are unable to discern the truth.' " [See Note 71]

This saying in Thomas contains no context or suggestion involving the Baptist. Whether its implication is that those addressed have come out to see Jesus, is uncertain. Originally, it may have referred to some unnamed prophet or teacher—or perhaps to no one in particular. But in Q3, it has been worked, with some variation, into the new scene between Jesus and John:

"²⁴After John's messengers had left, Jesus began to speak about him to the crowds: 'What was the spectacle that drew you to the wilderness? A reed-bed swept by the wind? ²⁵No? Then what did you go out to see? A man dressed in silks and satins? Surely you must look in palaces for grand clothes and luxury. ²⁶But what did you go out to see? A prophet? Yes indeed, and far more than a prophet. . . .' " [NEB]

The saying found alone in Thomas now refers in Q to John, within the context of Jesus' declaration about him. And what of other parts of the dialogue?

The saying in verse 28, that the least in the kingdom will be greater than John, also appears in a little different form in Thomas, again by itself (#46). It too has served as a piece in the Q composite dialogue. The parable in verse 32, the original meaning of which cannot be uncovered, has been pressed into service in somewhat strained fashion, to compare Jesus with John in their failed appeals to a stubborn generation. The original contrast was probably between John and the Q community. Even though John was regarded as a forerunner, his ascetic message seems not to have been embraced by the more liberal Q sect. The latter's lifestyle is now represented by Jesus' own outlook. In any case, says Q, this generation has rebuffed both the ascetic John and the more libertine Jesus.

John's opening question, "Are you the coming one?" might originally have been a question put by people to the Q preachers: Are these the last times? Can we expect the one who is to come—meaning the Messiah, or perhaps the Son of Man—or will there be further delay? Behind verse 22 may lie the community's original response: to quote passages from Isaiah about the poor rejoicing, about the expected signs and wonders that would attend the coming of God's kingdom, the healing of the blind, the deaf, the lame, the dumb. Yes, said the earlier Q, the kingdom was indeed coming, and it pointed to the preaching and healing activities of the Q prophets. In the new version, Jesus points to his own miracles, including the raising of the dead.

The final piece (7:35) in this complex—"And Wisdom is vindicated [proven right] by all her children"—is another indicator of the role of personified Wisdom in the thinking of the early Q community. It too seems to have been a separate saying that provided the punch line for the constructed dialogue. In its new setting it was used to describe Jesus and John, but earlier it may have referred to the Q community. Its members had been Wisdom's children, her spokespersons.

That little punch line also indicates something else. Both Jesus and John are presented as children of Wisdom. Though one was superior in importance to the other—John being relegated to the position of herald—no qualitative difference was envisioned between them. Both were seen as human preachers. Jesus was not touted as the Son of God, something beyond the status of any child of Wisdom. At this stage of Q, he was seen simply as the human founder of the movement. The reference to Jesus in the opening verse as "the coming one" creates a bit of an anomaly, but may simply be something that slipped in because John's preaching of an anticipated apocalyptic figure was so well established. While the phrase has messianic overtones, it is a striking feature of Q that nowhere is Jesus portrayed as the Messiah, and when he is eventually identified with the coming Son of Man (at a later stage of Q3), the link creates an awkward and unresolved incompatibility. This in itself indicates that Jesus is a later overlay.

Reorganizing Q

Thus the outlines of Q development seem clear. In the two earliest stages, no attribution of sayings to a Jesus can be uncovered. The wisdom sayings were probably designated as the words of Wisdom herself. The prophetic pronouncements would have reflected the activities of the Q preachers in general.

At the redaction of the Q3 stage, a handful of units, such as the dialogue between Jesus and John and the Beelzebub controversy, were fashioned from older pieces. A healing miracle previously ascribed to some Q prophet was recast as that of Jesus. And the set of three *chreiai* in which Jesus responds to bystanders' remarks would have been fashioned at this time out of discrete sayings from the Q1 stratum. But the vast amount of previous material would have been allowed to stand as before, though its order was probably rearranged. The whole document may have been provided with a simple heading identifying it as the words of the new Jesus.

Minor internal changes were likely made: the insertion of personal pronouns now that the words were placed in Jesus' mouth, some incidental reworking to reflect his role. The latest stage of the Gospel of Thomas indicates just such a process.

A few larger questions still remain to be answered. Where did the community's idea of a founder Jesus originate? How did such a figure arise in the Q mind if he was not based on an actual historical man? Further, why was he given the name Jesus, which in other circles possessed the full significance of its Hebrew meaning: Savior? For there is no soteriology in Q, no theory of redemption by Jesus. Q does not see its child of Wisdom as a redeeming figure. The Jesus of Q does not undergo a death and resurrection; he does nothing, beyond speak the sayings, to provide salvation.

Finally, what relationship is there between the Gospel of Mark and Q? For while it seems clear that Mark had no Q document to draw from, there are undeniably Q-like elements in the first Gospel. How are these to be explained?

18

Sectarian Developments in Q

Christianity as a Sectarian Phenomenon

One of the most profound and far-reaching insights in the history of New Testament scholarship came during the 1970s.

Previously, the interpretation of Christian origins had largely enjoyed a protected and rose-colored status. The internal workings of the Christian movement, it was claimed, had not been governed by the same forces which invested other religious and social groupings. Christianity was not to be regarded as the product of its time, and more than one scholar made that bold declaration in print.[76] If Paul or Luke issued a dictum on social behavior, if they championed the rituals and practices of the Christian communities, such things had developed within the Christian movement as a result of theological necessity, revealed through the spirit from God or Jesus' own teachings.

Theological correctness, current wisdom said, was permanent and timeless, isolated from its historical origins and ultimately proceeding from the will of God. Nothing in the personal experiences of the great figures of early Christianity, such as Paul or the evangelists, would have disturbed this inspired pursuit of the truth. The Christian movement as a whole had evolved along a path of divine inevitability, uninfluenced by the day to day social and political context around it.

When that snug little balloon was finally pricked, it collapsed immediately. Almost overnight, scholars began turning out books and articles showing that, in fact, the process worked the other way around. Christianity had been a thoroughly sectarian expression. Theological principles tended to be developed in order to justify and legitimate community practice. The religious construct which the movement evolved for itself served primarily to fill its needs as a social group. The way such a group viewed and interpreted its past was entirely determined by its life situation in the present.

The study of Christianity as a sect, one that followed universal rules of sectarian behavior, had finally arrived.

A sect is by nature a group which has set itself up in opposition to the rest of society. Or it has been forced into that position because its reform agenda, its new interpretation of events and of society's guiding principles, has not been accepted by the wider establishment. In this situation of isolation and conflict, the emerging group has to justify its stance, its new view of the world. The first audience at which that justification is directed has to be itself; only secondly is it aimed at the larger world.

The reaction of a sectarian community follows consistent paths. One path looks backwards. Support for the present is sought by a reconstruction of the past. The legitimacy of current faith and teaching, current ritual and practice, is strengthened if it can be shown that such things were there from the beginning; that they were established under divine auspices, in inspiring circumstances, and preferably by an heroic founder figure with a pipeline to the deity. The more inspiring and glorified that past, the greater will be the faith and determination of the present believers. This is especially needed at a time of conflict, or during a later generation when the fervor and loyalty of the initial period may be flagging. In keeping with the broader tendencies of human societies to seek meaning and stability for the present through myths of a sacred, determining past, the sectarian group seeks to sanctify its beliefs and practices by embodying them in hallowed and unimpeachable precedents.

Another path looks outward, beyond the battlements. A strong self-defense is needed for the sect in order to withstand attacks from a hostile environment. Theology is to a great extent determined by that conflict. Again, the rejection undergone by the sect is sanctified by being seen as the reflection of a similar rejection experienced by the founding members or glorified founder figure. Further strength can be gained by portraying that figure as having forecast the present time of troubles and girding his followers for it.

Finally, all these elements of sectarian response require a document in which to be recorded. The account of the community's formation, the story of its founder, his teachings and his example, the events and roots upon which the sect's theology is based: these things are set down in writing in what is known as a 'foundation document.'

Sociologists have shown this to have been an almost universal phenomenon of sectarian expression throughout history and around the world. New Testament scholars who have addressed this question have shown that early Christianity fits this mold like a glove.[77]

A Founder Figure for the Q Community

Does Q1 represent a distinct sectarian phase? To the extent that it reflects a Cynic-like philosophy and lifestyle, it represents a group message that has dissociated itself from the regular workings of society. Although there is no hint of violent contention with an establishment, conflict of some sort can be inferred from the fact that all counter-cultures inevitably experience friction with the mainstream culture. In Q1, there are allusions to alienation from parents and the need to 'take up a cross' to follow the group's way of life.

On the other hand, there is a notable absence of focus on glorified beginnings or a founder figure. Apocalypticism is absent. The kingdom of God being proclaimed seems little more than that found in popular Hellenistic philosophy.

But Q2 is a different case. Here we find a reflection of classic sectarianism. Hostility and reaction, a circling of the wagons. The transition from one to the other is abrupt, the gulf wide. It is difficult to believe that an early phase of the Q2 sect could have operated for a time under the atmosphere and principles embodied in the Q1 sayings. Its prophetic and apocalyptic outlook—which is hardly something that would have been abruptly adopted after a period without it—would imply that hostility should have been encountered almost immediately.

A natural conclusion would be that the essence of Q1 represents a foreign source, whether oral or written, one which first flourished in a non-Jewish milieu. The Jewish preachers of the new movement may have discovered and adopted it, perhaps making minor changes during assimilation, claiming it as the product of Wisdom. It would not have been the first time that Jews had identified pagan writings, or the ideas contained in them, as having an ultimate Jewish provenance.

But where is Q2's focus on the past, or a glorified founder? Here we have an intriguing kind of split. For the Q community, John the Baptist marked the inauguration of the new era of preaching. They had recognized him as a forerunner, if not an actual founder. (Had he been viewed as their founder, they would not have declared him to be of lesser stature than the least in the kingdom.) Still, he validated present teachings by locating them at the movement's inception. He had prophesied what the Q community was now prophesying, especially the coming of the Son of Man.

But perhaps his role was limited because the Q community had from the beginning possessed a proper and glorious founder, one larger than life, with a true pipeline to the Deity. That founder had been

Wisdom herself. With this personified communicating agent of God in place, John the Baptist's role would have been compromised. Luke/Q 7:35 implies that he had been relegated to the status of "child of Wisdom," a designation applied to all members of the Q community.

Ultimately, however, even Wisdom possessed deficiencies as an ideal founder. If she had not actually been on earth, she could only inspire the community and transmit its teachings from heaven. She could not have performed actions which reflected and predetermined those of the community. She had not herself engaged in controversy with the Jewish authorities. Most important, she had not spoken the sect's teachings in the flesh.

But was she about to do so?

It is recognized that several of the Q3 sayings have been recast from earlier Wisdom sayings. The best example is Jesus' lament for Jerusalem in Luke/Q 13:34, which is now thought to have originally been an oracle of Sophia/Wisdom. The hen is a material image for a divine being:

> "O Jerusalem, Jerusalem, killing the prophets and stoning those who are sent to you! How often would I have gathered your children together as a hen gathers her brood under her wings and you would not! Behold, your house is forsaken." [RSV]

Sayings such as this represent a genre of expression which pictures Wisdom as speaking directly to the world, no doubt within a sect like the Q community. It hears Wisdom's voice. Another saying, that 'only the Son knows the Father' (Q 10:22), is another way of speaking of the role of Wisdom, as God's authorized intermediary. That all these things were understood to have been spoken by personified Wisdom may be revealed by Luke's little slip in 11:49 that a Q2 oracle in the same vein as the above lament—messengers sent from God have been rejected and killed—was spoken by "the Wisdom of God." *By the time we get to Q3, all these things are regarded as spoken by Jesus.*

In other words, between Q2 and Q3, Wisdom has evolved into Jesus. In fact, Matthew, in his use of Q, shows a tendency to regard Jesus as the incarnation of Wisdom herself. Was such an outlook already present in the Q document he used: one perhaps Luke did not preserve as clearly because he had not the same interests?

The first step would have been to imagine that Wisdom had appointed a representative, one who had founded the community and spoken her sayings. He had been, as in Q 7:35, her child. Scripture was full of the voice of Wisdom speaking "by the gate." Her myths, in various biblical and apocryphal writings, contained the idea that she had come to earth and sought acceptance. Would a human embodiment of Wisdom not have been a natural development in the Q mind?

Ultimately, the very existence of the sayings collection itself would have induced the community to see it as having been spoken through a human mouth.

The critical requirement of the sectarian mentality is precedence. The Q people saw themselves as the latest in a long line of rejected prophets and messengers sent from God. This child of Wisdom would serve as the one who had first undergone that rejection, who had set the example for fortitude and defiance in its face. It was he who had first argued with the Pharisees. It was he who had made the authoritative pronouncements of faith and practice which continued to guide the community. As for the miracles, there is no question that the Q prophets, as preachers of the kingdom, would have claimed the performance of signs and wonders, for every sectarian movement of the time had to possess that facility. These, especially miraculous healings, were the indispensable pointers to the kingdom. To collect traditions about such miracles and assign them, with due exaggeration, to a founder, would enshrine them in the best possible light.

The Q community's new Jesus would have been a figure instantly recognizable. For he was the glorified embodiment of the Q preachers themselves. This is why he could be neither Messiah nor Redeemer. He could do only what the Q people themselves had done from the beginning, except that he did it better. He opened the door for the entry of men and women into the new kingdom.

Was it really possible for the Q community to believe that such a founder had existed, to interpret the community's evolving record in this way? After the great upheavals of the Jewish War which disrupted Palestine from one end to the other, killing or displacing three-quarters of the population and destroying so much, a denial of any new view of the past could hardly be verified. The question was probably not even raised.

One might wonder why John the Baptist could not have served as an heroic founder. It almost seems that Q2 had been priming him for just such a role. But perhaps he was too familiar. Perhaps it was known that he had not been a wisdom teacher, that he could not have spoken the Q1 sayings. It is also possible that by the time of Q3, a rival sect had already claimed John as its founder. This situation might further have induced the Q community to develop a founder of its own, one superior to John. The Baptist could now serve the secondary role of precursor and herald, one who fitted scriptural expectation. Such a role would, at the same time, put the rivals in their place.

Even Q2 had declared John a herald. But of the Son of Man, not a human teacher. And yet, in the aftermath of the Jewish War, perhaps those shoes John had referred to—which he was not worthy to untie— were seen as belonging to human feet.

When the Q document reached the redacted Q3 stage, it could now serve as a true "foundation document" for a classic sect. All it lacked was an actual biography of the founder. That deficiency would shortly be made up by the Gospel of Mark.

Are there precedents for a wholly invented founder figure? A later Christian Gnostic sect, the Elchasaites, is acknowledged to have probably begun much as did the present picture of Q's evolution. The Book of Elchasai (meaning 'Hidden Power') contained the record of the sect's inaugurating visions and teachings, but it later came to be understood as the record written by a man Elchasai, who had himself been the recipient of this knowledge from heaven. The group known as the Ebionites (the "Poor") seem to have given rise in some people's minds to the figure of "Ebion," if we can judge by the progression from Irenaeus (*Adv. Haer.* I.26,2) to pseudo-Tertullian (*Adv. omnes Haer.*3). As mentioned in the Introduction, the existence of the Chinese philosopher Lao-Tse, the reputed fountainhead of Taoism but about whom nothing is known, has been seriously questioned, as has that of Confucius (see Note 6). So too that of Lycurgus, the Spartan statesman to whom the invention of Sparta's social and political system was attributed. A more modern example is William Tell, a figure associated with the formation of the Swiss Federation in the 13th century. Tell did not put in an appearance in literature until close to 200 years after the event, and he is now known not to have existed.

The historicity of Moses is also far from certain, and even more so is that of older patriarchs like Abraham. The ancient world was full of local and national traditions about gods or semi-divine figures involved in the beginnings of communities and nations, none of whom would seriously be regarded as historical today. Whether a famous legendary figure such as the Greek Heracles could be said to have existed in any form resembling the later mythology about him is highly unlikely, and even if based on a *type* of hero or warrior in prehistoric times, this hardly qualifies him as an "historical figure."

What's In a Name?

One intriguing question in regard to the Q founder remains, and it will lead us to the great crossroads alluded to above, that Mark and the succeeding Gospels may ultimately have served as a biography of the Q Jesus. That question is this: Why was the imagined Q founder given the *name* Jesus?

Why did he appear with the same designation as the divine Lord of the Christ cults and some of those other spiritual Son figures dotting the early Christian landscape? After all, even though the name meant "Savior" the Q Jesus was not regarded as such—except perhaps in a general way, as the Q preachers themselves might be said to offer salvation to those who responded to their message. Would this have been enough?

Or was the term by now so widespread among Jewish sectarian circles across the empire that the offer simply couldn't be refused? This would imply that the Q community, at least by the decade or so following the Jewish War, was aware of the spiritual Christ cults flourishing in the wider world, and thus of the higher significance of the name. If so, did this impel that move toward divinity perhaps discernible in the final phases of Q3?

Another possibility. Could the latest stages of Q coincide with the earliest roots of Mark, allowing for some crossover influence of Mark on Q? Some scholars have speculated that this may have been the case.

But there is another way to approach the question. When Q3 first introduced a founder figure, was he called "Jesus" at all?

Even if the name nowhere appeared in the Q text, even if another designation had been used by the Q3 redactors in passages such as the dialogue between Jesus and John, Matthew and Luke, with Mark's Gospel in front of them, would inevitably have changed it to Jesus.

An alternative possibility. Since Matthew and Luke took up Q to amalgamate it with Mark probably no earlier than the end of the century, and perhaps after the Q community's demise or passage on to other things, some intervening hand may already have altered Q3's original designation for its founder. Who might have done this and why? While Mark is unlikely to have possessed a copy of the Q document itself, he was almost certainly (see next chapter) a part of the general kingdom milieu, and it may not have been too long after the Gospel was written that he or his community came into possession of a copy of Q itself. It may have been at this later time that the crossover influence from a newly-written Mark occurred. That is, the altering hand was someone in the Markan community who saw the Q document as a natural companion to the Gospel of Mark, and altered the name of Q's founder to correspond to Mark's humanized and historicized divine Christ named Jesus.

In fact, did Matthew and Luke each inherit the two documents, Q and Mark, from a common source: the Markan community? Did they arrive by the same post, so to speak?

This is, of course, speculation. But speculation based on a reasoned consideration of the evidence is a valid exercise, and can be used to offer possible explanations where no firm evidence exists. The practice is not unknown in New Testament research generally. There will be more to say on the question of the "Jesus" name and the interaction between Mark and Q in the next chapter.

19

Mark and Q: The Origin of the Gospels

The Construction of Mark

Traditional approaches to the Gospel of Mark have centered on dividing it between the ministry of Jesus and the passion story. Many scholars have postulated that the story of Jesus' trial and crucifixion had an independent existence in early Christian tradition; that it developed over the decades through oral transmission and was perhaps set down in some primitive written form. Mark, when he came to write his Gospel, it is said, took this pre-existing block of passion material, did some reshaping, and then constructed an elaborate preface. He fashioned a ministry out of other units of tradition which were circulating about Jesus but which had few if any narrative elements attached to them. In other words, Mark's teachings, miracles and stories about controversy with the establishment were separate pieces of tradition which he himself organized into a coherent sequence, giving Jesus a ministry which moved from Galilee to Jerusalem and led into the passion account.

Let's consider the arguments against a scenario like this. There is no evidence in the early record itself that the passion as a separate account with an identifiable sequence and set of events existed before Mark.[78] As we have seen, neither its details nor its overall picture can be found in the epistles and other documents of early Christianity, even in those containing a death and resurrection kerygma. It is not found in Q at any stage. As we shall see in Chapter 23, Mark's passion story can be shown to be his own literary construction, based on a biblical precedent. Neither its larger pattern, nor even its individual parts, which make sense only in the context of Mark's construction, can be derived through oral transmission. And virtually all of the story's details are taken from passages in scripture.

The other objection is that those separate units of tradition concerning Jesus' Galilean ministry, the miracles, the controversies, and especially the teachings, are either not to be found in the early record or are not associated with a Jesus figure. Paul's Jesus is never given an earthly ministry, let alone one located in Galilee. The epistles and other documents contain ethical maxims resembling those in the Gospels yet they are never identified as coming from a Jesus. There is a complete silence on any miracles attributed to him, or on conflict with the religious authorities. Even in Q, one is hard pressed to identify any association of these elements with a Jesus in the Q1 and Q2 layers.

Yet Mark did not invent out of nothing. Just as Paul brought new interpretations of his own to the prevailing intermediary Son faith and philosophy, so too did Mark perform an innovative recasting of the ideas and activities which were a part of his own world. All this suggests that we should discard the traditional division of the Gospel of Mark into ministry and passion, and substitute a division which cuts across the entire Gospel: one part based on the Galilean Tradition, the preaching of the kingdom as embodied in Q; the other part on the suffering Savior idea current in the Jerusalem Tradition and preached by Paul (though there is no sign that Mark had direct contact with Pauline activity or writings).

Cutting a Ministry from Q Cloth

It is probably safe to say that in any list of key debates in New Testament scholarship over the last half century, the question of whether Mark had a copy of the Q document is somewhere near the top. Those who argue against it cite the fact that Mark fails to include in his own Gospel virtually all the teachings which Matthew and Luke reveal were present in Q. This includes the radical, often enlightened sayings of Q1 and the powerful apocalyptic sayings of Q2. Though explanations have been offered as to why Mark would deliberately have chosen not to include any of these in his Gospel, such explanations are unconvincing, and all too often reflect oversubtle and sophisticated 20th century rationalizations. The appeal of such material within Mark's own context would have been too overwhelming for him to pass it up. Besides, the echoes of Q that do exist in his Gospel, which everyone acknowledges, are not substantially different from some of the things which he would supposedly have rejected. Thus, it seems safe to say that no copy of Q, at least in a form resembling the one used by Matthew and Luke, rested on Mark's writing table.

On the other hand, it is equally evident that the evangelist must have been familiar with the Q community and its traditions. The ministry of Jesus in Mark is cut from Q-type cloth. Mark's Jesus preaches the kingdom. His ministry is set in Galilee. It is intimately connected at its outset with John the Baptist who is portrayed as Jesus' herald. The nature of the preaching mission, the itinerant activities of the apostles in Mark, is much the same as the Cynic-style activities of the Q preachers. Mark is apocalyptic in the same way Q is. The Son of Man as an anticipated End-time judge appears in both. There are a few sayings in Mark which are almost identical to equivalents in Q. The drawing out of devils is an activity and an issue of contention in both. (Mark has his own Beelzebub scene.) He too condemns his generation for demanding a sign.

Thus the way to regard the Gospel of Mark, in its portrayal of Jesus as a preacher of the kingdom, is that it has carried Q one step further. If Q3, as demonstrated in the last chapter, has added a founder figure to its picture of the community's origins, one who instituted the Q teachings and activities, and if the very latest stage of Q reflects a tendency to provide the new founder with a biography, then Mark has given us the next step in the process. He has taken the 'biographical urge' and run with it.

At this point we need to clarify—or more finely nuance—the meaning of "the Q community" in the context of analyzing Mark. The preaching of the kingdom as epitomized in the Q document extracted from Matthew and Luke was undoubtedly a true "movement." That is, it was not restricted to one specific circle or community. Since an important element on the Q scene is the itinerant nature of the preaching missionaries, it must have covered a certain amount of territory. That territory may have extended outside Galilee and into Syria, for a tangential development on the original Q1 stratum of sayings, the Gospel of Thomas, ended up in northeast Syria. The community of the Didache (late first century), while it has no Q Jesus evident on its pages, is clearly part of the same itinerant prophet movement. It records teachings very reminiscent of early Q. The community of the Didache has also been located in Syria.

Consequently, it is possible to envision a widespread phenomenon covering many communities, not all of which would necessarily possess a copy of the Q document itself, or be as familiar with its elements as those which did. It is thus quite feasible that whoever produced the Gospel of Mark had no Q document to hand and yet was familiar with the general traditions which lay behind it—indeed, was a participant in those traditions. If some of Q's itinerant prophets visited the Markan community, if the Son of Man expectation was vital there, and if those visiting prophets as well as the Markan community leaders themselves were in the habit of employing various sayings such as we find in Q, then we have a state of affairs which could well have produced the content found in Mark.

Thus, we can picture Mark living in a Q-type community where Q-type preaching is part of the atmosphere, but he has no written document to refer to. He is familiar with the most prominent features of the current Q ethos: John the Baptist as the one who had inaugurated the kingdom movement, the expectation of the Son of Man, the healings and exorcisms which prophets everywhere claimed to perform. And he is conversant with the odd saying among those which have been recorded in the Q document.

In addition, it seems likely that he is party to another feature of the Q evolution as well. He is aware that at least some part of the kingdom movement possesses the "memory" of a founder: the same founder recorded in the Q document in its third stratum, the speaker of the sayings, the one who had first engaged the religious establishment in Galilee by proclaiming the "gospel of God" and the arrival of the kingdom. What name for that founder may have been in use at this time, what name was initially recorded in the Q document, cannot be determined. The name Jesus, or Jesus Christ, Mark could have derived from the other dimension he has brought to his "Gospel of Jesus Christ the Son of God," namely the kerygma of the suffering, dying and rising Savior. Certainly, he did not get the designation of "Messiah" (Christ) from Q thought or usage.

The older scholarly estimation that the Gospel of Mark was written in Rome has been to a great extent abandoned. All four Gospels are now generally regarded as coming from the Levant region, either from northern Palestine (including Galilee) or Syria. Burton Mack tentatively places Mark in Sidon or Tyre, but this may be too urban a location in view of the Q content. Some like to claim that the author of Mark did not have an intimate knowledge of Galilean geography, since his Jesus comes and goes in a sequence that does not make sense when plotted on a map. But this is not a serious objection in a story Mark knows is not intended to be history. In any case, we need not locate him too far from Galilee in order to allow for such geographical inconsistencies.

Almost all reconstructions of Q place John the Baptist's preaching of the Son of Man (Lk./Q 3:79) as the first unit in the collection. But a case might be made that it was preceded by another unit involving the more general preaching of John, as reflected in Luke 3:3-6. This unit may even have included, sometime in the Q3 stage, an account of the baptism of Jesus, with the descending dove and the voice from heaven identifying Jesus as God's Son, another touch of biography for the new Q founder. Mark may have drawn upon a knowledge of Q traditions like these for the opening of his Gospel (1:1-15). It has been pointed out that this part of the first chapter of Mark reads like an abbreviation of some longer account.[79]

Indeed, the Temptation Story in Mark (1:12-13) is so short it has almost no substance whatever, and one wonders what Mark thought he was conveying by its inclusion, or on what tradition he could have based it. This little unit is not the sort of thing that would circulate through oral transmission, and is certainly not to be regarded as based on an actual event. In fact, we can tell by Matthew's and Luke's much more involved, three-part story of the Temptation that it was a literary construction based heavily on scriptural precedents. Presumably they got it from Q, though each has made his own personal revision. Mark, not having Q to hand, and perhaps only vaguely remembering something of the sort, has inserted a skeletal distillation of it.

If all this sounds like rather mundane stuff as the genesis of sacred scripture, we must remember that the "sacred" part always comes later, and that most things in life have a genesis in mundane circumstances.

Turning the Q Founder into a Suffering Figure

If Mark's community, as reflected in his Gospel, is a part of the movement evidenced in the Q document, then he has built his picture of the ministry of Jesus on a Q foundation. But he has added a whole other dimension which is found nowhere in Q: a Jesus who suffers, dies and is resurrected.

That dimension is not confined to the appended passion narrative. Mark has worked in passion motifs all through the Q-style ministry which precedes it. To the teachings, the miracles, the controversies with the Pharisees, the apocalyptic expectation centering on the Son of Man—all of which are part of the Q experience and are associated in Q3 with a founder figure—to these Mark has added the passion element as part of the plot line. Thus Mark's Jewish establishment, reacting against Jesus' liberal teachings about ritual purity and Sabbath rules, against his claim that he has the right to forgive sins and generally act on his own authority, conspire to kill him. Mark expands the catalogue of Son of Man sayings which are part of Q's apocalyptic outlook by inventing prophecies by Jesus that the Son of Man (now himself) shall suffer, die and be resurrected (8:31, 9:31, 10:33-34). In the process, he ensured generations of bafflement on the part of modern New Testament scholarship over an "insoluble" Son of Man problem. Mark also associates the Q 'Jesus' with the Messiah and styles him Son of God, although he hedges this association—for reasons still obscure. He has Jesus admonish his disciples, along with assorted onlookers and exorcised demons, to keep such things secret.

Thus the Q founder has not only been given a biography, a family and hometown, a structured ministry in which to place all the elements associated with him in the Q document, he has been linked with the fundamental element of the Jerusalem Tradition. He has been brought to that city to undergo the death and resurrection which had always been part of that Tradition but was never identified with an earthly time and place. As we have seen, this entire other dimension of death and resurrection at Jerusalem, and the preparation for it which Mark has carefully inserted into his pre-passion ministry, are not to be found in Q or any of the wider circle of documents related to it (such as the Gospel of Thomas and the Didache). We are therefore justified in concluding—supported by the literary analysis of the passion narrative to come in Chapter 23—that the link between Q and Jerusalem is Mark's innovation, that no Q founder ever went (or was ever regarded as having gone) to Jerusalem, never got himself executed, and certainly never rose from his tomb.

Mark's Purpose

The great question in all of this is: Why did Mark create such a "Gospel" and how did he present it to his community?

Just as the Q-like picture of Mark's Gospel ministry can only be explained by assuming a certain participation on the part of Mark and his community in the kingdom preaching movement, the death and resurrection dimension to his Gospel must relate to the cultic Christ which people such as Paul were preaching. Mark betrays no intimate knowledge of Paul, and certainly does not reflect any of the distinctive Pauline christology or theory of redemption. His only direct point of contact with Paul may be the deriving of his Gospel's Last Supper scene from the Pauline myth of the sacred meal, the "Lord's Supper" in

1 Corinthians 11:23-26. Even here the connecting route is probably indirect. The words in Mark describing Jesus' establishment of the Eucharist are only roughly similar to those of Paul. This is perfectly in keeping with the haphazard development of a tradition which was not based on an historical event and not common to all early Christian expression. As for the empty tomb story, Mark shows no knowledge of the list of appearances Paul enumerates in 1 Corinthians 15:5-7; instead, he introduces his own characters in the form of the women.

Yet the cultic Christ is an intimate part of Mark's Gospel. Can we presume that Mark's community was a part of this cultic scene, that it shared a Pauline-type faith in a divine Son even if this was not directly due to contact with Paul? (We know of no proselytizing by Paul in Galilee or southern Syria, but he was far from the only one going about preaching the Son.)

One might ask how a Q-type community involved in the preaching of the kingdom had come to put one foot in the cultic Christ camp, especially at a time before any link between the two had been made. But perhaps this was one of those unusual happenings in history, a point of mutation that produces an unexpected swerve into bold new territory. The piece of writing known as the Gospel of Mark would be the consequence of that event, marking the inauguration of a new direction that was to shape the future of the western world.

The alternative is to suppose that Mark himself had come into contact with the cultic Christ movement and decided to link it with his own Q traditions in a new "Gospel." That is always possible (and it would make him the most influential individual in the history of the world—something he may be in any case). But would that personal contact have impelled him to go to the trouble he did, and would his community have accepted his product?

In fact, some of the content of the Gospel suggests that the Markan community as a whole was involved in a type of cultic Christ belief. Commentators recognize that some of Mark's scenes are meant as "lessons" for the community. The triple denial by Peter would show that even someone of the stature of a chief apostle could deny the Lord. The Gethsemane scene held the moral that doubts and fears could beset even the greatest among them. The inclusion of the Pauline sacramental Supper could have served a purpose similar to Paul's own: to provide a mythical precedent for the communal meal practiced by the community. None of these things would Mark have derived from the Q ethos, since they are not to be found there.

In sum, the geographical location of Mark's community, perhaps in southern Syria or northern Palestine, may have brought it into contact with both the Galilean Q movement preaching the kingdom, and the cultic Christ movement which we know was especially strong in the region of Antioch (northwestern Syria). People whose names have been forever lost could well have found both traditions appealing, they could have regarded elements in both as complementary.

One had a great moral teacher of the kingdom, a prophet of the imminent End they were all expecting, one who was identified as a child of Wisdom herself and as the Son of Man who would arrive to establish the kingdom. The other had a divine Son of God who was regarded as the Messiah, who had redeemed the world through a death and resurrection in the spiritual realm. The latter was a cult which also had a communal meal and preached an apocalyptic transformation of the world when their Messiah would arrive from heaven. Why not follow—and even integrate—both?

Nothing could better illustrate the sort of situation in which religious syncretism takes place.

Eventually, making a concrete association between the two must have struck someone as a grand idea. How to do it? By creating a story, a 'new truth' embodied in a symbolic tale constructed through the process of midrash. If the spiritual Christ inhabited scripture and spoke from there, if inspired gospels like Paul's were derived from elements of the sacred writings, what better source for 'details' of an earthly life than scripture itself: not only all those passages which traditionally had been interpreted as referring to the Messiah, but as many others as could be pressed into service? Such a Gospel would combine all the elements, finding parallels between the activities of Christ in the spirit world and the forces he encountered there, and those of the Q movement and its newly-envisioned founder.

Mark cleared his writing desk and started working.

History, the Gospel Jesus and the Q Founder

Could Mark have considered his story to be historically true? This seems highly doubtful, if only because he put it together himself out of discrete pieces and because the passion narrative was constructed out of passages from scripture. We can assume he was not building on any tradition of the Q founder's death in Jerusalem, since no such thing appears in Q, not even in what were probably the latest editions of the document used by Matthew and Luke.

Did Mark present his Gospel to his readership as actual history? That, too, seems doubtful. One could hardly fathom why he would want to perpetrate such a deception. The community would probably realize as well as he the passion's dependence on the sacred writings, and the most experienced among them could undoubtedly recognize midrash when they saw it—unlike most subsequent Christians.

For the Gospel to have been accepted at all implies that its author was a respected leader or teacher within the community, a specialist in scriptural study. His allegorical construction would have served to enhance the faith and understanding of the community in its dual involvement with the kingdom movement and belief in the spiritual redeeming Christ. Before long, that duality would fuse into a multi-layered unity—which is the way even modern critical scholarship, in its Twin Traditions concept, regards full-grown Christianity—and the new religion would be unable to look back over the receding, lost horizon and see its true beginnings in disconnected diversity.

A second question is this. If so much of the Gospel Jesus was an acknowledged fiction, how did Mark—and his community—relate his Jesus of Nazareth to the founder figure we see in the Q document, and with whom we have presumed they were familiar?

Since the community, at least initially, must have recognized Mark's story of Jesus of Nazareth as a symbolic tale of the cultic Christ linked in midrashic fashion with the Q founder, no problem should have arisen. Modern literature has numerous examples of historical fiction based on figures in history, in which the author would never suggest that the actual historical figure had undergone the experiences he portrays in his novel. Yet the author's fictional story line may well be designed to provide an insight into that historical figure's personality and significance, and by extension, our own understanding of ourselves and the world. If this historical novelist were to construct the details of his fictional story line from passages in scripture, we would call his product "midrash."

The Gospel of Mark may have had no greater purpose than this when first set down on paper. As such, it would have rested on the shelf of the Markan community, serving for its edification. But it would not have been regarded as an historical account of an historical figure who had actually undergone death and resurrection in Jerusalem. We might go so far as to say, in view of the lack of post-resurrection appearances in the first edition of Mark, that the latter 'event' symbolized the resurrection after death which the community members themselves could look forward to, as much as it allegorized the spiritual rising after death which the cultic Christ had undergone.[80]

A passing observation. We cannot assume that 'knowledge' of a Q founder was universal within the entire kingdom movement, because we have evidence against such a thing. We have noted before that the Didache, although the product of a community having obvious affiliations with the Galilean Tradition, nevertheless shows no sign of a founder Jesus (see Appendix 8). Not even John the Baptist puts in an appearance.

Most scholars have located the community of the Didache in Syria. If they are right, this would indicate that the kingdom movement was fairly widespread, but that the more specific Q traditions as embodied in the later stages of the written document were not. This silence in the Didache points to the development of the Q founder as being a narrowly-based event, perhaps confined to a circle in close proximity to the group possessing the document.

The Didache does, on the other hand, have a "servant/child Jesus" within its eucharistic prayers (ch.9) who seems to represent a type of spiritual "intermediary Son" idea. This would suggest that syncretism between the kingdom movement and the Christ cult, such as we see in the Markan community, was not an isolated phenomenon.

The Later Synoptics

Such a scenario would fit the development of the later Synoptics, those redactors of Mark. After a certain amount of time had passed—perhaps a couple of decades or so—a knowledge of Mark's allegorical creation spread to other communities, probably in the area of southern Syria. (Matthew is thought to be located here, Luke's provenance is more difficult to estimate.) In two different places, and probably at two different times—Luke is generally regarded as later than Matthew—in communities which may themselves have constituted further examples of Q and Pauline syncretism, two scholars of the scriptures came in contact with the Gospel of Mark and saw its possibilities.

Matthew and Luke also possessed editions of the Q document, with its 'Jesus' figure. Alternatively, as suggested in the previous chapter, the Markan community may in the meantime have acquired a copy of Q, and Mark and Q could have traveled together as complementary documents. One way to regard the Gospels of Matthew and Luke is that they were designed to make up the perceived deficiency created by Mark's failure to incorporate the Q material.

In view of the recasting of Mark by both later writers, incorporating the Q elements and creating a picture of Jesus which served their own purposes, we can assume Matthew and Luke were under no illusions that they were constructing or preserving an accurate record of history. It is possible that they and their communities regarded their Gospels as a general representation of the Q founder, whether they had known of such a figure previously or not. An intriguing question: even if they felt no compunctions about making changes to it, might Matthew or Luke have thought that the passion story of Mark's Gospel was historical?

Matthew carried the midrashic approach to new heights, pointing to Jesus doing this or that in order to fulfill such-and-such a scriptural passage. Again, it is difficult to say whether the evangelist had any concept of history in mind or whether he saw the principle of scriptural fulfilment as symbolic. Scripture was not only the medium which revealed the spiritual Christ, it may also have been seen as prefiguring the community's own experiences. For all the Gospels, at their most symbolic level, represent the faith and reform movement itself.

After a generation had passed following Mark's creation, there were multiple versions of the story of Jesus of Nazareth. Not too long after Luke, another community further north in Syria, possessing a Revealer Son and known later as the community of John, joined the company as well. Thus the scene was set in the wider Christian world for regarding Mark's figure and his story as historical. By this time, the political advantages in regarding them as such would have been compelling, as competing churches sought to ground their own beliefs in something more concrete than inspiration through the Spirit. At the same time, growing communities encompassing people of all walks of life may have felt the need for a more accessible and less esoteric Savior figure. The emergence of the Gospel Jesus of Nazareth onto the stage of history became an unstoppable force.

Dating Mark and Q

When was the Gospel of Mark written? Estimates range from 50 to 150 CE, both ends of the spectrum being equally radical and probably equally unlikely. The commonest date range is within a single decade, 65-75. Such estimates are based almost entirely on Mark's apocalyptic content, particularly the so-called Little Apocalypse in chapter 13.

There Jesus tells his disciples that of the great Temple buildings they are marveling over, not one stone will be left standing on another. Biblical literalists have no trouble envisioning Jesus as possessing true powers of prophecy and forecasting such a thing ahead of time. But the more sober-minded judge that this sentiment did not originate with a Jesus. Rather, it reflects Mark's knowledge of the fact that the Temple *had* been thrown down at the climax of the Jewish War (66-70). Or it suggests that Mark wrote shortly after the war's onset, and he did not need to be clairvoyant to see that the Romans would prevail and punish the Jews by destroying their Temple.

The most serious problem with the pre-70 scenario is that chapter 13 as a whole suggests that its author is allowing for the passage of a certain amount of time *after* the war before the End finally arrives. But it is unlikely that anyone of Mark's mindset, witnessing in the year 67 or 68 the build-up to the approaching cataclysm, or the disintegration of the Jewish situation as the Romans invaded Palestine and encircled the city, would not have been caught up in the drama of the moment and been convinced that the End, with the arrival of the Son of Man, was just around the corner. There would have been no motive or impulse to postulate any further delay.

That the delay occurred seems obvious in 13:5-13. Jesus' prophecy of false Messiahs best applies to the time between the war and the end of the century. To judge by some of the epistles, it was during this period and even beyond that discord within Christian communities was most active, with one faction calling another "antichrist" and warning of those who were leading people into false doctrine. Even in the Gospels of Matthew and Luke, such issues are still very much alive, and no serious scholar dates either of them before the year 80. In Mark 13:7, Jesus says that even after battles near and far, "the end is still to come." He talks of great wars between nations, of earthquakes and famines. In verse 10 he says: "Before the end, the Gospel must be proclaimed to all nations." This was a condition probably not even Mark would have considered fulfilled by the time of the Jewish War. The woes, the persecutions, the false Messiahs producing signs and wonders and misleading the faithful, these were part of the mythology of the coming age, its "birthpangs." All of this is yet to begin.

Thus it would seem that Mark's Jesus is accounting for a certain amount of time that has already passed after the war, during which the End has not arrived, though the atmosphere in the Markan community is that it can be expected some time soon. We know from the wider evidence that apocalyptic expectation was still rampant toward the end of the century. Revelation written in the 90s is evidence of that. Certain Jewish documents coming in the aftermath of the war, such as 4 Ezra, contain their own apocalyptic outlook, and these are not likely to have been fully written within only a few years. The legend that the emperor Nero was not dead but would return with armies from the east, the so-called *Nero redivivus* myth, must have required some time to develop after his death in 68. This myth seems to have been going strong in the latter years of the Flavian regime in the 90s.

Thus Mark's strong apocalyptic flavor is as consistent with a date around 85-90 as it is with one around 70. By way of analogy, historians a few hundred years hence would be guilty of a similar misconception were they to date every 20th century document which spoke of the fear of nuclear war as coming from the period of the Cuban missile crisis in 1962. That may have been the high point of such fears, but we know that they extended throughout the Cold War.

There are those who point out that Mark has Jesus promise (13:30) that "this generation will live to see it all," an encouragement to his community that the arrival of the kingdom and the Son of Man must be imminent. Certainly, 50 or 60 years is the outside time within which such a prediction made around the year 30 could still have had legitimacy. Yet if Mark were creating only a symbolic Jesus within a midrashic tale, such a limitation would not apply.

Another factor tending to keep Mark within the bounds of the first century is its close relation to the Q ethos. Dating the different strata of the Q document is notoriously difficult, though most Q scholars judge the bulk of it as pre-Jewish War.[81] In the Q2 prophetic layer, as in the warnings delivered to places like Capernaum, there is no suggestion that widespread destruction on the scale of the war has already occurred. Yet one element in Q seems to have the war behind it: Luke/Q 13:35. "Look, there is your house [meaning the Temple], forsaken by God." This may look back to a prophecy in Jeremiah 22:5, but it sees that prophecy as now fulfilled.

This verse is evidently a Wisdom oracle taken from some unknown wisdom book. It has been placed in the founder's mouth in the Q3 stratum. We don't know if the earlier version, when it was imputed to personified Wisdom, spoke in terms of an unfulfilled prophecy. If not, then even parts of the Q2 'Wisdom' stratum could be post-70.

If Q3 can be located in the decade or two after the Jewish War, when did the Q community or the movement as a whole die out? One might say that apocalyptic expectation *never* dies out, as we well know today, and millenarian ideas (the expectation of a thousand-year reign of the Messiah) were flourishing into the second century—as in

Papias—and beyond. If the Didache's provenance and dating near the turn of the second century is correct, a Q-type milieu still existed in Syria at that time, although elements of the Christ cult were creeping in. Beyond that point, the specific Q ethos is in evidence only in the later Synoptics.

If Matthew and Luke, based on a suggested dating of Mark around 85-90, are to be located within the first two decades of the second century,[82] this means the Q document still existed by that time, since they made use of it. But by then the Galilean-style kingdom movement, more than half a century old, may have run out of steam, and the Q document could have been its surviving legacy.

To return to the dating of Mark. If we place the first Gospel too early, especially in the 50-70 range, this creates the grand anomaly that no evidence of the possession of Gospel documents within the wider Christian world can be perceived for at least 75 years after the first one was penned. Quotations from written Gospels do not appear before the middle of the second century, in the writings of Justin Martyr and possibly the little epistle 2 Clement. (See Chapter 24 for a survey of the lack of knowledge of written Gospels in the writings of the Apostolic Fathers.) Even though we have allowed for the likelihood that the Gospels rested for a generation or two within the small circle of communities where they were produced, this long an interval seems difficult to accept. My own estimation of Mark as written toward the year 90 is partly due to a compromise between these considerations.

One also has to regard Ignatius of Antioch's very limited biographical data about Jesus as the first sign of a 'leakage' of ideas from Mark's creation beyond the immediate area where it was produced. Since Ignatius never appeals to a written Gospel to support his accusations against those who deny his basic biography of Jesus, we can assume he had not encountered a copy of such a document. Ignatius' letters, written during the overland journey to his death in Rome, are traditionally dated in the first decade of the second century. While that dating has been called into question (as part of a more radical dating of the Gospels to the mid-second century) I regard it as defensible. Thus, dating Mark around 90, with Matthew following perhaps a decade or so later, would mesh with Ignatius, living some distance further north, hearing the echoes of such writings some time early in the second century and finding the idea of an historical Christ an appealing concept. We must remember that he was part of a Son of God faith movement which had no central organization and no network of common doctrine and communication. A slow, patchy spread of the Gospel idea over succeeding decades makes sense, since it would be going against the established state of Christian belief (of the cultic Christ type) which did not have an historical Jesus.

Taking Stock of the Q 'Jesus'

Today, those who recognize that the Gospels' tenuous hold on historical reality has been broken by modern critical scholarship tend to voice a particular fallback alternative. Even if the Jesus of Mark's Gospel is entirely a fiction, they ask, even if the events of Jerusalem never happened, no trial before Pilate, no crucifixion or resurrection, even if there was no human figure lying at the genesis of the faith movement Paul was a part of, is it not conceivable that the Q Jesus was real, that there was a preaching rabbi in Galilee who said *some* of the things imputed to him in the Q document, but who never presented himself as the Son of God, never offered himself as a Savior much less the Messiah? Was he simply a teaching sage who sought to lead people into a more down-to-earth version of the long-awaited kingdom of God, and someone—such as Mark—linked him to the Christ cult?

Good question. However, in reviewing the evidence, we find that the early layers of Q contain strong indications that no Jesus figure was known at that time: passages which pointedly make no mention of him, the lack of hero-fixation that such a founder should have generated, the void even on his name in the early strata. The extended anecdotes concerning him are demonstrably later constructions. Indeed, if the later stage of Q was amenable to recording such anecdotes embodying Jesus' name and a touch of biography, why was early Q not so inclined, especially at a time when the memory of the preaching founder would have been closer and stronger? It is in the early stages that we would expect to find such things.

We might also ask whether it is feasible that the conglomeration of different types of sayings in the final Q document could at each step of the way be imputed to the same founder figure. It is one thing to reach the situation where a body of 'anonymous' sayings has been collected, and after the passage of time it is decided that they all must have originated from some figure in the past. Sectarian impulses often lead to such a development, and we can see examples of that sort of thing in history: in the collection of centuries of prophetic/kingly/priestly law in Jewish history imputed to the legendary figure of Moses, or in the intricate political and military system of the Spartans, developed through more than a century to deal with their overlordship of vast numbers of Helot serfs, imputed to the mind of one Lycurgus.

But it is another thing to imagine that as each new phase was reached, and newly occurring or acquired sayings were added to an older set, the Q compilers and their audience could simply impute them to the same Jesus. Even if the precise order of elements in Q is still less than securely established, there are strata which can be confidently declared sequential, or as proceeding from different sources. To say that the community was capable of adding, as it came along, each new element to the pile as the product of their founder, seems to require a greater degree of self-deception than one could accept.

Considering the movement as a whole, if a prominent teacher stood at its genesis, as speaker of a seminal body of sayings, that teacher should be a given in all the expressions of the movement found in the documentary record. We have seen that the Didache stands in some line with the Q community, yet the figure of a teaching, miracle-working Jesus is not to be found there. Revealingly, the Didache includes a body of ethical maxims which are often very similar to the Q1 sayings, and yet there is no attribution to a Jesus figure. This in itself indicates that their association with a Jesus in the Q document is a separate or local development, one the Didache did not share in, and that the introduction of a founder figure in Q came later than the Didache community's own tangential development. In the Gospel of Thomas, Jesus' hold on the sayings is tenuous, being limited to little prefaces which could well be secondary additions. Jesus made so little impact on the Thomas community that not even a primitive integration of him with the material itself, such as we find in Q3, was effected. Nor is there any trend toward biography in Thomas.

This review of the evidence provides strong indication that there was no Q founder in the initial stages of the movement, but that he was later added by some of the communities involved on the larger kingdom scene.

Further evidence will be added when we come to examine the references to Jesus in the works of the Jewish historian Josephus. Suffice to say for the moment, Josephus cannot support the fallback position on the existence of a Q Jesus, since his 'Testimonium' centers on the claim that Jesus was crucified by Pilate, a feature which the fallback position concedes has been relegated to Mark's Gospel fiction.

Part Seven

THE NON-CHRISTIAN WITNESS TO JESUS

20

Jesus Among Jew and Pagan

The Pagan Witness

After the silence on Jesus in the Christian documents themselves, the silence in the non-Christian writings of the first century may seem anti-climactic, but it is an important corroborative element within the puzzle picture. Even when references to Jesus start to appear in the second century and later, within both Jewish and Roman writings, these can be seen to be unreliable or inconclusive.

Much of the Gospel story has been relegated to fiction by recent critical scholarship, but if a genuine Jesus existed and had an impact which set the beginnings of a world religion in motion, we would have to presume that some features of his career, climaxing in an execution in Jerusalem, would have some basis in reality. Otherwise, the rise of Christianity as it is traditionally viewed would be inexplicable.

Consequently, for historians of the time, Jesus and the religion he began should have constituted a noteworthy event in the period of the early emperors. It is difficult to believe that he would have escaped the attention of at least some Jewish commentators. Nor was Palestine a backwater part of the empire, whose happenings were of no interest to those living beyond its borders. The land of the Jews lay in a strategic location on the route to Egypt. It was part of the bulwark against the hostile Parthians to the east. Its troubles seemed unending and its rebellious spirit must have been the source of many an imperial sleepless night on the Palatine. The two "Jewish Wars" which the empire fought to put down that rebellious spirit were Rome's heaviest military campaigns during the entire era. In the half century of escalating turmoil leading to the fall of Jerusalem in 70 CE, Judea was under a spotlight whose glare lighted up the whole eastern empire.

We should also remember that the Jews were a presence in their day unlike any other. Their Diaspora communities extended to every major city and many smaller ones. As a social group the Jews kept themselves separate and consequently visible. They maintained close ties with their homeland. The religion of the Jews was a focal point of interest in much of pagan society, and whether they were expressing admiration, resentment or ridicule, things Jewish were a going topic for many a Roman writer, poet and satirist.

If among these we begin our quest for the non-Christian witness to Jesus, the pickings are extremely slim. The first century philosopher Seneca (died 65 CE), the greatest Roman writer on ethics in his day, has nothing to say about Jesus or Christianity—even though Christians after Constantine made Seneca a secret convert to the faith and invented correspondence between himself and Paul. A little later, the Stoic philosopher Epictetus (c55-c135) espoused a "brotherhood of man" doctrine, aiming his message at the poor and humble masses (he was a former slave himself). But he had apparently not heard of his Jewish precursor. The historian Arrian preserved some of Epictetus' lectures but records no mention of Jesus. Book IV of his Discourses contains a bare remark about "Galileans" who meet death fearlessly, but we cannot be sure if this refers to Christians who preferred to die rather than sacrifice to heathen deities, or to Jewish Zealots in their political struggles with Rome. Epictetus' ethical views are so like those imputed to Jesus that some older scholars, such as Douglas Sharp in 1914 (*Epictetus and the New Testament*, p.136) seriously questioned whether he might have been a Christian.

In his witty epigrams, the satirist Martial (died c103) depicts the most diverse characters of his contemporary Rome, but Christians who believe in the deity of a crucified Jewish preacher are not among them. Martial's younger colleague Juvenal (died 138), a poet of broader and more bitter invective, also gives us a vivid picture of the foibles and fools of the empire's capital in his day, but he has no barbs for Christians either. The first of the satirists to pillory Christians is Lucian, who in the 160s wrote *On the Death of Peregrinus* in which he mocks them for their gullibility in accepting beliefs "without any sure proof." Here he refers to "him whom they still revere, the human fellow who was crucified in Palestine for introducing this novel cult to the world." By this time the Gospels were in circulation, and everyone knew what Christians now believed about their origins.

Epictetus' reference to "Galileans," if this means Christians, tells us nothing about whether the object of their worship was mythical or historical, and the same is true for a famous reference by Pliny the Younger contained in a letter to Trajan around the year 112. Pliny was prosecuting local Christians in the province of Bithynia in Asia Minor where he was serving as governor, and he writes to the emperor for advice on how punitive he should be with these obstinate fanatics who refuse to invoke the traditional gods, including the divine emperor. He tells Trajan that they seem to have "met regularly before dawn on a fixed day to chant verses alternately amongst themselves in honor of Christ as to a god," and to assemble later to take food "of an ordinary, harmless kind." Even subjecting them to torture, Pliny found "nothing but a degenerate sort of cult carried to extravagant lengths." We might have expected Pliny to refer to the "Christ" as a man crucified in Judea as a rebel, if that were the object of Christian worship, for this would have been unusual and of some interest to the emperor. However, he does not. In any event, any information Pliny is imparting or implying in this letter he has received from Christians.[83]

Pliny's uncle, Pliny the Elder, was a Roman writer on natural history. As part of a voluminous writing career, he assiduously collected reports on all forms of phenomena in nature, such as eruptions, earthquakes and all manner of astronomical events. (He was to meet his own death by suffocation when he ventured too close to observe erupting Vesuvius in 79 CE.) The elder Pliny recorded even legendary events, believed in by cultic or popular myth, such as the comet associated with Caesar's birth, events which he himself may not have regarded as factual. Yet he makes no mention of prodigies associated with the beliefs of Christians: no earthquake or darkening of the skies reputed to have occurred at the crucifixion of their founder, nor any star of Bethlehem that was supposed to have marked his birth. (Since Nero is reported to have had Christians executed in great numbers after the fire of 64, one might presume that Pliny would have been familiar with the sect.)

Popular Christian mythology is very likely the source of the first pagan reference we do find to Christ as a man executed in Judea by Pontius Pilate. The Roman historian Tacitus tells us in his *Annals* (Book 15, chapter 44) written around 115, that Nero, to dispel the rumors that he himself had ordered the city of Rome torched, produced substitute culprits, "a class of men loathed for their vices, whom the crowd styled Christians."[84]

Tacitus goes on in that passage of the *Annals* to give us a one-sentence background to the Christian movement:

> "Christus, the founder of the name, had undergone the death penalty in the reign of Tiberius, by sentence of the procurator Pontius Pilate."

Is Tacitus quoting an official record of an obscure crucifixion in Judea almost 90 years earlier, something he consulted in a Roman archive? This is highly unlikely. The Romans may have been famous for their efficiency and governmental bureaucracy, but that a record of every one of the countless crucifixions and executions they indulged in across the empire to maintain the peace resided for decades in some department in Rome is near impossible. We know of no record-keeping on such a scale. (As the scope of Jesus' activity and impact is reduced by modern scholars, to accommodate among other things the silence about him in the contemporary record, the chances that the Romans made a record of this particular execution is thereby reduced in turn.)

Was Tacitus a meticulous researcher? G. A. Wells points out (*The Jesus of the Early Christians*, p.187) that at least one modern historian has said that Tacitus was not in the habit of consulting original documents. In that very sentence about Christ, he refers to Pilate as "procurator." As Wells notes, this was the title of the post in Tacitus' day, but in the reign of Tiberius such governors were called "prefect." Had the historian consulted an archive, the record might have corrected his anachronism.

It is reasonable to suppose that, for this passing reference to an incident in his account of the reign of Nero, Tacitus simply reproduced what Christians of his day, those living in Rome or perhaps in the province of Asia which he governed a few years before writing the *Annals*, were beginning to say about their presumed founder. The bishop of Antioch had been executed in the arena scarcely ten years earlier. Might we speculate whether Ignatius could have brought to the Roman Christians the new conviction that the birth, passion and resurrection of Jesus had "truly" taken place "in the days of Pontius Pilate"? Tacitus would have had no compelling reason to check on this statement, and indeed no efficient way of doing so. Norman Perrin, in his *Introduction to the New Testament* (p.405), admits that Tacitus' information was probably based on police interrogation of Christians.

Suetonius is another Roman historian, writing around 120, who is assumed to have referred to Christians, this time in Rome during the reign of Claudius (41-54 CE). But his brief mention (*Lives of the Caesars*, Claudius, 25) is open to interpretation:

> "(Claudius) expelled from Rome the Jews who, under the influence of Chrestus, did not cease to cause unrest."

Who is "Chrestus"? Is this a misspelling of "Christus"? An unknown Jewish agitator with a very common name? Are these Christians at all, or simply apocalyptic-minded Jews anticipating the arrival of the Messiah? Is this figure supposedly on the scene, or is he merely the object of the agitators' beliefs? There is too much uncertainty here to take this as evidence of anything. Even if Chrestus refers to Christ, the original situation may have related to Roman Christians who followed a mythic Christ. Though we cannot tell from the passage itself, by the time Suetonius came to write he, too, may have been influenced by Christian hearsay in Rome about the reputed founder of the movement.

Obscure references in obscure historians such as Thallus and Phlegon, to supposed eclipses which may or may not be identified with some tradition about the darkness at Jesus' crucifixion, have in any case reached us exclusively through the filter of later Christian commentators. Origen and Julius Africanus may well have put their own spin on what the historians actually said; Africanus comes to us only second-hand. No case can be made based on references like this, and it is a mark of how thin the evidence really is that they would be considered of any evidentiary value.

The Jewish Witness

Does the Jewish side of the non-Christian record fare any better?

The Jewish philosopher Philo of Alexandria lived and wrote into the 40s of the first century. The foremost city of Egypt (and second in the empire) had the largest Jewish community outside Palestine. It was a center of Jewish learning, much of it reflecting the absorption of Hellenistic philosophy. Philo himself adapted Middle Platonism to the Jewish bible and created an allegorical picture of the universe and its workings. Alexandrian Jewish philosophy was, if not the father, the paternal uncle of much Christian thinking about the spiritual Christ. Philo was a mystic and not apocalyptically oriented, but the mythological transformation to which Christians are presumed to have subjected Jesus of Nazareth could not have failed to catch his attention over the 10 or 20 years he would have lived past the crucifixion. His writings show an interest in unusual sects like the Therapeutae and the Essenes, but of Jesus and the Christians he has nothing to say.

Justus of Tiberias was a Jewish historian writing in Galilee around the year 80, whose works have not survived to our day. But as Wells points out (*The Jesus Myth*, p.204), Photius, the Christian patriarch of Constantinople, had this to say on reading Justus' books in the 9th century: "This Jewish historian does not make the smallest mention of the appearance of Christ, and says nothing whatever of his deeds and miracles."

We can judge the references to Jesus in the Jewish Talmud as having no historical value. First of all, even though some remarks are attributed to rabbis who flourished around the end of the first century (none earlier), they were not written down before the third century or later. (Rabbinic tradition was entirely oral until about 200 CE.) Conflict with the Christian movement during the intervening period, during which the Christians themselves had developed an historical Jesus, could well have led to inventions and alterations in such Jewish references based on these new developments. Besides, a third or fourth century Jew would have been in no better position than a Christian to deny the already firmly established misinterpretation of the Gospels, nor can a later record of what first century rabbis were supposed to have said be regarded as any more reliable than the later Christian witness about many of its own first century traditions. There was also in medieval times a certain amount of censorship and emendation to the Talmudic manuscripts in the face of Christian persecution.

In any case, the Talmudic references are either so cryptic or off the mark that their identification with the Gospel figure is at best doubtful. One makes him the son of a Roman soldier, another presents him as a magician. He died by stoning in Lydda at Jewish hands, says one rabbi. (If not even Jesus' death by crucifixion was established in Jewish tradition, it is hard to see how any of it can be considered meaningful.) Another Talmudic mention places him a century later than Herod, and still another during the period of the Maccabean kings around 100 BCE.[85] Such things are hardly based on historical memory or reliable tradition. On wisps such as these, proof for the historical existence of Jesus cannot be based.

21

Flavius Josephus

In any survey of the non-Christian witness to Jesus, the Jewish historian Flavius Josephus occupies center stage. In fact, analyzing the two passages in the surviving manuscripts of Josephus which contain a reference to Jesus has become a major industry in the debate over his existence.

A young Joseph ben Matthias (he was born about 37 CE) fought in the Jewish War of 66-70 as a commander in Galilee, but was forced to surrender to the Roman general Vespasian. Recognizing the inevitability of Rome's rule, he threw in his lot with the enemy. He predicted—correctly—that Vespasian would become emperor, and spent the balance of his life in Rome as a client of the Flavian (Vespasian's) family. There, under the name Flavius Josephus, he wrote his two great histories, the *Jewish War* and the *Antiquities of the Jews*. Although he was mistrusted and even regarded as a turncoat by his fellow Jews, he attempted in his writings to serve as an apologist for the Jewish people. He died some time after 100 CE.

Soon after taking up his position in Rome, Josephus issued his first account of the Jewish War, that paramount catastrophe of Jewish history in which Judea was laid waste, much of Jerusalem was leveled, and the Temple and its sacrificial cult were destroyed, never to be reconstituted. *The Jewish War* was written in Aramaic for use in the east, designed to discourage further revolt against Rome. That initial version has been lost. It was followed not long afterward by an account in Greek of the same events, this time for a Greco-Roman readership. Josephus then spent the better part of two decades writing his nation's history, a free paraphrase of the Hebrew bible's historical books, with additions from other sources. The *Antiquities of the Jews* was issued in the year 93-94.

For modern historians, the works of Josephus have been the single most valuable source of information on first century Palestine, yet it is quite probable that we owe their survival through the Middle Ages to the Christian copyist or copyists who inserted those two passages about Jesus in the *Antiquities*, likely in the second or third century. That 'witness'—the first and longest passage is called the *Testimonium Flavianum*—was treasured by Christians for centuries, with the result that Josephus enjoyed a privileged position in the priorities of the medieval preservers of ancient non-Christian manuscripts.

Are those two passages in fact forgeries? Despite the efforts of modern commentators to protect them from dissolution under the light of examination, a good case can be made for saying that Josephus wrote nothing about Jesus and was probably unaware of any such figure. As in all matters of historical research, it may be very difficult to "prove" that Josephus made no reference to Jesus. But if the claim that he did so can be sufficiently undermined, or if one can demonstrate that both passages are unreliable or even unlikely to be his product, then at the very least they are removed from contention and cannot be used to discredit the argument, based on evidence within the Christian record itself, that there was no historical Jesus.

The *"Testimonium Flavianum"*

In Book 18 of the *Antiquities of the Jews* (18.3.3, or 18:63 in the alternate numbering system), one small paragraph follows an account of several misfortunes visited upon the Judean Jews by Pontius Pilate; it is followed by reports of certain scandals of the time in Rome, one of them involving Jews. In its present form, the paragraph reads:

> "Now about this time there lived Jesus a wise man, **if one ought to call him a man**, for he was a doer of wonderful works, (a teacher of such men as receive the truth with pleasure). He won over many Jews and many of the Greeks. **He was the Messiah.** When Pilate, upon hearing him accused by men of the highest standing among us, had condemned him to be crucified, those who in the first place had come to love him did not forsake him. **For he appeared to them alive again on the third day, as the holy prophets had predicted these and many other wonderful things about him.** And the tribe of the Christians, so called after him, continues to the present day."

It has been obvious to modern commentators for some time that Josephus could not have written the passages in bold type, since this would mean he subscribed to Christian doctrine. The line in brackets about the "teacher of truth" is also suspect. But what about the remainder? Could Josephus have written this 'distilled' Testimonium?

One common argument in favor is that such an "original passage" contains phrases and vocabulary characteristic of Josephus. But if a Christian copyist were seeking to create a convincing interpolation, he would try to employ Josephan fingerprints to make it appear authentic; and if he were introducing ideas similar to those expressed elsewhere in Josephus (such as the term "wise man" or "tribe" in the sense of a sectarian group) he would have precedents to draw on. If he were someone who worked with the manuscripts of Josephus on a long-term basis, such imitation might well become second nature to him.

Another standard argument in favor of a Josephan original is that if a Christian had constructed this passage in its entirety, he would not have limited himself to something so short to describe the career of his Savior. This argument can be set aside, for it would have to be applied to the scribe who supposedly added the extra elements to the presumed original. Why didn't *he* make his insertions longer? We cannot know the answer to either alternative.

G. A. Wells and others have argued that the continuity of the flanking passages works best when no passage about Jesus intervenes. The final thought of the previous paragraph flows naturally into the words of the one following, whereas the opening of the latter paragraph does not fit as a follow-up to the closing sentence of the Testimonium. This argument is somewhat tempered by the fact that since the ancients had no concept of footnotes, digressional material had to be inserted into the main text, as there was nowhere else to put it. However, one might ask whether the Testimonium should be considered digressional material, since it continues with the theme of Pilate's activities and about various woes which befall the Jews. One might also suggest that, digression or no, once Josephus had written it, his opening words in the subsequent paragraph ought to have reflected, rather than ignored, the paragraph on Jesus.[86]

Supporters of a Josephan original have pointed out that the distilled Testimonium has virtually no Gospel flavor, whereas the latter would be expected if these lines too were from a second or third century Christian interpolator. The miracles are only "wonderful works," the Jews are not overly demonized, the "winning over many Greeks" is not a feature of the Gospel picture. A number of explanations could account for individual points, but generally speaking, a good imitator of Josephus might be expected to avoid making it sound as though the passage is based on the Gospels. At the same time, the absence of any reference to the resurrection—even a skeptical one—in the "authentic"

Testimonium is an acknowledged problem. It is hardly likely that Josephus would have been ignorant of this central claim of the Christian faith, and even less likely that he would not have wanted to inform his readers of the Christians' outlandish belief that their founder had walked out of his tomb. On the other hand, one might postulate that bits of Josephus' original account of Jesus were dropped, and were replaced by the new Christian material.

The arguments thus far could conceivably go either way. However, there are two larger considerations which, in my opinion, tip the scales against the possibility that Josephus could have penned the present Testimonium, even in reduced form.

Witness to the *Testimonium Flavianum*

Most commentators who argue for an authentic original reconstruct it along these lines:

> "Now about this time there lived Jesus a wise man, for he was a doer of wonderful works and a teacher of such men as receive the truth with pleasure. He won over many Jews and many of the Greeks. When Pilate, upon hearing him accused by men of the highest standing among us, had condemned him to be crucified, those who in the first place had come to love him did not forsake him. And the tribe of the Christians, so called after him, continues to the present day."

This is invariably described as a "neutral" account. But such an evaluation is not realistic. A passage which describes Jesus as "a wise man" who "performed many wonderful works," who "won over many Jews and gentiles," who was perhaps a "teacher of the truth," cannot be described as neutral, and would hardly be viewed as such by Christians. And yet, the startling fact is that during the first two centuries when such a passage is claimed to have existed in all manuscripts of the *Antiquities of the Jews*, not a single Christian commentator refers to it in any surviving work.

This includes Justin (mid-second century), Irenaeus (late second century), Tertullian (end of second century), Clement of Alexandria (same), Origen (early third century), Cyprian (mid-third century) and Arnobius (late third century).

All these apologists are intimately concerned with defending Christianity against pagan hostility, yet not one of them draws on what may have been the sole example of a non-negative comment on

Christianity by an outsider before Constantine's conversion. If a figure of the stature of Josephus had said the things contained in the alleged "authentic" Testimonium, can one really believe that every Christian commentator for over two centuries would regard nothing in it as worthy of mention?

There is so much in this "neutral" account that Christians could have 'put a spin on' in defense of themselves and Jesus, so much that could have provided succor, support and even ammunition for what the Christian apologists were attempting to do in their writing. Origen alone spent a quarter of a million words contending against Celsus, a pagan who had written a book against Christian beliefs some half a century earlier. Origen draws on all manner of proofs and witnesses to the arguments he makes, including referring to Josephus. In Book I, chapters 46, 67 and 68 of *Contra Celsum*, Origen reports that Celsus had disparaged the miracles of Jesus, accusing Jesus of having learned his wonder-working tricks from the Egyptians. Origen counters this by claiming that Jesus' deeds were superior to anything contained in the Greek myths, and that Jesus performed his miracles in order to win people over to his commendable ethical teachings, something no Egyptian trickster could emulate. An appeal here to the declaration by Josephus, a respected Jewish historian, that Jesus had been a "wise man" who performed "wonderful works," would have served to place Jesus and his miracles in the favorable light in which Origen is trying to cast them.

The first sign of the existence of the *Testimonium Flavianum* comes with Eusebius, the church historian who wrote early in the fourth century. He quotes the passage exactly as we have it now, with all the pro-Christian elements intact. (Some have suggested that Eusebius himself may have been the originator of this passage.) From Eusebius' time and for the next 13 centuries, no one in Christendom doubted that Josephus had written that Jesus "was the Messiah."

John Meier (*A Marginal Jew*, p.79) offers a questionable explanation for the blanket silence on the Testimonium before Eusebius. Meier's argument is that the Christian Fathers would have recognized that Josephus did not accept Jesus as Messiah and Son of God, or believe that he had risen from the dead. The Testimonium witnessed to Josephus' unbelief and was therefore avoided. But should the apologists have found this disconcerting in a non-Christian? They dealt with unbelief every day, faced it head on, tried to counter and even win over the opponent. Justin's major work, *Dialogue with the*

Jew Trypho, did just that. Origen, in his own confrontation with Celsus, did not shy away from criticizing Josephus for attributing the fall of Jerusalem to God's punishment on the Jews for the death of James, rather than for the death of Jesus (see below). In fact, Origen refers to the very point which Meier suggests Christian commentators shied away from, that Josephus did not believe in Jesus as the Messiah. It hardly seems that the silence on *Antiquities* 18.3.3 by all the apologists prior to Eusebius can be explained in this way.

And what of that statement by Origen, that Josephus did not accept Jesus as the Christ? It is often claimed that it constitutes an oblique reference to an original Testimonium which was silent on such a thing. But rather than assume that Josephus' *silence* on the matter would impel Origen's comment, we should look for some *positive* piece of information in Josephus which might lead Origen to make such a statement. A good candidate is Josephus' declaration in *Jewish War* 6.5.4 that the Jewish messianic prophecies were really about the victorious emperor Vespasian. This statement might well have been sufficient to prompt Origen's comment that Josephus did not believe in Jesus as the Messiah.

Could Josephus Have Written the "Authentic" Testimonium?

Apart from the silence in the Christian commentators before the fourth century, there are other considerations which discredit the idea that Josephus could have penned even the reduced *Testimonium Flavianum*. But first, we can discount the fallback position which suggests that Josephus might have said something entirely negative about Jesus and Christianity, and that this was completely replaced by the Christian passage. Had Josephus said something hostile, it is very likely that someone such as Origen would have chosen to rebuke it. As noted above, Origen more than once makes negative comments about things he has read in Josephus, and there is no reason to think he would not have had something to say about an antagonistic passage in *Antiquities* 18.

Thus we are left with the claim that the reduced Testimonium is authentic, and that Josephus therefore knew of Jesus' existence. And yet the entire tenor of such an "original" *does not ring true for Josephus*. In the case of every other would-be messiah or popular leader opposed to or executed by the Romans, he has nothing but evil to say. Indeed, he condemns the whole movement of popular agitators and rebels as the bane of the century. It led to the destruction of the

Temple, of the city itself, of the Jewish state. And yet the 'authentic' Testimonium would require us to believe that he made some kind of exception for Jesus.

On what basis would he do so? If Josephus had possessed an intimate knowledge of Jesus, leading to some favorable estimation of the man that was markedly different from his usual attitude toward such figures, we would expect much more than the cursory account in *Antiquities* 18. The latter, in fact, amounts to little more than a bare summation of basic Gospel elements. In any case, most commentators conclude that Josephus had little familiarity with Christianity, so such an explanation would have to be discounted. Would Jewish sources have provided a favorable account of Jesus' teachings or activities? Hardly, and certainly not by the 90s, when Jewish leaders were laying anathemas on the Christians. Some raise the possibility that Josephus' information came from "official Roman records," but such a record would have been even less likely to present Jesus in a positive fashion.

Why, then, would Josephus have made an exception for Jesus? Did he have reports of Jesus' teachings, all of which he perceived as laudable? That is difficult to envision. By the late first century, if we can judge by the Gospels and even scholarly reconstructions of Q, any commendable teachings of Jesus would have been inextricably mixed with all sorts of inflammatory and subversive pronouncements and prophecies of a revolutionary and apocalyptic nature—whether authentic to Jesus or not. The latter would have been an expression of the very thing Josephus hated and condemned in all the other popular agitators of the period. It would be difficult to postulate a situation in which his knowledge of Jesus the "teacher" could have been so selective as to screen out the objectionable elements that would have been attached to him as well, and thus we are justified in concluding that *it is impossible that Josephus could have referred to Jesus as "a wise man."*

When we consider the phrase "(he was) a teacher of people who receive the truth with pleasure," which Meier (*A Marginal Jew*, p.61) and even Crossan (*The Historical Jesus*, p.373) regard as authentic, the claim for authenticity becomes intolerable, for how could Josephus refer to a man to whom all the various Christian expressions and expectations would have been attributed—including the destruction of the world—as a "teacher of the truth"?

The same objection applies to the phrase "a doer of wonderful works"—or even the possible alternative translation of "surprising" or "startling works." Such a phrase, in Josephus' mind, would have placed Jesus into the same class as those popular agitators such as Theudas the magician who promised to divide the river Jordan so that his followers could cross over it, or the unnamed Egyptian who claimed his command would knock down the walls of Jerusalem. Would Christian or any other reports filter out the healings (which Josephus could perhaps have accepted as believable or laudatory) from Jesus' reputed miracles over nature, or his Gospel prophecy that the walls of the Temple would tumble?

The very presence in the Testimonium of the phrase "wonderful works" indicates that some of Josephus' report would have been based on traditions about miracle-working by Jesus. This rules out a 'private pipeline' to some authentic picture of an enlightened sage. Instead, it opens the door to the possibility of a wide range of reports about dramatic and even revolutionary acts by Jesus, such as we find in both Q and the Gospels: working miracles in front of large crowds, challenging and condemning the religious authorities, or causing an uproar in the Temple. (If the story of the cleansing of the Temple were factual, such an incident would not have escaped Josephus knowledge, nor his reporting.) Factual or not, if such traditions were circulating about Jesus, this from Josephus' point of view would have brought him into association with the Zealotic rebels, bandits and general crazies who had infested the land of Israel prior to the great War and were most responsible for its devastating ruin. Could the historian have presented this Jesus in even a "neutral" way, could he have regarded him in any other light than just another detestable fanatic?

To judge by the Christians' own record in the Gospels and even some of the epistles, "the tribe of the Christians" toward the end of the first century was still a strongly apocalyptic one. It expected the overthrow of the empire and established authority, along with the transformation of the world into God's kingdom. What would have led Josephus to divorce this prevailing Christian outlook—for which he would have felt nothing but revulsion—from his judgment of the movement's founder?

The report in Tacitus, the persecution witnessed in Pliny's letter to Trajan, the *birkat ha-minim* (curse on the heretics) of the Jewish synagogues after Jamnia,[87] all testify to the hostility and vilification which Christian sects endured at this time. Yet an acceptance of the reduced Testimonium as authentic assumes that Josephus, alone of all our non-Christian witnesses, took an opposite stance. It assumes that when all about him were expressing condemnation, he could imply approval and even a touch of admiration for Jesus and the Christian tribe which "had come to love him and did not forsake him." For this is the overriding sentiment that emerges from the reduced Testimonium.

The final point to be stressed in this connection is that Josephus was writing under Flavian sponsorship. His readers were primarily Roman, some Jewish. What reason would he have had for being, in Meier's phrase, "purposely ambiguous"? He had nothing to fear from Christians, and no reason to consider their sensibilities. Regardless of what he may have thought about the character of Pilate, if Pilate had executed Jesus, then there had to have been—in official Roman and Flavian eyes—a justification for doing so. Crucifixion was a punishment for rebels, and Jesus' crucifixion would have been seen as part of Rome's ongoing campaign to deal with the problems of a troubled time in a troubled province.

Yet how, in the reconstructed Testimonium, does Josephus deal with the event itself? The words and their context give the impression that the crucifixion was due to "an accusation made by men of the highest standing among us," that this was the execution of a wise and loved man, a teacher of truth who was obviously innocent. Nothing could better reflect the Gospel image. But that would mean that Pilate had acted improperly, or that he had been misled or coerced by others. There could be no basis on which Josephus would be led to interpret the event this way, much less put it in writing for a Roman audience. There would have been no channel through which such a judgment would come to him that he would have accepted. And no way he could have avoided explaining himself if he did.

In his *Life* (65/363), Josephus declares that the emperor Titus himself "affixed his own signature to them [copies of the original Greek edition of the *Jewish War*] and gave orders for their publication." Josephus wrote at the behest of his Flavian patrons. Their motives were his motives. The official Roman outlook was largely his own outlook, at least where the War and the events which led up to it were concerned. The *Testimonium Flavianum*, in any version, makes no sense within such a Josephan world picture.[88]

The Galilean vs. the Jerusalem Jesus

In view of modern scholarship's division of Christian beginnings into two separate spheres of response to Jesus, further observations on the reliability of the *Testimonium Flavianum* are in order.

In any location outside Palestine and Syria, all the evidence concerning Christianity in the latter first century relates to the cultic expression of the Pauline type. Here Jesus is the cosmic Son of God, creator and sustainer of the universe, source of salvation through his death and resurrection. That evidence, as we have seen from writings like the pseudo-Pauline epistles, 1 Clement, Revelation, the Shepherd of Hermas, the Odes of Solomon, has nothing to say about the Galilean side of things, about the ministry as portrayed in the Gospels—nor about Jesus' death under Pilate.

If we can assume that Josephus, writing in the 90s, would reflect views of Jesus current in Rome at that time, how do we explain the fact that his "original" Testimonium says nothing about the cultic Christ of Paul, the redemptive Son of God who was an exalted divinity? Such cosmic descriptions and claims about the Son as are found in the first century epistles would have been a part of the Christian ethos which Josephus was exposed to. (Paul addresses the Roman congregation in those terms, indicating that this is the way Roman Christians regarded Jesus. 1 Clement, written in Rome and contemporary with Josephus, speaks in similar terms about the spiritual Christ.)

If Christians were going about talking of their founder in terms familiar to us from the epistles, this elevation of a crucified criminal to the very status of divine Son of the God of Abraham would hardly have been ignored by Josephus. For Josephus was intimately concerned with his Jewish heritage, its traditions and beliefs. The natural affront to Jewish sensibilities in the fundamental Christian doctrine about Jesus, its blasphemous association of a human man with God and the bestowing on him of all God's divine titles, would have received the closest attention from the historian, and inevitably his condemnation.

Nothing in the "authentic" Testimonium breathes a whisper of the Pauline Son of God. Instead, it sets its sights no higher than the Gospel-like picture of a remarkable sage who was crucified and gave rise to a new movement. With the addition of the resurrection, this is essentially Mark's amalgamation of Q with a passion narrative. This absence of any dimension relating to the cultic Christ is further evidence that the Testimonium is a product of second or third century Christian outlook, one in which the Gospel picture predominates, while the earlier cosmic Christ has receded into the shadows behind it.

In regard to the Jesus of Q, there are two ways of looking at the question. One is that if Josephus is writing history—however briefly— and the Jesus he is addressing was the founder (under whatever name) of a movement as extensive as the record makes it out to be, from Galilee through Syria, this should be reflected in what Josephus says. If Jesus had inaugurated a widespread counter-culture movement which prophesied the end of the world and delivered an innovative philosophy of life, and Josephus knew of him in that role—even if not to the extent of knowing what was "genuine" to this teacher—that role should have been reflected in the original Testimonium. Instead, the Jesus described there is simply an isolated figure, a "wise man" and a miracle worker. Apart from the difficulties in regarding this as Josephus' own evaluation, such an account would scarcely have done justice to the man who had presumably set so much in motion. (In the absence of a known founder figure, Josephus' silence on the subject of the movement itself may be understandable.)

We might note that Josephus presents another figure of lesser stature (in terms of the influence imputed to him) in much greater detail than the "authentic" Testimonium presents Jesus. This is John the Baptist (*Antiquities of the Jews*, 18.5.2). But if Josephus could know of and describe a figure like John, would he have been likely to neglect a proper treatment of the man who had given rise to the entire Q phenomenon? We should also note that not only does Josephus make no connection between John and Jesus, or between the Baptist's preaching and the Galilean kingdom movement, he places his account of John several chapters *later* than the point where the paragraph on Jesus is located. This also places John amid events of a period which lies too late (c34-37) to be able to include the standard dating range for the ministry and death of Jesus.[89]

The second way of looking at the question is even more telling. If Josephus were speaking of a Jesus who was supposedly the founder of the Q movement, and in view of the conclusion reached in Part Six that the story of the Markan Jesus is fiction, Josephus would not have been able to include the fact that he was crucified by Pilate, since no such event would have happened. Even the reduced Testimonium represents the *Gospel* picture, not an actual "wise man" who many today presume lay behind the Q document and the Q movement.

Thus, the picture of an "authentic" *Testimonium Flavianum* is further discredited, both by its failure to reflect the cultic Christ elements that would have been current among Christians in Josephus' Rome, as well as by its failure to present Jesus as he should properly have been portrayed by any historian of the time—as the founder of the kingdom of God movement in Galilee and beyond.

The Brother of Jesus, the One Called (the) Christ

The argument against the second passage referring to Jesus, in *Antiquities of the Jews* 20 (9.1), is more subtle and requires a consideration of external factors. This is the passage and its context as it now stands:

> "But the emperor, when he learned of the death of Festus, sent Albinus to be procurator of Judea. . . . But the younger Ananus who, as we have already said, had obtained the high priesthood, was of an exceedingly bold and reckless disposition. . . . Ananus, therefore, being of this character, and supposing that he had a favorable opportunity on account of the fact that Festus was dead and Albinus was still on the way, called together the Sanhedrin and brought before them **the brother of Jesus, the one called (the) Christ** [*ton adelphon Iēsou tou legomenou Christou*], James by name, together with some others and accused them of violating the law, and condemned them to be stoned. But those in the city who seemed most moderate and skilled in the law were very angry at this, and sent secretly to the king, requesting him to order Ananus to cease such proceedings. . . And the king, Agrippa, in consequence, deprived him of the high priesthood, which he had held three months, and appointed Jesus, the son of Damnaeus."

Let's consider the matter in point form:

(1) All manuscripts show essentially the same phrase. But we have nothing earlier than the 10th century, and by then one of the universal tendencies in manuscript transmission, that all copies of a well-known passage gravitate toward the best-known wording, as well as toward the inclusion of the passage itself, would have ensured that this reference to Jesus in its present form would long since have been found in all copies.

(2) On the surface, the phrase about Jesus serves to identify James. This inclusion of an identifying piece of information, say those arguing for authenticity, is something Josephus does for most of his characters. True enough, but this does not necessarily make the present phrase the original one. Josephus may have said something else which Christians subsequently changed. Or he may have written nothing. If he knew nothing else about James or chose to say nothing more, he would simply have used some equivalent to "a certain James" or "someone named James." And what in fact do we find in the Greek? The words referring directly to James are: *Iakōbos onoma autōi*. Translations

render this "James by name" or "whose name was James" or "a man named James." Such a phrase could have stood perfectly well on its own (with a slight change in grammatical form), and had the reference to a brother Jesus added to it by a Christian interpolator.

Without the reference to Jesus, the passage makes good sense and does not jar within the context. The passage is not about James—much less about Jesus. It is about the high priest Ananus and his fate. Ananus was deposed because he had executed "a man named James and certain others," an act which incensed some of the moderates among the influential Jews. The reader did not need to know anything else about those who had been stoned.

(3) The actual reference to Jesus contains a couple of suspicious features. One is that the key phrase, "him called (the) Christ" (*tou legomenou Christou*) is identical—except for being in an oblique case—to the one which concludes Matthew 1:16: *ho legomenos Christos*. The same phrase appears in John 4:25. These appearances in early Christian writings identify the phrase as one in use by Christians. Thus it could have been chosen by a Christian copyist inserting a phrase into Josephus, especially under the influence of its appearance in Matthew, the most popular Gospel from the mid-second century on.

The frequent translation of "*tou legomenou Christou*" as "the so-called Christ," with its skeptical and derogatory overtone, is in no way necessary, and is in fact belied by the usage of the same phrase in Matthew and John where it obviously cannot have such a connotation. The word *legomenos* is found in many other places in the New Testament without an implied derogation. Those using the term in their translations of Josephus betray a preconceived bias in favor of his authorship.

The second suspicious aspect of the reference to Jesus is that it comes *first* in the text. That is, the passage reads: "(Ananus) brought before them the brother of Jesus, the one called Christ, James by name, together with some others . . ." Why would Josephus think to make the *Jesus* idea paramount, placing it before the James one? James is the character that brought about Ananus' downfall, while mention of Jesus is supposed to be an identifying afterthought. It would have been much more natural for Josephus to say something like: "(Ananus) brought before them a man named James, who was the brother of Jesus, the one called (the) Christ . . ." On the other hand, if the phrase is the product of a Christian scribe, it may be understandable that he, consciously or unconsciously, would have given the reference to Jesus pride of place.

(4) As in the case of the *Antiquities* 18 passage, it is often claimed that a Christian scribe would have taken the opportunity to offer more about Jesus than a single phrase. But this is not a compelling argument. An interpolator would have recognized the limitations he faced. In a tightly-packed account of James' death and its repercussions on Ananus, there would have been no scope for an extended digression about Jesus. It would have destroyed the passage.

(5) In the *Antiquities* 20 reference we actually have a double identification: one for James, that he was Jesus' brother, the second for Jesus, that he was the one called the Christ. But would Josephus have been likely to offer this identification for Jesus? First of all, it implies that the historian had explained just what "the Christ" was at some previous point. (His readership was a Greco-Roman one, who would not be expected to have much familiarity with the idea.) The fact is, he has not, and certainly not in the *Antiquities* 18 passage, where the declaration "He was the Messiah" is rejected as a later and obvious Christian insertion.

Moreover, the entire Jewish tradition of messianic expectation is a subject Josephus seems to avoid, for he nowhere directly describes it, not even in connection with the rebellious groups and agitators in the period prior to The Jewish War. (His one clear reference to the messianic "oracles" of the Jews, the object of whom he claims was Vespasian [*Jewish War* 6.5.4], is in a different book, and is dealt with in very cursory fashion.) This silence and apparent reluctance would seem to preclude the likelihood that Josephus would introduce the subject at all, especially as a simple aside, in connection with Jesus.

In any case, if Josephus were merely looking for some quick way to identify this Jesus for his readers (one of many by that name in his chronicle), he would have a much easier, and less charged, way to do so. He would simply have to say, "the one who was crucified by Pilate." This is a point which it is claimed *did* appear in the "original" passage of *Antiquities* 18, one that would have been easily remembered by the reader. If Josephus had written the "authentic" Testimonium, with no reference to the Christ, the point about Pilate would have been the inevitable choice. (This ignores, of course, the consideration that no such crucifixion by Pilate actually took place.)

(6) It is possible that "brother of Jesus, the one called (the) Christ" began as a marginal gloss. Its shape and character would fit a notation in the margin made by an early copyist to supply an identification which Josephus lacked, a copyist bothered by the fact that the historian

had made no such link. Following the usual process, the margin notation would later have been transferred into the text itself.

This possibility, however, may be rendered unnecessary by the following scenario.

The "Lost Reference" to James and Jesus

In Origen three times and in Eusebius once, there appears the statement that Josephus believed that the calamity of the Jewish War (66-70) and the fall of Jerusalem was visited upon the Jews by God because of their murder of James the Just. This murder is briefly recounted in the *Antiquities* 20 passage we are considering, but the reader will note that no mention is made there of such an idea. We can discount the possibility that Origen has a copy which *does* show it, since the later Eusebius quotes the *Antiquities* 20 passage, and it is still not there. We must assume, therefore, that Origen and Eusebius have read it somewhere else in Josephus.

Here is Eusebius' quotation, in his *History of the Church*, 2.23.22:

"Josephus has not hesitated to testify this in his writings, where he says, 'These things happened to the Jews to avenge James the Just, who was a brother of Jesus the one called (the) Christ. For the Jews slew him, although he was a most just man."

Like Origen, Eusebius does not identify the location of this statement. Since no such thing can be found in any of our copies of Josephus, in any part of the *Antiquities* or *Jewish War*, we must assume that, wherever its location, it later disappeared or was removed. Note that this lost reference contains exactly the same phrase as the one in *Antiquities* 20, "brother of Jesus, the one called (the) Christ."

Was such a statement about the reason for the fall of Jerusalem authentic to Josephus, or was it a Christian insertion? If we consider Josephus the author, he was giving either his personal opinion or a current Jewish opinion. Both have been asserted by various scholars. But there are problems with either alternative.

Origen brings up the 'lost reference' to criticize Josephus for not saying that it was because of the death of *Jesus*, rather than of James, that God visited upon the Jews the destruction of Jerusalem. But more than half a century earlier, the Christian Hegesippus had said the same thing. As preserved in Eusebius, Hegesippus witnesses to a Christian view of his time (mid-second century) that it was indeed the death of James the Just which had prompted God's punishment on the Jews.

Now, if Josephus witnesses to a Jewish tradition that the murder of James had resulted in the fall of Jerusalem, why would Christians have subsequently taken over that view, rather than react as Origen later did and change it to the death of *Jesus*? Quite apart from that, why would Jews have adopted such a view in the first place? If James was a prominent *Christian* figure and brother of a supposed subversive who had been crucified, why would non-Christian Jews give him such an honor as to believe that God had wreaked upon them the greatest calamity in Jewish history simply because of his death? Moreover, this would imply that Christianity, and by extension Jesus' own status, *was supported by God*. Would Jews have believed such a thing? Hardly.

Would Josephus himself have subscribed to such a view? He would no more accept the implications just stated than would the Jews in general. Moreover, the blanket phrase "the Jews slew him" is too uncompromising. It contradicts Josephus' own account in *Antiquities* 20 with its very limited responsibility for the death of James. He would hardly have envisioned God punishing the entire Jewish nation for a murder he himself portrays as the action of an upstart high priest, a man whom other Jews promptly condemned and caused to be removed. In any case, had Josephus subscribed to such a tradition as is found in the lost reference, he would surely have provided his readers with a fuller, more laudatory account of the "one named James" over whose death God had destroyed the Jewish state and leveled his own holy Temple to the ground.

Finally, Josephus provides ample evidence of his own view of the cause of the calamity. Throughout the *Antiquities* he condemns the entire revolutionary movement beginning with Judas the Galilean (in 6 CE) for laying "the foundations of our future miseries" (*Ant.* 18.1.1). And while he can speak (with an eye on his Jewish audience) of God acquiescing in the destruction of city and Temple as a means of purifying them from the defilement caused by the actions of the Jewish Zealots, he is not likely, when writing for gentiles under Flavian patronage, to attribute the fall of Jerusalem to the motivations of the Jewish God using the Romans as a pawn for his purposes.

We must conclude that the lost reference, with its idea that God punished the Jews for the murder of James, is a Christian product, and an interpolation into a manuscript of Josephus. (Robert Eisenman, *James the Brother of Jesus*, p.395, suggests it was in the *Jewish War*.) Hegesippus witnesses to a widespread view of this sort among Christians in the mid-second century. But there is a very telling corollary to this. Why did those earlier Christians *not* impute the calamity to God's punishment for the death of Jesus, since to the later Origen—as well as to us—this seemed obvious?

The explanation is simple. The need to interpret the destruction of Jerusalem would likely have developed early, even before Hegesippus. At such a time, *an historical Jesus and historical crucifixion had not yet been invented*, or at least would not have been widely disseminated beyond a few early Gospel communities. Thus the idea would not have existed in the broader Christian world. Instead, James the Just, head of a prominent sect in Jerusalem which believed in a spiritual Christ, murdered by the Jewish high priest just before the War, would have been the natural, and perhaps only candidate available. And although the idea of an historical Jesus was under way by Hegesippus' time, the force of the original tradition about James' death might still have been operating, to be supplanted by the concept of Jesus' role only later. We find the first clear idea of it in Tertullian (*Adv. Jud.* 13) at the end of the second century. Origen a few decades later expresses his dissent with the old view (*Contra Celsum* I, 47; cf. 4:22).

This implies that the 'lost reference' must have been inserted into manuscripts of Josephus at a relatively early period, certainly within the second century. Any later than that, and the copyist would likely have reflected Origen's view, that the fall of Jerusalem was due to the death of Jesus, not of James.[90]

Certain consequences seem clear. The phrase "the one called the Christ," is demonstrably Christian in nature. Since the reference to Jesus is virtually identical in the two places, and one can be shown to be part of an interpolation, this increases the probability that the other is an interpolation as well. Because the insertion in *Antiquities* 20 is shorter and less essential to the context than the lost reference, the former is more likely to have been a copy of the latter. A Christian scribe, interpolating an entirely new passage into *Jewish War*, is not likely to have gone to the *Antiquities* for a phrase to describe James. He would simply have come up with one of his own.

Wells has an interesting observation to make. He suggests (*The Jesus Myth*, p.220) that if the phrase "the brother of Jesus, the one called (the) Christ" is an interpolation, we have no way of verifying that the "James" Josephus refers to is in fact James the Just. The man could easily have been some other "*Iakōbos*," murdered in Jerusalem in 62 CE, who was not a Christian. This would eliminate a problem, for two nagging questions have always lurked behind the *Antiquities* 20 reference. Why did Josephus not identify James more fully as an influential leader of the Christian sect, and why would important Jews of the city be so incensed over the murder of a Christian that they would agitate for the deposition of the High Priest?

A later Christian copyist, possibly influenced by the lost reference, might have made the assumption that the James in *Antiquities* 20 was indeed James the Just, brother of Jesus, and placed the phrase identifying him as such into the text. Or he may have placed it in the margin, from which point it was later inserted into the text. The copyist's assumption could have mirrored one that was already being made by Christians in general about the identity of the "one named James," making later traditions about the death of James the Just, as found in Eusebius' record of Hegesippus, simply fanciful elaborations based on the new reading of the phrase in *Antiquities* 20.

In view of all the arguments against the likelihood of authenticity for the reference in *Antiquities* 20, the reliability of this second pillar of the Josephan witness to Jesus collapses along with the first.

An Earlier Silence

There is one final observation to be made. In the section on Pilate in the earlier *Jewish War*, written in the 70s, Josephus outlines the same two incidents with which he began chapter 3 of Book 18 in the *Antiquities of the Jews*, incidents which caused tumult in Judea during the governorship of Pilate. In the *Antiquities*, these descriptions are immediately followed by the Testimonium about Jesus. In *Jewish War* (2.9/169-177) no mention of Jesus is included.

One is further intrigued by a similar situation in Tacitus. While the later *Annals* contains the passage about Jesus as a man who had "undergone the death penalty in the reign of Tiberius by sentence of the procurator Pontius Pilate," an earlier work in which Tacitus summarizes the reign of Tiberius contains no mention of either Jesus or Christians. In the *Histories* (5.9.2) Tacitus merely says that in Palestine at this time, "all was quiet."[91]

A coincidence? If the silence on Jesus in the earlier works of both Tacitus and Josephus casts doubt on the authenticity of their later references, then we have truly lost every clear non-Christian reference to Jesus as a human being before the latter half of the second century.

III : A COMPOSITE CHRISTIANITY

It would be interesting to speculate on the life and personality of the man who put together the world's most influential book. But we have so little to go on. Compared to the later Gospels, Mark is a bare-bones effort. Flashes of insight, touches of literary genius catch our eye as we make our way through this the simplest and crudest account of Jesus' life and death. Yet there is hardly enough to get a sense of the writer behind it. By contrast, a portrait of Matthew offers much richer potential, even if the personality that emerges is not an endearing one. It would also be interesting to know how long Mark outlived his moment of creation. Was he around to see his symbolic character and story take on a life of their own? Might he have come in contact with men like Ignatius who insisted to his face that yes, there was a Jesus Christ born of Mary and crucified by Pilate? Would he have set them straight? Perhaps he even came to believe it himself.

Once the Gospel of Mark is approached from the viewpoint that this is a literary creation from start to finish, using the building blocks of the Galilean and Jerusalem Traditions, the pattern of the construction becomes evident. Part Eight will examine in turn those Twin Traditions as used in Mark. Chapter 22 will survey each of the distinctive elements in the ministry of Jesus, its inauguration under John the Baptist, its teachings and apocalyptic preaching, miracle traditions and controversies with the religious authorities. It will identify each and all as features of the kingdom community's own experience and practice.

Chapter 23 turns to the second component of Mark's Gospel, the passion story, to show that in its broad outline it conforms to a recurring precedent found throughout centuries of Jewish writing: the tale known as the Suffering and Vindication of the Innocent Righteous One. This large scale overview passes to the fine detail of the trial and crucifixion scene, showing how so many pieces of it are taken directly from passages in the Psalms and Prophets. Through the process of midrash, Mark cut out verses from here and there and installed them as ready-made elements and details of his story. Other features and characters are invented plot devices to further the course of events.

Part Nine moves on to the second century. How much do the Apostolic Fathers in their surviving writings know of the Gospels and their content? Very little, as Chapter 24 will show. It will also examine Eusebius' report on the lost writings of bishop Papias, with his enigmatic references to "Mark" and "Matthew." Then on to a man who may have had more influence on Christianity's development than any other figure of the second century: the gnostic 'heretic' Marcion. He probably supplied the spur and the model for the Church's corpus of Paul's letters and the formation of the New Testament itself. His challenge also provoked a response in the writing of the Acts of the Apostles, now acknowledged to be largely if not entirely a fabricated picture of Christian origins to serve the purposes of the Roman Church.

Finally, Chapter 25 will turn to yet another manifestation of the diversity of Christianity in the first two centuries, in the writings of the Christian apologists. In a fitting climax to the Jesus Puzzle's picture of the missing historical Jesus, the accounts of the faith presented to the Greeks and Romans by the majority of those apologists will be shown to contain their own startling void on the human founder who was soon to conquer even pagan society and send its ancient religious traditions into oblivion.

Part Eight
THE EVOLUTION OF JESUS OF NAZARETH

22

The Gospels as Midrash and Symbolism

Preparing for a Ministry in Galilee

What does Jesus do in the Gospel of Mark?

The statement of Jesus' purpose, his mission in regard to his ministry on earth, is given very simply in Mark 1:14-15:

> "After John had been arrested, Jesus came into Galilee proclaiming the Gospel of God: 'The time has come, the kingdom of God is upon you; repent, and believe the Gospel.' "

Simple—almost mundane. A declaration like this could apply to just about any kingdom-preaching group one could envision plying its message across the land of Palestine in the first century. We can hear those words in the mouths of a multitude of preachers and prophets who believed that a time of judgment and transformation of the world—the long-awaited Day of the Lord—was imminent. Such a declaration would have been right at home in the Q community.

Mark has prefaced this statement with some preparatory material. At the head of his Gospel, he introduces John the Baptist, who misquotes a compound quotation from Malachi 3:1 and Isaiah 40:3 about a voice crying in the wilderness to prepare a way for the Lord. John arrives to preach repentance, a standard practice in announcing the imminence of the kingdom. But he is also a "herald." During centuries of expectation of the Day of the Lord, the moment when God himself would come to restore Israel to her former greatness and more, certain accompanying pieces of mythology had developed. One was that God's arrival would be preceded by the appearance of the prophet Elijah. In Malachi 4:5 this herald is specifically stated to be Elijah, and although the herald in Isaiah 40:3 refers only to an angelic messenger, Christians understood it to mean Elijah as well. Thus John the Baptist has become a stand-in for this expected precursor, since any group claiming that the kingdom was about to arrive had to be able to point to an Elijah-type figure to fulfill the scriptural expectation.

Whether John's quotation from the prophets stood as the first unit in Q is a matter of debate, but Q definitely contained the next Markan element about John: the Baptist's declaration that, "After me comes one who is mightier than I. I am not fit to unfasten his shoes. I have baptized you with water; he will baptize you with the Holy Spirit."

The reader may remember that this passage in Q ran a little longer and included some further description of the one to come, something a little more horrific. There, the one John heralded was due to baptize with fire. He would separate the wheat from the chaff, and the latter would burn in everlasting flames. John's prophecy in Q was almost certainly about the Son of Man, the End-time judge derived from Daniel 7. If John had ever said anything like this, he was probably referring to the arrival of God himself on the Day of the Lord.[92]

Mark brings this evolution of John's prophesying (from God to the Son of Man) a step further. Q's language shows that John was not prophesying a Jesus, preacher of the kingdom and founder of the community, who in any case cannot be discovered in early Q. But in Mark, as in Q3, this founder is now on the scene and John has become *his* herald. Thus, Mark has decided (if he is familiar with the longer tradition found in Q) that all the references to the baptism of fire and the winnowing of the wheat from the chaff have to be dropped. They would be unsuitable to such a Jesus.

This scene of John the Baptist's preaching, in Mark 1:2-8, cannot be regarded as in any way historical, since we can identify the successive stages through which it has evolved, from John possibly prophesying God, to Q2 making it a prophecy of the Son of Man, to Mark's turning it into a prophecy of Jesus himself. Such an evolution moves in lockstep with the community's view of itself, first as one awaiting the Son of Man, without a preaching Jesus, ultimately to Q3 and Mark who portray John as the herald of Jesus who himself becomes the Son of Man.

After the scene of John preaching, Jesus arrives and is baptized in the Jordan river by John. Two things happen. One is a graphic representation of the idea that the coming one will baptize with the Holy Spirit, for that investment of the Spirit—an effect of Christian baptism also envisioned by Paul—is symbolized by Mark as the actual descent of the Holy Spirit in the form of a dove into Jesus himself. This is followed by words out of heaven spoken by God. "Thou art my beloved Son in whom I am well pleased." This is a melding of two verses from scripture: Isaiah 42:1, "Here is my servant (child/son), whom I uphold, my chosen, in whom my soul delights," and Psalm 2:7, "You are my Son, this day I become your father." Paul's baptism also envisioned the initiate becoming God's son (eg, Galatians 4:5). Mark represents this by having God himself declare Jesus to be his "Son."

The baptismal scene, therefore, is not based on any historical incident. It is Mark's construction out of scripture. It symbolizes the community's own baptismal rite and its significant motifs. We can assume the Markan community possessed such a rite, otherwise Mark would have had no interest in portraying Jesus as being baptized, or in John as a baptist prophet.

This practice of drawing on scripture and combining two or more separate passages regarded as complementary and as strengthening each other (like two components of a manufactured alloy) is one of the central procedures in "midrash." Generally speaking, midrash was a traditional Jewish method of interpreting and using the scriptures to create new guides for behavior, to produce new readings of the old texts, to illustrate new meanings and spiritual truths. Often it was done through a retelling of ancient biblical tales set in contemporary circumstances. All these characteristics of midrash will become clearer as we examine how the Gospels were put together.

The baptismal scene is followed by the Temptation story, but in Mark this is so truncated that very little meaning can be drawn from it. Here Mark's memory, or familiarity with Q traditions, is evidently limited. But when we turn to Q as presented in Matthew and Luke, the purpose of the episode emerges.

The Temptation story is clearly not an historical incident, no matter what one's view of Jesus' existence. These three temptations of Jesus by the devil—to turn stones into bread so as to eat after fasting, to throw himself off the Temple's parapet and demonstrate that God will protect him, to bow down before Satan and receive dominion over the world—these serve to make moral points which relate to the community's concerns. How they are specifically to be interpreted has been a matter of debate. Don't be anxious over worldly needs, don't worry about death, don't aspire to political power or revolt, is one type of interpretation.[93] The point is that this set of temptations faced by Jesus symbolizes the ones which the community members themselves face. Jesus' response, as fashioned by Q and its redactors Matthew and Luke, represents the attitudes which need to be adopted in order to neutralize those temptations. Jesus thus serves as a model for the community, to represent their ideal mode of behavior.

Once again, some of the building blocks of this 'morality tale' are drawn from scripture: quotations from Deuteronomy and the Psalms. In midrashic fashion, different scriptural passages are brought together to illuminate the point the formulator of this composite 'lesson' wishes to make. The figure of Jesus can be entirely fictional, yet still serve to symbolize and teach the audience. Whether Mark felt he was conveying the moral entailed in the Q tradition by his drastically reduced reference to Jesus' temptation might be difficult to say.

In this one little preparatory sequence, then, we can see that Mark has constructed, out of precedents which he has altered and brought to new levels of meaning, an artificial picture which symbolizes various elements of the kingdom community. These are the expectation based on scriptural promises, popular mythology as in the anticipation of Elijah, the deeper significance of the community's rite of baptism, the difficulties and temptations it faced. All of it is focused on a single figure representing the community as a whole. Mark might have done without that artificial figure and cast these features in terms of the community itself. But that would have made for a much less interesting and effective product. Insights, lessons, deeper meanings are best conveyed when the focus is sharp and personalized, when a central character can speak, react, teach, undergo as an individual. With an individual it is much easier to understand, to learn from, feel emotion and involvement. Our own fiction, indeed fictional writing of any age, always serves to make more vivid the truths of human experience. Sectarian needs in the realm of faith are no different.

New Testament Methodology

Thus it would appear that the traditional ways of analyzing the elements of the Gospels have been unfounded. The standard approach has always been to attempt to identify what features of a given incident might be traceable to Jesus, to discover what authentic elements might lie at the origin of a tradition about him. Scholarship has sought to uncover evidence of how the preservers of such an incident might have altered it, how it was passed on through oral tradition and the changes which could be wrought in the process, and finally, how the Gospel writers might have reworked such a received unit of tradition for their own purposes. These matters are referred to by such terms as source criticism, form criticism, redaction criticism, and so on.

It would seem that none of it is based in reality. Not only have we seen that the epistles are resoundingly silent on traditions to do with Jesus' ministry, even in their barest fundamentals, we can see the process of Mark reworking Q traditions that had, in their previous incarnations, nothing to do with an historical Jesus or historical events. (That process is particularly clear in the assigning to Jesus of teachings which in earlier witnesses are not attributed to him at all.)

In other words, the whole idea of traditions originating with Jesus or in the immediate circles of response to him, subsequently to travel through oral transmission to the desks of the evangelists, has no support in the evidence. Instead, we see *literary* construction and reworking. We see creativity by the evangelist himself, usually applying something to Jesus—whether from scripture or earlier phases of the material—which had nothing to do with him. Jesus comes to life on the writing desk of Mark, or occasionally in rudimentary form at the hands of the Q3 redactors who have constructed little anecdotes for him out of earlier pieces of material which had stood on their own. When one looks behind the Gospel curtain, the mosaic of Jesus of Nazareth very quickly disintegrates into component pieces and unrecognizable antecedents.

This is not to say that one cannot trace an individual element's history of evolution and reworking, to arrive at some original basic form. This has been a mainstay of New Testament scholarship for generations. But an unargued assumption has also been applied: that those anterior processes lead one back through a chain which begins in many cases with Jesus himself, passing through the usage of the early church, eventually to reach the evangelists in their time. Such study has assumed that early Christian traditions were founded on a force located at ground zero, generated out of the figure of Jesus and the various responses to him. That force then expanded outward in a Big Bang which saw their independent molecules of tradition take on new shapes and meanings, at times attracting external molecules from other non-Jesus spheres, drawn into the Jesus gravitational field.

This, too, has no basis in reality. All those molecules came instead from variegated sources floating about in the atmosphere of the time. They came from the diffuse antecedents to Mark's own community, the wider scene of which his group was a part, as well as from the many-faceted sectarian impulses directed at reforming the ethics and rites and social conditions of the period. They came from the widespread expectation of God's kingdom, the hope of centuries.

As we saw in regard to Q1, they might even come from outside expressions, non-Jewish sources like that of the Cynics. But the focal point of all this material lay not in some common beginning or single figure of origin, it occurred at a later stage, when gravitational forces increasingly pulled these disparate elements together. To some degree, that process took place in later Q, but it was Mark who brought it to completion as an extension of the Q impulse.

Jesus as Prophet

If we continue the survey of what Jesus does in the Gospel of Mark, we see more of those varied elements being attached to the symbolic Jesus figure, a process that began even at the Q3 stage. In Mark, as in Q, Jesus is an apocalyptic prophet. He warns about the imminent End-time and what will happen when it arrives. This was a time of prophets, as Josephus reveals, and as John the Baptist represents.

In Mark and Q, Jesus speaks in a prophetic style going back to the biblical prophets. Declamations are prefaced by "Truly I say to you," (as in Mark 3:28). In Q, Jesus' denunciations of the Pharisees and others are launched with "Woe to you," a phrase found in Isaiah 5:8-24. Mark himself does not have specific "woe" sayings, although in 7:6 he condemns the Pharisees as "hypocrites," drawing on a quotation from Isaiah. "If you have ears to hear . . ." is another prophetic device, which we see in Mark 4:9. This mode of expression represents the widespread custom of preaching by the prophets of the Q and Markan communities, and no doubt of many others.

The Nature of the Kingdom

Similarly, Mark's Jesus preaches the kingdom. He gives his audience an insight into what the kingdom will be like and what processes are leading to its emergence. But we need to highlight a curious observation about that preaching. In both the Gospels and Q, expectations of the future are expressed in two quite different ways. One is blatantly apocalyptic. The Son of Man will arrive and wreak havoc on the world. Mark's "Little Apocalypse" in chapter 13 details the "birthpangs of the new age" (13:8): war, earthquake, famines. The Son of Man is coming at a time no one knows, but be ready for him! Don't try to take anything from the house, but make for the hills (13:14-16). There will be darkened sun and moon, falling stars. The prophets preaching this kind of kingdom must have made their listeners tremble—or scoff.

Beside those fulminations stands an entirely different expression of the kingdom. Most of this latter atmosphere is found in the parables. Here, as in the three parables of Mark 4, are images of quiet growth, seeds blossoming into plants and fruitful harvest. The seed is the word of preaching about the kingdom, the yield is the spread of the idea and its acceptance among many people. The kingdom becomes a tree on which birds may settle for shade.[94]

In Q, a famous parable (Lk./Q 14:16-24) describes how those originally invited to God's banquet, including the rich and privileged, have refused to come, and the master of the house has replaced them with the poor, the crippled, the blind, the lame. Not only does this epitomize the counter-culture nature of the Q movement and the expected reversal of fortune from society's present imbalance, it represents a kingdom in which joy and plenty are to be the lot of the previously unfortunate—now the new elect—a promise made in sayings like the Beatitudes.

Indeed, the two pictures of the future appear incompatible. It is difficult to impute them to the preaching of a single man—unless he was profoundly schizophrenic. Yet Q, followed by Mark and the other Synoptics, have brought them together under the same roof, seemingly impervious to the contradictions.

It seems impossible to reconcile the parables' picture of the kingdom with the apocalyptic one involving the Son of Man. In the former there is no mention of cataclysmic upheaval, no hint of the dread judge expected at the End-time. In Mark's apocalypse, rich and poor alike have much to fear and run from. In Q's picture (Lk./Q 17:34-5) there will be two in a bed, one will die. Two women will be grinding corn, one will be taken. There is no suggestion that it is the evil one of the two who will suffer such a fate. On the other hand, the kingdom of the parables seems to arrive peaceably. There is even the implication that simply through the preaching movement itself, with a bit of cooperation from all concerned, the kingdom is already at hand. This dichotomy of portrayal has led to generations of seesaw interpretation and debate about the precise nature of Jesus' concept of the kingdom. Was Jesus a thundering apocalyptic prophet, fixated on the coming end of the world in fire at the hands of the Son of Man? Or was he a calmer, more inward-looking seer who had no interest in apocalyptic images and imagined that the right people acting in the right ways could bring about an enlightened kingdom of God on earth—even now?

Of course, he was both and he was neither. These two disparate views of the coming kingdom were adopted by the Q community and by extension the Markan one. Through the imputation of both outlooks to an invented founder at the Q3 level, and to the composite Jesus of Nazareth in Mark's Gospel, both became attached to that artificial individual, one who served to symbolize all the expressions of the two communities.

Ultimately, the two outlooks go back to those two incompatible components of early Q, the enlightened 'wisdom' sayings of Q1 and the apocalyptic orientation of Q2. Once again we can see that the two are products of distinct sources which have been brought together in uneasy alliance. The nature of the Q preaching sect was fundamentally that of Q2, and was no doubt that way from the beginning. The sentiments of Q1 represent an external tradition, a harking back to the philosophy and practice of the Cynics. That tradition was adopted by the apocalyptic community in Galilee for reasons which can only be speculative. But come together they did, eventually to find their way into one mouth.

Jesus as Reformer

The Q and Markan communities belonged to a sectarian movement. As such they were in conflict with the establishment and its elitist expressions, the prerogatives and privileges it assumed for itself. A counter-cultural movement is usually universalist in its ideals. Those ideals state that everything is open to the common man and woman, and no one can claim an exclusive pipeline to authority or to the Deity.

Some of what Mark imputes to Jesus is indicative of the concerns of the community and the new reforms it championed. Jesus says to the paralyzed man (2:5): "My son, your sins are forgiven," and the lawyers respond: "This is blasphemy! Who but God alone can forgive sins?" The latter, of course, always refers to the self-appointed representatives of God, namely the religious establishment, who thus control the access to, and the cost of, such forgiveness.

Clearly, the Markan community has rejected that exclusivity. It claims the right for itself to seek God's forgiveness for sins. It is also rebelling against Sabbath strictures as imposed by the Pharisees. These regulations, too, are to be bent, perhaps even broken under some circumstances. "The Sabbath was made for the sake of man and not man for the Sabbath" (2:27). Human interests, even on the Sabbath, should come before rigid rules and the elitist proscriptions of the authorities. Thus Jesus heals on the Sabbath (3:1-6), regarding the saving of life and limb to be of overriding importance. The fact that this incident is portrayed by Mark as instigating the Pharisees' plot to do away with Jesus shows that such new attitudes on the part of the kingdom movement must have seemed disturbing and revolutionary to the religious authorities of Mark's time.

Evidently, that movement did not indulge much in fasting (Mark 2:18) or punishment of the body. The little parable in the dialogue between Jesus and John at the Q3 level has been used to illustrate a situation in which the founder (perhaps merely as "a son of man") came eating and drinking. This no doubt epitomizes the community itself. That community is far from elitist, far from turning up its nose at the less fortunate and 'sanitized' members of society. Mark 2:15-17 reveals a Jesus who eats with "tax-gatherers and sinners." Not only does the Markan community welcome all, it purposely invites those who are looked down on, and those who are "sick" (2:17). The practice of table fellowship with anyone who wishes to join is a mark of their new freedom and liberality. This community has rejected the purity regulations which all too often serve to ostracize those who are unable to meet the stringent requirements of being "clean." Eating with the "impure" is a mark of that rejection. Not washing one's hands before eating—a ritual purity regulation rather than a hygienic one—is a gesture of rejection of the whole elitist ethos. Even traditionally "impure" foods are declared to be clean (7:14-23).

Rather than regarding all these reform impulses as the product of a single man, who as a lone individual would have had difficulty in bringing about such a revolution in behavior and outlook, one ought to recognize them as the expression of the movement itself. They are part of the anticipation of the kingdom with its egalitarian promise and expectation of reversal, in which the exalted shall be humbled and the humble exalted. The Markan Jesus of Nazareth, like his forerunner in the Q founder, simply symbolizes in his own teaching the reform mindset of the entire kingdom movement.

Jesus and the Authorities

Those reform impulses inevitably led to controversy with the religious authorities, preserved in both Q and the Gospels as little exchanges between Jesus and members of the establishment. Such people are an ever-present force in Jesus' entourage. He is constantly surrounded by a coterie of scribes, Pharisees, lawyers and elders, who challenge and threaten him, express their dismay at everything he says and does, and bear the brunt of his condemnation. These little exchanges are called "controversy stories" and they have crystallized out of countless experiences on the part of the community preachers in one situation or another, in which opposition to their beliefs and practices have been expressed. In Q3 and the Gospels they are focused on the figure of Jesus.

A prominent controversy story found in both Mark and Q is the Beelzebub exchange (Mk. 3:22-26):

"The doctors of the law, too, who had come down from Jerusalem, said, 'He is possessed by Beelzebub,' and, 'He drives out devils by the prince of devils.' So he called them to come forward, and spoke to them in parables; 'How can Satan drive out Satan? If a kingdom is divided against itself, that kingdom cannot stand; if a household is divided against itself, that house will never stand; and if Satan is in rebellion against himself, he is divided and cannot stand; and that is the end of him.' " [NEB]

An accusation has been made against prophets of the community who are claiming to exorcise demons from people, and this is their counter. When accused of driving out demons by calling up the power of the prince of demons (Satan/Beelzebub), the Q and Markan prophets say that this makes no sense. If Satan allowed himself to be used to act against his fellow demons, they argue, the power of his own kingdom would be divided against itself and would collapse. The words of Jesus epitomize this argument with the religious establishment concerning a chief activity of the kingdom preachers.

Jesus as Miracle Worker

This brings us to what is perhaps the most significant activity given to Jesus in the Gospel of Mark: performing miracles, particularly those relating to healing.

One of the expected signs that the Day of the Lord was at hand would be the performance of miracles. Most important, God would confer upon men the power to heal sickness and physical disorders, including those caused by evil spirits. That expectation went back to passages such as those in Isaiah: "The eyes of the blind shall be opened, and the ears of the deaf unstopped; then shall the lame man leap like a hart, and the tongue of the dumb sing for joy" (35:5).

This healing would extend even to the resurrection of the dead. "But thy dead live, their bodies will rise again. They that sleep in the earth will awake and shout for joy." (26:19)

That healings of all sorts were part and parcel of the community's prophetic activity is shown by Mark's mission statement in 6:7-13:

> ". . . he summoned the Twelve and sent them out in pairs on a mission. He gave them authority over unclean spirits . . . They drove out many devils, and many sick people they anointed with oil and cured."

In Q's dialogue between Jesus and John, Jesus is asked by John's disciples, "Are you the one to come?" As demonstrated in Chapter 17, this passage is an artificial construction at the Q3 level. The original question put to the Q community may have been something like: "Is the kingdom really about to arrive?" The answer given by the Q prophets is placed in Jesus' mouth (Mt. 11:4-5) and its focus is upon miracles. In fact, it is virtually a recitation of the above passages from Isaiah:

> "Jesus answered: 'Go and tell John what you have seen: the blind recover their sight, the lame walk, the lepers are clean, the deaf hear, the dead are raised to life, the poor are hearing the good news."

One wonders if the Q and Markan prophets actually claimed to raise anyone from the dead. It is possible that there were claims of that sort, although Mark's portrayal may be based on expectation of prophetic fulfilment. Yet Acts (9:36-43) has Peter raising the woman Tabith from death, and even Paul raises a boy from the point of seeming dead (20:7-12). Acts as a whole is full of healing miracles by both Peter and Paul, indicating that this was the practice and expectation of the age.

Healing miracles are common in Hellenistic literature and they are very similar to Jesus' Gospel miracles both in substance and in literary style of reporting.[95] Accounts of miracles are found in the ancient Mesopotamian, Egyptian and Greek documents known as "magical papyri." The tales of heroes both legendary and historical included miracles allegedly performed by those figures, and the famous 'peer' of Jesus in the ancient world, Apollonius of Tyana, had many miracles imputed to him like those of Jesus.[96]

One strong indication that the healing miracles in Mark are symbolic of the community's own practices and do not represent historical incidents transmitted through oral tradition is that Mark's anecdotes are modeled on the accounts of miracles by Elijah and Elisha in 1 and 2 Kings. This is yet another example of midrash. Those accounts show the ancient prophets healing the sick and even raising the dead. Here is one such miracle in 1 Kings 17:17-24:

> "Afterwards, the son of this woman, the mistress of the house, fell ill and grew worse and worse, until at last his breathing ceased. . . . (Elijah) took the boy from her arms and carried him up to the roof-chamber where his lodging was, and laid him on his own bed. . . . Then he breathed deeply upon the child three times and called upon the Lord, 'O Lord my God, let the breath of life, I pray, return to the body of this child.' The Lord listened to Elijah's cry, and the breath of life returned to the child's body, and he revived. . . . (The mother) said to Elijah: 'Now I know for certain that you are a man of God and that the word of the Lord is on your lips.' "

Features of these biblical healing miracles (see also 2 Kings 4:18-37, in which the prophet Elisha raises a boy from the dead) are mirrored in the accounts of the raising of Jairus' daughter (Mk. 5:21-43) and the curing of the Syrophoenician woman's daughter (7:24-30). The last line in the quotation above shows that such miracles serve to authenticate the person and preaching of the prophet performing them. This is one of the main purposes of Jesus' miracles in the Gospels.

As part of the program of healing, Jesus gives his apostles the power to "drive out devils." One of the great superstitions of the age—one which Mark's Jesus is unable to rise above—was the pervasive belief in demons, the presence of evil spirits in the very air in which people moved. These demons were regarded as responsible for many types of illness, both physical and mental. They were held accountable as well for almost any unfortunate accident or natural disaster, even for developments within society which certain groups regarded as counter to God's wishes—and their own. (Consider the Church Fathers' belief that demons had orchestrated ahead of time the false rites of the mysteries to mimic the Christians' own.)

One of the attendant benefits of the kingdom would be the suppression, if not the complete destruction of all these harmful, hostile spirits. Exorcising demons from sick people was a sign that this overthrow of evil forces was imminent, and that the prophet-exorcist was indeed speaking and acting for God. The Beelzebub controversy, first formulated at the Q2 level, shows that the community practiced exorcism. Jesus symbolizes this activity.[97]

Another type of miracle common in antiquity was the 'feeding miracle,' and these too are imputed to Elijah and Elisha. They contain features which are directly copied by Mark in his construction of Jesus' feeding miracles. In 1 Kings 17:10-16, Elijah makes a single jar of flour produce endless cakes and a flask of oil never fail, in order to provide a source of food for a widow and her family. In 2 Kings 4:42-44, twenty barley loaves and a number of ears of corn are stretched by Elisha to feed a hundred men, with some left over.

These tales have been recast by Mark into his two accounts of Jesus' miracle of the loaves and fishes that are stretched to feed thousands, with a few baskets left over. This illustrates that other important device of midrash: take a biblical story and retell it in a new setting with new characters. For the community applying such a tale to itself, this procedure transferred all the associations attached to the old tale: God's involvement, the sense of significance for the community and the time it lives in, and most important, a continuity with the past. If Mark's community was essentially a gentile one, as many think, such a parallel linked those who regard themselves as a new Israel with their adopted Jewish heritage.

Miracle Collections

A common theory is that Mark and John had access to previously circulating collections of traditions about Jesus' miracles. These would have been similar to the 'biographies' of famous men (and gods) in the Hellenistic period, which often amounted to little more than a listing (called an "aretalogy") of miraculous exploits attributed to them.[98] But in the New Testament we have no way of telling if or when such collections had been assembled before the Gospels, or who they may have been imputed to. They may have been collections of miracles that were previously claimed by the community as witness to the kingdom. Some of them may have been the evangelists' own product.

That they are artificial literary creations, and not reflective of actual traditions about a Jesus of Nazareth, is evident when we view them as a set. Burton Mack (*A Myth of Innocence*, p.215f) describes the research of Paul Achtemeier[99] who showed that Mark contains two separate sets of five miracle stories which are identical in type and overall pattern. Each set begins with a sea-crossing miracle: the Stilling of the Storm (4:35-41) and Walking on the Sea (6:45-51). Each ends with an account of feeding the multitudes: the 5000 (6:34-44) and the 4000 (8:1-10). In between are one exorcism and two healing miracles.[100]

What the latter may have signified in the pattern is unsure, but the first and last had definite Exodus connotations, paralleling the crossing of the Red Sea and the miraculous feeding of the people in the wilderness of Sinai. Though the import of all the facets of this pattern may be lost to us, the overall conclusion to be drawn is not. The miracles of Jesus are the construction of the evangelist or his community. They confer a symbolic significance on the sect in relation to an important prototype in scripture, namely the Exodus story. Mark's miracles may have signified that the community could look upon itself as the new Chosen People, ready to enter a new Promised Land. Once again, a Gospel feature reveals itself as midrash, a reworking of biblical precedents to provide new meaning and import to the community itself. It is not in any way representative of history or traditions going back to a Jesus.

Jesus as Symbol

As asked at the opening of this chapter, what does Jesus do in the Gospel of Mark? In terms of his ministry, he does no more and no less than what the Markan community itself does. He symbolizes the community's relationship with God and its expectations for the future.

The overall view of much of the first century preaching movement, whether kingdom or cultic, was that God's relationship with the world had entered a new phase. He was establishing a new covenant, one that would supersede the old. The elements involved in establishing the old covenant had to be incorporated into the story of the new one. Jesus, as representative of the Markan community, had to be portrayed as a new Moses. His birth, when it came to be described by Matthew and Luke, had much in common with the birth tale of Moses. Jesus performs miracles similar to the ones attending the Exodus. The object was to show that Jesus, which is to say the sect itself, represented a new Moses and a new prophet. Israel entering the Promised Land prefigured the community's entry into the new kingdom of God.

The old covenant had also been marked by a blood sacrifice of animals, performed by Moses. In Mark, Jesus himself serves as the sacrifice required to establish the new covenant, and he speaks words at a Last Supper scene which are a close parallel to those spoken by Moses. It may have been features like this which drew Mark and his group to the Christ cult, with its sacrifice of Christ in the mythical realm. Those potential associations between the two Traditions would have been very appealing to a kingdom community that could open its mind to such symbolism.

Mark's Gospel was a religious statement. In a sectarian context, it justified and embodied the beliefs and practices of the community in poetic and symbolic terms. It also mirrored the darker side of its outlook, a resentment at the outside world's rejection of its reforms and doctrines. The plot against Jesus by the religious establishment, as well as Jesus' condemnation of the Jewish authorities and their values, undoubtedly mirrored a real-life situation. Jesus' fate in the Gospel may have reflected the conviction that, even if they kill us, we will rise again when the kingdom comes.

The spiritual Christ's crucifixion at the hands of the evil spirits in the higher world would have found a natural translation in Jesus of Nazareth's crucifixion at the hands of Jewish and Roman authorities on earth. But in the final analysis, the Christ cult may only have been Mark's trigger. He could almost have done without it.

23

The Suffering Righteous One and a Tale from Scripture

A Single Witness

For almost nineteen centuries, Christians, along with much of the rest of the world, have believed that their religion arose out of the events of the Gospel passion story. Jesus went to Jerusalem and was there arrested. He was tried by the Roman governor Pontius Pilate at the instigation of the Jewish authorities, crucified outside the city at a place called Calvary, and laid in a nearby tomb. Not everyone in the world over that length of time has believed that he actually rose from his resting place three days later, but they have always addressed the question by offering alternate explanations for the Christian perception that he had done so. In the modern era, it has even been postulated that Jesus did not actually die on the cross but was only in a coma, to be rescued later by his followers and revived.[101]

An entire faith movement, one of the world's major religions, is assumed to have been launched by those Gospel events. Yet if that were indeed the reality of history, we would face a profoundly astonishing situation. For the fact is, the story which presumably began so much is to be traced back to a single document, to the literary efforts of what may well have been a single individual.

We have already seen that until the time of Ignatius early in the second century, no one in the non-Gospel Christian record speaks of a trial and crucifixion by Pilate, of a death in Jerusalem or a rising from a tomb in that location. Moreover, contrary to popular belief, Mark himself has no corroboration. Christian tradition for the better part of two millennia has regarded the four Gospels as independent accounts of the events of Jesus' life and death, by persons in the know, providing a fourfold witness to those events. Most Christians today still believe that. But New Testament scholars know better, and they've known it for almost two centuries. They have come to realize that the

Gospels of Matthew and Luke, rather than being independent corroborations, are direct copies of Mark. Matthew reproduces almost 90% of Mark in his own text, Luke over 50%. As for the passion itself, those two later evangelists have shaped their accounts exactly as Mark did, with only a couple of minor alterations and additions. Even the extra source used by both, the Q document, had nothing to add to their passion story, since Q contained not a word about a trial, death and resurrection. It is as though Matthew and Luke knew nothing about the events at the end of Jesus' life, the events which brought salvation to the world and triggered the great explosion that became Christianity, until they encountered a copy of the Gospel of Mark.

Yet all of this should be regarded as an impossible situation. If something even remotely like those events had taken place and the Christian movement had begun in response to them, the Christian world could not fail to have been saturated with traditions about Jesus' death and rising, even if they contained much embellishment and inaccuracy, even if they were largely unreliable. Indeed, we would expect precisely that state of affairs. For the early record shows us that the Christian movement during its first hundred years was a sprawling, uncoordinated, diverse organism marked by division and incompatible theologies. We would expect that all those communities or regions would have preserved and developed their own angles on the passion events. They would inevitably have found different things to focus on, different characters or story elements to develop in relation to their own interests and faith.

Yet not only do we find none of this expected variety of passion traditions among the many Christian communities of the empire, we see no sign of any traditions at all for the first half century of the movement. That all these Christian groups could have lived and worshiped for that length of time, with no traditions or passion account of their own until one community, one person somewhere in Syria, decided to put down on paper the traditions which he had managed to acquire about the death of Jesus, cannot be accepted.

But Matthew and Luke show us precisely that. Even if their communities had not actually written such things down, they would surely have possessed their own oral descriptions of Jesus' passion and death. Those traditions would have been added to the mix when they came to rework Mark. Yet there is no sign of such a thing. The passion stories of Matthew and Luke follow in lockstep with that of Mark. Matthew adds a few minor details, such as the death of Judas, the guard at the tomb, the rising of some of the city's dead. Luke's notable addition is the hearing before Herod, when Pilate sends Jesus to be interviewed by the Tetrarch before finally passing judgment himself.

Of course, there are all sorts of ground-level changes which the two later evangelists have made, just as they have throughout the whole of their Gospels. They are constantly altering the words and details of Mark to reflect their own writing styles and editorial emphases. But the overall shape and content is precisely the same. We see no evidence of a passion tradition present in the Matthean or Lukan communities before the Gospel of Mark came along. And the epistles and other early writings show that no one else had one either.[102]

Robert Funk, in his *Honest to Jesus* (p.237-8) has this observation to make: "It is strange that no source outside the five gospels [he is including the Gospel of Peter, not Thomas] knows this same sequence of events, even in outline. . . . If the passion story were well known, it seems likely that others would have referred to it, at least in outline." What Funk fails to further observe is that no one has *any* sequence of events in regard to a passion story.

The traditionalist might claim that, well, since the story is true, once Mark's successors came to write down their version, it would conform closely to Mark's in any event. But those factors outlined above would ensure that even a 'true' story would, in the context of a widely diffused movement like Christianity, inevitably suffer change and differing emphasis, as well as the addition of 'untrue' embellishment.

We can demonstrate that principle by looking at what happens in Matthew and Luke after they run out of Markan material. The original Gospel of Mark ended at 16:8. The women have gone to the tomb and found it empty, the angel announces Jesus has risen and they run off in fear. From that point on, Matthew is completely unlike Luke. The post-resurrection appearances added by the two evangelists involve different characters and a different sequence of events. Luke's road to Emmaus scene has no counterpart in Matthew. The two evangelists cannot even agree on where Jesus appeared to his disciples. Matthew has such meetings take place in Galilee, in Luke everything happens in Jerusalem. Whether all of it is sheer invention on their part, or whether one chooses to believe that some of it is based on traditions which have developed since the supposed time of Jesus, the point is that those details, their setting, their sequence are dramatically different. *That* is the situation we should find in the Gospels in regard to the entire passion account.

The Position of the Fourth Gospel

And what of John, the fourth Gospel? Does this evangelist preserve something independent of the Synoptics? Considering that the Johannine theology and the teachings of Jesus are dramatically different from those of the other Gospels, one might expect that the Johannine community would have developed a passion story uniquely its own.

Yet John, too, lays out the events just as Mark does, and adds nothing new to the plot line, even if he introduces significant changes of interpretation to fit his own theology. For example, Jesus' death takes place on Passover eve, rather than on the following day as in the Synoptics, but this is not because John has inherited a different element of tradition. Most Johannine scholars are agreed it is because he wishes to play up the symbolism between the slaughter of Jesus on Calvary and the slaughter of the Passover lambs in the Temple, and so he fashions his version of the story to make the two coincide.

There has been a seesaw debate in New Testament scholarship over whether John is independent of the Synoptic Gospels or whether he too, like Matthew and Luke, has copied a Markan source. That the latter is the case can be shown by an observation which will start us on the road to establishing another principle: that the Markan passion account was not the product of oral transmission over the decades, but was set down for the first time *as a literary construction.*

Robert Funk (*op.cit.*, p.238) comes to the same conclusion. Because of its literary structure and intricacy, he discounts the possibility that the passion story in Mark was developed or transmitted in oral form. In other words, from its inception it was a written narrative. Someone first put it together 'on paper.'

One example of this intricacy serves to illustrate John's dependence on Mark. In a device known as "intercalation," Mark has a habit throughout his Gospel of sandwiching two parts of one anecdote around an intervening anecdote. The two interact to emphasize some point Mark is trying to make. In the passion story, the denial by Peter is split into two parts. The joint scene begins with 14:53-54:

> "Then they led Jesus away to the High Priest's house, where the chief priests, elders, and doctors of the law were all assembling. Peter followed him at a distance right into the High Priest's courtyard; and there he remained, sitting among the attendants, warming himself at the fire." [NEB]

Mark then shifts his attention from Peter to Jesus and goes through the interrogation of Jesus by the Sanhedrin and the exchange with the High Priest (14:55-65). That done, he returns to Peter and continues with the account of his denial (14:66-72) "three times before the cock crew." In this way, Mark has contrasted Peter's fear of persecution which leads him to deny any relationship to Jesus, with Jesus' own fearless admission that he is the Messiah and Son of God, for which he receives a death sentence.

And what does John do? He too divides the denial scene by inserting the High Priest's questioning of Jesus into the middle. In this case, he makes the break between Peter's first denial and the other two (18:15-27). That he would have done this simply by coincidence is so highly unlikely as to be rejected. The only conclusion to be drawn is that John depends on Mark for his passion story. Thus within the four canonical Gospels there are no multiple, independent corroborative versions of the key happenings which are supposed to lie at the base of the Christian movement and the story of Jesus. All we have is *one* story, *one* version, *one* pattern of incidents that have "preserved" the alleged central event of Christianity.

An Unknown Event

We will see in a moment that this story is entirely dependent on a culling from scripture of large-scale motifs and small individual passages which have been spliced together to create a narrative. Thus neither the overall shape nor the events themselves would seem to be grounded in a remembered history. A number of scholars have recently put forward a scenario to explain such a state of affairs.[103]

This scenario allows that most, perhaps virtually all, of the passion account in the four Gospels does not reflect what actually happened. The genuine historical details of what transpired at Jesus' trial and execution are assumed not to have survived in Christian consciousness, probably because they were unknown to his followers. Instead, the Jerusalem community created a narrative framework for the event of Jesus' death by drawing on scriptural passages mostly from the Psalms and Prophets, stringing them together to create a tale which could be told and transmitted through oral tradition, one that would reflect, through its scriptural make-up, traditional motifs and understandings for a new Jewish faith movement.

Those scholars have been forced to this conclusion because virtually every detail of the Gospel passion story can be shown to have a parallel in scripture, and because even the intermediate and large-scale structures of the account are scripturally determined. Also, no other details outside this scripture-based account surface anywhere in Christian tradition from that point on. They assume, therefore, that nothing concrete was known about Jesus' death.[104]

A number of evident objections to this theory offer themselves.

(1) Can "oral tradition" function and survive in such a framework? Does a preacher-prophet "tell" of an historical event to his own or his listeners' satisfaction by giving it an entirely scriptural content? If the speaker is preaching to a group of potential converts, does he communicate the details of Jesus' passion with a proviso at each step of the way: "Now, the gambling for Jesus' clothes at the foot of the cross, that too didn't really happen—that's from Psalm 22." How would the listener, especially a gentile, adjust to this kind of preaching and 'tradition' and how would he in turn pass it on to others?

(2) Why, in fact, would no details of the historical event of Jesus' death be known and added to those oral traditions, so that something other than scripture would show up in the passion account? Raymond E. Brown (*The Death of the Messiah*, p.14-15) calls it "absurd" to think that some information, some historical raw material, was not available, or could not be obtained by Jesus' followers after his death. Such a thought is certainly intuitive. And yet, the entire narrative can be broken down into echoes of scripture alone. That includes all the details *preceding* the time of Jesus' arrest, when the disciples were not yet separated from him. Why are the entry of Jesus into Jerusalem, the Last Supper, the Garden of Gethsemane, the arrest itself—namely, the part of the passion account when Christian witnesses were supposedly still on the scene—why are they equally saturated with scripture and just as lacking in hard historical material as the trial and crucifixion portions?

(3) If not even the basics were known, how could that death have made such an impact that people would feel impelled to set it in scripture? What would have captured the imagination of preachers and believers across the empire if no historical circumstances of Jesus' death were known? What could have been the fuel that launched this amazing response to Jesus in Jerusalem—especially since his teachings apparently made no impact there? Who would have noticed or cared if some simple Galilean peasant had come into the city with a few followers, done a bit of preaching, only to be seized and executed by the authorities under unknown circumstances? Who would have been

so overwhelmed by this event that they immediately ransacked scripture to create a story about him, delved into the full range of Greek and Jewish philosophy about intermediary forces between God and humanity, and turned this humble peasant teacher into the equivalent of the Logos and personified Wisdom? Who would have made him creator and sustainer of the universe and regarded that obscure death as the redemptive moment of God's salvation history?

Even if this scholarly scenario had merit, it founders on another consideration. If the actual historical details of the event of Jesus' death were unknown, and Christians were forced to go to scripture to articulate that event, *why*, among all the Christian communities spread across half the empire, did only one community, perhaps only a single person, decide to do such a thing—and then only after several decades had passed? Why did no other Christian groups, other exegetes, feel the need for some articulation of that unknown event? Why did the forces which impelled Mark to construct a midrashic story from scripture not operate in other locales, producing other tales of the passion which were quite different?

The inescapable conclusion would seem to be that no event of Jesus' death took place at Christianity's inception, and only with the construction from scripture of the first narrative of a Jesus of Nazareth, which the movement eventually adopted as history, was such an idea let loose in the world.

The Suffering and Vindication of the Innocent Righteous One

Apart from its many details which have been extracted from widely separated passages in scripture, the passion narrative as a whole follows a known generic model. That is, there is a type, or genre, of tale found throughout centuries of Jewish writing, both biblical and apocryphal, which bears a strong resemblance to the story of Mark's Jesus.

This tale tells of a righteous individual who is conspired against and falsely accused, who remains obedient to God and puts trust in him, who undergoes trial and suffering, finally to be condemned to death. At the last moment, God intervenes miraculously to rescue the protagonist and he or she is vindicated, shown to have been innocent of the charge. Finally, as a reward for the ordeal, the innocent one is raised or restored to a high position at court or in the community, and the adversaries are discredited. In later versions of the tale, the protagonist actually suffers death, but is exalted in heaven after death.

A detailed comparison of this type of tale with the well-known story of Jesus' passion is hardly necessary, though we will follow its course in the latter part of this chapter. Suffice to say that virtually every element of it is mirrored in the plot line of Mark's passion account.

This model is found in the Joseph narrative in Genesis 39-41, in the Book of Esther 3, in Tobit 1:18-22, Susanna, Daniel 3 and 6, 3 Maccabees 3, 2 Maccabees 7, the Wisdom of Solomon 2-5. The latter two involve exaltation after death, to which we might add the Suffering Servant in Isaiah 53, though this last does not contain the usual narrative elements present in the genre. All seem to be derive from an archetypal tale in pagan tradition called the Story of Ahiqar, which is at least as old as the fifth century BCE.

George Nickelsburg, in an influential article published in *Harvard Theological Review*, "The Genre and Function of the Markan Passion Narrative" (No.73 [1980] p.153-184) first laid out this genre and its components as the model for the passion story in Mark, and it has since become a commonplace to draw attention to it. Scholars refer to this model as The Suffering and Vindication of the Innocent Righteous One.

Burton Mack, in *A Myth of Innocence* (p.262-68), focuses on other critical factors that must be taken into account, further supporting the contention that Mark's Gospel is a literary construction and not a record of tradition. One is that major themes which Mark has introduced into the body of the Gospel, such as the plot against Jesus, the question of Jesus' identity and the various titles given to him in the course of his ministry, the anti-temple outlook, the failure of the disciples to understand, all these themes come to a climax and are resolved only during the passion scene. This literary shaping and interrelationship among the various narrative threads of the Gospel could not have been a product of oral transmission; such things can result only from careful construction at the hands of a skilled writer. Similarly within the passion narrative itself, so many details serve to build up a plot structure which works only on paper. As Mack points out, these cannot survive and be transmitted as independent stories or traditions, because they make sense only in the context of the constructed passion narrative as a whole.

But that "narrative as a whole" could not have existed before Mark, not only because there is no evidence for it in the wider record, but because its literary integrity is founded on the biblical model, and the details of that narrative have been extracted from scriptural passages.

We are led once more to the conclusion that the events which began Christianity, as envisioned by 19 centuries of Christian believers and world onlookers, are the product of one author, and had no existence until they took shape and came together on Mark's writing table.

We can now follow the tale recounted in Mark's midrashic construction, as he draws on motifs and passages from the Hebrew bible (equivalent to the Christian Old Testament).

Opening Scene

The passion story proper occupies Chapters 14 and 15 of the Gospel of Mark, but the sequence of events begins with Jesus' arrival at Jerusalem. This is the climax of the ministry Mark has created for Jesus, and so the entry into the city must be given some drama. Jesus directs two disciples to go to a nearby village where they will find a tethered colt, which they are to bring to him. This they do, and Jesus rides on the colt into the city, while bystanders carpet the road with cloaks and branches (palms) from nearby trees, some shouting "Hosanna! Blessed is he who comes in the name of the Lord!"

An historical scene? Turn to the prophet Zechariah, 9:9:

"Rejoice greatly, O daughter of Zion! Shout aloud, O daughter of Jerusalem! Lo, your king comes to you; triumphant and victorious is he, humble and riding on an ass, on a colt the foal of an ass."

An earlier verse, 2:10, declares a similar idea: "Sing and rejoice, O daughter of Zion; for lo, I come and I will dwell in the midst of you, says the Lord." Another prophetic passage also urges rejoicing, Zephaniah 3:14: "Sing aloud, O daughter of Zion; shout, O Israel! Rejoice and exult with all your heart, O daughter of Jerusalem! . . . The King of Israel, the Lord, is in your midst." Mark has turned these passages into the reaction of the crowd as Jesus enters the city, mounted on Zechariah's donkey. And what do they shout? A verse from Psalm 118 (verse 26a in the Septuagint wording): "Blessed is he who comes in the name of the Lord."

In perfect midrashic fashion, Mark has combined the ideas of all these passages and sculpted a narrative scene in which the disciples acquire the donkey, Jesus rides it into the city and the crowds rejoice and hail him, spreading palms worthy of a dignitary, even a king.

Matthew carries things even further. When he reworks Mark (21:1-5) he has the disciples bring back both a donkey *and* her colt. Why? Because the above passage in Zechariah can be read as referring to two separate animals. Exactly how Jesus can ride both is never illustrated, but Matthew is anxious to point out that all this is in fulfilment of the words of the prophet, and he quotes Zechariah directly.[105]

Cleansing the Temple

After a few verses, Mark gives us the dramatic scene in the Temple (11:15-17), where Jesus overturns the tables of the money-changers and pigeon-sellers, and bars passage through the Temple court. That such an event could have happened as Mark portrays it is virtually impossible. The outer court of the Temple was huge, and Jesus single-handedly could never have accomplished that degree of interference with Temple traffic. Nor could he have done it with impunity. Jewish and Roman authorities were constantly in attendance. Jesus calls the traders "thieves," but their activities were absolutely essential to the functioning of the Temple. It was they who made the public sacrifices possible. There was no thievery about it.

The scene is built on scriptural passages. Malachi 3:1: "The Lord whom you seek will come to his Temple." Hosea 9:15: "Because of their evil deeds I will drive them from my house." (Hosea was not talking about animal sellers.) Zechariah 14:21: "When that time comes, no trader shall be seen in the house of the Lord of hosts."

As for his condemnation of those traders, Jesus offers a quotation followed by his own comment. Both are from scripture. Isaiah 56:7 is placed in Jesus' mouth as a challenge: "My house shall be called a house of prayer for all nations." His follow-up thought is Jeremiah 7:11: "Do you think that this house . . . is a robbers' cave?" Again, Jeremiah is not talking about traders in the Temple, but those who commit atrocities and make sacrifices to Baal and then come into the Temple expecting to gain forgiveness. One of the features of the practice of midrash is that the context from which a passage is borrowed is never taken into consideration. Most times, if not all, the old context bears no relation to the new one which Mark creates for it.

This incident as a whole fits one of the key elements in the larger story pattern about the Suffering Righteous One. (Nickelsburg calls these "generic components.") This is the "Provocation" which induces the protagonist's enemies to act against him. Mark 11:18 spells it out: "The chief priests and doctors of the law heard of this and sought some way of making away with him."

That motif Mark continues to emphasize. "They began to look for a way to arrest him" (12:12). "The chief priests and the scribes were seeking how to arrest him by stealth, and kill him" (14:1). This is the "Conspiracy" element of the story pattern, and even here, the idea has specific connection with the Psalms. "Those who wish me dead defame me," says Psalm 38:12. "My enemies' rancor bursts upon me," says Psalm 71:10. And so on.

A Night of Betrayal

Mark brings the Conspiracy element to an inspired and insidious focus. The greatest conspirator of all is one whom the evangelist places next to Jesus himself, in the midst of his closest followers. The figure of Judas is undoubtedly one of the most powerful creations of world fiction, and probably none has had such terrible consequence. For two millennia, and almost single-handedly, he served to inflame Christian hatred of his race, for Judas was designed by Mark to represent the evangelist's view of the Jews as cold-hearted and perfidious. It is only with the late 20th century that Christian authority has pulled back in shame from that history of anti-Semitism, and Christian scholarship has come to the belated conclusion that Judas himself was probably an invention of Mark.

What scriptural passages might have spurred Mark's portrayal of Judas? Obadiah 7: "Your confederates mislead you and bring you low, your own kith and kin lay a snare for your feet." Psalm 41:9 says: "Even the friend whom I trusted, who ate at my table, has lifted up his heel against me." Psalm 55:12-13 laments over the friend and comrade who taunted the psalmist as though he were an enemy. Psalm 109 does the same over "the wicked and deceitful mouths (that) are opened against me," who attack without cause, returning evil for good, hatred for love. If Mark was familiar with the Pauline myth of the Lord's Supper (1 Cor. 11:23-26) with its "on the night he was delivered up," he may have decided to turn that neutral "handing over" (which Paul imputes to God) into Judas' act of "betrayal." Most modern translators of the Pauline passage have been willing to cooperate.

And Judas' price? Mark says only that the chief priests promised to give him money. Matthew is more specific (26:15). In his own survey of scripture he has lighted on Zechariah 11:12: "And they weighed out as my wages thirty shekels of silver." But the dissatisfied prophet, at God's suggestion, rejected the shekels and "cast them into the treasury in the house of the Lord." Matthew uses this as part of his scene of Judas' remorse and suicide (27:3-5) in which the betrayer "threw the money down in the Temple."

A Last Meal

Mark's creation of the Last Supper is undoubtedly more than simple midrash. If he is part of a community which has a communal, sacred meal—which seems likely—and if he knows the Pauline myth of the Lord's Supper, such elements would have contributed much to the scene of the twelve apostles gathered about Jesus for a final repast. But the concept of a new covenant established by Jesus would necessarily have required parallels to the scene of the old covenant established by Moses, as recounted in Exodus. Moses' words in 24:8, "This is the blood of the covenant which the Lord has made with you," would govern Jesus' words (14:24) at the Supper: "This is my blood of the covenant, which is poured out for many." Jesus himself is the blood sacrifice corresponding to Moses' animal sacrifice.

Jesus concludes the meal with the statement that he will not drink (wine) again "until I drink it new in the kingdom of God," a declaration of trust in Isaiah 25:6: "On this mountain the Lord will prepare a banquet of rich fare for all the peoples, a banquet of wines . . ."

From there, Jesus proceeds to the garden of Gethsemane and his ordeal begins.

Doubts and Agony

There are many finely-wrought elements to this simple scene, a piece of subtle crafting which places Mark in the ranks of the greatest writers of all time. Gethsemane's three-part structure, the contrast between the starkly agonizing Jesus and the oblivious, sleeping disciples, the inbuilt anticipation of the passion itself and the looming arrest, not to mention the various moral "lessons" Mark manages to convey about loyalty, obedience to God, a willingness to suffer for the faith, and much more—nothing could better illustrate the power and necessity of myth in the context of religious belief and commitment. Christianity owes its two-thousand year whirlwind career to the literary genius of Mark. Without Mark's creation, Paul and the Christ cult he spent his life preaching would have vanished into the sunken pits of fossilized history.

"How deep I am cast in misery, groaning in my distress," the writer of Psalm 42 (v.5) laments. Other psalmists had poured out their own expressions of misery: "I cry . . . but get no answer" (22:2); "Deliver me from the sword, my life from the axe" (22:20); "I am in distress and my eyes are dimmed with grief" (31:9). Mark had much inspiration to draw on from his scriptural well.

Luke, who for some reason trashed Mark's scene completely and destroyed every touch of poetry in it, took the line from Psalm 22:14 (LXX), "I am poured out like water," and turned it into a garish image of Jesus sweating drops of blood into the ground. Matthew in his own Gethsemane scene adhered closely to Mark. John, on the other hand, has discarded the whole thing, as part of his 'sanitization' of the Synoptic Jesus. The ability to feel human emotions like anguish and doubt was the last thing he wanted to grant to his own glorified divine Christ.

The Gethsemane scene, besides filling a dramatic role in Mark's unfolding passion story, is one of those "generic components" in the tale of the Righteous One, representing the motif of "Obedience" to God. Though Jesus, expressing the human side of his composite nature, asks in a moment of weakness that the terrible cup should pass him by, he sets aside those fears and tells his Father: "Yet not what I wish for, but what you wish of me." It was a line that would inspire centuries of Christian martyrs and faltering believers.

When Judas arrives to fill his role as betrayer through a kiss—a plot device which has never made sense to those who regard it as history rather than symbolism—the rest of the apostles give in to their own fears and flee the scene, leaving Jesus to face his fate alone. An incident like this is often held up as an example of a tradition which must be factual, since it is an embarrassing one. Why would the church, indeed the disciples themselves, want to invent such a shameful incident? Of course, in the context of Mark's midrashic piece of symbolism, echoing scripture and serving to convey lessons for the community, such a rationale does not apply. The disciples of his story had nothing to say about what might have been embarrassing to them. Their action was determined by Zechariah 13:7:

> "Strike the shepherd and the sheep will be scattered."

Surrounded by Enemies

> "Why did the gentiles rage, and the peoples plot futile things?
> The kings of the earth stand ready, and the rulers conspire together
> Against the Lord and his Anointed."

Psalm 2 is a Coronation Hymn, and verses such as these (1-2) reflect the unfortunate situation in which Israel historically found herself, standing at a geographical crossroads between all the great empires of the Near East. Putting on a brave face, and regarding God as ready and able to protect his Chosen (if only they would obey him properly) was often the only recourse the nation had. A Jesus surrounded by his enemies—the Jewish "people" and their religious leaders, Herod, one of the "kings of the earth" (though really only a Tetrarch) and Pilate the "ruler" (a governor, but virtually absolute in Judea)—is a situation which echoes the sentiments of Psalm 2.[106]

The first of those enemies is the Jewish Sanhedrin, before which Jesus is brought. From this point on, the Psalms become the major source for many of Mark's details, none more so than Psalm 22. The Septuagint version of verse 16 reads: "Synagogues (*synagogē*, assemblies) of the wicked have circled me round." Jesus is not only encircled by hostile chief priests, elders, scribes, the entire Council and the High Priest—just about every Jewish authority Mark can squeeze onto the stage—he is accused of trumped-up, contradictory charges (Mk. 14:55-60).

The Psalms are full of such sentiments about persecution. "Liars give evidence against me (27:12); "Malicious witnesses arose" (35:11); "Wicked men heap calumnies upon me" (109:2); and others. This is the "Accusation" component of the generic tale. The conspirators accuse the hero within the context of another component: the "Trial." In Mark, Jesus undergoes two trials. As in the opening verse of Psalm 2 (above), both the gentile and the Jew must be involved. Luke adds a kind of third trial, in the form of Jesus' interview with Herod (23:6-12), though this is almost a friendly affair to satisfy Herod's curiosity. Crossan (see Note 106 above) thinks it may have been included to give more graphic representation to the second line of Psalm 2: Herod is a "king" and he "conspires" with Pilate.

Trial by Jew and Gentile

In both trials, Mark introduces the motif found in Psalm 39:9: "I am dumb, I will not open my mouth." Psalm 38:13-14 sounds the same sentiments: "I am like a dumb man who cannot open his mouth. I behave like a man who cannot hear and whose tongue offers no defense." To the High Priest's trumped-up accusations (Mk. 14:60) Jesus "was silent and made no answer," and in the subsequent hearing before Pilate, Mark reiterates (15:5) that "to Pilate's astonishment, Jesus made no further reply."

John, incidentally, was not willing to keep his Jesus silent, and he crafted a lengthy and subtle discussion between Jesus and Pilate on the question of kingdoms and truth.

To the High Priest's questioning about who Jesus is, however, Mark has Jesus break his silence to make a capsule declaration. Between the question and the answer (14:61b-62), Mark manages to work in all three titles that have been applied to Jesus throughout the course of the Gospel—two of them accepted only reluctantly by Jesus. Now there is no holding back. Yes, Jesus is Messiah, and Son of God, and Son of Man. That is sufficient to bring down on him the charge of blasphemy and the judgment that he should be put to death. Whether such a declaration did indeed merit the charge and judgment has been debated in scholarship for some time. But neither these words, nor the entire scene, warrant such considerations. Mark and his community are laying claim to the symbolic significance of these titles. If the end of the world is indeed at hand, the sectarian group must regard itself as being at the center of all those expectations.

Both trials entail the component of "Condemnation," but the answer to the High Priest allows Mark to look ahead and provide the ultimate example of the all-important component of "Vindication." Like the later versions of the generic tale, Jesus' vindication will come after his death at the anticipated Parousia, when as the Son of Man he will be seen "seated on the right hand of God and coming with the clouds of heaven" (14:62).

Only in Matthew does Pilate wash his hands, mirroring a few Psalm references to hand washing, as well as Deuteronomy 21:6-8: "Elders shall wash their hands . . . and declare 'Our hands did not shed this blood'. " Finally, Jesus is delivered up for execution.

Abuse and Suffering

In the biblical tale, the hero is subjected to an "Ordeal" leading to death or the threat of death. Before his crucifixion, Jesus is first scourged and mistreated. While there are general references in Isaiah and the Psalms to being "abused by all men" (Ps.22:6) or "despised and rejected" (Isa. 53:3), each particular element of the Markan abuse has a scriptural precedent.

Isaiah 50:6-7: "I offered my back to the lash . . . I did not hide my face from spitting and insult." Pilate has Jesus flogged (15:15), and the soldiers spit on him (15:15), as the members of the Sanhedrin had earlier done (14:65). Micah 5:1 declares that "with a rod they strike upon the cheek the ruler of Israel," and so Mark has the soldiers "beat him about the head with a reed" (15:19). For other features of the abuse, Mark has looked to the Day of Atonement ritual of the two goats. The crown of thorns has been suggested by the thread of crimson wool laid on the head of the scapegoat. Dressing Jesus in a royal robe may reflect a further image of the red wool, though Crossan (*The Cross That Spoke*, p.128) thinks it "an allusion to Zechariah 3:1-5, an eschatological vision in which the high priest Joshua (Jesus!) has his filthy clothes removed and is robed instead with the sacerdotal garments."

Crucifixion

Chapter 8 pointed out the scriptural passages about "nailing" and "piercing" which would have suggested to Paul that the spiritual Christ had undergone crucifixion in the higher world. Zechariah 12:10, "They shall look upon him whom they have pierced." Psalm 22:16, "They have pierced my hands and my feet." And so on. Mark translates the "hanging on a tree" in the mythical realm to the cross mounted on the hill of Calvary outside Jerusalem. On the way to that execution, the evangelist introduces a memorable character, Simon of Cyrene, who helps an exhausted Jesus carry his cross. Generations of sermons focusing on this character more than justify Mark's intention here, to convey the lesson that Christians must share in the cross of Christ and help each other through adversity. While no scriptural passages readily suggest themselves as inspiration for this feature, it does reflect a frequent element within the tale's biblical model. There, various good-hearted people make an attempt to aid the hero, usually to no avail.

Once the crucifixion scene is under way, the text is thick with scriptural building blocks. Jesus' placement between two thieves is governed by Isaiah 53:12, "And he was numbered with the transgressors." Mark's passers-by hurl abuse at Jesus: "And those who passed by derided him, wagging their heads, and saying . . . 'save yourself, and come down from the cross!' Psalm 22:7-8 provides all three elements: "All who see me jeer at me, make mouths at me and wag their heads: 'He threw himself on the Lord for rescue; let the Lord save him'." Matthew, ever the stickler when it comes to scripture, adds (27:43) the specific thought in the Psalm's last phrase: "Let God deliver him now, if he wants him."

At the foot of the cross the soldiers gamble for Jesus' garments (15:24). Psalm 22:18 reads: "They divided my garments among them and for my raiments they cast lots." (While much scholarly study has gone into the Psalms, it is still not clear just when or in what situations they were written, though as a collection they are no doubt the product of a wide range of times and circumstances. Those plumbed by the evangelists naturally tended to be those which express some kind of distress and sense of persecution.)

From the cross, Jesus makes his anguished cry to God, a quote of the first verse of the ubiquitous Psalm 22: "My God, my God, why has thou forsaken me?" The generic tale often features a "Prayer" by the hero for deliverance or for vengeance. Mark allows Jesus to express neither of those hopes, but Luke's sentiment is more than appropriate: "Father, into thy hands I commend my spirit." In response to the cry in Mark, Jesus is offered vinegar to drink. Psalm 69:21 speaks of the psalmist receiving poison for food, "and for my thirst they gave me vinegar to drink." Only John addresses the question of the breaking of Jesus' legs—a regular practice in crucifixion—but it is to deny (19:33) that this was done, and perhaps the silence about this practice in the Synoptics is determined by the same need. Jesus' legs cannot be broken because there were too many 'interdictions' in the writings. Exodus 12:46 specifies that "You must not break a bone of (the paschal lamb)." Similarly, Numbers 9:12. Psalm 34:20 is adamant: "He guards every bone of his body, and not one of them is broken."

Reactions

While Jesus is still hanging on the cross, waiting to die, nature begins to react. Mark 15:33: "At midday darkness fell over the whole land which lasted until the ninth hour [three in the afternoon]." No record of such a phenomenon is to be found in the ancient world. Rather, its 'occurrence' is to be located on the pages of the prophet Amos. In forecasting the Day of Lord, he declares the word of God (8:9): "I will make the sun go down at noon and darken the earth in broad daylight."

When Jesus finally dies, further prodigies occur. The temple veil is torn in two from top to bottom, no doubt a symbol of God's displeasure with Israel and the passing away of the Temple's religious supremacy. Matthew adds an earthquake, drawing from the prophet Joel (2:10): "Before them the earth shakes, the heavens shudder. . . ." To which Joel has also added ". . . sun and moon are darkened, and the stars forbear to shine," another midrashic element supporting the darkness at noon motif. These prodigies are signs of God's reaction and thus of "Vindication."

But the reactions include human ones as well. Mark has the centurion at the cross declare (15:39) that "Truly, this man was (the)

Son of God." While Mark may be conveying a lesson here about faith and who possesses it, he is also providing the final components in the tale of the Suffering Righteous One: "Reaction" and "Acclamation." Bystanders and enemies marvel at what has taken place, and often praise the hero. The latter admit that they were wrong, as in the Wisdom of Solomon 5:4-5: "Fools that we were . . . he is one of the Sons of God."

Burial & Rising

Jesus had to be buried that evening, for Deuteronomy 21:22-23 prescribed that "(the hanged man's) body shall not remain all night upon the tree, but you shall bury him the same day." Joseph of Arimathea, who petitions Pilate for the body of Jesus and lays him in a tomb, is another Markan invention to further the plot line. Jesus had to be buried by his friends so that they would have access to the tomb and witness his resurrection. For this purpose, Mark also invented the characters of Mary Magdalene, Mary the mother of James, and Salome. They serve only to witness Mark's empty tomb, but once come to life on his pages they take on an ever expanding role in the later Gospels as witnesses to the risen Jesus himself. There is no sign of such women in the wider record of the first century.

Matthew is the only evangelist to introduce guards at the tomb. This seems not to be based on any scriptural precedent. Perhaps he felt that one evident objection to his story could be that without such a guard, the followers of Jesus might be accused of having stolen the body. That is in fact the rationale he supplies in the text (27:62-66). The Gospel of Peter also has an elaborate "guard at the tomb" scene, and these guards witness the actual resurrection of Jesus, a feature which no canonical evangelist supplies.

Jesus' rising from the tomb is also a sign of his Vindication and Exaltation. It fulfills a scriptural "prophecy" of Hosea (6:1-2):

"Come, let us return to the Lord, for he has torn us and will heal us, he has struck us and he will bind up our wounds; after two days he will revive us, on the third day he will restore us, that in his presence we may live."

The tale of Jonah also contains a similar motif: "For three days and three nights (Jonah) remained in the fish's belly" (1:17). From there he prayed, "Thou didst bring me up alive from the pit, O Lord my God," and God fulfilled the prophecy by having the fish spew Jonah out.

As we noted earlier, most early Christian witness outside the Gospels reveals no concept of Jesus rising from the dead to spend time on earth. In fact, just about everyone except Paul writes as though Jesus simply ascended to heaven immediately after death. What is Mark seeking to convey here? Some read an ambiguous meaning into 16:7, that part of the scene when the women go to the tomb and find it empty. Does the angel's message to the disciples, "He will go on before you into Galilee and you will see him there, as he told you," imply later physical appearances to them? Or might it simply refer to the Parousia, when Jesus will arrive as the Son of Man? Was it only the later evangelists who came up with the idea of a bodily resurrection and an appearance to his followers "in the flesh"? The tale of the Suffering and Vindicated Righteous One contained no such feature. If Mark had this innovative idea in mind, why did he not include actual post-resurrection appearances in his story?

We will probably never know.

Part Nine
THE SECOND CENTURY

24

The Remaking of Christian History

After the events "recorded" in the Gospel of Mark, Jesus of Nazareth and the great panoply of characters surrounding him sleep in a silent limbo for many decades. Their "resurrection" comes only at the beginning of the second century, when Mary and Pontius Pilate steal from the shadows onto the pages of Ignatius of Antioch's letters. That resurrection is rather a whimper than a bang, for it would be many decades more before the Gospel events emerge fully into the light.

Justin Martyr, in the 150s, is the first Christian writer to make identifiable quotations from the Gospels, and to declare that he is doing so, though it is possible that he knows only Matthew and Luke. Even at that, he does not refer to them by name, calling the documents he is quoting from "memoirs of the Apostles."[107] Moreover, his quotations for the most part do not agree with our present texts. Some have suggested that Justin was merely quoting from memory, or that he did not trouble to reproduce the exact wording of his sources. Some have postulated that he was working from a "harmony," an artificially created Gospel combining features and passages from more than one of the canonical Gospels into a single synthesis. Justin's pupil, Tatian, was later (c170) to compose the most famous harmony of all four Gospels, known as the *Diatessaron*.

A harmony, however, assumes that a number of Gospels are in widespread circulation and use prior to such a synthesis, and this is precisely what is lacking in the evidence prior to Justin. It is more likely that Justin is working with two or three Gospels that have only just emerged into wider Christian consciousness, and that they were to undergo further evolution and revision before arriving at the forms we know today. It is also apparent that the names now attached to those "memoirs of the Apostles" had not yet been applied. In Justin's day, they were simply anonymous. The first witness to a fourfold Gospel account of the life and death of Jesus, under the names of Matthew, Mark, Luke and John, comes only with Irenaeus around 180.[108]

In the writings of the Apostolic Fathers prior to Justin Martyr, we have no clear witness to any use of written Gospels. Those who have studied this matter[109] have concluded that the echoes of Gospel material occasionally found in the Fathers are derived from floating oral traditions or perhaps small collections of sayings; these elements would have found their own way into the written Gospels.

We will look at the four major Apostolic Fathers represented in surviving writings of the time: Ignatius of Antioch, Clement of Rome, Polycarp of Smyrna, and the writer of the Epistle of Barnabas.

Ignatius of Antioch

As noted in chapter 6, Ignatius is unlikely to be familiar with a written Gospel, for he would surely have pointed to one in support of his declaration that Jesus had been born of Mary and crucified by Pilate. Nor does he appeal to the idea of apostolic tradition, never suggesting that his biography about Jesus is knowledge that has been transmitted over the generations through apostolic channels. Nowhere in all of his seven letters, written around the year 107 while he was being brought to Rome for execution, does Ignatius quote a single teaching of Jesus, nor a miracle, nor any detail of the passion under Pilate which he so ardently defends.

All this would suggest that the biography he puts forward is of recent vintage, and that few if any other details of Jesus' human life are known to him.

Clement of Rome

A decade or so before Ignatius, the epistle known as 1 Clement was sent to the Christian community in Corinth from the Christian community in Rome. Tradition later identified the writer with Clement, bishop of Rome toward the end of the first century. Most scholars today doubt that he was the actual writer, though the letter may have been dispatched during his tenure. It is usually dated around 96 CE. In chapter 13, 'Clement' says:

"Let us remember especially the words of the Lord Jesus, which he spoke in teaching kindness and forbearance. For he said this: 'Be merciful, that you may obtain mercy. Forgive, that you may be forgiven. As you do, so shall it be done to you. As you give, so shall it be given to you. As you judge, so shall you be judged. As you are kind, so shall kindness be shown to you. Whatever measure you mete out, so it shall be measured to you.' "

Though many of these sentiments are to be found in the Synoptics, they nowhere appear as a block like this. Is Clement paraphrasing, or perhaps writing from his memory of a written Gospel? If so, his memory is exceedingly selective, for only a few verses later (14:4) he says: "It is written, 'the kind-hearted will inhabit the earth, and the innocent will remain upon it, but the transgressors will be rooted out of it.' " This is not a quotation from the Beatitudes, or even from oral tradition; it is Proverbs 2:21-22. The "it is written" refers, as always in this period, to the Jewish scriptures. Clement must be unfamiliar with Jesus' thoughts in the same vein, as presented in Matthew's Sermon on the Mount and Luke's Sermon on the Plain. Clement also shows himself to be unfamiliar with the Gospel teachings of Jesus on many other topics discussed in his letter.

When Clement comes to describe Jesus' suffering (ch.16) we must assume that he has no Gospel account to paraphrase or quote from memory, for he simply reproduces Isaiah 53. His knowledge of Jesus' passion comes from scripture. Clement's ignorance on other Gospel elements has been noted at earlier points in this book.

What, then, of the "teaching" of chapter 13, to which can be added 46:8: "Remember the words of the Lord Jesus, how he said: 'Woe to that man; it would be better if he had never been born, than that he should lead astray one of my chosen ones," a saying similar to one in Matthew and Luke? Since Clement knows so little of oral traditions about Jesus, must these be regarded as referring to an earthly ministry?

We have seen in the Pauline letters that the heavenly Christ was regarded as giving instructions to prophets through revelation. Clement shares in the outlook that sees Christ's voice as residing in scripture. In Chapter 22 he declares: "For it is (Christ) himself who summons us through the Holy Spirit, with the words: 'Come, children, listen to me, and I will teach you the fear of the lord.' " This is Christ speaking— and teaching—through a passage from Psalm 34 (11). Clement says that Christ "spoke" the teachings in chapter 13, using the same verb (*elalēsen*) that he uses in chapter 16, where the Holy Spirit "spoke" the description of the passion in Isaiah 53. Evidently Clement perceives the two sources as being the same.

The "teaching" of chapter 13, and Clement's phrasing of it, is reminiscent of the field of popular maxims. We know that this kind of moral directive belonged among the ethical commonplaces of the day. The saying in 46:8 (above) has all the flavor of an admonition thundered out by Christian prophets. In Clement's world, these things have come to be associated with revelations from the spiritual Christ, just as were Paul's "words of the Lord." Koester (*Ancient Christian Gospels*, p.15) acknowledges that Clement's sources were probably oral, rather than any version of a written Gospel.

Polycarp of Smyrna

Bishop Polycarp of Smyrna was a friend of Ignatius, though he outlived the latter by half a century. He was martyred, if modern scholarly deductions are correct, in 155. Polycarp's single surviving epistle seems to be made up of two pieces, one (ch. 13) written before he learned of Ignatius' fate in the arena, the other (ch. 1-12) some time later, perhaps as much as a quarter of a century.[110]

Even at that later time Polycarp seems unfamiliar with a written Gospel. In 2:3a he speaks of "the Lord in his teaching" and proceeds to quote part of the block of maxims found in 1 Clement 13. That quote, along with the lead-in words, is acknowledged to be a borrowing from Clement's letter and not from a Gospel. Koester (*op.cit.*, p.20) claims that Polycarp "corrected" the text of 1 Clement to coincide with the wording in the Gospels of Matthew and Luke, but this is not true of at least half the phrases, leading one to suspect that the other "corrections" are simple coincidence. (Alternatively, the present versions in Matthew and Luke may proceed from the wording familiar to Polycarp, or later copyists of Polycarp may have, consciously or unconsciously, altered some of the phrasing to match their familiarity with the Gospel versions—a not uncommon occurrence.)

In two other places (2:3b, 7:2) Polycarp uses further sayings found in the Gospels, but the former is not an exact match. Never does Polycarp refer explicitly to written documents. Koester admits (*op.cit.*, p.20): "It is remarkable that Polycarp never uses the term 'gospel' for these documents, and that the words of Jesus are still quoted as if they were sayings drawn from oral tradition."

Unlike Clement, Polycarp makes it clear (7:1) that he believes Jesus came to earth in the flesh. But like Clement, he has no account or traditions to draw from in regard to Jesus' passion. In referring to those 'events' (8:1) he, too, can only quote passages from Isaiah 53.

The Epistle of Barnabas

The Epistle of Barnabas has been dated anywhere between 90 and 125.[111] Like Polycarp and Clement, 'Barnabas' has no documents or traditions to draw on when he wishes to describe Jesus' passion (5:2, 5:12, 13). He, too, has recourse to Isaiah (50 and 53) and the Psalms (22 and 119). While Barnabas has a greater sense than any of the other early Fathers that Jesus had been on earth (5:10, 11), he has little of substance to say about that incarnation. He speaks of Jesus as teaching the people of Israel and of his miracles and wonders (5:8) but he never itemizes any of those teachings or miracles. The latter were expected of the Messiah, so the writer may simply be assuming that such things had happened.

In 5:9 he says that Christ had chosen apostles, but he describes those apostles unlike any portrayal found in the Gospels, calling them "sinners of the worst kind." He seems to base this on a saying whose source he does not identify: "He came not to call saints but sinners." This saying appears in Jesus' mouth in Mark 2:17, but there it applies to Jesus' general audience, not to his apostles. Barnabas quotes other things whose sources are unknown, and it is possible that this saying, too, is from some writing now lost, or is a unit of oral tradition that has come to be applied to Jesus. Barnabas is not likely to have known Mark and yet misapply this saying so badly, or to so misrepresent the character of the apostles in that Gospel.

His only other quotation of a saying found in the Gospels (Mt. 22:14) is 4:14: "It is written that many are called but few are chosen." "It is written" tells us that Barnabas looks upon the source as a sacred writing. In Barnabas' time, this could not have included the Gospel of Matthew—had it even been written by then.

Barnabas is also ignorant of any teachings of Jesus concerning dietary laws, or on what will happen at the End-time, or on "hearing the word of God"—all of which are topics he addresses in his letter. Like the Didache, this epistle contains a Two Ways section of moral teaching (ch. 18-21) but none of it is attributed to Jesus. In fact, these directives are referred to as "the precepts of the Lord, as they are set forth in scripture" (21:1). Thus Barnabas' concept of Jesus as a teacher would seem to be a theoretical one, not grounded in actual historical memory or record. He goes so far as to say that scripture is the means by which God has made the past known (5:3, compare 1:7)—including, we are to assume, Jesus' own experiences. He even suggests (5:12) that we know the Jews were responsible for Jesus' death because scripture says so! It is God, not historical memory, which has identified the Jews as those who killed his Son.[112]

Thus, we are confronted with a situation in which four different Christian writers over a period of some 40 years, ranging from Alexandria to Antioch to Asia Minor to Rome, show no knowledge of written Gospels—and this up to a period of some 60 years after the standard dating of Mark. Even the little homily known as 2 Clement, erroneously attributed to Clement of Rome and usually dated a little before the writings of Justin, quotes only sayings allegedly spoken by Jesus; it draws on no narrative events such as might be found in a written Gospel.[113] If Jesus had lived and undergone the experiences portrayed in the Gospels, and if those Gospels had been set down beginning as early as 70 CE, it is difficult to understand how the situation revealed by the Apostolic Fathers could have existed. Though the Fathers are beginning to draw on sayings and maxims which they attribute to Jesus, their abysmal ignorance of the basic content of the Gospels, especially in regard to the passion, would suggest that such documents and their dissemination are a late phenomenon.

Papias

In his *History of the Church* (Bk.III, ch.39) Eusebius quotes and discusses certain fragments of Papias, who was bishop of the city of Hierapolis in Asia Minor during the early second century. These and other fragments preserved by ancient commentators have been taken from Papias' most famous (and perhaps only) work, called *The Sayings of the Lord Interpreted*. This lost document has been dated between 110 and 140, with majority opinion lying somewhere in the middle of that span.

Modern catalogues of the various fragments of or about Papias usually list as No. 1 a quotation from Irenaeus in the late second century (*Against Heresies* Bk.V, 33.3-4). This fragment closely parallels a passage (29:4-8) in 2 Baruch, a Jewish apocalyptic work written around the turn of the second century CE. The passage is about the fertility of vineyards during the anticipated reign of the Messiah. (Both the Messiah and his reign lay, in Jewish perspective, in the future.) Papias, according to Irenaeus, has attributed it to Jesus, as a forecast of his own thousand-year reign when he returns from heaven.

This attribution to an historical Jesus of a passage taken from a Jewish writing illustrates not only the unreliability of Papias' own judgment or the traditions he is using about what Jesus had said, it is a good example of the widespread phenomenon of attaching current wisdom, ethical and prophetic material—even that contained in non-Christian sources—to the figure of Jesus, as the latter progressed from myth to history. It casts doubt on everything Papias says, or is reported to have said. Alternatively, if Irenaeus is mistaken, it casts doubt on all the later traditions about Papias and his writings, including in Eusebius.

To this observation one must add the bizarre nature of some of the preserved fragments. No. 3, from Apollinaris, contains a fanciful and gruesome account of the death of Judas. No. 11, from Philip of Side, a fifth century Christian historian, has Papias relating how Barsabas, a candidate along with Matthias to replace Judas (see Acts 1:23-6), was forced to drink snake poison and yet survived unharmed. The same fragment records that, according to Papias, the dead raised by Christ survived until the reign of Hadrian (117-138 CE). Clearly, Papias as a witness to anything is highly suspect.

But back to Eusebius. His extended discussion of Papias, known as Fragment 2, starts with a quote from Papias' "Prologue" which includes a confusing reference to a chain of apostolic tradition going back to the earliest apostles, through which Papias claims to have received some information about Jesus. Nothing secure can be derived from this passage.[114] Eusebius also includes some fantastic miracle traditions and most important, a reference to documents Papias says he had heard about which were attributed to "Mark" and "Matthew."

Here is that reference as quoted, in two parts, by Eusebius:

"This, too, the presbyter [or elder] used to say. 'Mark, who had been Peter's interpreter, wrote down carefully, but not in order, all that he remembered of the Lord's sayings and doings. For he had not heard the Lord or been one of his followers, but later, as I said, one of Peter's. Peter used to adapt his teaching to the occasion, without making a systematic arrangement of the Lord's sayings, so that Mark was quite justified in writing down some things just as he remembered them. For he had one purpose only - to leave out nothing that he had heard, and to make no misstatement about it.' "

Eusebius goes on:

"Such is Papias' account of Mark. Of Matthew he has this to say: 'Matthew compiled the Sayings in the Aramaic language, and everyone translated them as well as he could.' " [trans. G. A. Williamson, *Eusebius: A History of the Church*, p.152]

A number of fairly secure conclusions can be drawn from these quotations.

(1) Papias himself had not seen these documents, let alone possessed copies of them. In regard to "Mark," this is information he has received from "the presbyter." Although Papias is not specific when he gets to "Matthew," it is likely that the same situation applies there as well. Besides, if he possessed documents containing sayings and deeds of Jesus as recorded by Jesus' very followers, he would not likely have disparaged such written documents in favor of oral tradition, as he does at the end of Eusebius' quote from his Prologue: "For I assumed that what is derived from books does not profit me as much as what is derived from a living and abiding voice." Thus, it would seem that all of this information comes to Papias second-hand and is recounted from memory. He can witness to nothing else than that certain collections of material were circulating sometime in the early second century, which some people were now assigning to an historical Jesus, as recorded by legendary apostolic figures who had come to be regarded as his followers.

(2) Those collections may or may not have circulated under the names of "Mark" and "Matthew." Papias does not specify that this is what they were called, but simply who the reputed compilers were.

(3) It is highly unlikely that these two documents are to be equated with the canonical Gospels now known as Mark and Matthew. In the latter case, Papias states clearly that it was a compilation of sayings. This rules out a narrative work. If it was in Aramaic, it could not be the Gospel of Matthew, since that was a work composed originally in Greek and based on the Greek Gospel of Mark. Scholarship has abandoned any suggestion that Matthew or any other Gospel existed at an earlier stage in Aramaic. Not even Q, the document used by Matthew and Luke, can be demonstrated to have been written at any stratum in anything other than Greek.

As for Papias' "Mark," this is referred to as a record of Peter's recollections of "the Lord's sayings and doings," but not "in order" nor with the purpose of "constructing an ordered arrangement of the Lord's sayings." While the "doings" suggest anecdotes about deeds of Jesus— probably miracles—the reference to lack of "order" and "arrangement" rules out the narrative Gospel of Mark. Rather, what is suggested is a loose compilation of sayings and anecdotes, probably something along the lines of the Q document which contained sayings and a few miracle and controversy stories reflective of the community's activities. That this was a haphazard, unorganized collection is further suggested by all the apology about it which Papias expresses. This in turn suggests that such a collection may have had nothing to do with a Jesus figure originally, and only seemed "unordered" as a picture of his ministry when it was assigned to such a figure.

In view of all this, it is surprising how many New Testament scholars insist on regarding these remarks as referring to the canonical Gospels of Mark and Matthew, and how they try to rationalize those remarks in order to do so.[115]

(4) Many scholars also assume that Papias possessed copies of these documents, and even that he discussed the Gospel sayings of Jesus in his work. This is patently impossible. Not only does Papias' own language, as quoted by Eusebius, rule this out, not a single one of the fragments (over a dozen) preserved from his *Sayings of the Lord Interpreted* includes any saying from the canonical Gospels. If Papias had actually discussed *anything* from the Gospels we know, there can be no doubt that Eusebius, having Papias' work in front of him, would have thrown a spotlight on it. If sayings and deeds of Jesus as found in Mark and Matthew had been a feature of Papias' work, later commentators like Philip of Side would hardly have limited themselves to the often ridiculous and repugnant things Papias does have to say.

(5) Whatever Papias' second-hand description referred to,[116] it is quite possible that traditions like these were drawn on later when it came time, probably a little after Justin, for the Church to decide who might have written the Gospel accounts of Jesus of Nazareth.

Marcion and the Gnostic Appropriation of Paul

Many have been the attempts to provide a simple definition of Gnosticism. In the fullest flowering of this religious movement in the second century, from Mesopotamia to Gaul, there were many sects and many different varieties of doctrine, but the commonest features of gnostic belief were these. Something had gone wrong in heaven within the workings and evolution of the various parts of the Godhead, and the creation of the world of matter and humans had resulted. This was a great misfortune, since the world was an evil place. As part of that heavenly malfunction, pieces of divinity had fallen into matter and now resided in a certain class of human beings. Through varied processes of revelation and salvation—usually including a heavenly revealer-savior who descended to earth—these 'gnostic' humans were discovering their true natures. Through this secret knowledge, or "gnosis," they were learning how they could reascend to their rightful home in heaven and rejoin the Deity.

An essential part of the full-blown gnostic myth was the idea that an evil god or rebel angel had created the material world of humans and now ruled over it. Some gnostics equated this evil god with the God of the Old Testament, Yahweh himself. For reasons that are still obscure, Gnosticism grounded its features in the Jewish scriptures, particularly Genesis. This it combined with Greek philosophical speculation based on the creation myths outlined in Plato's *Timaeus*. Whether this means that the movement grew out of radical Jewish circles which had adopted esoteric features of Greek philosophy, or whether it began with gentiles who syncretized with Jewish thought, is uncertain. (This question lies at the heart of the great debate over the origins of Gnosticism.)[117] But in that Jewish-grounded thought world, the true, highest God stood over and above the traditional God of the Jews, and the latter was regarded by many gnostics as an evil sub-deity. The most prominent advocate of this idea was Marcion.

Marcion came to Rome around 138 CE from Sinope on the Black Sea and joined the Christian Church of Rome. Before long, however, he had adopted the gnostic ideas of Cerdo, who hailed from Syria, that the evil creator-god was Yahweh and that Jesus Christ had come to reveal the true Father, the good God who was higher than the God of the Old Testament. Marcion's Christ was docetic, he remained true spirit even on earth, but through his death he had broken the power of the evil Yahweh and freed mankind from the Jewish Law. For these beliefs Marcion was expelled from the Church in 144. Within ten years he had established his own Church to rival the Roman one, and soon the Marcionites had spread over much of the empire.

Marcion rejected Judaism and its scriptures as the product and embodiment of the evil creator. This rejection probably accelerated the Roman Church's own movement in the opposite direction: to adopt the Jewish scriptures and claim them as Christianity's own heritage. Marcion formed his own set of authoritative writings embodying the truth—the earliest "canon"—made up of a shorter version of the Gospel of Luke,[118] and ten letters of Paul. In Paul, Marcion saw many 'gnostic' ideas which he claimed supported his own doctrines. This appropriation of Paul and the formation of the first recorded Pauline corpus also spurred the Roman Church to move toward establishing its own canon of officially approved documents, which would include four Gospels and a Pauline corpus of 13 letters.[119]

Those four Gospels were no doubt subjected to some reworking in the period from Justin to Irenaeus (150-175). Not only does the longer, canonical version of Luke not show up until this time, it would seem that the final, ecclesiastical redaction of the Gospel of John, reworked to soften its dangerously 'gnostic' elements and add the Logos hymn in a new Prologue, comes from this period. John Knox has suggested (*op.cit.*, p.140) that the choice of the four canonicals out of a burgeoning field of available Gospels (see Note 4) was not a chance affair. It was not so much that these four were chosen *because* they were regarded as more authentic, but that they made the best available candidates for creating a canon; they could be beaten into shape to provide support for the beliefs then current in orthodox circles and to counter Marcionism.

That counter became an ambitious, multi-pronged attack, spread over the third quarter of the second century. Not only would Paul be rehabilitated and rescued from the gnostics, but a wider apostolic base of authority would be established. The Church proceeded to collect documents from Christian communities all across the empire and turned them into epistles written by the actual apostles of Jesus: Peter, John, James, Jude. These gave authority to the legendary Twelve and fitted Paul and the Church into a broad apostolic stream which would wash away Marcion and his claims.

But the greatest weapon in the war against the Marcionite heretics literally created early Christian history.

The Acts of the Apostles

One of the reactions to Marcion and his appropriation of Paul seems to have been the composition of the Acts of the Apostles, sometime around the middle of the second century. By attaching Paul securely to the Jerusalem apostles, by giving him speeches which held not a trace of heresy—they are identical in tone and content to those put in Peter's mouth—and by ignoring the very fact that Paul had written letters which the Marcionites were declaring gave support to their own doctrines, the Church of Rome reclaimed Paul for itself.

At the same time, Acts created a unified view of the Christian apostolic movement in its spread across the empire, arising out of "Golden Age" events in Judea. Such a picture clearly linked the idealized beginnings of the movement with the Roman Church and not the Marcionites. The construction of Acts was carried out in conjunction with the expansion of the Gospel of Luke over the earlier version used by Marcion, and the two documents were linked under one 'author' (whom I will refer to as "Luke").

A detailed study of Acts is beyond the scope of this book, but we can survey its essential features which support the above scenario.

In pondering the date of Acts, scholars must face the fact that no clear evidence of it surfaces before 175, in Irenaeus (*Against Heresies*, Bk.III, ch.12:1-15). Justin, in his *Apology* and *Dialogue with the Jew Trypho*, never once refers to it, nor does anyone before him. (See the extensive discussion of the witness to Acts in Ernst Haenchen's *The Acts of the Apostles: A Commentary*, p.3f.) Several scholars lean toward a date well into the second century. John Knox's mid-second century date (*Marcion and the New Testament*, p.124) is seconded by J. T. Townsend ("The Date of Luke-Acts," in *Perspectives on Luke-Acts*, p.47f). Others place it a little before Marcion: J. C. O'Neill at 115-130 (*The Theology of Acts*, p.21), Burton Mack around 120 (*Who Wrote the New Testament?* p.167).

But one of the most effective arguments in favor of a post-Marcion composition of Acts is put forward by Knox (*op.cit.*, p.119-123). Marcion chose an early form of the Gospel of Luke as his 'canonical' Gospel. Would he have done so if it were already attached to the Acts of the Apostles, a document which portrayed Paul in a way that directly contradicted Marcion's own view of Paul? Marcion claimed that Paul was independent of Jesus' original disciples and was thus free of the "Jewish corruption" (in Marcion's eyes) which those apostles had brought to Jesus' teaching. Yet an Acts of the Apostles integrated with the Gospel of Luke would have discredited that very claim, making it highly unlikely that Marcion would have chosen to use Luke at all.

It is often argued that, since the author of Acts shows no sign that he is familiar with Paul's letters, this must date Acts earlier than the formation of the first corpus of Pauline epistles. But whether a corpus had been formed or not, if that author knew anything of Paul (and how could he not, if he undertook to write a 'biography' of him?) he had to know that Paul was famed as a letter writer. Thus, no matter when Acts was written, its silence on the letters of Paul must be deliberate.

In the scenario of a mid-second century composition of Acts, the reason for the silence would have been the fact that those epistles had been appropriated by Marcion. Perhaps the Church's own corpus, through which Paul would undergo rehabilitation, had not yet been completed. Thus Acts' silence on the Pauline letters cannot be used to date the document. In addition, since evidence for the longer, canonical Luke cannot be found before Justin, and the two documents, Luke and Acts, surface only later in a close twinning which contains evidence that they were written/revised by the same author, it seems justified to date both Luke and Acts post-Marcion.

Scholars have long noted that Acts contains a markedly primitive view of Christian theology. Like the Gospel of Luke, it has no explicitly redemptive interpretation of the death of Jesus. (In Luke, only if one appeals to the longer version of Jesus' eucharistic words found in some manuscripts—probably later accretions under the influence of other Gospels—is anything to be found on the subject of soteriology.[120]) Paradoxically, this 'primitive' quality in both Acts and the standard Luke fits not the mid or late first century, when the Pauline type of cultic Christ was still the predominant expression of Christianity. Rather, it fits the mid-second century, when the new Gospel picture of Mark's virtually human Jesus (see Note 80) had eclipsed the Pauline cosmic Son of God and redemptive Christ. Rather than the Christ of Luke-Acts being "pre-Pauline," as it is sometimes styled,[121] it is *post*-Pauline, when the Q-like Jesus of the Synoptics had supplanted the spiritual Christ of the cultic movement.

Even the Marcionites had little appreciation for the cosmic Son Paul had really preached. They focused instead on using Paul to support their view of the Gospel Jesus as a preacher of the true God over the Jewish creator-god Yahweh. Thus the author of Acts, living at a time when Paul lay under a tainted and obscuring cloud of heretical adoption, probably knew little and understood less of the actual content of Paul's letters, making it easy to simply ignore them. That Paul was not widely known by the Christian world as a whole is something scholars have recently come to realize. Justin has not a word to say about Paul, and only with Irenaeus, once the canon including the Pauline epistles had been put together by the Church of Rome, does he emerge with any force in orthodox circles. This state of affairs during the first hundred years after Paul supports the picture of Christianity as a diverse movement with no central coordination or common tradition.

Contradicting Paul

Luke's disregard of the epistles and ignorance of their content would have created the other striking feature of Acts: the contradiction of so much of its details with the information contained in Paul's own writings. Acts portrays Paul, upon his conversion, as immediately subordinating himself to the apostles in Jerusalem, but the epistles show him operating quite independently and in occasional conflict with them; he fails even to contact them for three years (Gal. 1:18). Paul in Acts is a faithful observer of the Law, going so far as to circumcise Timothy (16:3). Yet Paul in the epistles maintains that the Law has run its course and should be suspended (Gal. 3:23-25).

There are major discrepancies between the account in Acts (15:4-29) concerning the so-called Apostolic Council in Jerusalem and Paul's description of these events in Galatians 2. If the regulations stated in Luke's version had truly been agreed upon, Paul's difficulties over circumcision and table fellowship with the gentile would have evaporated. Luke reflects what had been resolved by his own time, and in true sectarian fashion he is anxious to have it grounded and legitimized in a decision by the original apostles.

Some of the details concerning Paul which Luke has provided have been judged likely to be fiction: that he was a trained rabbi who studied under Gamaliel (Acts 22:3), that he was a Roman citizen—which would make the final quarter of Acts pure invention, since Paul is sent to Rome as a result of his claim of Roman citizenship and the granting of his appeal to Caesar.[122] Even Acts' statement that Paul hailed from Tarsus has been questioned. None of these facts are supplied by Paul, and situations reflected in his letters would belie the first two. As for charismatic activities, Paul provides no support for the idea that he performed miracles on the scale of those described in Acts, much less raised anyone from the dead (20:9-12).

Much of the Pauline chronology of Acts is incompatible with Paul's movements as constructed from the letters. Acts' repeated portrayal of Paul proceeding first to Jewish synagogues at each center he visits and there preaching his message unsuccessfully, has no support in the epistles, where Paul's preaching to the Jews seems to lie entirely in his past. In Acts, Luke is anxious to portray the Jews as constantly rejecting the word of God, in order to reinforce his picture of the gentiles inheriting the promises of "eternal life" (13:46) which the Jews have forfeited. This was very much the self-image of second century Christianity, by then almost entirely gentile in makeup—at least within centrist circles such as Rome.

Paul gives no support to the incident of his own conversion on the Damascus Road; this may have been a legend that developed before Luke's time or else was invented by him. Earlier writers who speak of Paul nowhere refer to the long sea voyage with its dramatic shipwreck.

As noted above, some consider that this episode (Acts 27-28) may be entirely fictional, emulating a popular element in contemporary Hellenistic romances.[123]

The great disruptive debates in which Paul was engaged in his letters are nowhere in sight in Acts. Though Luke may have possessed pieces of tradition concerning early apostolic activity and about Paul— whether accurate, legendary, or tendentious is impossible to say—there can be little doubt that in constructing his account of the beginnings of the Christian faith movement, his sole purpose was to create a picture which would serve the needs of his own time and his own situation. That purpose had nothing to do with faithfully reproducing history.[124]

Opening a New Window in Acts

Acts' picture is generally taken as a window onto the early Jerusalem community and its beliefs, but few details of that picture enjoy any corroboration in the early record. There is a tendency among scholars to suggest that the 'primitive' view of Jesus in Acts—he is not overtly described as divine, nor even as a 'savior'—indicates that this early group of apostles around Peter and James did not hold Jesus to be an actual divinity. But we have noted before that such a claim is unsupported by Paul, who in his letters clearly links the Jerusalem apostles with his own cultic view of Christ's death and resurrection. He provides no indication that the former's attitude toward Jesus differed so markedly from his own. In 1 Corinthians 15:11, he says: "This is what we all proclaim, and this is what you (the Corinthians) believed."

Neither Paul nor any other epistle writer mentions the great collective visitation of the Holy Spirit to the apostles at Pentecost (Acts 2:1-4). Rather, Paul's view of the Spirit, as witnessed in passages like 2 Corinthians 11:4, is a matter of personal revelation to individuals. Luke has focused that widespread phenomenon of the early prophetic movement onto a single, representative dramatic event.

The great martyrdom of Stephen with its picture of the "Hellenist" community in Jerusalem (6:1-7:60) sounds not an echo in the early evidence. Some now regard Stephen as a fictional character. Luke, again in sectarian fashion, is representing the largely gentile nature of the faith in his own time as having had an archetypal existence in a group in Jerusalem during the earliest days of the movement. There are suspicious parallels between Luke's account of Stephen's death and descriptions of James the Just's murder in the year 62, as described by Hegesippus, recorded in Eusebius (*History of the Church*, II,23).

Scholars admit that no sources can be identified for Acts. We know of no documents Luke might have used for his information, nor is there any sign from features of style or form that he is incorporating sources unknown to us. The speeches are clearly constructed by the author.[125] Virtually all of them have the same tone and content. All indications are that Luke, in writing Acts, is composing and not compiling.

Thus, Acts opens a window, not onto earliest Christianity, but onto the Christian ecclesiastical movement centered in Rome during the mid-second century, one which was seeking to establish a new orthodoxy based on the historical Jesus recently generated by the Gospels. But there was something else on the scene as well, something notably different from either the Roman Church or its gnostic rivals: the expression of Christianity embodied in the second century apologists. To that, in the final chapter of this book, we now turn.

25

Jesus in the Christian Apologists

The second century was the period of formative growth for Christianity as we know it. Gospels which had their roots in the very late first century were spreading throughout the Christian world, and by the time of Justin were coming to be accepted in many circles as historical accounts. The Acts of the Apostles was written sometime around the middle of the century to provide a unified picture of Christian beginnings and the apostolic movement, one to fit the new scenario created by the Gospels. Acts joined Paul to the Jerusalem apostles in a way which took away his independence and undercut Marcion's claim that Paul had held doctrines compatible with his own. Widely diverse pieces of writing were collected from communities all over the Christian world, most of them in the form of epistles, though one or two may have been recast to fit that form. It is possible that some had their names ascribed to them only at that time, names of legendary apostles of the Christ now regarded, thanks to Mark, as having been disciples of the Gospel Jesus. As for Paul himself, a corpus of his genuine letters, along with others written in his name, was put together, in imitation of an earlier, more limited collection by Marcion. These diverse writings by early cultic Christians were now assumed to have been speaking of the Jesus of the Gospels.

Much of this work of collection and rehabilitation was performed by the Church of Rome, and there is no doubt that this undertaking, with its focus on the new historical Jesus, was a major factor in that Church's eventual ascendancy to a position of power over the previously fragmented Christian world. The recognition of such a political advantage was no doubt a key factor in the enthusiasm with which the idea of an historical Jesus was embraced and promoted. The next two centuries were to see the Roman bishopric assert its hegemony over all strands of the Christian movement, both "orthodox" and "heretical." Once it gained real political power, anything falling into the latter category was systematically exterminated.

But the second century scene, for much of its course, was anything but united in the new views of Jesus and Christian history. This is nowhere so evident as in the Christian apologists of the period 130-180, men like Justin Martyr, Tatian, Theophilus of Antioch, Athenagoras of Athens. Once again, as in the first century, we encounter diversity, a lack of common doctrine, no centralized authority and a weak concept of apostolic tradition. We also encounter a telling range of silence on the reputed founder of the movement.

The Apologists as Platonic Philosophers

Those who study the apologists have made some surprising observations. They note how little continuity these writers show with earlier traditions. Their ideas often have nothing in common with those of the epistles and even the Gospels. There is no dependence on Paul. Moreover, such writers seem not to move in ecclesiastical circles. Even Justin, though he worked in Rome, has nothing to say about bishops and church organizations. And almost all of them before the year 180 (Justin being the major exception) are silent on the Gospels and the figure of Jesus contained in them. In fact, one could say that they pointedly ignore, and even deny, any historical figure at all.

Scholars specializing in the second century have characterized the Christianity of the apologists as essentially a philosophical movement. Whereas the premier expression of Christian development in the first century, the one belonging to Paul and the Jerusalem group, was an essentially Jewish, apocalyptically oriented phenomenon, that of the apologists, who were all located in cosmopolitan centers of the empire, was grounded in Platonic philosophy and Hellenistic Judaism.

Justin, the apologist about whom we know the most, came to Christianity after having investigated all the other popular philosophies of his day: the Stoics, Peripatetics (begun with Aristotle), the Pythagoreans. Finally, he was schooled in Middle Platonism, the predominant philosophical outlook which colored everything else in this era, especially in its strongly religious concerns about the nature of Deity and its relationship to humanity. When Justin encountered Christianity, he judged it to be the best version of contemporary philosophy. In Rome, he seems to have had no connection with any ecclesiastical body, but set up his own school, teaching Christian philosophy in the manner of pagan philosophers of the time.

What was this 'Christian philosophy' as presented by the apologists as a group? There is no question that it had roots in Judaism. It preached the monotheistic worship of the Jewish God, a God presented as superior to those of the pagans. For information about this God it looked to the Hebrew scriptures. It placed great value on a mode of life founded on Jewish ethics—again, something presented as superior to the ethical philosophy of the pagans. At the same time, it derived from Platonism the concept of a Son of God, a 'second God' or Logos (Word), a force active in the world and serving as an intermediary between God and humanity. In the second century even more so than in the first, this idea of the Logos was floating in the air of most Greek philosophies as well as Hellenistic Judaism.

Thus the religion of the apologists has been styled "Platonic-biblical" or "religious Platonism with a Judaistic cast," although it was in the process of wresting away from those Jews the ancient promises of their God and even their own scriptures. It would seem to have grown out of mixed pagan and Jewish Diaspora circles which had immersed themselves in Greek philosophy. (Justin and others, including the gnostic movement, provide evidence of heretical Jewish sects, with many gentiles attached, which had evolved a great distance from traditional Jewish loyalty and thinking.) There is little to suggest that the apologists' religion proceeded out of the first century branch of Christian development surrounding Paul. Nor is there any of the Gospels' focus on the Messiah or the end of the world, and the apologists' views of salvation are rooted in Greek mysticism, not Jewish martyrology for sin. Instead, the two expressions seem like separate branches of a very broad tree.

Justin, and whoever recast the Gospel of John to include the Prologue, with its hymn equating the Logos with Jesus, came to believe that the intermediary Word, the spiritual Son of God, had been incarnated in a human figure as recounted in the Gospels. But is this true of the apologists as a whole?

The astonishing fact is that of the five or six major apologists up to the year 180—after that, Irenaeus, Tertullian, Clement of Alexandria and Origen are all firmly anchored in Gospel tradition—none, with the exception of Justin, introduces an historical Jesus into their defenses of Christianity to the pagan.

Theophilus of Antioch

Consider Theophilus of Antioch. According to Eusebius, he became bishop in that city in 168, but one has to wonder. In his treatise *To Autolycus*, apparently written toward the year 180, he tells us that he was born a pagan and became a Christian after reading the Jewish scriptures, a situation common to virtually all the apologists.

But what, for Theophilus, is the meaning of the name "Christian"? The Autolycus of the title has asked him this question. He answers (I.12): "Because we are anointed with the oil of God." Though the name "Christ" itself means Anointed One, from the anointed kings of Israel, no reference is made to Christ himself in regard to the meaning of "Christian." In fact, Theophilus never mentions Christ, or Jesus, at all. He makes no reference to a founder-teacher; instead, Christians have their doctrines and knowledge of God through the Holy Spirit. Along with the pronouncements of the Old Testament prophets, he includes "the gospels" (III.12), but these too are said to be the inspired word of God, not a record of Jesus' words and deeds. When he quotes ethical maxims corresponding to Jesus' Gospel teachings, he presents them (II.14) as the teaching of those gospels, not of Jesus himself.

And what is Theophilus' Son of God? He is the Word through whom God created the world, who was begat by him along with Wisdom (II.10). He is the governing principle and Lord of all creation, inspiring the prophets and the world in general to a knowledge of God. Yet Theophilus has not a thing to say about this Word's incarnation into flesh, or any deed performed by him on earth. In fact, he hastens to say (II.22) that this is not a Son in the sense of begetting, but as innate in the heart of God.

Here he seems to quote part of the opening lines of the Gospel of John, the Word as God and instrumental in creation, but nothing else. Is this from the full-blown Gospel, or perhaps from the Logos hymn John drew upon? (The name "John," the only evangelist mentioned, could be a later marginal gloss inserted into the text; but see below.) The writers of the "gospels," Theophilus says, are inspired men, not witnesses to an historical Jesus.

As for redemption, all will gain eternal life who are obedient to the commandments of God (II.27). There is no concept in Theophilus of an atoning sacrificial death of Jesus, a death he never mentions. And when challenged on his doctrine that the dead will be raised—Autolycus has demanded: "Show me even one who has been raised from the dead!"— this Christian has not a word to say about Jesus' own resurrection. He even accuses the pagans of worshiping "dead men" (I.9) and ridicules them for believing that Hercules and Aesclepius were raised from the dead (I.13). All this, in answer to an Autolycus who has asked: "Show me thy God."

Athenagoras of Athens

Athenagoras of Athens, who worked in Alexandria, wrote around the same time, though one ancient witness places him a few decades earlier. He was a philosopher who had embraced Christianity, but he shows no involvement in any church, or interest in rituals and sacraments. In *A Plea For the Christians* addressed to the emperor, he says this of his new beliefs (10): "We acknowledge one God . . . by whom the Universe has been created through his Logos, and set in order and kept in being . . . for we acknowledge also a Son of God . . . . If it occurs to you to enquire what is meant by the Son, I will state that he is the first product of the Father (who) had the Logos in himself. He came forth to be the idea and energizing power of all material things."

Unfortunately, in the course of 37 chapters, Athenagoras neglects to tell the emperor that Christians believe this Logos to have been incarnated in the person of an historical Jesus. He dissects contemporary Platonic and Stoic philosophy, angels and demons, as well as details of various Greek myths, but he offers not a scrap about the life of the Savior. He presents (11) Christian doctrine as things "not from a human source, but uttered and taught by God," and proceeds to quote ethical maxims very close to parts of the Sermon on the Mount: "Love your enemies; bless them that curse you . . . ." Other quotations he labels as coming from scripture, or from "our teaching." Are these ethical collections that are unattributed to Jesus? Athenagoras never uses the term "gospel." He speaks of "the witness to God and the things of God" and enumerates the prophets and other men, yet he ignores what should have been the greatest witness of them all, Jesus of Nazareth.

With no incarnation, there is in Athenagoras' presentation of the Christian faith no death and resurrection of Jesus, no sacrifice and Atonement. Eternal life is gained "by this one thing alone: that (we) know God and his Logos" (12). In fact, the names Jesus and Christ never appear in Athenagoras. Yet he can say (11), "If I go minutely into the particulars of our doctrines, let it not surprise you." One might be forgiven for regarding this as blatant dishonesty.

The Epistle to Diognetus

The anonymous *Epistle to Diognetus* is often included with the Apostolic Fathers. But it is really an apology, a defense of Christianity addressed probably to an emperor, either Hadrian or Marcus Aurelius. Most scholars lean to an early date (*c*130). The writer goes so far as to say that the ultimate God sent the Logos, his Son, down to earth, but no time, place, or identity for this incarnation are provided. The name Jesus never appears. The Son revealed God, but is not portrayed as a human teacher.

We find an allusion (9) to the Atonement: "He (God) took our sins upon himself and gave his own Son as a ransom for us," but his description of this act is based on scripture. No Gospel details are mentioned, no manner of the Son's death (if that's what it was), no resurrection. All this is in response to Diognetus' "close and careful inquiries" about the Christian religion. The final two chapters of the sole surviving manuscript of *The Epistle to Diognetus*, which contain a reference to apostles and disciples of the Word, have been identified as belonging to a separate document, probably a homily from the mid to late second century.[126]

Tatian

We turn now to Tatian, a pupil of Justin. He was converted to Christianity, he says, by reading the Jewish scriptures. At a later stage of his career, after apostatizing to the heretical sect of the Encratites and going off to Syria, Tatian composed the famous *Diatessaron*, the first known harmony of the four canonical Gospels. But while still in Rome, some time around 160, he wrote an *Apology to the Greeks*, urging pagan readers to turn to the truth. In this description of Christian truth, Tatian uses neither "Jesus" nor "Christ," nor even the name "Christian." Much space is devoted to outlining the Logos, the creative power of the universe, first-begotten of the Father, through whom the world was made—but none to the incarnation of this Logos. His musings on God and the Logos, rather than being allusions to the Gospel of John, as some claim, contradict the Johannine Prologue in some respects and may reflect Logos commonplaces of the time. Resurrection of the dead is not supported by Jesus' resurrection. Eternal life is gained through knowledge of God (13:1), not by any atoning sacrifice of Jesus.

In Tatian's *Apology* we find a few allusions to Gospel sayings, but no specific reference to written Gospels and no attribution of such things to Jesus. Instead, all knowledge comes from God himself. Tatian says he was "God-taught" (29:2). He does, however, make a revealing comment about mythical stories, which I will return to in a moment. Finally, around the year 155, the first Latin Apologist, Minucius Felix, wrote a dialogue between a Christian and a heathen, entitled *Octavius*.

It too presents a Christianity without an historical Jesus, and in fact contains some startling features in this regard. It will be examined in some detail later in this chapter.

Apologizing for the Apologists

As one can see by this survey, if one leaves aside Justin Martyr there is a silence in the second century apologists on the subject of the historical Jesus which is almost the equal of that in the first century epistle writers. Commentators on these works, like those studying the earlier epistles, have struggled to come up with explanations.

One is that the apologists were concerned first and foremost with preaching the monotheistic Father, the God of the Jews, while debunking the Greek myths with their all-too-human and morally uninspiring divinities. This is true. But it should not have precluded them from devoting some space to the most essential feature of the faith, and besides, the apologists have no reluctance about bringing in the Son of God in the form of the Logos. In fact, the apologists as a group profess a faith which is nothing so much as a Logos religion. It is in essence Platonism carried to its fullest religious implications and wedded with Jewish theology and ethics. The figure of Jesus of Nazareth as the incarnation of the Logos is a graft, an adoption which was embraced only by Justin and the later Tatian.

The glaring anomaly which must be explained is this: how can an apologist be giving his pagan readers a meaningful picture of the Christian faith when he leaves out the most central of its elements, the figure of Jesus and what he had done for salvation? How was the reader to understand the history and origins of the movement without him?

Inevitably, commentators have been led to conclude that the omission—indeed, the suppression—of Jesus was deliberate. Pagan philosophers like Galen had challenged Christian thinkers that their faith was based on revelation rather than reasoned philosophical argument. They had ridiculed the idea of a crucified god. The heathen attitude had made it impolitic to speak of Jesus of Nazareth, and so he needed to be kept in the closet.

Too many common sense arguments tell against this explanation. First, a writer like Athenagoras is quite adept at reasoned, sophisticated argument. Why not apply such talents to a justification of the faith's principal tenet? If the world at large is maligning Jesus, surely the overriding need is to rehabilitate him, not hide him away. Second, this blatant suppression of Jesus, the misrepresentation of everything from the name "Christian" to the source of Christian ethics, amounts to nothing less than a *denial* of Christ. The apologist is constructing a picture which excludes the central elements of the faith, falsifying his presentation, leaving no room for Jesus. He has gone beyond silence in stating, "I have said all there is to say." In an age when Christian pride and fortitude required that any penalty be faced—even the ultimate one—rather than renounce the faith, this gutting of Christian doctrine would have smacked of betrayal. It would have horrified believers and quickly discredited the apologists in Christian eyes. Could any of them really have chosen to defend the Name by expunging it?

Moreover, who would they be fooling? Any pagan who knew the first thing about Christianity would surely have been familiar with the figure of Jesus of Nazareth as the movement's founder. An 'apology' for the faith which left him out would readily be seen for the sham that it was, thus foiling the whole object of the exercise. Besides, Justin, the most prominent of the apologists, felt no qualms about placing Jesus at the center of his exposition. Tatian was someone who cared not a fig for the objections or sensibilities of any pagan. And beyond the year 180 no Christian writer felt any need or pressure to suppress Jesus.

Another important consideration is that the apologists were arguing for the superiority of Christian ethics and its monotheistic view of God. If Jesus had been the source of these teachings, their stature would have been raised by being presented as the product of a great teacher; while at the same time, the attribution to Jesus of this estimable body of ethics and theology would have gone a long way toward redeeming him in pagan eyes for whatever Christians might have been claiming about him which met with their disapproval. The fact that no one but Justin has incorporated the teaching, human Jesus into his appeals to the pagan is too bizarre a situation. No, some other explanation for the silence of almost the whole of the apologetic movement must be sought.

A clue to the solution of this puzzle lies in Tatian's *Apology*. In chapter 21 he says, "We are not fools, men of Greece, when we declare that God has been born in the form of man [his only allusion to the incarnation] . . . Compare your own stories with our narratives." He goes on to describe some of the Greek myths about gods come to earth, undergoing suffering and even death for the benefaction of mankind. "Take a look at your own records and accept us merely on the grounds that *we too tell stories*" (my italics).

This may well be a reference to the Christian Gospels. But if Tatian can allude to the incarnation in this way, why does he not deal with it openly and at length? His comment is hardly a ringing endorsement, or a declaration that such stories are to be accepted as history. The way Tatian compares them to the Greek myths implies that he regards them as being on the same level. Certainly, he does not rush to point out that the Christian stories are superior or, unlike the Greek ones, factually true. Nor can we get around the fact that he pointedly ignores those Gospel stories in the rest of his *Apology*. (He was to change his mind by the time he composed the *Diatessaron*.) Furthermore, he ignores them even though his language clearly implies that the pagans were familiar with them.

Rejecting the Gospel Graft

There seems to be only one way to interpret all this. We can assume that most, perhaps all, of the philosopher-apologists had encountered the Gospel story and its figure of Jesus of Nazareth. But with the exception of Justin, they had chosen not to integrate him into their own faith, not to identify this reputed historical founder-teacher with their divine Logos and Son of God, not to regard him as the source of Christian teachings.

This is possible only if the Logos religion the apologists subscribed to, especially at the time of their conversion, was lacking the figure of Jesus of Nazareth. Only if they could view the Gospel story and its central character as a recent graft, a fictional, symbolic tale like those of the Greeks, was it possible for them to reject it, to feel that they could be presenting the Christian faith legitimately. Only if it were possible for pagans to regard the story of Jesus as a myth like their own religious myths, was it acceptable for the apologists to present to them a Christianity which ignored or rejected the figure of Jesus.

As a mix of Platonism and Hellenistic Judaism, the apologists' branch of Christianity had become prominent throughout the empire in the second century. As we have seen, this Platonic Christianity defined itself in ways which had nothing to do with an historical Jesus. Nor is it likely to have grown out of Paulinism, as they have almost nothing in common.

If development had been as scholars present it, a shift in emphasis from the first century style of Christianity to one based on Greek philosophy and Hellenistic Judaism, the figure of Jesus would hardly have been dropped; he would have been integrated into the Platonic picture. This is not a Christian 'utilization' of Greek philosophy. The apologists' faith *is* the religious Platonism of the time brought into a Jewish theological and ethical setting (which rendered the Logos and the faith "anointed," or Christian). It is significant that none of them (possibly excepting Theophilus) have connections with a church.

Such a picture supports the view that Christianity, for its first 150 years, was a mosaic of uncoordinated expressions. It was a variegated organism which took root and flowered across the landscape of the empire, a widely divergent mix of Jewish and Greek features. As time went on, the distillation of Jesus of Nazareth out of certain pores in this organism spread inexorably across its entire skin, until by the year 200 he was firmly entrenched in every aspect of the faith.

The Conversion of Justin

Even Justin Martyr gives evidence of this picture. After reaching Rome in the 140s, he encountered the Gospel story and embraced the historical man-god it told of. In his apologetic writings, penned in the 150s, Jesus and the Gospels occupy center stage. For Justin, the Word/Logos "took shape, became man, and was called Jesus Christ" (*Apology*, 5). But he has left us a record of the nature of the faith he joined before his encounter with the story of a human Jesus.

The *Dialogue with the Jew Trypho* was written after the *Apology*, and the latter can be dated to the early 150s. But the action of *Trypho* is set at the time of the Second Jewish Revolt in the 130s, and scholars are confident that this represents the time of Justin's conversion, which he describes in the opening chapters.

By the sea near Ephesus Justin encounters an old man, a Christian philosopher. After a discussion of the joys and benefits of philosophy, the old man tells of ancient Jewish prophets who spoke by the Divine Spirit. These prophets, he says, had proclaimed the glory of God the Father and his Son, the Christ. (This was the interpretation of the Hebrew bible in Platonic terms.) Wisdom could come only to those who have it imparted to them by God and his Christ.

At this, says Justin (8:1), "a flame was kindled in my soul; and a love of the prophets and of those who are friends of Christ possessed me." Justin does not even say—despite the best attempts of some commentators—that he felt a love for Christ himself, for in the Christianity to which he was converted Christ was a philosophical concept. He was a part of the Godhead in heaven, a Logos-type entity. This Christ is a Savior by virtue of the wisdom he imparts (8:2). This is

Justin's concept of salvation here, for he goes on to conclude the story of his conversion by saying to Trypho: "If you are eagerly looking for salvation, and if you believe in God, you may become acquainted with the Christ of God and, after being initiated, live a happy life." Later, under the influence of the Gospels, Justin laid increasing emphasis on the redeeming value of Christ's death and resurrection, but in the basic Logos religion the Son saves by revealing God.

Where is Jesus of Nazareth in all this? The old philosopher had not a word to say about him, nor about any incarnation of the Son. We are fortunate that Justin did not recast the memory of his conversion experience in the light of his later beliefs based on the Gospels. In those opening chapters of the *Dialogue with Trypho* we can see that all the apologists came to the same Christian faith: a Platonic religious philosophy grounded in Hellenistic Judaism which failed to include any historical Jesus.

Trypho himself may be a literary invention, but Justin puts into his mouth (8:6) a telling accusation, one which must have represented a common opinion of the time: "But Christ—if he has indeed been born, and exists anywhere—is unknown . . . And you, having accepted a groundless report, invent a Christ for yourselves. . . ." Trypho also expresses the opinion that the incarnation is incredible and even Justin (*Apology* 13) admits that "sober-minded men" are of the opinion that "Christians are mad to give a crucified man second place to God." As we shall see, even some Christians might agree.

In passing, it should be mentioned that one of the earliest surviving apologies, that of Aristides to the emperor Antoninus Pius, a short and minor work written in Syriac around 140, is clearly dependent on some Gospel account. It speaks of God born of a virgin, having twelve disciples, pierced died and buried, then rising after three days. This apology comes from a different milieu, one located in the Palestine-Syria area (where the Synoptic Gospels were written), for it has nothing to say about the Logos or Greek philosophical concepts.

Minucius Felix: A Smoking Gun

I have left until last the most fascinating of all the apologies, a document which could well be called a 'smoking gun.' The little treatise *Octavius* was written in Rome, or possibly North Africa, in Latin. It takes the form of a debate between Caecilius, a pagan, and Octavius, a Christian, chaired and narrated by the author, Minucius Felix, by whose name the work is now usually referred to.

There has been a long and seesaw debate as to when *Minucius Felix* was written. A clear literary relationship exists with Tertullian's much longer *Apology*, written around the year 200. But who borrowed from whom? A good general rule says that the later writer tends to expand on what the earlier writer wrote, not chop drastically, especially since in this case it would mean that Minucius Felix had cut out many important Christian dogmas and every single reference to the Gospel Jesus—and this, well into the third century, when no one else had any qualms about speaking of such things. This and other arguments considered, the earlier dating between 150 and 160 is much preferable.

In this dialogue, the names of Christ and Jesus are never used, though the word "Christian" appears throughout. Nor is there any allusion to the Son or Logos. Octavius' Christianity revolves around the Unity and Providence of God and the rejection of all pagan deities, the resurrection of the body and its future reward or punishment. In regard to the latter, no appeal is made to Jesus' own resurrection as proof of God's ability and intention to resurrect the dead. Not even in answer to the challenge (11): "What single individual has returned from the dead, that we might believe it for an example?" Much of Octavius' argument is devoted to countering the calumnies against Christians which Caecilius, representing general pagan opinion, enumerates: everything from debauchery to the devouring of infants, to Christian secrecy and hopes for the world's fiery destruction.

But here is where it becomes interesting. For no other apologist but Justin has voiced and dealt with one particular accusation which the writer puts into the mouth of Caecilius. The list of calumnies in chapter 9 runs like this (partly paraphrased):

"This abominable congregation should be rooted out . . . a religion of lust and fornication. They reverence the head of an ass . . . even the genitals of their priests. . . . *And some say that the objects of their worship include a man who suffered death as a criminal, as well as the wretched wood of his cross; these are fitting altars for such depraved people, and they worship what they deserve.* . . . Also, during initiations they slay and dismember an infant and drink its blood . . . at their ritual feasts they indulge in shameless copulation."

Remember that a Christian is composing this passage. (The sentence in italics is translated in full.) He has included the central element and figure of the Christian faith, the person and crucifixion of

Jesus, within a litany of unspeakable calumnies leveled against his religion—with no indication by his language or tone that this reference to a crucified man is to be regarded as in any way different from those other items: disreputable accusations which need to be refuted. Could a Christian author who believed in a crucified Jesus and his divinity really have been capable of this manner of presentation?

In Octavius' half of the debate, he proceeds eventually to the refutation of these slanders. But here are some of the other things he says along the way.

In ridiculing the Greek myths about the deaths of their gods, such as Isis lamenting over the dismembered Osiris, he says (22): "Is it not absurd to bewail what you worship, or worship what you bewail?" In other words, he is castigating the Greeks for lamenting and worshiping a god who is slain. Later he says (23): "Men who have died cannot become gods, because a god cannot die; nor can men who are born (become gods). . . . Why, I pray, are gods not born today, if such have ever been born?" He then goes on to ridicule the whole idea of gods procreating themselves, which would include the idea of a god begetting a son. Elsewhere (20) he scorns those who are credulous enough to believe in miracles performed by gods.

How, without any saving qualification, could a Christian put such arguments forward, since they would confute and confound essential Christian beliefs *in his own mind*, and leave himself open to the charge of hypocrisy? It is one thing for the puzzled commentator to claim that silences in the apologists are due to their desire not to discourage or irritate the pagans with long and confusing theological treatises on subjects they are prejudiced against, or because they are not aiming to provide a comprehensive picture of the faith. But when an apologist makes statements which flatly contradict and even defame ideas which should be at the very heart of his own beliefs and personal devotion, such explanations are clearly discredited.

How does Minucius Felix deal with the accusation that Christians worship a crucified man and his cross? As he did in Caecilius' diatribe, the author inserts his response into the midst of his refutation of other calumnies about incestuous banquets and adoration of a priest's genitals. Here is the manner and context in which he deals with the charge of worshiping a crucified criminal (29):

> "'These and similar indecencies we do not wish to hear; it is
> disgraceful having to defend ourselves from such charges. People
> who live a chaste and virtuous life are falsely charged by you with

acts which we would not consider possible, except that we see you doing them yourselves. [2]Moreover (*nam*), when you attribute to our religion the worship of a criminal and his cross, you wander far from the truth in thinking that a criminal deserved, or that a mortal man could be able, to be believed in as God. [3]Miserable indeed is that man whose whole hope is dependent on a mortal, for such hope ceases with his [the latter's] death . . . ."

Before going on, we should first note that verse 2, following as it does on the sentiments of verse 1 (which the Latin word "*nam*" emphasizes), makes it clear that the writer regards this accusation as being in the same vein as the other "indecencies" he is at pains to refute. And what is the refutation he provides? It is to heap scorn on those who would believe that a crucified criminal, a mortal, should be thought of as a god. Where is the necessary qualification that no Christian could surely have remained silent on? Where is the saving defense that in fact this crucified man was not a mere mortal, but was indeed God? Some claim that this is what Minucius is implying, but such an implication is so opaque, it can only be derived from reading it into the text. Octavius' words certainly do not contain it, although they do imply that the writer knows of some Christians who believe such things, but he has no sympathy with them.

The translator of this work in the 19th century collection of *Ante-Nicene Fathers* (on which my own translations are based) includes the following in his summary preface at the head of chapter 29: "For they believe not only that he was innocent, but with reason that he was God." Such an idea is nowhere to be found in the text, and the context of the charge and its response, again, cannot reasonably be said to imply it. Nor do the other things Minucius says which scorn different aspects of the Christian faith (such as gods being born in the present time or performing miracles) allow us to draw such an implication. To verse 2 the translator offers this wishful footnote: "A reverent allusion to the Crucified, believed in and worshiped as God." What one cannot believe is missing, one will read into the text, no matter what.

A more recent scholar, G. W. Clarke (*Ancient Christian Writers #39*, 1949) makes this observation in an end note: "A remarkable avoidance of any mention of the Incarnation. Indeed, so anxious is Minucius Felix to avoid admitting such a difficult doctrine that he gives the appearance of denying it." Indeed he does. And while Clarke compares this to Arnobius' "coyness" on the same topic, that later (*c*300) Christian apologist was in no way reluctant or dishonest in admitting the doctrine, even though he lived at a time of greater persecution. "We worship one who was born a man. What then? Do you worship no one who was born a man? . . . But he died nailed to the cross. So what? Neither does the kind and disgrace of the death change his words or deeds" (*Against the Heathen*, I.37 & 40).

Minucius goes on in this passage to cite the folly of heathen peoples who *do* "choose a man for their worship," but he makes no such admissions for Christians. As to the accusation of worshiping crosses, he says dismissively: "We do not adore them, nor do we wish for them." He goes on to admonish the pagan for being guilty of using signs of crosses in their own worship and everyday life. There is not a hint that for Minucius the cross bears any sacred significance or requires defending in a Christian context.

From this refutation of the calumny of Jesus and his cross, he proceeds ("Next . . .") to challenge those who accuse Christians of the slaughter of children. There is nothing in the way Minucius has dealt with the supposed heart of the Christian faith to differentiate it from all these surrounding horrors. The disparaging tone is unredeemed.

One commentator, H. J. Baylis (*Minucius Felix*, p.148) in addition to expressing his regret that the writer has been so silent in defending the person of Christ, also laments the fact that he missed a golden opportunity to refute the charge about licentious feasts and cannibalistic initiation rites by describing the Eucharist. He could have defended, says Baylis, the sacramental significance and pure conduct of this Christian *agapē* (love feast) over Jesus' body and blood. Baylis finds it equally "odd" that in speaking of the sources of the "truth about the Godhead" (38), Minucius is silent on the teachings of Jesus himself, or Jesus' own status as Son within that Godhead.

The survival of this document, with its out-and-out dismissal of the central tenets of Christianity, is perhaps surprising, but it was no doubt possible only because a certain veiled ambiguity could be read into a verse like 29:2 above, and by letting this perception override the derogatory tone and jarring silence of the passage and document as a whole. Baylis has labeled 29:2 "oblique," but Minucius' stark language rules out any such escape route. This scholar, too, reads into Minucius' defense something which is not evidently there: "Yes, we adore one who was crucified, but he is neither a criminal nor a mere man." Those who will allow historical documents to say what they seem to be saying will recognize that *Minucius Felix* is a true 'smoking gun' pointing to a Christian denial of the historical Jesus.

To the dispassionate eye, Minucius Felix is one Christian who will have nothing to do with those, in other circles of his religion, who profess the worship of a Jesus who was crucified in Judea under the governorship of Pontius Pilate, rumors of which have reached pagan ears and elicited much scorn and condemnation. To claim that a whole generation of apologists would falsely convey such an exterior to those they are seeking to win over, that they would deliberately indulge in this kind of Machiavellian deception, is but one of the desperate measures which modern Christian scholars have been forced to adopt in their efforts to deal with a record that stubbornly refuses to paint the picture they all want to see.

Defending the Apologists

The apologists were not fools. Their literary and polemical talents were considerable. They were versed in a wide range of ancient knowledge, in the intricate subtleties of contemporary philosophy. That they could design careful and elaborate pieces of apologetic writing that yet deliberately contained such devastating omissions and weaknesses as we have seen in Minucius Felix, in Theophilus, in Athenagoras, in Tatian, is not feasible.

If an author like Minucius Felix is being silent for political reasons, why would he choose to place in the mouth of his pagan spokesperson accusations concerning the very thing he is deliberately silent on? Why would he allow the opponent such critical and derogatory declarations about the central object of Christian worship when he has already decided he must deny himself the luxury of answering them? Why would he place in the Christian's *own* mouth, as he does in chapters 21 and 23, sweeping and scornful statements which go against elements of the Christian faith with no possibility of offering saving qualifications? There is not even an attempt, through veiled language and implication, to assuage the 'knowing' Christian reader, to show that such saving exceptions are present in his own mind. In fact, his uncompromising treatment of these faith subjects is tantamount to a denial of them.

At the end of *Minucius Felix* the writer portrays his pagan character as converting to Christianity. But what is the use of converting someone like Caecilius to a religion which has had all its essential elements concealed? When Caecilius arrives "on the morrow" for his first lesson as a catechumen, Octavius will be forced to say, "Oh, by the way, there were a few details I left out yesterday." If a Christian makes his appeal to a pagan according to philosophical and logical principles, how will he then turn around and subsequently present the Christian mysteries and dogmas which he must be aware go counter to such principles? His own argumentation will then stand in danger of being turned against him. His dishonesty will place himself and his faith in a dishonorable light.

It must be stressed that nowhere in the literature of the time is there support for the standard scholarly rationalization about the apologists' silence on the figure of Jesus. Nowhere is it discussed or even intimated that these writers have in fact deliberately left out the essential elements of the Christian faith in their defenses of it, for reasons of political correctness or anything else. The occasionally quoted account of Origen in the third century, that he sometimes expounded his ethical views without labeling them as Christian, since he feared his listeners' hostility to the very name of Christianity and Christ, is not applicable here. In such cases Origen was not identifying himself as a Christian at all, he was not offering a defense of Christianity, even in a limited way. If he had been, he would certainly not have left himself open to challenges he was not allowed to answer. His own writings are proof of this. Origen does not conceal Jesus or his resurrection. He counters every scoff and calumny of Celsus with all the resources at his disposal.

This is true also of Tertullian, writing his apology around the year 200 and borrowing, or at least using as inspiration, parts of the work of Minucius Felix. Tertullian indulges in no such cryptic concealment. In his own day, the hostility to Christianity was no easier than it had been a generation earlier when Felix wrote, or a mere two decades since Athenagoras and Theophilus had penned their defenses. Tertullian's work is full of vivid references to Christ's incarnation, to his death and resurrection. Near the end of his account of "that Christ, the Son of God who appeared among us," he declares: "Let no one think it is otherwise than we have represented, for *none may give a false account of his religion* . . . . We say, and before all men we say, and torn and bleeding under your tortures we cry out, 'We worship God through Christ!' " Apparently, if we believe modern commentators, the bulk of the second century apologists possessed no such conviction, no such courage.

Certainly, Tertullian would have had no sympathy with their alleged policy of concealment. The above quotation may even be a veiled condemnation of them, if he were familiar with the works of Athenagoras or Tatian or Theophilus. Or it may have been directed at

Minucius Felix himself, whose apology he would have felt constrained to expand on and fill in the painfully missing blanks.

As a final note, we might ask: where are the writers (for we might expect there to be some) who openly and in unmistakable words reject the figure of Jesus, with no possibility of ambiguity? Until we realize that no such document would ever have reached us through 2000 years of Christian censorship. For probably the same reason, we possess no pagan writing which discusses the case for rejection of the historical Jesus. Even Celsus (who does not do this) survives only piecemeal in Origen's great refutation of him. On the other hand, it is likely that even leading pagan thinkers like Celsus would have had no way to verify or disprove the circulating Christian story and narrative accounts of Jesus of Nazareth, nor would they have possessed the exegetical tools and abilities to disprove Christian claims through a study of the documents themselves. In any case, all of these documents, given the poor state of communication and availability of materials in the ancient world, would hardly have been accessible to someone who might think of undertaking such a task.

POSTSCRIPT

The image of Jesus of Nazareth walking the roads of Galilee, healing and working wonders, bringing a message of hope, trust in God, and the anticipation of a new world, is deeply imbedded in the Western mind. The fate he suffered when he went to Jerusalem is perhaps the most powerful and enduring tale the world has ever fashioned. That composite picture of a man whom historians have always found elusive and enigmatic, but whom believers have ever been able to embrace as a personal friend and deity, has been the sustenance of a sizeable portion of the world's population for the better part of two millennia.

Jesus has always been larger and more substantial than the often crude, disjointed and contradictory picture presented in the Gospels. He has been continually reinvented and re-envisioned for each new phase of the Christian evolution. Paradoxically, as the cracks and fissures in the Gospel structure widen, and the coherence of the early Christian record undergoes increasing disintegration, liberal scholars are creating ever more sophisticated portraits of the enlightened sage who is supposed to lie behind it all. But a rescue operation of this magnitude needs a secure base on which to establish itself, and the very dismantling of the age-old witness to Jesus which has led to such unprecedented discrediting of the Christian myth, has left a vacuum which it may not be possible to fill.

We are in a transition period. While the old structure has collapsed, New Testament scholarship still considers that it can salvage enough pieces to build a new, more modest house in which to install the reputed fountainhead of Christianity. But even the foundations have disintegrated. The roots of Q are too amorphous to provide the basis on which to set a renewed Christian religion on a second 2000-year run. As for the epistles, they have opened their doors to reveal an alien universe, one which later ages thought had been buried forever. If the defining element of Christianity, the faith of apostles like Paul, had nothing to do with an historical man, will the remnant from Q, the gleanings of declared authenticity within that hypothetical document, be sufficient to recreate anything like the old vitality? That seems doubtful.

Why has it taken so long? And why has it happened in the late 20th century? In the spring of 1995, the Jesus Seminar met to debate and vote on the historicity of the resurrection as embodied in the New Testament record. Papers and articles (see the March/April 1995 issue of *The Fourth R*) pointed out that views of Christ's resurrection among early Christians went through an identifiable evolution during the first several decades after Jesus' passing. Paul, they said, envisioned only a spiritual "awakening" of Jesus by God, something that happened in heaven after Jesus' physical death on earth. Later, as expressed in the Gospel of Mark, Christians began to regard that awakening as the physical rising of Jesus' body from its tomb, although it was not a body that was seen again. The sojourn on earth for a time, the physical appearances to disciples, came still later, in the Gospels which built on Mark, a further expansion on the idea of resurrection. Thus the Christian tradition of a bodily resurrection of Jesus after death, the Seminar concluded, was an evolution of faith and literary activity, and had no foundation in history or historical witness.

All this has lain in plain sight for centuries. What happened in the past generation or two which allowed the scales to fall, and the documentary record as a whole to be seen for what it is? In my own life experience I have seen a good part of the Western world pass from the last phase of the Middle Ages (wherein much 'medieval' thinking still survived) to an unprecedented secular outlook. Believers may still make up a majority of the population, but as a whole, in its collective image of itself, society has become predominantly secular and scientific, unaccepting of religious control over its institutions and expressions. (Which is not to say that the pendulum could not swing again.)

That turning point occurred sometime around the year 1960. It was perhaps one of those points of 'punctuation' in the long evolution of the human mind. Ancient credulity gave way to a new skepticism, a new willingness to ask questions and think the unthinkable. New Testament scholarship soon after World War II had begun to do both, to see the Christian documents as embodying human conditions and human motivations far more than it reflected the will of God or divine truth. That trend came to a climax during the 1980s, in the formation of the Jesus Seminar, an association of progressive scholars under Robert

Funk, based in California. For the first time in history, scientific and skeptical examination of the Christian record by mainstream biblical scholars led to shocking conclusions about the reliability of the Gospels and the things attributed to Jesus, even about the fundamental nature of Jesus himself. And for the first time, such controversy within the ranks of scholarship reached the media and the pulpit.

The first ten years of the Seminar saw the toppling of major pillars of the Christian faith, and the substitution of a new concept of a human Jesus. But that new figure has been largely a scholarly exercise, and shows little sign of capturing the public imagination, let alone the hearts and souls of believers. Ironically, it has gained the interest more of the agnostic bystander with a passion for history. In even the enlightened pews there has been, more than anything else, an intense disquiet and even outright revolt at the prospect that Jesus may not have been divine after all, and did not undergo a death that was sacrificial.[127] To consider that he may not even have been historical is probably more than any Christian denomination could countenance.

But there is no going back. Fundamentalism, still thriving in North America and parts of the third world, will no doubt keep the Gospel Son of God alive for a time, but once the dissolution of the Christian record as a reliable and historical set of documents makes its way fully into public consciousness, it is hard to see how Christianity as a vital force in society will be able to continue.

What will replace it is difficult to say. Many people who have abandoned traditional religion style themselves "spiritual." If by "spiritualism" we speak not of some supernatural dimension and inscrutable link to divine or philosophical entities whose existence cannot be shown, but rather of the deep and fascinating potential which lies within the human organism itself and its links with the living, knowable world, if we speak of it as the product of natural evolution in an observable and understandable universe, the outlook for the future may be bright. Whether this is to be defined by the term "spiritualism" or by a word such as "humanism" should not matter, so long as we cease to search for meaning in the sphere of fantasy, or extrapolate the best in ourselves onto an idealized, larger-than-life individual or heavenly force (which the Jesus Seminar is still trying to do). Instead, we need only find it in the earth-based capacity of every human individual.

Acknowledgments

I have always felt that credits are best placed after a work, whether it be a film, a broadcast, or a book. The eager reader may not attend to such preliminaries, whereas in the calm of completion—hopefully in a state of satisfaction—the credits may actually be of some interest. Accordingly, I would like to acknowledge and thank those who helped me to polish the manuscript and caught many a flaw in structure, style and clarity. Those reader-editors were David Blackwell, Pat Hutcheon, Peggy Krachun, Angela Beale and Penny Sanger. And, of course, Dr. Robert Price of the Jesus Seminar and the Institute of Higher Critical Studies, who gave me valuable advice on points of interpretation and graciously provided a quote for the cover. If any detail of the book fails to live up to their good advice, the responsibility is entirely my own.

It is the practice of scholarship to make brief reference to the views and works of others in the field in the course of presenting one's own argument, whether for support or in the spirit of debate, and I would like to thank those I have quoted for the use of such views, without which practice no field of study can advance.

I would also like to acknowledge the generous contribution of many people who made the publication of this book possible, including members of the Humanist Association of Ottawa. I and the publisher also drew on the considerable talents of Richard Young in the creation of the cover and Greg Singer in the design of the text, and I extend my sincere thanks to all.

Finally, my thanks and appreciation to Canadian Humanist Publications for placing their faith, not in some higher power, but in the very human and imperfect efforts of one who came to this study through unorthodox channels and who would never claim to have all the answers.

Earl Doherty
September 1999

APPENDICES

Appendix 1
Two interpolations in the New Testament epistles
[page 15]

I: 1 Thessalonians 2:15-16

Many commentators (see below) have dismissed the italicized verses in the following passage as an interpolation by some later editor or copyist. They do so on two grounds.

One is the very apparent allusion to the destruction of Jerusalem in verse 16, an event which happened several years after Paul's death. Here is the passage in its entirety, courtesy of the New English Bible:

> "[14]You [those in Thessalonica] have fared like the congregations in Judea, God's people in Christ Jesus. You have been treated by your countrymen as they are treated by the Jews, [15]*who killed the Lord Jesus and the prophets and drove us out, the Jews who are heedless of God's will and enemies of their fellow-men,* [16]*hindering us from speaking to the gentiles to lead them to salvation. All this time they have been making up the full measure of their guilt, and now retribution has overtaken them for good and all.*"

The finality of God's wrath would seem to signify an event on the scale of the first Jewish War (66-70) when the Temple and much of Jerusalem were destroyed—not, as is sometimes claimed, to the expulsion of Jews from Rome (apparently for messianic agitation) by Claudius in the 40s. The apocalyptic statement in verse 16 is unlikely to be applied to a local event which the Thessalonians may or may not have been aware of several years later. Besides, Paul's reference in verse 14 (which is usually taken as the end of the genuine passage) is to a persecution by Jews in Judea, and even the killing of Jesus was the responsibility of Jews in that location. Offering a local event in Rome as a punishment for either crime seems inappropriate. There are also those who question whether any such persecution of Christians took place prior to 70 (see Douglas Hare, *The Theme of Jewish Persecution of Christians in the Gospel According to St. Matthew*, p.30f), indicating that perhaps even verse 14 is part of the interpolation, by someone who had little knowledge of the conditions in Judea at the time of Paul's letter. (Birger Pearson—see below—suggests this.)

It has been pointed out that there are no variant texts of 1 Thessalonians without the disputed passage. Since this is so, it is claimed, the insertion would need to have been made very early (soon after 70) when there would hardly have been enough time for the evolution from the mythical to the historical Jesus phase. But this is an unnecessary assumption. Recently (see *The New Testament and Its Modern Interpreters*, 1989, p.207f), scholars have begun to abandon the old idea that the first corpus of Pauline letters was assembled no later than the year 90. They now see such a collection as coming around the time of Marcion in the 140s. (See Chapter 24.) Even though Romans and 1 Corinthians seem to have been known by the turn of the second century to Fathers such as Ignatius, the first witness in the wider Christian record to 1 Thessalonians itself (beyond the writer who used it to compose 2 Thessalonians, probably in that city) comes after the first corpus was formed.

Thus the interpolation in 2:15-16 could have been made quite late. Even into the second century, Christian anti-Semitism remained high and the catastrophic events of the first Jewish War were very much alive in the memories of both Jews and gentiles in the eastern empire. The inserted passage was probably the product of someone in Thessalonica, before the letter entered the corpus. It is even barely conceivable that verse 16 refers to the outcome of the Second Jewish Revolt (132-5), when Bar Kochba was crushed, the Jews were expelled from Palestine, and a Roman city was built over the ruins of Jerusalem.

The second reason scholars tend to reject this passage as not genuine to Paul is because it does not concur with what he elsewhere expresses about his fellow Jews, whom he expects will in the end be converted to Christ. The sentiment in these verses is recognized as an example of "gentile anti-Judaism" and "foreign to Paul's theology that 'all Israel will be saved'." (See the Pearson article below, p.85-6.)

It has also been noted that in Romans 11, within a passage in which he speaks of the guilt of the Jews for failing to heed the message about the Christ, Paul refers to Elijah's words in 1 Kings, about the (unfounded) accusation that the Jews have habitually killed the prophets sent from God. Here Paul mentions no responsibility on the part of the Jews for the ultimate atrocity of the killing of the Son of God himself. This would be an inexplicable silence if the passage in 1 Thessalonians were genuine and the basis of the accusation true.

These are some of the scholars who have pronounced the passage an interpolation:

- Birger A. Pearson: "1 Thessalonians 2:13-16: A Deutero-Pauline Interpolation," *Harvard Theological Review* 64 (1971) p.79-94.
- Burton Mack: *Who Wrote the New Testament?* p.113
- Wayne Meeks: *The First Urban Christians*, p.9, n.117
- Helmut Koester: *Introduction to the New Testament*, vol.II, p.113
- Pheme Perkins: *Harper's Bible Commentary*, p.1230, 1231-2
- S. G. F. Brandon: *The Fall of Jerusalem and the Christian Church*, p.92-93
- Paula Fredricksen: *From Jesus to Christ*, p.122

II: 1 Timothy 6:13

1 Timothy 6:12-14 reads ("Paul" addressing "Timothy"):

"[12]Run the great race of faith and take hold of eternal life. For to this you were called and you confessed your faith nobly before many witnesses. [13]Now in the presence of God, who gives life to all things, and of Jesus Christ, [who himself made the same noble confession and gave his testimony to it before Pontius Pilate,] [14]I charge you to obey your orders irreproachably and without fault until our Lord Jesus Christ appears."

1 and 2 Timothy and Titus (called "the Pastoral Epistles") were written in Paul's name so as to claim the authority of the famous apostle for the views the writer is advocating. Most critical scholars date them between 100 and 125. They can be a product neither of Paul nor of his time. As J. L. Houlden says (*The Pastoral Epistles*, p.18): "Neither in vocabulary and literary techniques nor in atmosphere and teachings is it plausible to suppose that these writings come from the same pen as the main body of Paul's letters." The Pastorals reflect the beginnings of a church system which only came into existence around the beginning of the second century: a bishop, supported by a group of elders and deacons. As well, all sense of immediate expectation of the Parousia (the "coming" of Christ at the End-time) has passed. The Church is becoming acclimatized to the world and a future.

Timothy's confession of faith before many witnesses (verse 12) is interpreted as referring to one of two possible occasions: either the baptismal ceremony upon his conversion to the faith, or his ordination as a minister. Commentators usually choose the former, since baptism is the more likely event at which one could be said to be "called to eternal life." The sacrament was publicly administered before the congregation, providing the "many witnesses" referred to. Timothy is confessing his faith before God and fellow Christians. The content of that statement of faith no doubt had to do with a belief in Christ.

The way the reference to Pilate is introduced into the text (the clause in square brackets in the quote above) shows that it is intended as a parallel to Timothy's confession in the previous sentence. But there is much to be concerned about in this assumption. (See J. H. Houlden, *The Pastoral Epistles*, p.100-1; J. N. D. Kelly, *The Pastoral Epistles*, p.143.) Jesus' situation on trial before Pilate is scarcely the same as Timothy's at his baptism, or even at an ordination. Timothy's confession is before God and friendly witnesses; Jesus' is not, and it puts Pilate in parallel to God, which is at best inappropriate, at worst irreverent. Jesus' declaration before Pilate is presumably a statement about himself, which is an awkward equivalent to the believer's declaration of faith in Jesus. With these difficult features in such a comparison, one might wonder what would have led the original writer to think of making it.

Commentators discount the possibility that the occasion of Timothy's confession was before a magistrate, when he might have been on trial for his Christian beliefs. No such event, from which the writer could have drawn, appears in the genuine Pauline letters. Besides, such a trial would hardly be called a summons to eternal life. However, we must consider the possibility that a later copyist may have misinterpreted things in this way. Perhaps by some time further into the second century a tradition had grown up that Timothy had been prosecuted for his faith. This may have prompted such a copyist to insert the idea that, just as Timothy had declared before hostile magistrates his faith that Jesus was the Son of God and Messiah, Christ before a hostile Pilate had declared these things about himself. Such an editor may have felt that while "God" (in verse 13) had a qualifying phrase, "who gives life to all things," something was lacking after "and of Jesus Christ," and the comparison with Jesus' trial was what came into his mind.

It has also been pointed out that in the account of the trial before Pilate in the Synoptic Gospels, Jesus barely says anything, maintaining a stoic silence. His simple agreement, "It is as you say" in answer to the question "Are you the king of the Jews?" is hardly a "noble confession" to inspire such a comment as we find in 1 Timothy 6:13.

However, John, when he came to revise the Synoptic passion story, had Jesus engage in a dramatic debate with the Roman governor, which could well have been the source of the comment. Since attestation for the Gospel of John is lacking during the period to which the Pastorals are usually assigned, this would suggest that the clause is an interpolation from a later point in the century, when John was more widely known. The Pastorals are not included in the earliest corpus of the Pauline letters, so the fact that there is no manuscript evidence of the letter without this reference to Pilate does not pose a problem.

Moreover, only a few verses later (6:16), when speaking of God, the epistle makes this sweeping statement: "No man has ever seen or ever can see him." If the man Jesus of Nazareth had recently been on earth, standing before Pilate, a man who had in fact seen and come from God, one would not expect the writer to have said such a thing.

The possibility of interpolation is supported by something suspicious which occurs a few verses earlier. In six places in the Pastoral letters the writer uses the phrase "wholesome teaching." In five of these, there is no indication of the source of such teaching. In fact, the first time the phrase appears, in 1 Timothy 1:10, the writer (speaking as Paul) says that such teaching "conforms with the gospel entrusted to me, the gospel which tells of the glory of God." This pointedly ignores any identification of Jesus as the source of the teaching.

But in 1 Timothy 6:3 an unexpected phrase intrudes:

> "If anyone . . . teaches differently and does not agree with wholesome words—those of our Lord Jesus Christ—and with pious teaching, I call him puffed up and ignorant."

The phrase "those of our Lord Jesus Christ" (*tois tou kuriou hēmon Iēsou Christou*) has the look of a scribal notation originally made in the margin, which was later inserted into the text. (This was a common occurrence in the transmission of ancient manuscripts.) If it were part of the original writer's text, the word "those" (*tois*) would have been redundant and would not likely have been written. Rather, it conveys the impression of an after-thought. The whole thing seems carelessly done, because the insertion fails to cover the succeeding phrase, "and with pious teaching," which we would expect to find identified with Jesus as well.

Note that taken by itself, the passage in 6:3 is not required to be an interpolation in order to maintain that the Pastorals know of no historical Jesus. Even if *tois tou kuriou hēmon Iēsou Christou* is part of the original text, it need imply no more than that the "teaching" is considered to be revealed through the spiritual Christ, in much the same sense as Paul's "words of the Lord." (See also the discussion concerning 1 Clement in Chapter 24.)

We have here a very likely interpolation made some time after the letter was written, and it occurs just a few verses before another phrase, the one about Pilate, which seems similarly out of place. It is admittedly in my own interest to regard the reference to Pontius Pilate in 1 Timothy 6:13 as an interpolation, but there are clearly good reasons for doing so.

Appendix 2
A conversation between Paul and some new converts
[page 25]

Scholarship has long suggested that Paul's silence on all things to do with Jesus' human life and career results from his "lack of interest" in the man, and his view that such things are "irrelevant" to his theology about Jesus. If we were to assume a steadfast refusal by Paul to gather or preach information on any aspect of Jesus' earthly life and teachings, we could envision something like the following scene. The setting is some rich Greek's house in the Diaspora, with a mix of converts and interested friends and bystanders gathered about Paul on a warm summer evening. Their conversation might go something like this:

DEMETRIOS (the host and owner of the house): So, Paul, tell us more about Jesus the Savior. I have heard that he taught the people with great authority about the coming kingdom of God, and how we should all love one another.

PAUL: Yes, I have heard rumors to that effect, but I consider such things to be unimportant, and as it happens I am not familiar with any of his teachings.

DEMETRIOS: I see. But your mission is to gentiles like ourselves, is it not? Surely Jesus himself included gentiles in his own ministry and directed his apostles to go out and preach to them? I would certainly like to think that he did.

PAUL: I suppose that's possible. I don't have any first-hand information.

HERMES: You have performed signs and wonders for us, Paul, which convinces us that the Lord is indeed speaking through you. I understand that Jesus himself performed great feats over nature and once fed thousands with a few loaves of bread. My friend Ampliatus heard about that when he was in the east.

PAUL (clearing his throat): Oh, I don't concern myself with such things, and you shouldn't either. They're quite insignificant, and you don't need to know about them to believe in the risen Son of God.

JUNIAS: When I heard you would be here, Paul, I told my sick mother that perhaps you would come around to see her and expel the demon that is making her ill. I, too, have heard from a relative in Galilee that Jesus expelled demons and healed many people—

HERODIAN (interrupting in some agitation): Yes, the demons have been especially active in my own household. My brother has contracted a fever, and just last week the roof of my workshop collapsed for no reason—

PAUL (with a placating gesture): There is no doubt that evil spirits beset us on all sides, my friends, and we must have faith that God will deliver us from them. As to reports of healings by Jesus, perhaps he did, but then, every wonder-worker in the country makes such claims, so perhaps we should not place too much importance on such things.

OLYMPAS: You have told us about the coming End, Paul, and I look forward to our promised deliverance from this sorry world, but I am greatly frighted by what may happen. Did Jesus reveal anything to his disciples about what things would be like when he comes back from heaven?

PAUL (somewhat miffed): Who knows? Anyway, one can't rely on what those so-called 'men of repute' in Jerusalem are spreading around. After all, they're only fishermen. Besides, as I have told you, I have information on the subject directly from Christ himself—

AGRIPPA (a Jew): Some of my Jewish friends have heard of your preaching, Paul, but when I invited them to join us at table, they said they could not break their purity regulations and eat with gentiles. Did Jesus follow such strict rules and refuse to eat with the unclean?

PAUL (exasperated): I have no idea.

CRISPUS (looking a little pained): I have a Jewish friend, too, who is a follower of Christ. But he says that even the gentile has to be circumcised—(pained expressions all around)—and follow every aspect of the Jewish Law if he wishes to become a member of your faith in Christ. Is that so? Did Jesus specify such a requirement?

PAUL: My friends, my friends, why all these foolish questions? What Jesus may have said or done in the course of his life is completely immaterial. I have already informed you of the only thing that matters, Christ's own suffering and death, and his rising from the dead. These are the things that have brought us salvation!

DEMETRIOS (hastily, sensing some perplexity and unease among his guests): Yes, my friends, the Lord's passion is surely what we should be focusing on, and what he went through in his terrible ordeal. Tell us about that, Paul. Was he tortured and scourged before they crucified him?

PAUL (shrugging): I assume he was. The Romans do that to everyone they crucify.

GAIUS (spitting in disgust): Yes, and they break the condemned man's legs to make him die more painfully. I suppose they did that to Jesus?

PAUL: I don't know. I wasn't there.

ARCHIPPUS: Tell us what he said, Paul, when they put him up on the cross. Even now the authorities are persecuting new believers in Christ and I wonder if we'll suffer their hatred, too, just as Christ did. Did he speak? Did he stand fast? Did he condemn them for what they did?

PAUL (curtly): I didn't ask. But let me tell you about what the Lord revealed to me personally—

JULIA: Oh, how I envy you, Paul! You who have been to Jerusalem and could stand on the very spot where Jesus was crucified. That would give me the shivers. You must have felt his presence. Is that when he spoke to you?

PAUL: My dear lady, I've never been to Calvary. I couldn't find the time when I went to see James and Peter. It's only a little hill, after all.

PERSIS: But the tomb, Paul. Did you not see that? Are there still signs of the Lord's resurrection? Do Jesus' followers pray there every Easter?

PAUL (throwing up his hands): As to that, I couldn't say. But one tomb is much like another, don't you think? Why fill your heads with such paltry details? We should better focus on the eternal significance of these events—

DEMETRIOS (noting nervously that a couple of his guests had quietly slipped away): Well, I am sure we all agree that Paul has been very enlightening on the subject of Christ Jesus. Perhaps we should retire to the atrium for aperitifs and he can tell us more. . . .

Appendix 3
Ignatius of Antioch and docetism
[page 56]

Chapter 6 quoted a passage from Ignatius' letter to the Trallians, in which he declares his faith in certain basic biographical data about Jesus:

"Close your ears, then, if anyone preaches to you without speaking of Jesus Christ. Christ was of David's line. He was the son of Mary, who was really (*alēthōs*) born, ate and drank, was really persecuted under Pontius Pilate, was really crucified. . . . He was also truly raised from the dead." (Epistle to the Trallians 9:1f)

Commentators have regularly claimed that in passages like these, Ignatius is battling an heretical doctrine which had emerged within the Christian movement around the end of the first century. This doctrine is called "docetism" (DAW-suh-tism). It supposedly started from the conviction that a divinity, such as Jesus would have been, could not truly enter into matter, that the very idea of God in human flesh was repugnant and indeed impossible.

Thus, goes the argument, views of Jesus of Nazareth had to be revised. An early docetic, Cerinthus, is said to have held that the spirit of the divine Christ entered a human man, Jesus son of Mary and Joseph, at the time of his baptism, and left him just before the passion and crucifixion. At no time was the divine Son of God contaminated by installing himself within that human nature. (We do not have any works of Cerinthus, only references to him and his doctrine in the writings of Christian apologists almost a century later. This leaves room for subsequent confusion or revision as to what Cerinthus actually believed, why he believed it, and when he did so.)

Later, it is said, the docetic stance shifted. The Son of God *had* been born and lived his own life in the world, but this life had been within a body which only "seemed" (this is the meaning of the Greek verb *dokein*, from which the term "docetism" is derived) to be human flesh and blood. Though he appeared to be a man to those around him, he was really a phantom, and thus his sufferings, his bodily experiences, were not real.

But there are problems with such an interpretation of passages like Trallians 9. First of all, the net is cast too broadly. William R. Schoedel (*Ignatius of Antioch*, p.124-5), while maintaining that Ignatius' opponents were docetists, recognizes that such passages suggest that "Ignatius had in mind a denial of the passion more thoroughgoing than our argument has so far indicated." He acknowledges that what some seem to deny "is the very reality of Christ's death," and thus of the incarnation. The opposing view offers not simply a docetic Christ, it offers something which gives Christ "no place in our lives" (epistle to the Magnesians 9:2).

Consider Magnesians 11:1:

> "I wish to warn you not to fall into the snare of stupid doctrine, but to be convinced of the birth, passion and resurrection, which took place at the time of the governorship of Pontius Pilate."

This is not an exhortation to reject a docetic interpretation of things. Schoedel admits it is "relatively anemic as an anti-docetic statement." Rather, Ignatius is making a firm declaration that such events did indeed happen. In the Trallians passage earlier, the bishop of Antioch wants Christians to "close their ears" to anyone who has no historical Jesus to preach, not just to the one who preaches that Jesus of Nazareth did not genuinely suffer. And why are Mary and Pilate so prominently included as part of this anti-docetic net? Such figures would be accepted even by docetists. By way of analogy, we might say it is like two adult brothers who argue about the details of an incident which took place in their boyhood home. If one maintains that it was a flower vase they broke and the other that it was Mom's best teapot, neither one is likely to argue the fact that it all took place on Elm Street. This is an accepted part of the background, and no one would be interested in disputing it.

On the other hand, we do find passages in Ignatius which specifically address a docetic position, but they are separate from the more sweeping arguments about the historicity of Jesus. Look at Trallians 10, for example, which follows on the passage in Trallians 9 quoted earlier:

> "It is asserted by some who deny God . . . that his sufferings were not genuine."

Why would Ignatius address the same point again if he has just covered it? Compare the similar situation in Smyrneans 1 and 2, where a general discussion of Jesus' biography (this time including a reference to Jesus being baptized by John the Baptist) is again separate from a specifically docetic discussion.

In Smyrneans 5:2, Ignatius castigates those blasphemers who deny that Jesus "ever bore a real human body." In both these passages he tries to counter them using anti-docetic arguments. (These are in terms of the effect such heretical views would have on Christians' own sufferings: if Christ's were not real, how can there be any value to our own?) This is something he does not do in the more general passages. The word *alēthōs*, "really" or "truly," is often labeled an anti-docetic term, but it can equally mean "in actuality."

This is not to say that certain anti-docetic touches do not creep into arguments like the declaration of Trallians 9; "ate and drank" has that flavor. But it would be no surprise if Ignatius fails to keep his heretical opponents rigidly separate. It may be that they were not always two distinct groups. Rather, the milieu in which Jesus of Nazareth was emerging into history included many who resisted it, some with outright denial. (See 1 John 4:1f, where certain "spirits" labeled Antichrist deny that "Jesus Christ has come in the flesh," while 2 John 7 condemns a similar denial.) But that milieu also included some who preferred an incarnated Jesus who had not been a true human being. This latter view was the direction followed by the gnostics.

My own view of the development of docetism is dependent on the above scenario. Rather than envision, after the passage of some 70 years during which everyone accepted Jesus of Nazareth as a real human being, that some people would suddenly raise the objection that he could *not* have been human after all, it would make better sense to see such an objection in the context of a newly emerging historical Jesus. It was only when the dying and rising Christ of Paul was turned into an historical figure who had lived in historical time did the problem of a god possessing real human flesh and undergoing real human suffering arise.

Before that, Christ was looked upon as a spiritual entity who had undergone spirit-world suffering in the heavenly realm at the hands of the demon spirits. But if, at the time of Ignatius—and Cerinthus, who is said to have lived around Ignatius' time—the idea was emerging that he had been on earth, had suffered and died under Pilate, shedding real human blood on a cross outside Jerusalem, this is when the objections would have begun, for some would have found it philosophically unacceptable that a divinity could enter flesh and truly suffer. Others like Ignatius would have had no problem with it—indeed, they embraced such a doctrine, since it brought Jesus closer to their own suffering. (Proper Platonism be damned!) Gnostics, in particular, found repugnant any idea that their savior figure had operated in flesh, and so their soteriology tended to keep him at a distance. When more gnostic savior figures merged with the Christian Jesus as the second century progressed, their view of Jesus of Nazareth was usually defined in docetic terms, and they tended to shy away from "biography" Gospels in which he was dangerously portrayed as undergoing human experiences.

Note: The above translations are based on those by Maxwell Staniforth, in the Penguin Books edition of *Early Christian Writings*.

Appendix 4
A Gospel-based interpolation in the Ascension of Isaiah 11
[page 108]

Chapter 10 examined a composite Jewish-Christian document from the late first century, the Ascension of Isaiah, which contains passages about the descent of the Son (chapters 9 and 10) that show no trace of an incarnation to earth or knowledge of the Gospels. Nothing prepares the reader, therefore, for the extended passage 11:2-22 found in one of three manuscript lines. (This work has been translated with commentary by M. Knibb in vol.2, p.143-176, of *The Old Testament Pseudepigrapha*, ed. J. H. Charlesworth.)

There are three classes of surviving manuscripts of the Ascension of Isaiah: Ethiopic, second Latin, and Slavonic. The first is thought to be based on one Greek text, the other two on a different Greek text. There are notable differences between the Ethiopic on the one hand, and the second Latin and Slavonic on the other. Also, the latter pair include only the second section of the work, known as the Vision of Isaiah, chapters 6 to 11, which is the part we are concerned with.

In the Ethiopic text there is an unusual passage in 11:2-22, not a word of which appears in the other two. It recounts (as part of Isaiah's vision of the future) first the birth of the Lord to Mary and Joseph in Bethlehem. This passage agrees with no Gospel Nativity scene. Here Jesus is born in his parents' house, to a Mary who has not been forewarned of who this infant is. Lacking any details concerning Herod, magi, census, manger, shepherds, etc., it would seem to be an early, more primitive formulation of a birth story. The passage goes on to make bare reference to the great signs and miracles the adult Jesus performed in Israel, how the children of Israel turned against him, how he was handed over to the "ruler" (Knibb presumes that this must be Pilate) to be crucified, and how he descended to the angel in Sheol. It then concludes (verse 20): "In Jerusalem, I saw how they crucified him on a tree, and how after the third day he rose and remained (many) days. And I saw when he sent out the twelve disciples and ascended."

Knibb (*op.cit.*, p.154) remarks that "the primitive character of this narrative makes it difficult to believe that it did not form part of the original text." Elsewhere (p.146), he suggests that the Greek text on which the second Latin and Slavonic manuscripts were based was a "revision" of the one on which the Ethiopic was based, and that the 11:2-22 passage had been cut from the latter because of its "legendary features." But this would not seem to make much sense. Why would a "reviser" choose to delete this key passage, the only one in the Vision which has anything to say about Jesus' life on earth? Why would such details be seen as "legendary," implying that they were undesirable? If they seemed primitive to a later editor, experience has shown that when a Christian copyist or redactor does not like something, he changes it to make it conform to current outlook. Rarely does he drop it altogether— or reduce it to a phrase, such as is found at that point in the other versions.

A better explanation would be that the Latin and Slavonic texts are earlier, and that the Greek text behind the Ethiopic has enlarged upon an earlier Greek version lying behind the others. Even within the Ethiopic text of 11:2-22, we can detect signs of incremental expansion and revision. For example, in 11:21, in referring to how long Christ remained on earth after rising, different manuscripts in the Ethiopic have varying lengths of time, one being "forty days," no doubt under the influence of Acts. In general, the Ethiopic seems to show expansions on more primitive passages in the other two.

It can be argued that the Ascension of Isaiah reveals an evolution from a spiritual Christ operating in a supernatural setting, to a physical Christ living a life in an earthly setting. A document is being periodically revised (by multiple redactors in different versions) to reflect new developments in thought and doctrine, even if not every detail is always brought up to date. The Ethiopic manuscripts can contain a brief account of Jesus' life on earth, and yet not have descriptions of the Son's descent enlarged to include an earthly dimension. Perhaps it was felt to be implicit—as some modern scholars would assume.

Appendix 5
Hebrews 8:4 - "If he were on earth . . ."
[page 122]

This startling verse in chapter 8 of the epistle to the Hebrews is one which most commentators manage to gloss over or ignore completely. The writer is speaking of Jesus' ministry in the heavenly sanctuary and begins to compare him to the earthly high priest. At verse 4, he says:

"Now, if he had been on earth, he [Jesus] would not even have been a priest . . ."

No matter how one tries to detect a qualification to this phrase, there is no denying that the writer seems to be saying that Jesus was never on earth. The Greek is "*ei men oun ēn epi gēs*," which is literally: "Now, if accordingly he were on earth . . ." The verb *ēn* is the imperfect, which is strictly speaking a past tense, and the NEB (the translation above) chooses to reflect this. But the meaning is probably present, or at least temporally ambiguous, much like the conditional sense in which most other translations render it: "Now if he were on earth (meaning at this time), he would not be a priest."

However, the writer has failed to qualify this statement in any way. He does not say, if he were *now* on earth (instead of earlier), if he returned to earth, if he were still on earth; not even: "While he was on earth, he was not a priest . . ." The writer says nothing which shows any cognizance of the fact that Jesus *had* been on earth, recently; that it was on earth where an important part of his sacrifice, the shedding of his blood, had occurred. (In contrast to most modern commentators, who regularly feel constrained to point this out.)

The point he is making in this verse is that Jesus on earth would have nothing to do, since there are already earthly priests performing the duties which the Law prescribes, and they do so "in a sanctuary which is only a copy and shadow of the heavenly" (8:5). Yet how could any writer say that Jesus would have nothing to do on earth when he did, in fact, have so much to do? Could he imply that earth is the scene only of human duties in a human sanctuary when here was where Jesus had performed his sacrifice, shed his blood—presumably on a hill called Calvary outside Jerusalem? It is difficult to understand how a writer could express himself this way without at least a qualification, something which would give a nod to Jesus' recent presence in the physical arena.

Attempted explanations for this verse are inadequate. If Jesus had actually been on earth and conducted a sacrifice on Calvary (of himself), why would the writer bother to make the trivial observation that he wouldn't do it *now*, since there are priests on earth who do the equivalent with animals? In any case, those priests on earth had been performing such sacrifices for centuries, including during the time of Jesus' presumed incarnation. No, making the statement at all seems to preclude the idea that Jesus had ever performed a sacrifice in the earthly realm.

Paul Ellingworth has glimpsed the edge of the abyss and hastily drawn back. In analyzing this passage (*Hebrews*, p.405), he questions the normal interpretation of the imperfect *ēn*, and with it the NEB translation—which he admits "is grammatically possible"—because it "could be misunderstood as meaning that Jesus had 'never been on earth'." He claims that this "goes against the context." But that "context" is the assumption over the last 19 centuries that an historical Jesus existed, one who had been to earth; in fact, such a context is not to be found in Hebrews, but has instead been imposed upon it.

The writer goes on in 8:6 to point out that Jesus' present ministry in heaven is far superior to the earthly one of the high priest, an idea which takes no account of (and would seem to denigrate) the fact that Jesus had recently conducted an earthly ministry himself. Finally, the verses which lead into 8:4—and it is a major motif of the whole chapter—show that the writer's point is the assigning of a counterpart role to each of the two parties, the one being superior to the other: Jesus in the heavenly sanctuary, the human priests in the earthly one. Here again is an illustration of the point made in Chapter 12, that writers like that of Hebrews set up Platonic-type comparisons based on the separate and complementary relationship between the two spheres, between the higher and lower worlds, and if Jesus had in fact operated in both, the contamination would have destroyed their carefully crafted antitheses and required at least some direct reference to the discrepancy.

A similar silence on Jesus' recent presence in an earthly body which would have destroyed the writer's point is to be found in 1 Corinthians 15:44-49. Here, in contrasting the spiritual body of Christ, the man of heaven, with the material body of the earthly Adam, Paul fails to specify that the body of Christ he is speaking of was the spiritual one he took on *after* his resurrection, when he departed from the material world and left behind the earthly body like Adam's. (Paul's point is that resurrected humans will take on a heavenly body like that of Christ.) Commentators declare that Paul is *implying* this, but this does not change the fact that Paul gives no hint of such an implication.

Appendix 6
The location of the myths of the Greek savior gods and of Christ
[page 123]

Where did the Greeks and Romans envision the activities of their cultic gods had taken place? If Christianity's original Jesus was a savior god of the same nature, had he undergone his crucifixion in the same realm? Was this regarded as the higher spiritual world, the lower layers of the heavens in a Platonic universe? Or was it part of a primordial past on earth, a sacred time before history?

There is no doubt that before Platonic thought came to pervade the philosophical analysis of the universe a little before the turn of the Common Era, the Greek myths would have been relegated to a primordial past. Some of them would have stayed there, as in more traditional mythology about semi-divine superheroes like Heracles. But in regard to the salvation cults, were the myths of their gods transferred to a Platonic higher world (even if just above the earth) and did Christianity follow suit? I have shown in the text that the evidence leads strongly in that direction, and will enlarge on some of it here.

As discussed in Part Four, the presentation of the gods' activities in earthly or even human-sounding terms does not in itself rule out the upper world, since the lower material world and its characteristics were seen as derived from heavenly counterparts and archetypal spiritual models. Unfortunately, the only writings which address the myths of the mysteries are by sophisticated philosophers and not by priests or devotees of those cultic beliefs. Invariably such writers express themselves according to the principle laid down by Plutarch in the late first century CE:

> "Therefore, Clea, whenever you hear the traditional tales which the Egyptians tell about the gods, their wanderings, dismemberments, and many experiences of this sort . . . you must not think that any of these tales actually happened in the manner in which they are related." (*Isis and Osiris*, ch.11 / 355B; Loeb edition, p.29)

In other words, the mythical stories are allegories and not historical happenings in any sense. (In pre-Hellenistic versions of this myth, Osiris was identified as a legendary early king of Egypt, but the Greek cultic religion which grew out of him transcended that 'historical' identity.) Plutarch speaks (ch.54 / 373A) of the myth of Osiris' body being dismembered by Typhon, and of Isis wandering in search of its various parts, as something that is done 'repeatedly.' He thus regards it not as a single event which has taken place in a sacred past. The body of Osiris is equated with the Logos, a symbolic rendering of the Logos' activity as 'immanent' in the world, in the sense of it being an intermediary between the highest sphere of the timeless, changeless God and the sphere of temporal, changing matter. Though Plutarch does not present it in such terms, this is akin to the idea of the 'descending redeemer,' and of the cultic savior god who operates in some lower celestial sphere which impinges on the material world.

The fourth century philosopher Sallustius also regards the myths of savior gods like Attis as allegories of "timeless processes." Julian the Apostate of the same period, again in terms of allegory, speaks of the descent of the savior god Attis to a level which is described this way:

> "For it is there, they say, that the substance which is subject to change mingles with the passionless revolving sphere of the fifth substance." (*Orations V: Hymn to the Mother of the Gods*, 165C; Loeb edition, p.461)

Julian's Neoplatonic philosophy envisioned an intermediate layer of the universe in which divine beings or essences take on the characteristics of the material world; it was a sphere of overlap. Julian goes on to suggest that other elements of the myth of Attis represent characteristics that are even closer to the material world, and yet even this "does not mean matter itself, but the lowest non-material cause which subsists prior to matter." This area of the universe is "the

connecting link between forms embodied in matter beneath the moon"
and "the cause that is set over matter." He also styles Attis as a
demigod who "seems to lean and incline toward matter," being lower
than the "unchanging gods." All of this suggests an intermediate sphere
where gods can get close to the material world and do things which
have an impact upon it.

Highly esoteric stuff, almost unintelligible to the modern mind—
and, of course, totally unreflective of actual reality—which only the
philosopher may have thought to understand. It may say little about
how the average devotee of the cults looked upon such things, but it
demonstrates that the thinking of the era (something not to be regarded
as unified, however, or governed by any central authority) revolved
around Platonic images of the universe, and not around concepts of a
primordial past.

E. R. Goodenough (*By Light, Light*, p.14-15) sees the way in which
Plutarch handles the Isis/Osiris myth as reflective of the mystic's
search for spiritual ascent, for achieving the sought-for union with
God. Such mystical views were part of the Platonic structure of the
universe and had nothing to do with the sacred past concept.

Even in Apuleius' *The Golden Ass*, in the "allowable" report he can
give the reader on his introduction into the rites of Isis, he says:

> "I entered the presence of the gods of the under-world, and the gods
> of the upper-world, stood near and worshiped them." (trans. Robert
> Graves, *Penguin Classics*, 1950, p.241)

These gods and demigods exist in the 'now' and are described in terms
of their present manifestations. This is in much the same sense that
Christ is a present force in the thought of Paul, a mystical "body" in
which believers now share.

The myth of the god Mithras slaying the bull, within the Greek cult
which arose in Hellenistic times, has been explained (David Ulansey,
The Origins of the Mithraic Mysteries) as a mythical reflection of an
astronomical discovery by Hipparchus concerning the precession of the
equinoxes. This discovery was made in the late second century BCE.
Mithras, originally a Persian god later associated with the Greek god
Perseus who had his own constellation in the heavens, was the deity
regarded as responsible for this great, overriding manipulation of the
cosmic structure. The myth of the bull-slaying personified the removal
of the previous position of the spring equinox out of the constellation
of Taurus the Bull, effected by the constellation of Perseus (Mithras)

which was positioned right above it in the sky (*op.cit.*, p.83). If this view is correct, such a myth is by nature an upper-world occurrence and not an event of the sacred past. The myth may have been the product of the Stoics of the period, who were great astrologers and proponents of astral religion, allegorizing natural forces as the activity of celestial gods—once again illustrating the philosophic orientation of the times.

When we turn to Christian myths about the activities of Christ, the evidence there, too, points to a higher world concept. Paul's "rulers of this age" are the demons who have controlled humanity and its sphere up to the present time. Those demons were located in the "air" between the earth and the moon. Christ's death as an act which is about to consign the demons to destruction and restore the unity of the universe they have broken is less likely to have been envisioned as a primordial event in the dim prehistoric past than one taking place in an ever-present upper world. In any case, the Christian version of salvific processes, as outlined in Chapter 10, was not strictly Platonic, in the way Julian and Sallustius and Plutarch saw it—timeless allegories—but processes that were seen as part of God's ongoing workings of salvation history. Thus, they had to be compatible with that time line and could not be relegated to some prehistoric earthly past.

The Ascension of Isaiah represents itself as the record of a vision given to the prophet Isaiah, who lived in the 8th century BCE. The descent of the Son to be crucified by the "god of that world" is thus a *future* event, and cannot be located in a primordial past. The position of Christ's redeeming sacrifice in the epistle to the Hebrews is clearly located in a Platonic upper world sanctuary, and post-dates the Sinai cult on earth, to which it is compared in fine detail. (The writer's thought places it "at the completion of the ages" [9:26].)

That sacrifices could be offered in heaven is also demonstrated in the Testament of Levi, third part of the Testaments of the Twelve Patriarchs, a Jewish document with "additions" which scholars have labeled Christian. In chapter 3, sacrifices are depicted as being offered to God in a heavenly temple, by angels of the third heaven. This layer of heaven contains an archetypal sanctuary whose copy is the temple on earth. Here the archangels "offer propitiatory sacrifices to the Lord in behalf of all the sins of ignorance of the righteous ones" (as in the earthly rite on the Day of Atonement). "They present to the Lord a pleasing odor," although they are declared to be "bloodless." (See H. C. Kee, "Testaments of the Twelve Patriarchs" in *The Old Testament*

Pseudepigrapha, vol.2, p.789.) Sacrifices in heaven involving blood are, however, found in later Kabbalistic thinking.

Finally, the 'Descending-Ascending' redeemer concept as found in Gnosticism and elsewhere (together with its strong echo in the Gospel of John) is a process of revelation which occurs in a contemporary sense. It is part of a salvation system of mystical ascent through layers of the universe, aided by knowledge imparted from the heavenly redeemer, not through connections with primordial divine actions in a distant earthly prehistory.

In sum, then, the thinking of the age points strongly to a Platonic, spiritual world setting for both the myths of the mystery cults and the sacrifice of early Christianity's Christ.

Appendix 7
The priority of Mark and the existence of Q
[page 144]

This Appendix does not attempt to present a comprehensive case for either question, but to provide a summary of the principal arguments in favor of both.

The Priority of Mark

As a general rule, when two documents are similar in content and layout, and one is longer than the other, the longer one tends to be an expansion of the shorter. Matthew and Luke are considerably longer than Mark, and both seem to follow Mark's layout and content. The standard (and virtually only) alternative to the priority of Mark has been the priority of Matthew (a suggestion going back two centuries to the "Griesbach hypothesis").

In this case, however, one must provide a reasonable explanation for why Mark, if he is writing later and using one or both of the other Synoptics as his source, has cut out so much. He has stripped away the genealogies and nativity stories, gutted the Temptation scene, discarded the bulk of the teachings—including almost all the parables, as well as the most prized of Christian ethics such as those contained in Matthew's Sermon on the Mount. He has excised many of Matthew's details surrounding the crucifixion, the guard at the tomb, the post-resurrection appearances, the "preach to all nations" directive (Mt.

28:19) and much else. A convincing rationale for this degree of drastic reduction, along with a feasible setting in which it could have taken place, has yet to be put forward.

It is also the case that Matthew is more theologically developed than Mark, showing greater sophistication in his soteriology and use of titles for Jesus. The Matthean and Lukan grammar is an improvement over that of Mark, and Markan passages compared to the other two often contain a "harder" reading; that is, Mark's versions entail problems which Luke and Matthew have evidently 'smoothed out.'

The strongest weapon in the arsenal of those who reject the priority of Mark is the so-called "minor agreements" between Matthew and Luke. When all three Synoptics present the same saying or incident, it is sometimes the case that Matthew and Luke will have similar or identical wording, whereas Mark will differ from them both. This, it is claimed, shows that copying must have taken place between Matthew and Luke, rather than either or both of them from Mark.

But there are a number of other reasonable explanations for this phenomenon. Helmut Koester (*Ancient Christian Gospels*, p.175) suggests that subsequent alteration of the text of Mark may account for it no longer showing an agreement with the other two. Later scribes may have altered Luke's wording to agree with Matthew's (a common sort of occurrence in manuscript reproduction). And so on. The point is, measured against the arguments in favor of Markan priority, something like the minor agreements do not have an overwhelming weight, and the alternatives inevitably face their own, even greater, difficulties. As Koester says (*op.cit.*, p.130), "the rejection of the two-source hypothesis solves nothing and creates new riddles for which even more complex and more improbable hypotheses have to be proposed."

The Existence of Q

No one will deny that within the material in Matthew and Luke which they do not share with Mark (ie, which they have not taken from him) a great deal of it is extremely similar, as though both are drawing on another literary source. In many cases, the similarities are too close to be put down to a common drawing on oral tradition. If the existence of a separate written document is to be denied, some other explanation must be offered for this common material. The most frequent suggestion is that Matthew himself wrote this extra material, and that Luke used Matthew's Gospel and copied it from him. (This hypothesis exists within the context of Markan priority; ie, that both Matthew and Luke used Mark.) Two scholars advocating this position are Michael Goulder and John Shelby Spong.

There are several arguments telling against this possibility.

(1) The common material—otherwise assigned to Q—never appears in the same context in Luke as it does in Matthew, not even with similar lead-in lines. (This applies to the vast majority of the common material, which constitutes simple sayings; it excludes the three or four more extended anecdotes which, in the Q hypothesis, are indicative of a later layer of Q redaction: see Chapter 17.) If Luke is copying all these sayings from Matthew, it is strange that he never once borrows any element of Matthew's contexts as well.

(2) In Matthew, the common sayings material is arranged in very carefully organized blocks, whereas in Luke it is broken up into more disjointed pieces, and notably not in Matthew's order. If Luke is using Matthew, this rearrangement—especially the breaking up of Matthew's masterful Sermon on the Mount—is difficult to understand. There is also a marked inconsistency in relation to this observation: When Luke copies the *narrative* material from Mark (and from Matthew, in the scenario under consideration) he carefully maintains the order of his source(s), but when he is presumably copying the extra sayings material from Matthew, he radically mixes up its order. Why the two different approaches? Rather, the differences between the two evangelists in the order of their common (Q) material is best explained by seeing Matthew as the one who has rearranged it from the common source to create his organized blocks, whereas Luke has more closely followed the original order of that less organized source.

(3) When the same saying differs in wording between Matthew and Luke, sometimes Luke has the more primitive form, sometimes Matthew. If Luke were copying from Matthew, we would expect that in virtually all these cases it would be Matthew that would possess the less developed form. (Luke might 'improve' on Matthew, but he would hardly be likely to rework him in a more primitive direction.) The mix indicates that they are both drawing on a common source and that both evangelists have sometimes 'improved' the sayings they use.

(4) Although the question of the order of material within the three Gospels is a complex one, and not always conclusive, one aspect of it is compelling. When Matthew and Luke agree in their sequence, it is always when they both agree with Mark; the explanation being that they have both derived their common sequence from Mark. But in that

material which is common only to themselves, they never agree in its sequence. This would indicate that Luke is not copying from Matthew.

(5) Quite apart from the common (Q) material between them, if Luke has Matthew in front of him, why has he left out significant elements peculiar to Matthew? Why has he changed every element of Matthew's Nativity scene, but for its location in Bethlehem (which both would have derived from the prophecy in Micah 5:2, that the future king of Israel would be born there)? Robert H. Stein (*The Synoptic Problem*, p.102) asks: "Why would Luke have omitted such material as the coming of the wise men? Would not the presence of such Gentiles at the birth of Jesus been meaningful for Luke's Gentile-oriented Gospel? Why would he have omitted the flight to Egypt and return to Nazareth; the story of the guards at the tomb and their report; the unique Matthean material concerning the resurrection; and so on? Added to this is the observation that if Luke had before him Matthew's birth account and genealogy, one wonders if he would not have sought in some way to "harmonize" the one we have in his Gospel with the Matthean version."

Stein observes that it is, of course, impossible to get inside the mind of any given writer to know why he might or might not have done something, but he also maintains that we are still entitled to argue for those things which appear more probable when all known factors are taken into consideration. I would agree that this can often be a valid approach in the field of historical research; otherwise, we would lose helpful opportunities for deductive reasoning in situations where more exact evidence is not available.

Apart from a comparison of the documents to determine whether Luke copied Matthew, there is another important consideration in this matter. If no Q document existed, Matthew becomes the originator of the common material. This creates two significant problems.

The first is the difficulty in envisioning that someone of Matthew's mentality could have originated many of the sayings assigned to Q. Matthew was a hidebound traditionalist who emphasized the saying placed in Jesus' mouth that "not a letter, not a stroke, will disappear from the Law" (5:18). He was a fulminating prophet who painted a chilling, pitiless picture of the final judgment by the Son of Man, amid "wailing and grinding of teeth" (25:30-46). He penned the most heinous line in all of world fiction: "His blood be upon us and upon our children" (27:25). He was humorless, intolerant, virulently anti-Jewish—even if he was likely Jewish himself. Who can imagine that from his mind and pen could come: "Love your enemies, bless those who curse you . . . If someone strikes you on the right cheek, turn and offer him your left . . . Be merciful, even as your Father is merciful"?

The second problem is, if Matthew invented all the 'Q' material, why is it not consistent with the material he has drawn and reworked from Mark? Why does it, as a block, have its own distinctive internal fingerprints: the strong Cynic character, the void on any death-resurrection-redemption kerygma that saturates the rest of the Gospel? Why would it not all simply blend in with the elements of the majority part?

If there were no Q, we face a notable problem with the Gospel of Thomas. Those sayings in Thomas similar to the Q1 stratum would have no roots in the past but would instead have to be traced to Matthew. Yet too good a case has by now been made which rules out a dependence of Thomas on the Synoptic Gospels. (See Stephen J. Patterson: *The Gospel of Thomas and Jesus*, p.9-16; J. D. Crossan, *The Birth of Christianity*, p.117-118; H. Koester, *Ancient Christian Gospels*, p.84-85.)

If it is suggested that Matthew did not originate all this material, but drew it from some other source, then one has simply reinvented Q. The concept of Q is in any case much preferable to the idea that a small handful of evangelists were responsible for virtually all the Gospel content, for it opens up much wider headwaters for understanding the various types of ideas that flowed into Christianity and were eventually deposited in the Gospels. If it is acceptable to envision the Gospel of Mark as reflecting the ethos and traditions of a Q-style preaching movement based in Galilee, it is hardly a quantum leap to envision that ethos as embodied in a document which Mark himself happened not to possess (perhaps because it was not as far along in its evolution), but which later came into the hands of Matthew and Luke.

Appendix 8
The absence of an historical Jesus in the Didache
[page 64, 192]

At several points in this book, we have touched on the silence in the Didache about an historical Jesus: as the source of the ethical teaching—some of it closely resembling that of the Gospels—

contained in the "Two Ways" section (ch. 1 & 2); as the standard by which the itinerant prophets' authority and teachings are to be measured (ch. 11); as the one who will arrive at the Parousia (ch. 16); as the institutor of the community's thanksgiving meal (ch. 9 & 10). Neither is that meal a sacramental one, linking the bread and wine with Jesus' death. In fact, the Didache as a whole has nothing to say about a death and resurrection.

The only mention of Jesus comes in the eucharistic prayers of chapters 9 and 10, where he seems to be no more than a spiritual conduit to God, a revealer of "the life and knowledge thou hast made known to us through thy servant (or child) Jesus." In other words, a version of the "intermediary Son." As such, he is part of the baptismal formula quoted in 7:1:

". . .immerse in running water 'In the Name of the Father, and of the Son, and of the Holy Spirit.' "

In the Didache we can detect no idea of apostolic tradition, no appeal to any authority or correctness of doctrine going back to Jesus or any originating phase of the movement. The document as a whole is thoroughly theocentric—centering on God, not Jesus. Everything is done in the name of "the Lord," meaning God.

Yet here is where some scholars claim to find a reference to Jesus. John Dominic Crossan, in his *Birth of Christianity* (p.377), suggests: "The *Didache* has a calculatedly ambiguous use of *Lord* to mean "the Lord God" and/or "the Lord Jesus." But this spiriting in of Jesus under a cloak of alleged ambiguity is unfounded, for a careful consideration of its usage in this document shows that "the Lord" *always* refers to God.

Perhaps the most important use of this term is in 11:8. "Not everyone who speaks in the spirit is a [true] prophet but only if he has the character [*tropoi*] of the Lord" (Crossan's translation). Maxwell Staniforth, in the Penguin translation (*Early Christian Writings*, p.233), expands that last phrase to: "unless they also exhibit the manners and conduct of the Lord." Literally, the Greek is *ean echei tous tropous kuriou*, "unless they have the ways of the Lord."

Both of these scholars, and others, make the assumption that this refers to Jesus. But keep in mind that the document comes from the late first century, long after Jesus would have passed from the scene. Any lifestyle of Jesus would lie in the past, and if appealed to would probably be cast in terms of a past phenomenon. The phrase above lacks this past dimension and has a very present flavor. Whatever this *tropos* is, it seems to be a standard which operates in the present.

By way of comparison, look back a few verses to another phrase, twice repeated. "Receive (the itinerant preacher) as (you would) the Lord" (11:2), and "Let every apostle who comes to you be received as the Lord" (11:4). For both the Didache's writer and its readers, there can be no question of receiving Jesus at this time, since he is long gone, and yet the sense of present receiving, of present—if theoretical—opportunity to receive "the Lord" *now*, is very much there. If the intention were to draw a parallel between how the community should receive the itinerant prophet and how it would have received Jesus in the days when Jesus himself was traveling from place to place, that past concept would likely be reflected in the choice of words.

Both of the above verses have illuminating antecedents. Before 11:4, verse 3 says: "As regards apostles and prophets, act thus according to the ordinance of the gospel" (trans. Kirsopp Lake, *The Apostolic Fathers* [Loeb], p.327). Lake observes that this ordinance is not known, nor its source, and "gospel"—virtually all would agree—does not refer to a written gospel but simply to the preached message. But if Jesus can be imagined in the very same verse as arriving at the door, if it is he who is held up in the key verse of 11:8 as the very model by which *behavior* is to be judged, surely he as the source of the teaching itself would spring to mind—and pen—here, as the *author* of the ordinance, rather than the impersonal "gospel."

Look at the initial half of 11:2: "But if the teaching (of the itinerant prophet) be for the increase of righteousness and knowledge of the Lord . . . (receive him as [you would] the Lord)." Knowledge of the Lord. Especially in conjunction with the term "righteousness." Could anything echo more strongly of traditional Jewish concepts, and terminology, about learning of God and his ways? If Jesus of Nazareth were implied here, it seems clear that to distinguish it from the natural understanding of the phrase as referring to God the Father, a specific departure from Crossan's "calculated ambiguity" would have to be made. Instead, the constant and pervasive use of "the Lord" with no designation anywhere that this term also encompasses Jesus, seems to rule out any such meaning or ambiguity.

Back to 11:8 and its *tropoi* of the Lord. If the sentiment seems to lie very much in the present, what could the phrase mean? One might think that the writer is not likely to be speaking of *God's* manner and conduct—although an earlier verse to be examined shortly seems to say that very thing, and even 1 Peter 1:15 can speak of being "holy in all your behavior, even as the One who called you is holy." (The scriptural reference subsequently quoted makes it clear that this is a reference to God.)

In any case, there is a much more natural way of interpreting 11:8. Bauer's Lexicon offers as a translation of *exein tous tropous kuriou,* "have the ways that the Lord himself had, or *which the Lord requires of his own*" (my italics). Just as we would say that "following the ways of the Church" does not refer to the actual behavior of the Church hierarchy, but rather to the requirements laid down by the Church, so surely does the Didache's phrase mean that the itinerant prophets must exhibit—not Jesus' past behavior, but a conduct in their *own* present as required *now* by "the Lord." The idea of Jesus' "ways" thus evaporates, and we are left with no reference at all in Didache 11 to either the example of Jesus' conduct or his teachings in relation to that of the itinerant prophets.

A careful examination of the roughly two dozen times the title "Lord" is used in the Didache leads to the conclusion that it is exclusively a reference to God, never to Jesus. Some uses are obviously so, and since the writer or redactor fails to make any distinction for a separate application to Jesus, we are led to assume uniformity. Here is a passage from the Two Ways section which opens the document (using Staniforth's Penguin translation with the odd alteration in the direction of the literal):

> "Never speak sharply (to) servants who hope in the same God as yours, lest they cease to fear the God who is over you both; for he comes not to call men according to their rank, but those who have already been prepared by the Spirit. And you, servants, obey your masters . . . as the representatives of God . . . See that you do not neglect the commandments of the Lord, but keep them as you received them. . . ." (4:10-13)

This certainly looks like an unbroken chain of reference to God the Father, complete with Old Testament allusions. God is spoken of as "coming" and acting through the Spirit. This is a community which regards its message as God's product, imparted by revelation. It is silent on any figure of Jesus in its past as arriving or imparting anything. Its commandments, its rules of behavior, have been received from God, not Jesus. A little earlier, the text says:

"Give him (he who speaks the word of God) the honor you would give the Lord; for wherever the Lord's attributes (or nature, *kuriotes*) is spoken of, there the Lord is present." (4:1)

Kuriotes is a word referring to God (see Bauer's Lexicon); the context is entirely of God. This meaning and these sentiments cast their long shadow over the verses in chapter 11 considered above, where "receive him as the Lord," and "unless they have the ways of the Lord," can be seen as a reference to God. Again, this is a community which regards itself as an emissary of God and a recipient of his direction. The personality and direction of Jesus is nowhere evident.

Not only are the Didache's apostles welcomed as one would welcome God, not Jesus, they come and speak in his name, not Jesus' name: "Everyone who comes in the name of the Lord is to be made welcome." Parts of the eucharistic prayer tie the concept of "name" unambiguously to the Father, again with Old Testament allusions:

"Thanks be to thee, holy Father, for thy sacred Name which thou hast caused to dwell in our hearts." (10:2)
"Thou, O Almighty Lord, hast created all things for thine own Name's sake." (10:3)

Therefore, we can make a clear interpretation of this earlier part of the prayer:

"No one is to eat and drink of (the) Eucharist but those who have been baptized in the name of the Lord; for concerning this also did the Lord say: 'Give not that which is holy to the dogs.' " (9:5)

Not only is baptism conferred in God's name, but a saying attributed to Jesus in the Gospels (Mt. 7:6) must be regarded as attributed to God in the Didache. Those who would object to this need merely look at 14:3, which offers another "saying" of "the Lord." This one is not a Gospel saying but a quote from the Old Testament book of Malachi. Scripture is the word of God, regarded as things he "says," and the saying in 9:5 is probably, prior to its induction into Matthew (7:6), from some writing now lost.

Furthermore, we have in the Didache two references to the "gospel" of "the Lord." One is general: "Be guided by what you have (*echete*: have, not "read" as Staniforth translates) in the gospel of our Lord" (15:4). Koester (*Ancient Christian Gospels*, p.16-17) acknowledges that such references are unlikely to mean a written Gospel, but rather the oral message and instruction issued by the charismatic apostles of the community. This extends even to the other reference, a specific citing of the Lord's Prayer (8:2), which is a little different from Matthew's and is considered earlier. This citing is prefaced by: "Pray as the Lord commanded in his gospel."

In view of the continuous and unqualified use of the term "Lord" as applied to God in this document, and the lack of any general appeal to the teaching of Jesus, we have every reason to take this as a reference to God, to the message and instruction the itinerants carry which is regarded as coming from him, whether through inspiration or scripture. (See also my argument above that since "the gospel" in 11:3 is not attributed to Jesus, that it has no specific sense other than *God's* gospel.)

Thus the Didache provides evidence that the "Lord's Prayer" was indeed something which was seen to come from "the Lord," meaning God, and was only later, through the evolution the Q document underwent, placed in the mouth of Jesus by Matthew and Luke. A prayer like this, probably formulated at some time in the Didache community's past or contained in the traditions they inherited, would now be part of such a gospel, one "commanded" by God. (Note the reference in 4:13 above to "the commandments of the Lord," which the context identifies as God.)

As discussed in Chapter 19, the presence of the "servant/child Jesus" in the eucharistic prayers, and of "the Son" in the baptismal formula, shows that certain elements of the spiritual Christ movement—but not the death and resurrection concept—have crept into the Didache community. There is also a passing use of the term "Christ" in 12:5: "If someone [ie, the itinerant prophet] does not wish to cooperate, he (or she) is a Christ-peddler" (Crossan's translation, *op.cit.*, p.374).

But if this "Christ," along with the "servant/child Jesus" of the eucharistic prayers, is to be equated with an historical Jesus who began the movement of which the Didache community is a part, why does that same Jesus not appear in all the other places in the Didache examined above? Why is he not credited with the teachings, with the "gospel"? Why is he not the standard by which the itinerant prophets are measured? By the same token, if "the Lord" is claimed to be, at least some of the time, a reference to an historical Jesus, how can this human man be exalted to the extent of receiving God's own divine title, and yet fail to be linked in the community's thinking with any of its activities or traditions?

Rather, we are looking at one particular offshoot of the widespread kingdom movement reflected in the Q document. The Didache community had, like the early stages of Q, no human founder or source of its teachings. But unlike Q, it has absorbed ideas of Messiah and Son (purely spiritual versions) in the course of its own evolution. This probably took place in Syria, where the idea of the intermediary Son seems to have been especially strong.

NOTES

Introduction (pages 1 to 8)

1   *[page 1]* The terms "CE" and "BCE" stand for "the Common Era" and "Before the Common Era." They are a modern substitution for AD and BC which in international scholarly work are considered too specific to a Christian world view.

2   *[page 4]* Traditions: In this context, anything to do with beliefs, customs, teachings, experiences, perceived memories which are preserved by a group or cultural entity, either orally or in writing, and passed on to others over time. Thus the singular "Tradition" refers to the collectivity of such things, or the collective idea of a group or entity.

3   *[page 5]* Hellenistic: period and characteristics of the ancient civilization in the eastern Mediterranean and Near East following the conquests of Alexander the Great in the 4th century BCE, extending to the Roman conquests in that area at the end of the first century BCE. It was marked by the superimposition of Greek culture on the older states of the Near East, with particular focus on the larger cities such as Alexandria (in Egypt), Antioch (NE corner of the Mediterranean), and Ephesus (western Asia Minor/Turkey).

4   *[page 6]* The Christian New Testament (the official canon of sacred writings) is comprised of two main categories of documents. In the first category, the four Gospels, Matthew, Mark, Luke and John, are regarded as giving testimony to Jesus' life and death, while the Acts of the Apostles purport to describe the immediate response to those events and the course of the first few decades of the apostolic movement, most of it centering on Paul. Although the Gospels are incompatible with each other in many of their details, they and Acts have been regarded for almost two millennia as essentially historically reliable. However, modern scholars no longer consider the Gospels to have been written in the initial apostolic period, and the traditional names attached to them are not regarded as an accurate identification of their authors (see Chapters 14 and 24).

The term "gospel" is the English translation of the Greek *euangelion*, meaning "good news." In the literature it can refer to the orally preached message of apostles like Paul (in which case it is usually spelled with a small 'g'), or it can refer to the written accounts of Jesus' life and death which embody that message (in which case it is usually spelled with a capital 'G'). By the end of the second century, many more Gospels than the canonical four were in circulation among various Christian groups across the empire. Most of that extensive catalogue has been lost, or is preserved only in unearthed fragments or quotations in the early Christian writers. Most of them were judged heretical or inferior to the chosen four and were eventually suppressed. While Mark, Matthew, Luke and John are written in narrative form, many non-canonical Gospels comprised sayings collections or dialogues, with no narrative framework.

The second category within the New Testament is a miscellaneous collection of epistles. While the "epistle" takes the form of a letter, usually to some community or other, it was designed to be read out to the congregation of that community and often embodied teaching or polemical material. More will be said on the nature of the epistles in Chapter 1. Most of the epistles of the New Testament are attributed to Paul, others to apostles who appear in the Gospels as followers of Jesus, or to reputed relatives of Jesus. In ancient times, the epistle to the Hebrews became assigned to Paul, but later was regarded as anonymous. Its final verses (13:22f), with its Pauline references, is regarded by many as a later addition. The New Testament closes with the Apocalypse of John, a prophecy of the future cataclysmic overthrow of the present world order.

5 [*page 6*] Synoptic(s): literally "seen together," referring to the three Gospels of Mark, Matthew and Luke, with their great similarity of material, such that they can be compared side by side. "They are similar in outline, contents, order and wording. Most impressive are the verbal agreements, which are almost total in some passages" (*Harper's Bible Dictionary*, p.1009). See Appendix 7 for arguments on the position that Mark was the first Gospel written.

6 [*page 8*] See Charlotte Allen, "Confucius and the Scholars," *Atlantic Monthly*, April 1999, p.79-83. From that article: "Most Sinologists these days would agree that Confucius, if he existed at all, has left little concrete evidence of what he was like, and that the traditional biographical material associated with him is largely legend. It is also accepted academic wisdom that the *Analects* (. . .a collection of 497 sayings and short dialogues written down by his disciples after his death . . .) was put together over several generations. . . . If it turns out that Confucius never existed, or that the *Analects* was composed over several centuries, the faith of many New Confucians is likely to be rattled a bit but not destroyed." Allen summarizes Professor Lionel M. Jensen's view (*Manufacturing Confucianism: Chinese Traditions and Universal Civilization*) that it was the Jesuits in the late 16th century who turned "the spiritual and ethical traditions of the *ru*, China's elite scholarly class . . . (into) a full-fledged religion centered on the person of its supposed founder, Confucius . . . using the model of Christian theology, which centers on the person of Jesus Christ." An invented founder used to recast the traditions of another invented founder? As we go through this book, the similarities in the Christian situation will become evident, as will the universal human

tendency to impute national and religious traditions which originate in multiple sources over a period of time to a single innovator at a single point in history.

Chapter 1: A Heavenly Christ *(pages 11 to 22)*

7
  [*page 13*] More radical views of the Pauline corpus regard even fewer letters as genuine, or none at all. Such an interpretation goes back to F. C. Baur and the Dutch Radical School of the 19th century, but is making a comeback in some circles today. While it is likely that liberal scholarship will eventually enlarge the extent of later editing and interpolation it would allow within some of the "genuine" letters of Paul, it is too soon to overthrow the basic reliability of the standard seven. I would regard them as in principle defensible, and in this book accept their core authenticity.

8
  [*page 18*] The term "mythological" as employed in New Testament studies can have a more specific meaning than the popular sense of relating to legends or mythical stories. It may refer to features given to deities, spiritual forces, etc. which relate to their functioning in the heavenly world or in relation to other spiritual things. For example, saying that Jesus was "pre-existent" with God in heaven before the creation of the world or that he gained power over the spirit forces in the heavens are "mythological" features. There may be some variance in usage among commentators, but this is the way the term will be used in this book.

9
  [*page 19*] Some aspects of the Buddha in later philosophy about him might be said to rival the divine Jesus in scope, but these took much longer to develop after the Buddha's passing.

10
  [*page 20*] Biblical anthropomorphisms (human images applied to God) have been rooted out by writers such as Philo of Alexandria and the translators of the Targums (versions of the bible in Aramaic) because it was regarded as unseemly to represent God as possessing human attributes. James Dunn (*The Parting of the Ways*, p.188f) notes that Paul shows not the slightest discomfort in applying to Jesus passages from the Hebrew scriptures which originally referred to God. The hymn in Philippians 2:6-11 is a clear echo, he says, of Isaiah 45:23, which is "one of the strongest assertions of Jewish monotheism in the whole of the scriptures." He goes on to declare: "That a Jew should use such a text of a man who recently lived in Palestine is truly astonishing."

11
  [*page 21*] *A Myth of Innocence*, p.96-102; *Who Wrote the New Testament?* p.75f.

12
  [*page 21*] In his *Who Wrote the New Testament?* Burton Mack judges the group in Jerusalem around Peter and James as "not a congregation of the Christ cult kind" (p.103). This suggestion, that the Jerusalem apostles did not regard Jesus as divine, is an increasingly common view which is not borne out by the evidence in Paul. In 1 Corinthians 15:3-8 Paul not only

links the Jerusalem group with his own gospel that Jesus had died for sin and risen (elements which are part of the "cultic" picture), but he gives no indication that their interpretation of Jesus differed so fundamentally from his own. Is it really possible that if Peter had no concept of Jesus as God, he would associate with a man who was doing something that would have been horrifying to his apparent Jewish loyalties and sensibilities? The issue evidenced in Galatians 2, of whether Jews could eat at the same table as gentiles, would be insignificant beside the dispute that would have set Peter and Paul at each other's throats over whether a Galilean preacher should be converted into the divine Son of the God of Abraham! (See also Note 41.)

13 [*page 22*] The cultic presentation of Jesus' crucifixion does not fit the "noble death" scenario. The latter is classically of the warrior or teacher who dies for his country, his followers, his teachings. These things focus on a life, a cause; in Judaism, it is invariably for the sake of the Law. This is precisely what is missing in the Christ cult, which has nothing to do with Jesus' life, teachings or followers. Dying for sin is not in the same category, especially when placed in the spirit realm; this is a mystical, spiritual concept.

Chapter 2: A Conspiracy of Silence (pages 23 to 30)

14 [*page 26*] A passage often appealed to as a declaration by Paul that he has abandoned interest in Jesus' earthly life is 2 Corinthians 5:16. But such an interpretation is not justified when the passage is examined: "Just as from now on we know no man according to the flesh (*kata sarka*) so too, even if we have known Christ according to the flesh, we do so no longer."

Whatever Paul means by this rather cryptic sentence, it contains no reference to an earthly life of Jesus. Among others, C. K. Barrett (*Second Epistle to the Corinthians*, p.170-1) recognizes that the second "according to the flesh" does not describe an attribute of Christ, but Paul's action of "knowing," and thus "the view, based on a false interpretation of this verse, that Paul had no interest in the Jesus of history, must be dismissed." It is the attitude of humans toward other humans, and toward Christ, which has been filtered through "the flesh"—their own—and Christ as an entirely spiritual figure remains unaffected.

The NEB translation shows that any allusion to an historical Jesus needs to be abandoned: "With us, therefore, worldly standards have ceased to count in our estimation of any man; even if once they counted in our understanding of Christ, they do so now no longer."

Have we come full circle to Paul's declaration? Does our understanding of Christ—based for 1900 years upon the worldly standard, the historical "flesh" created in the Gospels—need to be set aside? Paul was more of a prophet than he realized.

15
[*page 26*] The Jesus Seminar, led by Robert W. Funk, is an association of New Testament scholars based in California, formed in the 1980s to apply modern critical analysis to the documents of the Christian record. Membership is open to scholars around the world, though most of those on its roster are American. The Seminar spent several years judging the likelihood of authenticity for the sayings attributed to Jesus in the Gospels, followed by a few years spent judging the historical authenticity of the acts attributed to Jesus in the Gospels, including the resurrection. At their meetings, balloting by members on each point of discussion is carried out using a system of colored beads dropped into a voting box. Red: Jesus undoubtedly said/did this. Pink: Jesus may have said/done this or something like it. Gray: Jesus did not say/do this, though there may be a little similarity. Black: Jesus said/did nothing like this. Resulting judgments are stated in terms of color determined by percentages. The Seminar has recently turned its primary attention on Paul and his letters.

16
[*page 30*] See Burton Mack, *A Myth of Innocence*, p.87, n.7; Werner Kelber, *The Oral and the Written Gospel*, p.206: "These sayings could have come from Jesus, but they could just as well have been prophetically functioning sayings of the Risen Lord." Rudolf Bultmann, in a classic statement of the idea (*History of the Synoptic Tradition*, p.127) refers to various prophetic sayings in the Gospels: "The Church drew no distinction between such utterances by Christian prophets and the sayings of Jesus in the tradition, for the reason that even the dominical sayings in the tradition were not the pronouncements of past authority, but sayings of the risen Lord, who is always a contemporary for the Church." This common type of rationalization, that the early Church did not differentiate between the words of the Risen Lord and the teachings of Jesus on earth, simply masks the fact that the idea of the latter nowhere appears in the early record.

Chapter 4: Apostles and Ministries (pages 39 to 46)

17
[*page 40*] The Greek has the pronoun "he" in this sentence, but most translations insert "God" based on the context and Paul's practice; others leave the "he" but none I am aware of read it as "Jesus."

18
[*page 41*] Sometimes Paul refers to a vision of Christ (though nothing on the scale of Acts' Damascus Road experience, which he never mentions), but in most cases he declares that his calling and his gospel come from God (eg, Gal. 1:16, 1 Cor. 1:1, 2 Cor. 1:1, 3:6, 10:13, 1 Thess. 2:4, Romans 1:1; cf. Col. 1:25, Eph. 1:1, Titus 1:3).

19
[*page 42*] The only rival apostle named in Paul's letters is Apollos of Alexandria, who also appears in Acts 18:24-28. In 1 Corinthians 1 and 2, Paul speaks of rival "cliques" which have formed within the Corinthian congregation around himself and around Apollos. He goes on (1 Cor. 1:18-24) to defend his position against those who do not subscribe to his

theology of the cross, which he calls "the wisdom of God" as opposed to "the wisdom of the world." I would argue that this attack is directed at other Christian apostles who do not believe in a sacrificial Son but rather in a Son who is a Revealer of wisdom, and this includes Apollos himself. See my website article, "Apollos of Alexandria and the Early Christian Apostolate," at <www.magi.com/~oblio/jesus/supp01.htm>

20 [*page 42*] Note that this appearance in 1 Cor. 15:5 is to the full Twelve. If these were the Gospel Twelve and that account were correct—Judas having dropped out (at the end of a rope)—it would only have been to eleven. More than one commentator has fussed over this little 'inaccurate detail' (eg, E. P. Sanders, *The Historical Figure of Jesus*, p.277).

Even the term in Acts 6:2, imbedded in a piece of tradition whose reliability is uncertain, is ambiguous. We might postulate that the Twelve are a group within the Jerusalem sect who are charged with certain duties, and that their number was chosen as a symbolic representation of the twelve tribes of Israel. They may also have had a symbolic function anticipating the coming Parousia, for the Gospels record the apocalyptic expectation that the Apostles shall sit on twelve thrones to judge the world when Jesus returns as the Son of Man.

The same symbol of the twelve tribes is undoubtedly the source of the idea we find in Revelation 21:14, the only clear mention of "the twelve" as apostles in the first century, and that right at its end. Yet Revelation gives us no historical Jesus, and such apostles need not be linked to an earthly Master. That "twelve" is a mystic number and not a part of history is shown by the context: the heavenly Jerusalem possesses twelve gates bearing the names of the twelve tribes of Israel, and a city wall with twelve foundation stones; upon these stones are inscribed "the names of the twelve apostles of the Lamb." It was probably such symbolic thinking which created the tradition that Jesus had twelve apostles, with the added factor that some body in the primitive church had been labeled the Twelve.

21 [*page 45*] For example, "According to the newspaper this morning, the President went to Chicago." The President is not fulfilling the newspaper account, that account is informing the reader of the President's actions. Just as scripture informed Paul about the Christ and his activities.

22 [*page 45*] Some scholars have offered a way around the apparent problem. Paul, they claim, is not saying that he heard this from Jesus' own mouth, but that he received an account from others of words which *derived* from Jesus. In other words, "from the Lord Jesus" *(apo tou kuriou)* refers to the "remote antecedent," the originator of the information being passed on. So that a more accurate translation of Paul's meaning might be: "I received (words) of the Lord (through others) which I passed on to you . . ."

Much of this argument hinges on the use of the preposition *apo* ("from"). A different preposition, *para* (also "from"), is usually used when a writer or speaker is referring to the immediate source of the thing received, such as someone who has told him something directly; whereas *apo* is more frequently used when referring to the ultimate source of the information, passed through some intervening stage of transmission.

The only problem with this solution is, these usages were not strict, and right in the Gospels we can find cases where *apo* is used to refer to the *immediate* source, such as Matthew 11:29 where Jesus says: "Take my yoke upon you and learn *from* me." In Colossians 1:7 we find the same thing: "You learned (God's truth) *from* Epaphras." Thus, nothing prevents us from taking "*apo tou kuriou*" (from the Lord) as referring to a direct reception of information from Christ himself by Paul—which can only mean in the sense of revelation.

There is an additional consideration. If Paul is referring to Jesus as the remote source, the originator of the saying, he is creating a rather awkward redundancy in this passage. Paul is about to tell his readers that Jesus spoke certain words. Would he have been likely to preface it with a statement which declares that Jesus spoke these words? No, it makes much better sense all round if Paul is saying what the words plainly seem to be saying: that he knows these words of Jesus because he has received a report of them directly from the Lord himself. As such, the passage falls into the same category as Paul's other "words of the Lord," all of which are the product of revelation.

Chapter 5: Apocalyptic Expectations *(pages 47 to 54)*

23

[*page 48*] The Greek word "*apokalupsis*" means "a revelation," with the connotation of uncovering something which God has hitherto hidden from human knowledge. In modern scholarly study of the period, a second word is often brought in to make the phrase "apocalyptic eschatology." The latter word is from the Greek "*to eschaton*" meaning "the end," since the thing being revealed is usually something to do with the end of the world. This End is regarded as imminent and one which will arrive in a cataclysm. In fact, the word "apocalyptic" by itself has come to possess all these connotations and is more often used alone. As a noun, it encompasses the beliefs, the literature, the phenomenon itself in both its Jewish and Christian manifestations.

Ultimately, the type of thought encompassed by this word goes back to Persian Zoroastrianism which expected a violent confrontation on the heavenly scene between the forces of good and the forces of evil. The views of the Essenes, especially those of Qumran whose outlook is reflected in some of the Dead Sea Scrolls, are thought to be heavily dependent on Persian apocalyptic antecedents. In the first century CE apocalyptic expectation is also expressed in Jewish documents such as 1

Enoch and 4 Ezra. In Christianity, it comes to a climax in the Gospels and Revelation.

24 [*page 50*] "LXX" is an abbreviation for the Septuagint, the Greek translation of the Hebrew bible made in Egypt in the 3rd and 2nd centuries BCE. Because there were significant differences in this translation over its Hebrew original, scholars can tell that in virtually all cases in which early Christian writers quote scripture, they are using the Septuagint rather than the Hebrew version. This sometimes creates the curious anomaly that Jesus has the words of the LXX in his mouth, rather than the Hebrew, something that would have been very unlikely had he had a rabbinical background and preached in Aramaic, as most scholars today assume. It has also been their custom to assume that Jesus did not speak Greek.

25 [*page 50*] Scholars claim that there is one passage in the New Testament epistles (though they admit that it is *only* here in the entire corpus) which contains a clear reference to the End-time coming of Jesus as a *second* coming: Hebrews 9:27-28. But is such a reference to be found even here?

> "[27]And as it is the lot of men to die once, and after death comes judgment, [28]so Christ was offered once to bear the burden of men's sins, and will appear (literally, he will be seen, or will reveal himself) a second time (*ek deuterou*), sin done away, to bring salvation to those who are watching for him." [NEB]

If the *ek deuterou* in verse 28 means "a second time," the parallel with verse 27 is destroyed. Verse 27 is saying "first men die, and after that (or 'next') they are judged." There is no sense here of a second time for anything; the writer is simply offering us a sequence of events: death, followed by judgment.

Why not make verse 28 offer a sequence as well? "Christ was offered once (his sacrifice), and after that (next) he will appear to bring salvation." The idea of appearing "a second time" would be intrusive here. Since the writer is presenting his readers with some kind of parallel between verses 27 and 28 (note also the "once" in both parts), it seems unlikely he would introduce an element which does not fit the parallel, especially one he does not need. *Ek deuterou* can have the alternate meaning of "secondly" or "next in sequence," like the similar word *deuteron*, which appears in this sense in 1 Corinthians 12:28. Just as a person's death is followed by judgment, so is Christ's sacrifice followed by his appearance, but with no indication of the length of time between the two. As long ago as the turn of this century, Vaughan (quoted in *The Expositor's Greek Testament*, Hebrews, p.340) translated verse 28: "Christ died once and the next thing before him is the Advent."

Thus even in Hebrews 9:27-28 it seems there is no Second Coming of Christ.

Chapter 6: From Bethlehem to Jerusalem *(pages 55 to 64)*

26   *[page 57]* Compare also 1 Corinthians 9:5. Here is a literal translation: "Have we not the right to take along a sister (*adelphēn*), a wife, as do the rest of the apostles and the brothers (*adelphoi*) of the Lord and Cephas?" Look at the word "sister." No one would say that Paul is referring to his own or anyone else's sibling. He means a fellow-believer of the female sex, and he seems to use it in apposition to (descriptive of) the word "wife." Indeed, all translations render this "a believing wife" or "a Christian wife."

This, too, should cast light on the meaning of *adelphos*, both here and elsewhere. It refers to a fellow-believer in the Lord. The more archaic rendering as "brethren of the Lord" conveys exactly this connotation: a community of like-minded believers, not "siblings" of each other or anyone else. Thus, a "brother of the Lord," whether referring to James or the 500, means a follower of this divine figure, and in 1 Corinthians 9:5, Paul would be referring to some of these members of the Jerusalem sect.

Finally, it is not impossible that the phrase "the brother of the Lord" in Galatians 1:19 began as an interpolation or marginal gloss. Some later copyist, perhaps when a 2nd century Pauline corpus was being formed and after James' sibling relationship to the new historical Jesus had been established, may have wished to ensure that the reader would realize that Paul was referring to James the Just and not James the Gospel apostle.

27   *[page 58]* E. M. Sidebottom (*James, Jude and 2 Peter*, p.79) claims that the absence of a reference to Jesus by James "would be natural in his brother," but this is unsupported by any reasoning as to why this would be so. Helmut Koester (*Introduction to the New Testament*, vol.2, p.247) wonders whether the silence in Jude was "chosen for polemical reasons." What these might have been is not said. J. N. D. Kelly (*The Epistles of Peter and Jude*, p.233) suggests that this same writer's reticence was due to "humility and reserve." Regrettably, the letter itself gives no evidence of such traits, with its doom-laden condemnation of those who follow rival beliefs and practices which make them "brute beasts." Besides, no one would expect or value such "reserve." The "avoidance of presumption," another suggested reason by Kelly, is not a strong characteristic of early Christian writers either.

28   *[page 60]* Not only would a preacher of the kingdom be expected to perform miracles, his views on the coming End-time would have been eagerly sought. All these things would have been inseparable within the one package, determined by popular expectation and universal practice among Jewish and Christian prophets. Every Christian document of the first century, from Q to the Didache to the New Testament epistles, speaks of some kind of apocalypticism, with miracle working not far behind.

It thus becomes a highly dubious proposition for modern critical scholarship to construct an "authentic Jesus" who has these fundamental elements stripped away. The Jesus Seminar's presentation (working from Q and the Gospel of Thomas: see Part Five) of a teaching sage who is too progressive to indulge in miracle working or too enlightened to share in the apocalyptic expectations of his age, speaks more for the needs and preferences of the modern scholarly mind than it does for an historically accurate picture of a presumed first century preacher of the kingdom. Selective interpretation of certain features in teachings like the parables, while ignoring the explicitly apocalyptic elements which stand alongside them, have served to highlight and impute to Jesus the concept of "the kingdom within you now," while divorcing it from the less enlightened (to our minds) dimensions of End-time anticipation and hopes that were the mark of the period.

We shall see that the 'prophetic' layer of the Q document (Q2) contained both apocalyptic preaching and traditions of miracle working, including raisings from the dead (see Lk./Q 7:22). These things modern critical scholarship regards as having been imputed—falsely—to Jesus as early as the 50s of the first century. (My view on that point will be seen to differ.) All these observations show that if Jesus had been an historical figure preaching the kingdom of God, traditions about him working miracles and forecasting the End-time would have started to circulate early on, and should have been accessible to writers like Paul and the author of the epistle of James.

29 [*page 62*] Because the Temple was a volatile place, with Roman soldiers always stationed in the immediate vicinity (the major Jerusalem fortress, the Antonia, with its Roman garrison, overlooked the Temple itself), some scholars, eg, F. W. Beare, in his *Commentary on Matthew*, p.416, argue for the impossibility of such an incident.

30 [*page 64*] A careful study of the use of the term "Lord" in the Didache shows that it always refers to God. For an extensive discussion of this point and of the general lack of an historical Jesus in the Didache, see Appendix 8.

31 [*page 64*] Burton Mack (*Who Wrote the New Testament?* p.87) regards the Last Supper as part of the later mythology about Jesus, and not an actual historical event. He calls this scene "not historical but imaginary," a creation of the Christ cult surrounding meal practice "in keeping with their mythology."

Chapter 7: The Passion Story *(pages 65 to 76)*

32 [*page 69*] The Gospel incident of the release of Barabbas is entirely unbelievable. The claim that Pilate had a custom at festival time of setting

free one prisoner of the public's choosing is flatly rejected by many scholars. Apart from there being no evidence for it, it goes against all Roman policy and character, and certainly does not fit what we know of Pilate himself from other sources.

33
[*page 71*] See the March/April 1995 issue of *The Fourth R*, the magazine of the Westar Institute and the Jesus Seminar.

34
[*page 71*] In a comprehensive study of the meaning of *ōphthē*, a passive aorist (past tense) of the verb *horaō*, to see, the *Theological Dictionary of the New Testament* (vol.V, p.358) points out that in this type of context the word is a technical term for being "in the presence of revelation as such, without reference to the nature of its perception." In other words, the "seeing" may not refer to actual sensory or mental perception. Rather, it may simply be "an encounter with the risen Lord who reveals himself . . . they experienced his presence." If what we have here is more an experience of Christ's "presence" than a full-blown hallucinatory vision, this would make it easier to accept that so many individuals and even large groups (such as the "more than 500 brothers" in 1 Corinthians 15:6) could imagine that they had undergone such an experience.

It is far from clear, therefore, that Paul is describing anything more than a series of experiences in which many people, most of them within a group already formed for a religious purpose, felt a conviction of faith in the spiritual Christ, experiences which may well have grown in the telling. We could note, too, that Paul's own "seeing" may not be an account of his conversion experience. When he refers to his conversion, or "call" (usually by God), he never describes it in the dramatic terms of a vision, and certainly not in the way Luke casts the event in Acts when he has Christ appear to Paul on the road to Damascus. Paul's "seeing" in 1 Corinthians may be a 'confirming' experience subsequent to his call, just as the other ones he lists must be, since those apostles were already believers. When self-styled prophets, including modern evangelists, make their claims to speak with the voice of God, they inevitably support and justify their claims by an appeal to personal experiences of that God, to wonders or miracles they have known or been a part of. Paul and the others *needed* the "seeings" he recounts here—and they duly received them.

35
[*page 76*] See, for example, Robert Funk, *Honest to Jesus*, p.237-8; John Dominic Crossan, *The Birth of Christianity*, p.251; John Shelby Spong, *Liberating the Gospels*, p.249; Burton Mack, *A Myth of Innocence*, ch. 9.

Chapter 8: The Word of God in the Holy Book *(pages 77 to 86)*

36
[*page 79*] For example, 1 Enoch 62:5-7: "And pain shall seize them when they see that Son of Man sitting on the throne of his glory. Kings, governors, and all the landlords shall (try to) bless, glorify, extol him who

rules over everything, him who has been concealed. For the Son of Man was concealed from the beginning, and the Most High One preserved him in the presence of his power; then he revealed him to the holy and the elect ones." (Translation by E. Isaac in *The Old Testament Pseudepigrapha*, vol.1, p.35.)

Some commentators have tried to see this section of 1 Enoch, known as the Similitudes of Enoch (ch. 37-71) as a Christian composition, because they identify the Son of Man as a Christian element. But this, along with the concept of a spiritual Messiah, must be seen as ideas not exclusively Christian but of Jewish sectarian provenance. The Son of Man reached the Gospels and Jesus only through the (Jewish) Q community when the latter invented a founder figure and applied its Son of Man to him; Mark later expanded on this Q tradition in his Gospel.

37 [*page 80*] This verb in Isaiah 53 for "delivering up," in the context of God doing the delivering, is the same as that used in 1 Corinthians 11:23, in Paul's account of the Lord's Supper: "on the night he was delivered up." As will be seen in Chapter 11 when examining that Supper, the implication is that the "delivering" there is also by God, and not within the historical situation of the Gospels. The link with Isaiah 53 also supports the contention that Paul, in recounting this scene in 1 Corinthians 11:23-26, is speaking of matters which have come to him through revelation.

38 [*page 83*] In Barrett's *Epistle to the Romans*, p.20. C. E. B. Cranfield (*International Critical Commentary*, Romans, p.60) allows that *kata* as meaning "in the sphere of" is a possibility. But he prefers to read "*kata sarka*" as encompassing the idea of "ongoing nature," something broader than simply the idea of "in his life span." Cranfield thus inadvertently points to an idea which is non-historical, fitting the timeless realm of myth.

Chapter 9: The Intermediary Son *(pages 87 to 94)*

39 [*page 89*] Philo of Alexandria is the foremost example of the input of Greek ideas into Jewish thought, a phenomenon which produced an important type of philosophy and culture during this period, called "Hellenistic Judaism."

40 [*page 89*] There are those who maintain that "Wisdom" was simply a poetic way of expressing certain of God's activities, but most scholars will admit that the portrayal of Wisdom in the biblical and extra-biblical literature makes her a distinct divine personage or force. See, for example, Helmer Ringgren, *Word and Wisdom*, p.118, 132, etc.

41 [*page 91*] D. Moody Smith notes (in *Harper's Bible Dictionary*, under "Logos") that "it is not immediately obvious why a man sent from God, even the Messiah of Israel, should have played such a role," referring to the Logos' role as God's agent in creating the world. He is quite right.

That Jews, no less, could assign to a crucified preacher the creation of the universe is beyond belief. But of course they did nothing of the sort. They assigned that role to the spiritual Son in heaven, just as thinkers before them had assigned it to God's Wisdom and others to the intermediary Logos. The historical man entered the picture only when the heavenly son was later thought to have come to earth and lived a life told of in the Gospels. Cosmic beliefs about a supposed historical man were much easier to accept when applied long after the 'fact,' and easier still when created by a largely gentile mind.

On the matter of presumed Jewish response to a human Jesus, one of the common observations about groups in the 2nd and 3rd centuries which are styled "Jewish-Christian" is that they did not regard Jesus as a divine figure. The Ebionites, for example, saw Jesus as a prophet Messiah but not the Son of God. But all these groups flourished only after the first century, and the record of fragments from their documents (as in Epiphanius and Hippolytus) comes from the 3rd and 4th centuries. There is great difficulty in tracing Ebionite views back into the 1st century, especially to the Jerusalem community known to us through the letters of Paul. It is by no means easy to support views like that of Burton Mack (see Note 12), that this original Jerusalem group around Peter and James did not regard Jesus as divine. In fact, Paul provides evidence of quite the opposite.

Thus, our evidence that Jewish-Christians regarded an historical Jesus as simply a human prophet arises only after the figure contained in the Gospels had come to be widely known and accepted as historical. In fact, certain preserved fragments suggest that earlier Jewish-Christian sects did indeed envision a heavenly origin for Christ, though not as a Son of God. "They (the Ebionites) say that he was not begotten of God the Father, but created as one of the archangels . . . that he rules over the angels and all the creatures of the Almighty." (Epiphanius, *Refutation of All Heresies*, 30.16,4; see E. Hennecke, *New Testament Apocrypha*, vol.1, p.158.)

These observations support the view that Jews, as a general rule, were unable to associate a human man with God. Once Jesus was brought to earth and given a human identity, Jewish groups who were part of the Christian faith (and carried along like everyone else by the juggernaut of the Gospel Jesus) could no longer accept divinity for such a figure and had to reduce him to human dimensions.

Such an attitude surfaces as early as Justin, whose character Trypho the Jew, in *Dialogue with Trypho*, serves to represent the outlook and opinions toward Christianity current in Justin's day, when the historical Jesus was beginning to make inroads into the thought of the time. In chapter 88, Justin puts these words into Trypho's mouth: "For you utter many blasphemies, in that you seek to persuade us that this crucified man ought to be worshiped." Such an attitude in the 2nd and 3rd centuries, whether among Jews or Jewish-Christians, was not likely to have differed from that of the 1st century, and thus the entire picture of Christianity beginning with a response to a human Jesus by great numbers of Jews, elevating him to the status of a pre-existent divinity with all of God's titles, must be dismissed.

42 *[page 94]* Hugh Montefiore (*Hebrews*, p.63) suggests that this practice of putting scriptural texts into Jesus' mouth was "the tradition of the early church." What he does not recognize is that this tradition was based on the fact that there was no earthly ministry or body of sayings to draw from. Graham Hughes (*Hebrews and Hermeneutics*, p.62) makes the assumption that such Gospel sayings were well known to the author and that he chose to "give expression" to them by appropriating Old Testament "forms" of these sayings. This is an example of a not infrequent practice among commentators of offering a 'definition' which serves to make something seem its opposite. Here, Hughes suggests that the absence of the sayings is really a quotation of the sayings in their 'Old Testament prefigurations.'

Chapter 10: Who Crucified Jesus? *(pages 95 to 108)*

43 *[page 97]* As in his *Birth and Rebirth, Myth and Reality, The Myth of the Eternal Return*, etc.

44 *[page 99]* Like Romans 1:3 (examined in Chapter 8) Hebrews 7:14 is a passage that speaks of Christ's 'racial' lineage and points toward scripture as the source:

> "For it is very evident (*prodēlon*) that our Lord is sprung (the verb *anatellein*) from Judah, a tribe to which Moses made no reference in speaking of priests."

This statement is made in the midst of a theological argument, not a recounting of historical facts. Hebrews presents Christ as a new High Priest, one who supplants the old cultic system which was run by the priestly class of the tribe of Aaron, the Levites. The writer finds Christ's "archetype" in Melchizedek, who was also not a member of the Levites (what tribe he may have been of is not stated). The point is, Christ must be of a new line in order to create a new order of priesthood.

Where does the writer find confirmation that the new High Priest is indeed of a different line than the Levites? How does he support this very necessary claim that Christ is "sprung from Judah"? There is no appeal to historical facts or apostolic traditions concerning Jesus of Nazareth, no reference to Mary or Joseph, no mention of his lineage as recounted in the Gospels of Matthew and Luke. The word "*prodēlon*" means "clear, manifest" to the senses or to judgment (compare 1 Timothy 5:24, 25); it does not mean "a matter of historical record." It fits the sense of "clear to someone who knows the scriptures," which in itself fits the thought world of the entire epistle.

The verb *"anatellein,"* to spring (by birth), is also the language of scripture. It is used in several messianic passages, such as Ezekiel 29:21 ("a horn shall spring forth") and Zechariah 6:12. Hebrews never says that Jesus is a descendent or "son" of David; the latter figure the epistle shows no interest in. The author simply needs scriptural support for the concept of a priest arising from a tribe which has never "had anything to do with" the old cult (7:13), a priest who can establish a new law to supplant the impotent old one, and a new hope (7:18 and 19). To confirm Jesus' role as High Priest, the writer turns to nothing in history, he draws on no deed or saying from the story of Jesus' life, but delves instead (7:17) into the timeless pages of scripture: "Thou art a priest forever, in the succession of Melchizedek." This line from the all-important Psalm 110 he takes as God's word to Jesus. Buchanan, in his Anchor Bible Commentary (*Hebrews*, p.253) admits that "the author may not have received the information from local tradition at all . . . (but) from his use of scripture."

45
[*page 100*] The concept of a paradigm in heaven who determines the fate of his counterparts on earth can be illustrated by examples from Jewish apocalyptic. As noted in Chapter 5, Daniel 7:13-14 introduces a vision of the "one like a son of man," a heavenly figure who is brought before the throne of God following the overthrow of the last of earth's great empires. This figure receives power and dominion from God, an act which signifies (so an angel informs Daniel) that the righteous elect of Israel, the "Saints of the Most High," shall receive such a sovereignty over the earth. Some regard this "one like a son of man" as an angel, others simply as a poetic image of the saints he represents. Still others suggest he is a supernatural figure who serves as a heavenly representative for the saints on earth. Here the issue need not be resolved. Whatever the writer had in mind, Daniel's figure can serve as an example of the paradigm who undergoes an experience in heaven which guarantees a corresponding experience on earth by his human counterpart.

In the Similitudes of Enoch (1 Enoch 37-71), as seen earlier (Note 36), the figure called the Elect One or Righteous One—also Son of Man and Messiah—is revealed to be waiting in heaven. Soon he shall appear on earth to render judgment, he will raise the oppressed and overthrow the wicked rulers and those who reject the Most High (God). He is the champion of a group on earth, the suffering righteous and elect. In the Elect One dwells those qualities, holiness and righteousness, shared by his earthly counterparts. They await the changes he will bring, including their own glorification and reception of eternal life. However, this Righteous One (a 'spiritual Messiah' idea among Jews!) is not a sacrificial figure; the Enochian sect had not evolved in that direction.

But we will see (on page 104) that whoever wrote the christological hymn quoted by Paul in Philippians 2:6-11 has done just that. Here we have a divine being who "shared in God's very nature," who humbled himself and in obedience accepted death. As a consequence, "God raised him to the heights," where he received the homage of all powers and beings on earth and in heaven. The implication is that this self-sacrificing divinity (who operates in the celestial spheres, not on earth) is a paradigm for believers on earth, who will similarly be exalted as a consequence of their own obedience and death. As Morna Hooker puts it ("Philippians 2:6-11," in *Jesus und Paulus*, p.151f): "Christ becomes what we are (likeness of flesh, suffering and death), so enabling us to become what he is (exalted to the heights)."

46 [*page 101*] Some of those who judge "rulers of this age" (1 Corinthians 2:8) to be a reference to the demon spirits: S. G. F. Brandon (*History, Time and Deity*, p.167), C. K. Barrett (*First Epistle to the Corinthians*, p.72), Jean Héring (*The First Epistle of St. Paul to the Corinthians*, p.16-17), Paula Fredriksen (*From Jesus to Christ*, p.56), S. D. F. Salmond (*Expositor's Greek Testament*, Ephesians, p.284). Paul Ellingworth (*A Translator's Handbook for 1 Corinthians*, p.46) says: "A majority of scholars think that supernatural powers are intended here."

And so did the ancients. Origen regarded the *archontōn* of 1 Cor. 2:8 as evil spiritual beings, as did the gnostic Marcion. Ignatius uses the term in an angelic sense in his epistle to the Smyrneans, 6:1.

47 [*page 103*] *Theological Dictionary of the New Testament*, VII, p.128. The angels "have flesh or at least appear to have it" (*op.cit.*, p.143), though it is a different "corporeality" between humans and angels (see Jude 7).

48 [*page 105*] For the suggestion that "death on a cross" is a Pauline addition, see, for example, Norman Perrin, Dennis C. Duling, *The New Testament: An Introduction*, (2nd ed.) p.61.

Two further observations about this hymn are interesting. This divinity seems to have received the name of "Jesus" (Savior, or Yahweh saves) only at the time of his exaltation, following his death. One also wonders why the composer stated three times that this Jesus took on a 'likeness' to humanity (assuming the form of a slave / bearing the human likeness / revealed in human shape). This may have been necessitated by the poetic structure of the hymn, which has its lines grouped into two mirror-like halves, a structure called "chiastic." But if the hymnist needed some material to fill one or two available lines, why did he not devote them to some details about the incarnated life which these verses are claimed to refer to?

49 [*page 105*] In his latest book, *The Jesus Myth*, Wells takes a step in the opposite direction, allowing for the existence of a "Q Jesus," the founder figure which modern scholarship declares can be unearthed from the roots of the Q document. I disagree with that position, and offer specific arguments against it in the final section of Chapter 19.

Chapter 11: The Mystery Cults *(pages 109 to 116)*

50 [*page 109*] For example, Walter Burkert: *Ancient Mystery Cults*, p.3.

51 [*page 110*] See Justin Martyr, *First Apology* 54, 66; *Dialogue with Trypho* 70, 78; Tertullian, *De Corona* 15, *On Prescriptions Against Heretics* 40.

52 [*page 110*] See David Ulansey, *The Origins of the Mithraic Mysteries*, p.40-45.

Chapter 12: Three Views Through the Window in Scripture *(pages 117 to 125)*

53 [*page 119*] *Theological Dictionary of the New Testament* I, 198-209; IX, 592.

54 [*page 119*] J. D. Quinn, in the Anchor Bible Commentaries (*Titus*, p.65) has put it clearest when he says: "The phrase *pro chronōn aiōniōn* refers to the timeless order in which God himself lives, in contrast to the *chronoi aiōnioi* (as in Romans 16:25) through which the world has passed." James Barr (*Biblical Words For Time*, p.138) hesitates over this interpretation, noting that the concept of "God's time" as something distinct from normal time is "hardly represented in the Bible." This is true, if only because the bulk of the Old Testament has been little or not at all influenced by Platonism. But he goes on later to allow that God's eternal realities and institutions are usually expressed as being fundamentally different from those which inhabit normal time, and that usually the word *aiōnios* is used to describe them.

55 [*page 121*] Moffat in *International Critical Commentary*, Hebrews, p.xlii; Dods in *Expositor's Greek Testament*, Hebrews, p.332.

56 [*page 121*] Moffat: "The writer breathed the Philonic atmosphere (of Middle Platonism) in which the eternal Now over-shadowed the things of space and time, but he knew this sacrifice had taken place on the cross, and his problem was one which never confronted Philo, the problem which we moderns have to face in the question: How can a single historical fact possess a timeless significance?" (*op.cit.*, p.xliii)

But the writer of Hebrews never gives any indication that "he knew" of such an earthly sacrifice, nor that he faced a problem which Philo did not. Hebrews never asks or addresses Moffat's question, or other "problems" like it.

Nor does Hebrews support G. A. Buchanan's attempt (Anchor Bible, *Hebrews*, p.xxv) to get around the epistle's Platonic pattern. Buchanan declares that the relationship between heavenly prototypes and earthly antitypes is "understood in terms of historical sequence and faith that is foreign to Platonism." But in Hebrews no such understanding can be detected. It is true that in regular Jewish biblical exegesis, prototypes in scripture could be seen as anticipating later antitypes "that were also historical and earthly." But this is clearly not the course followed by this epistle, which focuses all its attention on the work of Christ in the spiritual world. It never bends its Platonic principles to accommodate history or an earthly sacrifice. These things it never mentions.

57 [*page 121*] Héring (*Hebrews*, p.86) simply translates the verb into the past tense, without comment. Montefiore (*Hebrews*, p.166) suggests that the coming into the world refers to Christ's "human conception or his human birth," and that the writer regards the Psalm as reporting Jesus' words to the Father at such a moment. Ellingworth (*Hebrews*, p.499) assumes that the writer hears Christ speaking through scripture prior to his incarnation. All this is something that has to be read into the epistle's words, for of birth and incarnation in an historical setting it has nothing to say.

58 [*page 122*] Romans 1:3, 9:5; Ephesians 1:15; Colossians 1:22; 1 Timothy 3:16; Hebrews 5:7; 1 Peter 3:18, 4:1.

59 [*page 122*] It is often claimed that Hebrews 5:7 refers to an incident in the life of Jesus, namely the passion scene in the garden of Gethsemane. However, some recognize the problems in such an interpretation.

At Gethsemane, Jesus' anguished plea that the cup of suffering should pass him by was in fact not answered by God, which contradicts the point the writer wishes to make. From 4:14 on, he is anxious to show that Jesus is qualified to be a High Priest for human beings, and one of his tasks, like the earthly high priest, is to petition God on their behalf. The reference in 5:7 is designed to show that on the latter score Jesus has already proven himself. For "in the days of his flesh" his prayers to God on his own behalf were answered.

Not that the writer of Hebrews envisions his Jesus as having successfully avoided death through prayers to God for such a thing. Rather, those prayers asked that Jesus be delivered out of death (that is, brought up from it) and that he be perfected through suffering and obedience in order to serve as the source of humanity's salvation. And in fact, says the writer, this request was granted.

Any tradition about Jesus at Gethsemane which bore a resemblance to the Gospel account would not fit Hebrews' idea here, for the Gospel Jesus had prayed, in a moment of human weakness, that the cup be removed. This writer would never want to suggest that such a prayer was in any way answered, or was even a worthy one, much less that it made Jesus qualified to be the ideal High Priest. Scholars who face this discrepancy usually downplay the link to Gethsemane.

Where, then, did the idea in 5:7 come from? In the case of this epistle, the answer is clear: from scripture. Buchanan (*op.cit.*, p.98) suggests that "offering up petitions" is drawn from Psalm 116:1, which uses the same words (in the Septuagint version). Montefiore (*op.cit.*, p.97), while noting that it does not appear in the Gospel description, sees the phrase "loud cries and tears" as an enlargement on Psalm 22:24: "when I cried to him, he heard me" (again in the wording of the Septuagint). Reflecting scholarship in general, Ellingworth (*op.cit.*, p.285) admits that 5:7 represents "a generalized use of the language and pattern of Old Testament intercession." He allows that it does not refer to Gethsemane—though he considers that it must refer to *some* historical event.

Chapter 13: A Riotous Diversity (pages 126 to 140)

60
[*page 129*] The NEB translates the heart of the passage this way: "For this deliverance was first announced through *the lips of* the Lord *himself*; those who heard *him* confirmed it to us . . ." The words in italics are not present in the Greek, which provides a good example of how translations can import Gospel preconceptions into the epistles where they are not to be found.

61
[*page 130*] It should be pointed out that Hebrews 5:12 also refers to the teaching received at the time of the movement's inception, but rather than this being Jesus' own teachings, such things are referred to as "God's oracles," a phrase which clearly points to revelation. Nor do the "rudiments" of faith and ritual which are listed immediately afterward (6:12) say anything of an historical ministry of Jesus.

62
[*page 132*] For a discussion of the question of layering in 1 John, and its priority over the Gospel, see my website article "A Solution to the First Epistle of John" at <www.magi.com/~oblio/jesus/supp02.htm>

63
[*page 134*] For an extended treatment of this document, with many quotations from its verses, see my website article "The Odes of Solomon" at <www.magi.com/~oblio/jesus/supp04.htm>

64
[*page 135*] The sole appearance of "Christ" in one manuscript is thought to be an emendation of "Lord" (God) which appears in other manuscripts.

65
[*page 137*] Philo's Heavenly Man: "There are two kinds of men. The one is Heavenly Man, the other earthly. The Heavenly Man being in the image of God has no part in corruptible substance, or in any earthly substance whatever; but the earthly man was made of germinal matter which the writer [of Genesis] calls "dust." For this reason he does not say that the Heavenly Man was created, but that he was stamped with the image of God, whereas the earthly man is a creature and not the offspring of the Creator." (From *Allegorical Interpretation of the Law* 1,31, translated by C. H. Dodd.)

66
[*page 137*] See the comprehensive listing in the *Theological Dictionary of the New Testament*, VIII, p.412f.

67
[*page 139*] It has been rather naively suggested that those Jews from all over the empire who were living in Jerusalem at the time of the first Pentecost (Acts 2:5) may have been converted in large numbers and

subsequently went back to convert their fellow Jews at home in equally great numbers.

68 [*page 139*]Quotation taken from Francis Watson, *Paul, Judaism and the Gentiles*, p.93. Ambrosiaster is a name given to the unknown author of a commentary on the Pauline epistles, written at Rome in the latter 4th century. The work was later ascribed to Ambrose.

Chapter 14: Excavating the Roots of Q *(pages 143 to 150)*

69 [*page 147*]Note that the designations Q1, Q2, Q3 do not represent separate documents, but indicate different strata of material within the reconstructed totality of Q used by Matthew and Luke. Such designations also refer to the surmised state of the document at each of those stages of development, although this must be seen as the simplification of a reality in which numerous little additions and revisions were no doubt made to the Q document between a couple of extensive overhauls.

70 [*page 149*]Burton Mack (*The Lost Gospel: The Book of Q and Christian Origins*, p.138-9) regards 'to accept one's cross' as meaning "bear up under condemnation," and as having had "a long proverbial history behind it" (within the Cynic tradition). The cross "had become a metaphor for the ultimate test of a philosopher's integrity." Robert Funk (*Honest to Jesus*, p.235) regards Q 14:27, along with Gospel of Thomas #55 which adds "like me" or "as I do" to the carrying of the cross, as possibly a "veiled reference" to Jesus' death, but he allows that both could be taken in a non-literal sense. David Seeley ("Jesus' Death in Q," NTS 38 [1992] p.223f) places the saying in the context of contemporary Cynic-Stoic philosophy about the pupil who should be willing to follow his master into any hardship, even death. He also admits that "Jesus' death is not explicitly referred to in 14:27." Earlier he says that "not one of the passages in which prophets are mentioned refers to Jesus' death. Such a reference must be assumed." Once again preconception determines the course of interpretation. Rudolf Bultmann (*History of the Synoptic Tradition*, p.161) regards the saying as referring to no more than "a sense of vocation." He also suggests the idiom may have grown up "among the Zealots, whose followers would have to reckon with the cross."

Chapter 15: The Gospel of Thomas *(pages 151 to 154)*

71 [*page 151*]Translations by Thomas O. Lambdin, in *The Nag Hammadi Library*, p.124f.

72 [*page 152*]Helmut Koester, in *Trajectories Through Early Christianity* (p.126-28), put forward a good argument for locating the Gospel of Thomas, in its final form, in the Edessan region in the 2nd century because only there do we find the name Thomas associated with the name Judas and the designation Twin ("Judas Didymos Thomas" in the introductory line). The general appearance of such traditions in that region cannot reasonably be dated to the 1st century. Later (*Introduction to the New Testament*, vol.2 p.152), Koester tried to pull Thomas into the 1st century because of the lack of influence apparent in Thomas from the canonical Gospels. But the canonical Gospels show little "influence" in *all* Christian writings before well into the 2nd century (see Chapter 24).

73　　[*page 154*] The dating of the Gospel of Thomas is a fluid affair in modern scholarship. Those most anxious to find within its Q-like stratum corroboration for the picture of the historical Jesus derived from Q tend to regard that stratum as part of a "Common Sayings Tradition" (CST) and date it as a collection of its own to the mid-1st century. The remaining mystical/gnostic sayings are regarded as coming later and were added to the CST. Others protest that the latter group of sayings, being hardly of a full-fledged gnostic quality at all, could as easily proceed from the 1st century as well. True enough, but that both types of sayings found in the complete Thomas are hardly likely to proceed either from the same man or from the same point in time, seems a natural conclusion, especially as one of the two types is related to a set of sayings found elsewhere. There must be a sequential relationship between the two types, and since the CST element in Thomas can be aligned with Q1 which is reasonably to be dated to the mid-1st century, it seems safe to date earliest Thomas, ie, the parallels to Q1, as coming from more or less the same time.

The more important question is: when is the very latest layer of redaction involving the figure of Thomas likely to have taken place? The attribution of the collection to a recording of Jesus' sayings by Thomas, as well as #13, which elevates Thomas in importance over other apostles like Peter and Matthew, must come from a time when Christian communities were in competition with each other as to who had the most authoritative pipeline back to Jesus. In other words, when the idea of apostolic tradition, a chain going back through certain apostles and their appointees to the Master himself, was in full swing. For such a state of affairs there is no evidence before the 2nd century. First century documents like the Johannine epistles and the Didache, even the letters of Ignatius in the early 2nd century, are pointedly lacking such a feature. (The claim that 1 Corinthians 1-2 gives early evidence of groups claiming apostolic authority for secret wisdom is unfounded, for the epistle itself never links that wisdom to an historical teaching Jesus; in fact, Koester is not the only one to express surprise that no teachings of Jesus are appealed to in the dispute Paul is embroiled in at Corinth concerning himself and Apollos. For the latter, see Note 19.) Since it is also likely that the concern for tracing traditions back to Jesus through an apostle is something that arose almost in conjunction with the development of an historical Jesus, we can thus locate the addition of the "Jesus said" layer of attribution to the period of the Thomas attribution, namely in the first half of the 2nd century, and probably more toward the middle of it.

Chapter 16: A Counter-Culture Movement in Galilee *(pages 155 to 168)*

74   [*page 159*] Burton Mack is probably the best known advocate of Jesus as a "Cynic-style sage" (*Who Wrote the New Testament*, p.40; *A Myth of Innocence*, p.67-69, 73-74). F. Gerald Downing wrote an influential article "Cynics and Christians" (NTS 1984, p.584-93). It revived an early 20th century trend of observation about the similarities between the wandering Cynics and the activities of early Christians. In that article he details a selection, from "a mass of material," of "often quite detailed overlaps in the message proclaimed by some Cynics and that proclaimed by some early Christians." J. D. Crossan (*Birth of Christianity*, p.333f) hedges on identifying Jesus as 'Cynic,' claiming irrelevance.

Chapter 17: Introducing Jesus to Q *(pages 169 to 174)*

75   [*page 171*] The Dialogue Between Jesus and John (Luke/Q 7:18-35):

"[18]John too was informed of all this by his disciples. Summoning two of their number [19]he sent them to the Lord with this message: 'Are you the one who is to come, or are we to expect some other?' [20]The messengers made their way to Jesus and said, 'John the Baptist has sent us to you: he asks, "Are you the one who is to come, or are we to expect some other?" ' [21]There and then he cured many sufferers from diseases, plagues, and evil spirits; and on many blind people he bestowed sight. [22]Then he gave them his answer: 'Go,' he said, 'and tell John what you have seen and heard: how the blind recover their sight, the lame walk, the lepers are clean, the deaf hear, the dead are raised to life, the poor are hearing the good news. [23] And happy is the man who does not find me a stumbling-block.'

"[24]After John's messengers had left, Jesus began to speak about him to the crowds: 'What was the spectacle that drew you to the wilderness? A reed-bed swept by the wind? [25]No? Then what did you go out to see? A man dressed in silks and satins? Surely you must look in palaces for grand clothes and luxury. [26]But what did you go out to see? A prophet? Yes indeed, and far more than a prophet. [27]He is the man of whom Scripture says,

"Here is my herald, whom I send on ahead of you,
And he will prepare your way before you."
[28]I tell you, there is not a mother's son greater than John, and yet the least in the kingdom of God is greater than he.'

"29When they heard him, all the people, including the tax-gatherers, praised God, for they had accepted John's baptism; 30but the Pharisees and lawyers, who refused his baptism, had rejected God's purpose for themselves.

"31'How can I describe the people of this generation? What are they like? 32They are like children sitting in the market-place and shouting at each other,

"We piped for you and you would not dance."

"We wept and wailed, and you would not mourn."

33For John the Baptist came neither eating bread nor drinking wine, and you say, "He is possessed." 34The Son of Man came eating and drinking, and you say, "Look at him! a glutton and a drinker, a friend of tax-gatherers and sinners!" 35And yet God's wisdom is proved right by all who are her children.' " [NEB]

Chapter 18: Sectarian Developments in Q *(pages 175 to 182)*

76
   [*page 175*] See H. G. Meecham, *The Epistle to Diognetus*, p.1.
77
   [*page 176*] Christianity as an expression of sectarianism is dealt with in many books, such as:

Francis Watson: *Paul, Judaism and the Gentiles*, p.38-48

Graham N. Stanton: *A Gospel For a New People: Studies in Matthew*, p.89-107

J. A. Overman: *Matthew's Gospel and Formative Judaism*, passim

Philip E. Esler: *Community and Gospel in Luke-Acts*, p.16-22, 46-70

Robin Scroggs: "The Earliest Christian Communities as Sectarian Communities" in *Christianity, Judaism, and other Graeco-Roman Cults*, II, ed. J. Neusner. (A seminal piece of writing on this subject, 1975.)

   Some books quoted by the above scholars on the sociology of sects:

Bryan Wilson: *Religion in Social Perspective* (1982)

Lewis Coser: *The Functions of Social Conflict* (1956)

P. L. Berger and T. Luckmann: *The Social Construction of Reality* (1966)

Chapter 19: Mark and Q: The Origin of the Gospels *(pages 183 to 198)*

78
   [*page 183*] John Dominic Crossan (supported by a "red" [agree] vote of 26% at the October 1995 meeting of the Jesus Seminar) points to an existing non-canonical Gospel as containing the very first constructed passion story, namely the recently recovered Gospel of Peter. Imbedded within that incomplete work (the portion before the washing of hands by Pilate is lost, as is the ending in a post-resurrection appearance of Jesus) Crossan sees an antecedent he calls the "Cross Gospel" which he believes was the first passion narrative written, and on which Mark drew for his own story. The other evangelists are also supposed to have drawn upon it

in conjunction with their use of Mark. Crossan has outlined this theory in two books, *The Cross That Spoke* and *Who Killed Jesus?*

A majority of scholars in the field, however, regard GPeter in its entirety as dependent on the canonicals, though there are good arguments for seeing GPeter as having its own early and late strata. There are problems on both sides of this dispute, and even were Crossan right, it would not of itself alter the basic picture of the Jesus Puzzle, though I think such a complicating factor is unnecessary.

It is also particularly difficult to imagine the various Synoptic evangelists using the "Cross Gospel" and changing or leaving out so much. That Gospel offers an actual depiction of the resurrection, and yet all four canonical evangelists choose not to provide one of their own; it has a 'good' thief crucified with Jesus, yet only Luke makes such a distinction; it has a prominent 'guard at the tomb' scene, and yet only Matthew among the canonicals has such a thing, and that much reduced. In any case, without having the early part of the GPeter with its (presumed) ministry of Jesus, it is impossible to relate GPeter to the Q movement or to compare it overall with Mark. (For a fuller discussion of Crossan's views on the Gospel of Peter, see my website review of his latest book, *The Birth of Christianity*, at: <www.magi.com/~oblio/jesus/crossbr.htm>.)

[79] *[page 187]* There have been a number of proposals outlining a possible unit in Q (on the Appearance of John and the Baptism of Jesus) preceding the normally accepted one: David R. Catchpole, "The Beginning of Q: A Proposal" in NTS 38 (1992), p.205-221; Dieter Lührmann, "The Gospel of Mark and the Sayings Collection Q" in JBL 108/1 (1989), p.51-71; J. Lambrecht, "John the Baptist and Jesus in Mark 1:1-15: Markan Redaction of Q?" in NTS 38 (1992), p.357-384. Most of these postulate that Mark is abbreviating such an initial unit in the Q document. The idea, however, makes better sense in the *absence* of a Q document on Mark's desk, but in a context of him being familiar with these Q traditions; the impression of "abbreviation" is because he is not working from their fullest record in the Q document itself but from his community's general familiarity with the role of John and his alleged preaching. Lambrecht (p.381) cites Streeter: "Thus at the outset we are struck by the fact that the first thirteen verses of Mark, so unlike his usual picturesque diffuseness, read like a summary of a longer and fuller account."

[80] *[page 192]* It is true that the Gospel of Mark does not portray its Jesus in the elevated fashion of the Christ cult. Indeed, it is sometimes pointed out that Mark's Jesus is scarcely divine, certainly not overtly so. He is not the Logos or personified Wisdom of the epistles, the emanation and image of God involved in the process of creation. None of these things are present in Mark's Gospel, and even the soteriology is primitive. Mark barely develops the concept of Atonement or vicarious suffering, and simply says

(10:45) that Jesus has come to surrender his life "as a ransom for many." This is not too much different from the concept developed in 4 Maccabees (early first century?) that the righteous martyr's suffering and death will be considered by God to have a redemptive efficacy on all of Israel.

Mark's Jesus, in the matter of his resurrection, is a quantum leap further, but even this element may owe some of its flavor to the idea that resurrection was the destiny of the righteous elect of Israel. Thus while Mark was almost certainly impelled to create his suffering and rising Jesus as a result of some contact with the Christ cult, he has given him a more human grounding in the Q setting. Besides, the constraints of the Gospel story with its earthly location would preclude any total translation of the cosmic Christ of Paul onto the Galilean scene. If Mark's Jesus feels constrained to keep his Messiahship a secret, it is even less likely that he would want to discuss his pre-existence with God in heaven or his role in creating the universe.

81

[*page 195*] Dieter Lührmann ("Mark and Q" in JBL 108/1 [1989], p.59): "The final redaction of Q must be situated about AD 60, because nothing in the material in Q indicates an acquaintance with the affairs which immediately preceded or made up the Jewish War." He overlooks or differently interprets Luke/Q 13:35, with its reference to Jerusalem's "house" (meaning the Temple) which "has been forsaken." This seems an obvious reference to the destruction of the Temple in 70 at the climax of the Jewish War, and some scholars take it as such.

82

[*page 196*] Burton Mack allows that Luke and Acts were written about 120 (*Who Wrote the New Testament?* p.167)

Chapter 20: Jesus Among Jew and Pagan *(pages 199 to 204)*

83

[*page 201*] Some have called into question the authenticity of this letter of Pliny, noting its closing remarks about the fact that, prior to the government campaign against the Christians, so many people had been converting to Christianity that pagan rites had declined, animal sacrifices had been abandoned, and meat sellers had no market for their wares. This picture of Christian success seems not only extreme, the passage is reminiscent of the scene in Acts 19, where Demetrius the silversmith complains that Paul's preaching is winning over so many that his business of making and selling images of the goddess Diana is in jeopardy.

84

[*page 202*] Popular views of Christians could be grotesque, envisioning ritual murder of children, cannibalism and assorted abominations committed during their clandestine rites. Ideas like these are a common form of excess which the prejudiced and uninformed often visit upon groups they are mistrustful of. Christians themselves have held a carbon copy of such views toward the Jews, in the Middle Ages and not-so-middle ages.

The official basis of such prejudice was the Christian refusal to sacrifice to the state gods and acknowledge the divinity of the current emperor. Such worship was looked upon as one of the ordinary and essential duties of life, necessary for a safe and spiritually healthy society. Disavowal of them was a crime, requiring severe punishment. The charge of "atheism" and disloyalty to Rome was natural; Christians were seen as undermining society and corrupting ancient wisdom. (Jews were traditionally granted an exemption in being allowed to modify their obeisance to the emperor so as not to contravene their religious principles, but no such loophole was extended to the Christians.)

85
[*page 204*] In the Gemara (Sanh. 107b), Jesus is said to have been persecuted by the Maccabean king Alexander Jannaeus (103-76 BCE). Elsewhere in the Gemara (Shab. 104b), the husband of Jesus' mother is identified as Pappos ben Jehudah, who in the Talmud is said to have been a contemporary of rabbi Akiba, who flourished in the early second century. (See J. Klausner, *Jesus of Nazareth*, p.22; and R. Travers Herford, *Christianity in the Talmud and the Mishnah*, p.35-40.)

Chapter 21: Flavius Josephus *(pages 205 to 222)*

86
[*page 207*] On some of the above points, Charles Guignebert (*Jesus*, p.17) has this to say: "It may be admitted that the style of Josephus has been cleverly imitated, a not very difficult matter, but the short digression, even with the proposed corrections [referring to the Testimonium], interrupts the thread of the discourse into which it is introduced." Guignebert judges, after a consideration of both references to Jesus in Josephus, that "It seems probable that Josephus did not name Jesus anywhere" (p.18). This was a more common evaluation in the earlier part of this century (Guignebert's book was published in 1956) than in the latter part. Recent scholars seem more determined to retain a Josephan witness to Jesus in some form.

87
[*page 212*] According to Jewish tradition, after the Jewish War with its destruction of city and Temple (70 CE) a group of Pharisaic scholars under Johanan ben Zakkai met at Jamnia (Jabneh), a Palestinian city near the coast of the Mediterranean south of Joppa. There they reconstituted a "Council" to direct Jewish culture and religious observation in the absence of a Temple cult and without a focus on Jerusalem. It was a turning point in the history of Judaism, in that it marked the emergence of rabbinic Judaism as the normative form. It is also viewed as the official "parting of the ways" between Judaism and Christianity as a Jewish sect.

The council at Jamnia is traditionally dated around 90 CE, but there are some who question whether such a meeting took place. A. J. Saldarini ("Johanan ben Zakkai's Escape from Jerusalem: Origin and Development of a Rabbinic Story," JSJ 6 [1975] p.189-204) regards it as a legend. See J. A. Overman, *Matthew's Gospel and Formative Judaism*, p.38-39.

88
[*page 213*] In a few places—almost all of them in the earlier work, *Jewish War*—Josephus expresses the opinion that the actions of the Zealots in the years leading up to the conflict, their murders and mayhem, and especially their defiling of the Temple's purity, led God to acquiesce in the destruction of city and Temple by the Roman invaders as a means of purification. While Josephus is primarily concerned with justifying Rome's actions and providing a lesson to the world at large—that rebellion against Rome is futile—he also keeps his eye on his own countrymen and their interests. Thus he sometimes offers comments and explanations in terms of Jewish concerns about prophecy, ritual purity and divine providence, and these explanations do not always coincide with others expressed elsewhere.

89
[*page 215*] In the *Antiquities of the Jews*, the passage about John the Baptist comes after the death of Herod Antipas' brother Philip, which can be dated to 33/4, and before the expedition by Vitellius, the Roman legate of Syria, against the Arab king Aretas, dated 37. This latter event was in response to Aretas' attack on Galilee, which was brought about by Herod's repudiation of his first wife, Aretas' daughter, in order to marry Herodias, wife of one of his half brothers, whom she agreed to divorce. According to the Gospels, the execution of John was the result of his condemnation of this marriage, and if it came after the death of Philip in 33/34, this would force Jesus' career to be placed after that year, allowing just enough time—or perhaps not—for the crucifixion to have happened shortly before Pilate's recall to Rome in 36.

A date this late for the crucifixion creates problems in early Christian chronology, including in matters relating to Paul. E. P. Sanders (*The Historical Figure of Jesus*, p.286f) tries to solve the problem by pointing out that in this section of the *Antiquities*, Josephus does not always present events in proper chronological order. Sanders notes that the appointment of Pilate, which can by other sources be reliably dated to 26 CE, precedes mention of the death of Germanicus in 19 CE (though both of these are mentioned in passing, tied to other subjects). From inconsistencies like this, Sanders suggests that the uproar involving the Baptist and Herod's marriage to Herodias may have taken place earlier than the period between the two datable events of Philip's death and Vitellius' expedition. But a gap of five years or more between that expedition and the death of John which supposedly set off the chain of events leading to it seems excessive.

Sanders supports his argument by further noting that the *Testimonium Flavianum* comes between two events that can be dated in 19 CE, the death of Germanicus (found a few chapters before the Jesus reference), and the Isis and Jewish scandals in Rome (found right after the Jesus reference). He points out that strict chronology would require dating both Pilate and Jesus to an earlier period surrounding the year 19—which the odd scholar has done. Thus he opts for regarding Josephus as not putting things in proper chronological order. But a more likely explanation is that Josephus had no placement of Jesus at all, and the Christian interpolator was the one who got his Jesus out of place. (Somewhat like Luke, who failed to make his birth of Jesus compatible with the death of Herod the Great in 4 BCE and the local census of Quirinius in 6 CE, which the evangelist seems to have identified with his fictional Augustan census.) The interpolator of the *Testimonium* would have faced a problem, in that he had to choose between linking Jesus to the passage on Pilate, or to the later one on John the Baptist, two figures whom Josephus had unfortunately separated by a few chapters. He chose the one on Pilate.

90 [*page 221*]Why was the "lost reference" lost? Some suggest it may have been removed because of Origen's complaint, but in that case it is much more likely that it would have been *changed* to reflect that complaint. That is, we would find the reference saying that it was on account of the death of *Jesus*, rather than of James, that Jerusalem fell. However, the better explanation would be that the "lost reference," being an interpolation, was made only in certain manuscript lines, probably of *Jewish War* and probably in the east, and that these lines died out. Once the reference's imitation (if that's what it was) became interpolated into the *Antiquities*, it would have undergone its own fate, in this case surviving and spreading westward into all copies of the latter document.

91 [*page 222*] J. D. Crossan (*The Birth of Christianity*, p.9) points this out without comment. The relevant passage in the *Histories* is admittedly a short one, since the work as a whole is concerned with a later period.

There are those who question the authenticity of the passage in Tacitus' *Annals* which refers to Jesus. Even though it is hostile and even contemptuous toward Christians, Christian sources do not speak of a persecution by Nero as a result of the great fire for another two centuries.

Chapter 22: The Gospels as Midrash and Symbolism *(pages 225 to 239)*

92 [*page 226*]See David R. Catchpole: "The Beginning of Q: A Proposal." NTS 38 (1992) p.214-15, 220.

93 [*page 228*]See John Kloppenborg, *The Formation of Q*, p.250f.

94 [*page 231*]Mack (*A Myth of Innocence*, p.159) quotes a passage from Seneca: "Words should be scattered like seed; no matter how small the seed may be, if it once has found favorable ground, it unfolds its strength and from an insignificant thing spreads to its greatest growth" (*Epistles* 38:2). Clearly, the parables of the kingdom imputed to Jesus have much in common with the wider expression of this period, including within pagan circles, making the link of Q1 to a Cynic precedent not an unlikely one.

95 [*page 235*]See, for example, Mack, *A Myth of Innocence*, p.209-11.

96
[*page 236*] Apollonius of Tyana was a neo-Pythagorean who lived until about the year 98. He was said to have been sired by the Egyptian god Proteus, to have preached one true God, performed miracles, healed the sick, cast out demons, raised the dead. Following his own death, it was claimed he had himself risen from the dead, appeared to his followers to discuss immortality with them, and made a bodily ascent into heaven. The satirist Lucian in the middle of the 2nd century makes a brief reference to him. His 'biography'—in which it is impossible to separate fact from legend—was written around 220 by the Sophist Flavius Philostratus. See Philostratus: *Life of Apollonius*, trans. and ed. by C. P. Jones, G. W. Bowerstock (1970); and *The Life and Times of Apollonius of Tyana*, by Charles P. Eels (1967).

97
[*page 237*] It is ironic that the Old Testament contains nothing about evil demons, and certainly not in connection with sickness, so that healings in scripture were not cast in terms of expelling them from the sufferer. But the forces of darkness gradually loomed ever larger in Jewish thought— and Hellenistic as well—during the intertestamental period (after about 200 BCE), as did the concept of Satan as prime leader of these forces. The chief of devils, under the influence of Persian demonology, evolved out of less evil antecedents in Jewish heavenly mythology.

Thus by the time of Christianity, evil spirits had become an obsessive preoccupation for many. Ephesians 6:12, with its grim lament about the fight "against the superhuman forces of evil in the heavens," reveals the tormenting effect which such superstition could have. Mark's healing Jesus had to be cast in such a context, forever saddling Christianity with a Son of God who himself believes in these forces and even converses with them. It is perhaps the most embarrassing feature of Gospels which on the whole are not marked by an excess of rationalist thought.

98
[*page 237*] See Helmut Koester, *Introduction to the New Testament*, vol.1, p.134-5.

99
[*page 238*] Paul Achtemeier, "Toward the Isolation of Pre-Markan Miracle Catenae," JBL 89 (1970), p.265-291.

100
[*page 238*] In the first set: the Gerasene demoniac's spirit expelled (5:1-20), Jairus' daughter raised (5:21-43), woman with hemorrhage cured (5:25-34). In the second set: the blind man at Bethsaida cured (8:22-26, this being out of sequence), the spirit in the Syrophoenician woman's daughter expelled (7:24b-30), the deaf-mute cured (7:32-37). The identification of these two sets goes a long way toward understanding why Mark has two feeding miracles which are very similar (The Feeding of the 5000 and the Feeding of the 4000). Scholars used to wonder whether he had inherited two slightly different traditions of the same incident and felt compelled to include them both. Now we may conclude that he repeated himself deliberately because of the requirements of his miracle patterns.

Chapter 23: The Suffering Righteous One and a Tale from Scripture
(pages 240 to 258)

101 [*page 240*]Hugh R. Schonfield, in a famous bestseller in 1966, *The Passover Plot*, argued that Jesus may have participated in a conspiracy in which he was drugged before the crucifixion in order to appear dead. While a respectable scholar in his own right, Schonfield was a little too accepting of most details in the Gospel story as historical.

102 [*page 242*]For that matter, Matthew and Luke, and by extension their communities, show little sign of possessing a developed set of traditions about Jesus' ministry. The structure of their pre-passion story follows Mark's general outline and content, supplemented by the Q material which they have differently fitted into the Markan pattern. Luke has several elements which are unique to himself, notably parables such as the Good Samaritan and the Prodigal Son, but these are probably best seen as his own invention, if only because one would expect that such powerful and effective examples of teaching, if they were the product of Jesus (as the Jesus Seminar tends to think), would be known to the other evangelists.

103 [*page 244*]For example, John Dominic Crossan in *The Birth of Christianity*; John Shelby Spong in *Liberating the Gospels*.

104 [*page 245*]Crossan has recently said: "If there were, from the beginning, a detailed passion-resurrection story or even just a passion narrative, I would expect more evidence of it than is currently extant. It is totally absent from the Life Tradition [my "Galilean side"] and it appears in the Death Tradition [my "Jerusalem side"] as follows. On the one hand, outside of the gospels, there are no references to those details of the passion narrative. If all Christians knew them, why do no other Christians mention them? On the other hand, within the gospels, everyone else copies directly or indirectly from Mark. If one story was established early as history remembered, why do all not "copy" from it rather than depend on Mark? Why do Matthew and Luke have to rely so completely on Mark? Why does John, despite his profound theological innovation, depend so completely on synoptic information?" (*The Birth of Christianity*, p. 521).

105 [*page 249*]Two millennia of Christian tradition has regarded these close correspondences between the Old Testament and the Gospel story of Jesus as a situation of prophecy and fulfilment. However, no scholar worthy of the name today will advocate that all these passages in the Hebrew bible are actually presagings of the particular events of Jesus' passion experience.

106 [*page 253*]I am indebted to John Dominic Crossan in his *The Cross That Spoke* for this reading of Psalm 2:1-2, along with a couple of the more esoteric points in this midrashic survey of Mark's passion narrative.

Chapter 24: The Remaking of Christian History (pages 259 to 274)

[107] [*page 259*] References in Justin to "memoirs of the Apostles": *Apology 1*, 66:3, 67:3-4; *Dialogue with Trypho*, 13 times, eg, 100:4, 101:3, etc.

[108] [*page 260*] Irenaeus, *Against Heresies*, Bk.III, ch.xi, 8. The Gospels are four in number, he says, because "there are four zones of the world in which we live, and four principal winds . . . and it is fitting that she [the Church] should have four pillars."

[109] [*page 260*] For example, Helmut Koester's groundbreaking search for Synoptic references in the writings of the early Fathers, *Synoptische Überlieferung bei den apostolischen Vätern* (1957), concludes that almost all such references come from a pre-Gospel layer of tradition.

[110] [*page 262*] See P. N. Harrison, *Polycarp's Two Epistles to the Philippians*.

[111] [*page 263*] The later ascription of the epistle of Barnabas to the apostle who accompanied Paul on some of his journeys is not considered feasible today. The epistle is usually seen as the product of a learned Jew of Alexandria, since its earliest attestation is by Clement and Origen in that city. But this is a Jew who has disowned his ancestral religion and claimed the sacred writings of the Jewish heritage for Christianity. Others would say that he is in fact a gentile writing to other gentiles who have thoroughly absorbed Judaism and who see themselves as the inheritors of a new covenant which the Jews have forfeited. That latter view might well sum up the fundamental nature of Christianity once it had broken ties with its Jewish parent.

[112] [*page 264*] Following his quotation from Isaiah 53 to illustrate how Jesus had died to forgive sins, Barnabas tells his readers (5:3): "Therefore we ought to give thanks to the Lord that he has made known [ie, through scripture] the things that are past, that he has enlightened us about the things of the present [literally, that are here now] and given us some understanding of the future."

In other words, Barnabas is stating that we know of Christ's experiences on earth through the scriptures, in passages like Isaiah 53. Near the start of the letter (1:7) he has declared the same principle: "Through the prophets (God) has made known to us things which are past and present and some measure of the future." It would seem that there is no recent history in Barnabas' mind which also tells of Christ's experiences. Knowledge of the past comes through scripture and scripture alone. (Staniforth's translation of 5:3, *Early Christian Writings*, p.198, that the writings "give us an *insight* into the past" is fanciful; the Greek verb *gnōridzō* is not so accommodating.)

This restriction to scripture as the source of Barnabas' knowledge about Jesus' life explains a curious phenomenon in the epistle. The writer seems to be implying that scripture has foretold the events of Christ's life, and yet the second half of that equation is never itemized. Though he regards scripture as "prophecy," we are never pointed to a concrete equivalent in history which constitutes the fulfilment of the prophecy. The actual experiences of Jesus on earth are theoretical. That is, the writer seems to be deducing their existence from scripture and then labeling scripture as a prophecy of them, but they are given no independent support or illustration through comparison to a recorded account or oral tradition. Elsewhere, he is at pains to show how ancient Hebrew institutions prefigured counterparts in current Christian belief and practice. This is one of the chief aims of his letter, the purpose of his allegorical interpretation of scripture: to show that the scriptural "past" is fulfilled in his Christian "present." But when he gets to the description of Christ's passion in scripture, the corresponding fulfilment in the experiences of Christ 'on earth' go undetailed, unidentified in terms of specific historical content. (This is in contrast to the later Justin, who directly compares scriptural 'prophecy' with the corresponding 'events' described in the "memoirs of the Apostles.")

113
[*page 264*] See H. Koester, *Ancient Christian Gospels*, p.18.

114
[*page 265*] An adequate discussion of this would be lengthy, given the acknowledged lack of clarity in Papias' description of how he sought out information from "elders" who in turn had derived their knowledge either from apostles of Jesus or from followers of those apostles. The exact meaning of "elder," or whether Papias uses it with a consistent meaning, the number of stages intervening between himself and the "disciples of the Lord," along with much else about this passage, is a matter of debate. So, too, is the identification of the "elder John" he refers to, whether this is the same as the supposed apostle John, or is perhaps the elder who gave Papias his information about "Mark" and "Matthew."

Irenaeus' claim that Papias knew the apostle John of the Gospels is almost certainly based on this uncertain reference to someone whom Papias may not be identifying as a follower of Jesus. Whole chains of early Christian inference and claims about the early period of the Christian movement were based on shaky foundations such as these. In addition, some of the remarks assigned to Papias suggest he is writing late in the first half of the 2nd century, which makes the feasible number of stages between himself and the presumed apostles of a Jesus on earth too great to suppose that he could have known any of them.

115
[*page 267*] For example, J. Kleist (*Ancient Christian Writers*, p.111) suggests that the complaint about "order" in Papias' "Mark" was a criticism that the Gospel was so short. W. R. Schoedel (*Apostolic Fathers*, vol.5, p.106) describes past opinions about Mark's deficient "order": that it was "the abrupt beginning, the incomplete ending, the admission of 'trivial' points," and so on. These are not definitions of "order" one would

normally arrive at if preconception did not require something that could be applied to canonical Mark.

116 [*page 267*] Schoedel (*op.cit.* p.106) points out that the style of the quote of Papias about Mark, in "the rhetorical balance of the lines," is the same as the Prologue which Eusebius quotes earlier. Schoedel observes: "This means that Papias has reworked whatever he received from 'the elder' (John?). It is impossible, then, to distinguish between Papias and his source at this point." Not only is Papias reporting the elder's account from memory, he has recast it in his own words. In sum, how such traditions originated about Mark as the interpreter of Peter in regard to this collection of "sayings and doings," or about Matthew as collector of certain Aramaic sayings, and whether the "elder" Papias refers to had anything to do with the formation of those ideas or whether he filtered ideas that had preceded him, is now impossible to say. The highly uncertain state of the fragments of Papias allows us to continue to maintain that no Christian writer before Justin gives evidence of a knowledge or use of written Gospels.

117 [*page 268*] What also remains obscure is the exact relationship of Gnosticism to orthodox Christianity and its Gospel-based Jesus of Nazareth. Investigators are coming to realize that the older idea that Gnosticism grew out of the early Christian movement is no longer tenable. Some gnostic documents have a savior figure who bears no relationship to the Gospel Jesus; such documents may even be pre-Christian at their roots (see Chapter 13). In some areas, such as Egypt and northern Syria, gnostic forms of Christ/Son belief were on the scene well in advance of more 'orthodox' versions of Christianity. (See Walter Bauer's *Orthodoxy and Heresy in Earliest Christianity*.) What is more certain is that the two branches of belief were interacting with one another by the early 2nd century, and that some gnostic sects began to equate their savior figure with the newly-emerging historical Jesus. They leaned toward making him a docetic Christ (only "seeming" to be human) and generally regarded him as a revealer figure rather than a sacrificial savior of the Pauline type, though they usually made room for some significance in a death and resurrection.

118 [*page 268*] Tradition, from the writings of heresiologists like Tertullian who wrote to discredit Marcion, says that Marcion used a gutted text of Luke's Gospel, ridding it of passages he didn't like. But another view, espoused by John Knox in *Marcion and the New Testament* (p.77-106), argues that the text Marcion used, or based his own upon, was an early version of Luke, one that was subsequently reworked and expanded by the church of Rome. (That expansion included the whole of chapters 1 and 2.) We can arrive at some of the contents of Marcion's Luke only through Tertullian's detailed refutation of the arch-heretic.

119 [*page 268*] Marcion's corpus of Paul included all but the Pastorals (1 & 2 Timothy and Titus). Modern scholars have lately been questioning the older assumption that a corpus of Paul's letters was first put together in the late 1st century—not including the Pastorals which were written in Paul's name only in the 2nd century—and are focusing on Marcion as the first recorded evidence of the assembly of such letters into a fixed collection. See H. Gamble, "The Canon of the New Testament" in *The New Testament and Its Modern Interpreters*, p.205f, although Gamble believes that Marcion may be reworking some earlier, unspecified collection which had only gradually come together. See also Jonathan Z. Smith in *Drudgery Divine*, p.110, n.44, who discusses scholarly views on the question and supports the idea of a 2nd century corpus in reaction to Marcion. As early as 1934, Walter Bauer (*op.cit.*, p.221-2) not only regarded the first Pauline corpus as a product of Marcion, he believed it possible that Marcion himself had collected many of the letters of Paul from various Christian communities in his travels from Sinope to Rome. More radical theories about the Pauline letters include the idea that the Marcionites may have forged them all, or drastically recast more primitive documents going back to Paul, and that it is these Marcionite constructions, with later editing by the Roman Church, which Christianity has inherited.

120 [*page 271*] See C. Moule, "The Christology of Acts" in *Studies in Luke-Acts*, p.171. See also "Re-Reading Talbert's Luke" in *Cadbury, Knox and Talbert: American Contributions to the Study of Acts*, p.221.

121 [*page 271*] See Hans Conzelmann, "Luke's Place in the Development of Early Christianity" in *Studies in Luke-Acts*, p.308.

122 [*page 272*] E. R. Goodenough is one scholar among many who reject one or both items as entirely fictional. See *Studies in Luke-Acts*, p.56-7.

123 [*page 273*] One of the traditional puzzles in Acts, which seemed to point to some source document used by Luke, was the recurrence in certain passages (16:10-17; 20:5-15; 21:1-18; 27:1-28:16) of a narrative style which employed the first person plural, the so-called "we" passages. "We set sail from Philippi after the Passover season. . . ." "When we had parted from there and set sail, we made a straight run and sailed to Cos. . . ." Were these from a diary, perhaps by one of Paul's companions? If so, how did it survive the shipwreck recounted in the later chapters? Was Luke trying to heighten the sense of authenticity by putting things in the first person? If so, why only spottily?

The puzzle was solved when Vernon Robbins, following earlier hints by scholars such as H. J. Cadbury, made a splendidly simple observation (see *Perspectives in Luke-Acts*, p.215-229). All such passages in Acts begin with and mostly encompass sea voyages. This led Robbins to a survey of the depiction of sea voyages in ancient literature where he found that "One of the features of (sea voyage narratives in Greek and Roman literature) is the presence of first personal *plural* narration. Undoubtedly the impetus for this is sociological: on a sea voyage a person has accepted a setting with other people, and cooperation among all the members is essential for a successful voyage. Therefore, at the point where the voyage begins, the narration moves to first person plural." Luke is employing a common stylistic device of Hellenistic literature.

124 [*page 273*] E. R. Goodenough opens his article "The Perspective of Acts" (*Studies in Luke-Acts*, p.51) with this statement: "Many years ago Kirsopp Lake said to a class that if Acts is not a basically sound historical document we know nothing of the origins of Christianity." Modern study of Acts has all but reached that point. It has also reached a similar point in the study of the Gospels, and Lake's remark will have to be expanded.

125 [*page 274*] Ironically, one of the sources we *can* identify does not generate confidence in Acts' historical reliability. Paul's famous speech to the Greeks at the Areopagus in Athens (Acts 18:22-31) is closely modeled on a Hellenistic/Stoic type of speech about the true knowledge of God, to which Luke has tacked on a relevant Christian ending. (See Martin Dibelius as quoted by Philipp Vielhauer, "On the 'Paulinism' of Acts," in *Studies in Luke-Acts*, p.34.)

Chapter 25: Jesus in the Christian Apologists *(pages 275 to 292)*

126 [*page 280*] See H. G. Meecham, *The Epistle to Diognetus*, p.66.

Postscript *(pages 293 to 295)*

127 [*page 295*] For close to 2000 years, Christians have accepted that Jesus' sacrificial death on Calvary was a redeeming act which conferred salvation on the believer. Chapter 10 discussed the principle of paradigmatic relationships between divine figures and their experiences in the heavenly realm, and those of their human counterparts on earth. That homologic parallel guaranteed, through its pattern of "likeness," a beneficial effect on the believer, usually to do with the afterlife. But how did the sacrifice itself function? Why was the shedding of Jesus' "blood"—whether spiritual or material—regarded as efficacious? Why would it persuade or enable God to confer forgiveness of sin and eternal salvation?

The surprising fact is that nowhere in all the biblical writings is this question addressed. No writer of the Old or New Testaments makes an effort to explain it. Hebrews 9:22 states: "Under the law almost everything is purified with blood, and without the shedding of blood there is no forgiveness of sins" [RSV]. A few verses earlier, the author concludes (through a somewhat deficient argument) that to ratify a covenant with God, a death must occur involving the shedding of blood. However, no explanation accompanies these statements.

In Israelite religion, communion with God, especially in the matter of intercession, purification and propitiation, took place through the blood sacrifice of animals, millions of them over the centuries. Other ancient cultures were not far behind. The origins of this practice and the thinking behind it are lost in beginnings far older than recorded history. Although there were other, less sanguinary gifts people could offer to placate and intercede with the gods, blood sacrifice was at the center of the divine-human relationship. At some early time, the sacrifice of animals seems to have grown out of and supplanted the sacrifice of humans. The legend of Abraham and Isaac in which God demands the sacrifice of Abraham's son, then relents and instructs him to offer the lamb instead, is regarded as a mythical story symbolizing the changeover in the dimly remembered past from human to animal sacrifice. That human sacrifice survived in at least isolated cases in Israelite history is indicated by the traditions recorded in Judges 11:30-40 and 2 Kings 16:3 and 21:6. Such practices had their roots in those among the Canaanites, from which the Israelite population is now regarded as having been largely derived. (See Norman K. Gottwald, *The Hebrew Bible: A Socio-Literary Introduction*, p.215-16.)

Biblical and other records show that during the first half of the first millennium BCE, the Phoenicians (related to the Canaanites) living on the Mediterranean coast of Syria in cities like Sidon and Tyre still occasionally sacrificed children to their gods, and the Carthaginians (of Phoenician stock) continued to do so into Roman times.

It would not have occurred to the ancient mind that there was anything reprehensible about a god who required the blood sacrifice of animals to effect purification or expiate sin because it would have been looked upon as part of the natural workings of the universe, which probably even the god had no power to change. This may be why neither the Old Testament nor the New makes any attempt to explain how the sacrifice of Jesus brought about the expiation of sin. It may have been regarded as one of God's mysteries.

The practice of blood sacrifice, even of animals, is a primitive concept which no one in the 20th or 21st centuries would regard with anything but aversion, yet the principle itself still lies at the heart of the Christian religion and is still vigorously defended in that context. The focus on Jesus' love and willingness to make the ultimate sacrifice on behalf of humanity does not solve the problem.

NOTE: Should there be a future change in the Jesus Puzzle website address (as quoted in a few of the above Notes), the reader may enter <The Jesus Puzzle> using any Internet Search engine.

SELECTED BIBLIOGRAPHY

This is neither an exhaustive bibliography on the subjects dealt with in the book, nor a complete listing of all works consulted. It includes all works cited, except for a few very old publications. Abbreviations of Journals and Bible Commentaries: *ABC* - Anchor Bible Commentary. *ANRW* - Aufstieg und Niedergang der römischen Welt. *HTR* - Harvard Theological Review. *JBL* - Journal of Biblical Literature. *NCB* - New Century Bible. *Nov. Test.* - Novum Testamentum. *NTS* - New Testament Studies. (ET = English Translation.)

Achtemeier, Paul. "The Origin and Function of the Pre-Markan Miracle Catenae." JBL 91 (1972) p.471-491.

— "Toward the Isolation of Pre-Markan Miracle Catenae." JBL 89 (1970) p.265-291.

Anderson, Hugh. *The Gospel of Mark: A Commentary.* NCB, Oliphants, London, 1976.

Angus, S. *The Mystery Religions and Christianity.* John Murray, London, 1928.

Ante-Nicene Fathers. 10 vols. 1870-72. Reprinted Eerdmans, Grand Rapids, 1951-78

Barnard, L. W. *Justin Martyr, His Life and Thought.* Cambridge University Press, 1967.

— *Athenagoras.* Beauchesne, Paris, 1972.

Barr, James. *Biblical Words For Time.* SCM Press, London, 1969.

Barrett, C. K. *The Epistle to the Romans* (2nd ed.) A&C Black, London, 1991.

— *A Commentary on the First Epistle to the Corinthians.* Harper & Row, New York, 1968.

— *The Pastoral Epistles.* Clarendon, Oxford, 1963.

Bauer, Walter. *Orthodoxy and Heresy in Earliest Christianity* (first published 1934). ET: SCM, London, 1972.

— *A Greek-English Lexicon of the New Testament and Other Early Christian Literature.* (2nd ed.) Chicago, 1979.

Baylis, H. J. *Minucius Felix.* Society for Promoting Christian Knowledge, London, 1928.

Beardslee, William A. *Literary Criticism of the New Testament.* Guides to Biblical Scholarship, Fortress Press, Philadelphia, 1970.

Beare, F. W. *The First Epistle of Peter.* Blackwell, Oxford, 1970.

— *The Gospel According to Matthew: Commentary.* Blackwell, Oxford, 1981.

Bellinzoni, A. F. *The Sayings of Jesus in the Writings of Justin Martyr.* Brill, Leiden, 1967.

Benko, Stephen. "Pagan Criticism of Christianity During the First Two Centuries A.D." ANRW II.23, p.1055-1118.

Blackman, E. C. *Marcion and His Influence.* SPCK, London, 1948.

Boman, Thorlief. *Hebrew Thought Compared with Greek.* SCM Press, London, 1960.

Bornkamm, Gunther. *Paul.* Harper & Row, New York, 1970.

Brandon, S. G. F. *The Fall of Jerusalem and the Christian Church.* SPCK, London, 1957.

— *History, Time and Deity.* Manchester University Press, 1965.

— *The Trial of Jesus of Nazareth.* B. T. Batsford, London, 1968.

Brown, Raymond E. *The Epistles of John* (ABC vol.30). Doubleday, Garden City, NY, 1982.

— *The Death of the Messiah.* Doubleday, Garden City, New York, 1994.

Buchanan, G. *To the Hebrews* (ABC vol.36). Doubleday, Garden City, NY, 1972.

Bultmann, Rudolf. *The History of the Synoptic Tradition.* ET: Harper & Row, New York, 1963.

Burkert, Walter. *Ancient Mystery Cults.* Harvard University Press, 1987.

Cameron, Ron. *The Sayings Tradition in the Apocryphon of James.* Fortress Press, Philadelphia, 1984.

Campbell, Joseph. *The Masks of God: Occidental Mythology.* Penguin Books, 1976.

Carr, Wesley. "The Rulers of This Age: 1 Corinthians 2:6-8." NTS 23 (1977) p.20-35.

Catchpole, David. "The Beginning of Q: A Proposal." NTS 38 (1992) p.205-221.

Chadwick, Henry, ed. and trans. *Contra Celsum.* Cambridge Univ. Press, 1980.

Charlesworth, James H., ed. *The Old Testament Pseudepigrapha* (2 vols.) Doubleday, Garden City, NY, 1983-1985.

— *The Odes of Solomon*, the Syriac texts with translation and notes. Scholars Press, Chico, Calif., 1977.

Collins, John J. *Between Athens and Jerusalem: Jewish Identity in the Hellenistic Diaspora.* Crossroad, New York, 1983.

— *Daniel. With an Introduction to Apocalyptic Literature.* Eerdmans, Grand Rapids, 1984.

— *The Apocalyptic Imagination.* Crossroad, New York, 1982.

Couchoud, Paul-Louis. *The Creation of Christ* (*Le Mystère de Jésus*). F. Rieder, Paris, 1924.

Cross, F. L. *The Early Christian Fathers.* Duckworth, London, 1961.

Crossan, John Dominic. *The Historical Jesus: The Life of a Mediterranean Jewish Peasant.* HarperSanFrancisco, 1991.

— *The Birth of Christianity. Discovering what happened in the years immediately after the execution of Jesus,* HarperSanFrancisco, 1998.

— *The Cross That Spoke: The Origins of the Passion Narrative.* Harper & Row, San Francisco, 1988.

— *Who Killed Jesus? Exposing the Roots of Anti-Semitism in the Gospel Story of the Death of Jesus.* HarperSanFrancisco, 1995.

Cullmann, Oscar. *Christ and Time: The Primitive Christian Conception of Time and History* (rev. ed.) Westminster Press, Philadelphia, 1964.

Dart, John. *The Jesus of Heresy and History: The Discovery and Meaning of the Nag Hammadi Gnostic Library.* Harper & Row, San Francisco, 1988.

Davies, Stevan L. *The Gospel of Thomas and Christian Wisdom.* Seabury Press, New York, 1983.

Dillon, John. *The Middle Platonists: 80 BC to AD 220.* Cornell University Press, Ithaca, NY, 1977.

Downing, F. G. "Cynics and Christians." NTS 30 (1984) p.584-593.

Dunn, J. G. *The Parting of the Ways Between Christianity and Judaism.* Trinity Press, Philadelphia, 1991.

— *The Evidence for Jesus.* SCM Press, London, 1985.

Edwards, Richard A. *A Theology of Q: Eschatology, Prophecy and Wisdom.* Fortress Press, Philadelphia, 1976.

Ehrman, B. D. *The Orthodox Corruption of Scripture: The Effect of Early Christological Controversies on the Text of the New Testament.* Oxford University Press, 1993.

Eisenman, Robert. *James, the Brother of Jesus.* Viking, New York, 1997.

Eliade, Mircea. *A History of Religious Ideas* (3 vols.) Univ. of Chicago Press, 1978.

— *Birth and Rebirth.* Harper, New York, 1958.

— *Myth and Reality.* G. Allen & Unwin, London, 1964

— *Myth of the Eternal Return* (*Cosmos and History*). Princeton University Press, 1978.

Ellingworth, Paul. *Epistle to the Hebrews.* Eerdmans, Grand Rapids, Mich., 1993.

Epp, E. J. and G. W. MacRae, ed. *The New Testament and Its Modern Interpreters.* Fortress Press, Philadelphia, 1989.

Esler, Philip F. *Community and Gospel in Luke-Acts.* Cambridge University Press, 1987.

Eusebius. *A History of the Church from Christ to Constantine.* Trans. G. A. Williamson, Augsberg, Minneapolis, 1965.

Filoramo, G. *A History of Gnosticism.* Blackwell, Oxford, 1990.

Frazer, Sir James George. *The Golden Bough. A Study in Magic and Religion* (Abridged ed.) MacMillan, New York, 1951.

Fredriksen, Paula. *From Jesus to Christ: The Origins of the New Testament Images of Jesus.* Yale University Press, 1988.

Freke, Timothy and Peter Gandy. *The Jesus Mysteries. Was the 'Original Jesus' a Pagan God?* Thorsons, London, 1999.

Friedman, R. E. *Who Wrote the Bible?* Summit Books, New York, 1987.

Funk, Robert. *Honest to Jesus.* Polebridge Press, Sonoma, Calif., 1996.

— and Roy Hoover. *The Five Gospels. The Search for the Authentic Words of Jesus,* HarperSanFrancisco, 1997.

— and the Jesus Seminar. *The Acts of Jesus. The Search for the Authentic Deeds of Jesus,* HarperSanFrancisco, 1998.

Furnish, V. P. *Jesus According to Paul.* Cambridge University Press, 1993.

Gager, John G. *Kingdom and Community: The Social World of Early Christianity.* Prentice-Hall, Englewood Cliffs, N.J., 1975.

Goodenough, E. R. *By Light, Light. The Mystic Gospel of Hellenistic Judaism.* Philo Press, Amsterdam, 1969 (reprint of 1935 edition).

— *An Introduction to Philo Judaeus* (2nd ed.) Blackwell, Oxford, 1962.

Gottwald, Norman K. *The Hebrew Bible: A Socio-Literary Introduction.* Fortress Press, Philadelphia, 1985.

Grant, Frederick C. *Hellenistic Religions: The Age of Syncretism.* Liberal Arts Press, New York, 1953.

Grant, R. M., ed. *The Apostolic Fathers* (6 vols.) T. Nelson, New York, 1964-1968.

— *Theophilus of Antioch.* Clarendon Press, Oxford, 1970.

Grayston, Kenneth. *The Johannine Epistles.* Eerdmans, Grand Rapids, 1984.

Guignebert, Charles. *Jesus.* University Books, New York, 1956.

Haenchen, Ernst. *The Acts of the Apostles: A Commentary.* Westminster, Philadelphia, 1971.

Hamerton-Kelly, R. G. *Pre-Existence, Wisdom and the Son of Man: A Study of the Idea of Pre-Existence in the New Testament,* Cambridge, 1973.

Harrison, P. N. *Polycarp's Two Epistles,* Cambridge University Press, 1936.

Hedrick, Charles. *The Apocalypse of Adam.* Scholars Press, Chico, Calif., 1980.

Hennecke, E.; W. Schneemelcher, ed. *New Testament Apocrypha* (2 vols.) ET: Westminster Press, Philadelphia, 1963.

Herford, R. Travers. *Christianity in Talmud and Midrash.* Reference Book Publishers, Clifton, N.J., 1966 [first published London, 1903].

Héring, Jean. *Hebrews.* Epworth Press, London, 1970.

Hooker, Morna. "Philippians 2:6-11" in *Jesus und Paulus,* Vandenhoeck & Ruprecht, 1975, p.151-164.

Houlden, J. L. *The Pastoral Epistles,* Penguin Books, 1976.

— *A Commentary on the Johannine Epistles,* A&C Black, 1973.

Horsley, Richard A. *Sociology and the Jesus Movement.* Crossroad, New York, 1989.

Hughes, Graham. *Hebrews and Hermeneutics.* Cambridge University Press, 1979.

Jacobson, Arland. *The First Gospel: An Introduction to Q.* Polebridge Press, Calif., 1992.

— "The History of the Composition of the Sayings Source Q." SBL Seminar Papers, 1987.

Jonas, Hans. *The Gnostic Religion* (3rd ed.) Beacon Press, Boston, 1963.

Josephus. *Works.* Loeb Classical Library (10 vols.) 1926-65.

— *Complete Works.* trans. W. Whiston, Kregel, Grand Rapids, 1973.

Julian (the "Apostate"). *Orations 4 and 5* in *The Works of the Emperor Julian.* Loeb Classical Library (Greek & English), Harvard University Press, Cambridge, Mass., 1980.

Keck, Leander E., ed. *Studies in Luke-Acts.* Abingdon Press, Nashville, 1968.

Kee, Howard C. *Community of the New Age. Studies in Mark's Gospel.* Westminster Press, Philadelphia, 1977.

— "The Function of Scriptural Allusions in Mark 11-16." in *Jesus und Paulus,* Vandenhoeck & Ruprecht, 1975, p.165-188.

Kelber, W. H., ed. *The Passion in Mark: Studies on Mark 14-16.* Fortress Press, Philadelphia, 1976.

— *The Oral and the Written Gospel.* Fortress Press, Philadelphia, 1983.

Kelly, J. N. D. *A Commentary on the Epistles of Peter and Jude.* A&C Black, London, 1969.

— *A Commentary on the Pastoral Epistles,* A&C Black, London, 1963.

Klausner, J. *Jesus of Nazareth.* George Allen & Unwin, London, 1947.

Kloppenborg, John S. *The Formation of Q: Trajectories in Ancient Wisdom Collections.* Fortress Press, Philadelphia, 1987.

— *Q Parallels: Synopsis, Critical Notes, and Concordance.* Polebridge Press, Sonoma, Calif., 1988.

— "The Sayings Gospel Q and the Quest of the Historical Jesus." HTR 89 (1996), p.307-344.

Knox, John. *Marcion and the New Testament.* Univ. of Chicago Press, 1942.

Koester, Helmut. *Introduction to the New Testament* (Vol.1: *History, Culture and Religion of the Hellenistic Age.* Vol.2: *History and Literature of Early Christianity*). Fortress Press, Philadelphia, 1982.

— *Ancient Christian Gospels: Their History and Development.* Trinity Press, Philadelphia, 1990.

— *Synoptische Überlieferung bei den Apostolischen Vätern.* Akademie, Berlin, 1957

— "Apocryphal and Canonical Gospels." HTR 73 (1980), p.105-130.

— "History and Development of Mark's Gospel" in *Colloquy on New Testament Studies: A Time for Reappraisal and Fresh Approaches,* Bruce Corley ed., 1983, p.35-57.

Lake, Kirsopp, trans. *The Apostolic Fathers* (2 vols.) Loeb Classical Library (Greek & English). 1912-13.

Lambrecht, J. "John the Baptist and Jesus in Mark 1:1-15: Marcan Redaction of Q." NTS 38 (1992) p.357-384.

Laws, Sophie. *A Commentary on the Epistle of James.* Harper & Row, San Francisco, 1980.

Layton, Bentley. *The Gnostic Scriptures.* Doubleday, New York, 1987.

Lease, Gary. "Mithraism and Christianity." ANRW II.23.2, p.1306-1332.

Lieu, Judith. *The Theology of the Johannine Epistles.* Cambridge University Press, 1991.

Long, A. A. *Hellenistic Philosophy.* Duckworth, London, 1977.

Lührmann, D. "The Gospel of Mark and the Sayings Collection Q." JBL 108/1 (1989) p.51-71.

Maccoby, Hyam. *Paul and Hellenism.* Trinity Press Int'l, Philadelphia, 1991.

Mack, Burton. *A Myth of Innocence: Mark and Christian Origins.* Fortress Press, Philadelphia, 1988.

— *The Lost Gospel: Q and Christian Origins.* HarperSanFrancisco, 1993.

— *Who Wrote the New Testament? The Making of the Christian Myth.* HarperSanFrancisco, 1995.

McKnight, Edgar V. *What Is Form Criticism?* (Guides to Biblical Scholarship), Fortress Press, Philadelphia, 1969.

Meecham, H. G., *The Epistle to Diognetus.* Manchester Univ. Press, 1949.

Meeks, Wayne. *The First Urban Christians. The Social World of the Apostle Paul.* Yale University Press, 1983.

— "The Man From Heaven in Johannine Sectarianism." JBL 91, p.44-72.

Metzger, Bruce. *The Canon of the New Testament: Its Origin, Development and Significance*, Oxford University Press, 1987.

Montefiore, Hugh. *A Commentary on the Epistle to the Hebrews*, Harper & Row, 1964.

Nickelsburg, George. *Jewish Literature Between the Bible and the Mishnah.* SCM, London, 1981.

— *Resurrection, Immortality and Eternal Life in Intertestamental Judaism.* Harvard University Press, 1972.

— "The Genre and Function of the Markan Passion Narrative." HTR 73 (1980), p.153-184.

Nock, A. D., ed. and transl. *Concerning Gods and the Universe* (*Sallustius, Neoplatonist*). Cambridge University Press, 1926.

O'Neill, J. C. *The Puzzle of 1 John.* SPCK, London, 1966.

— *The Theology of Acts in its Historical Setting.* SPCK, London, 1970.

Orlinsky, H. M. "The So-Called Servant of the Lord in Second Isaiah" in *Studies in the Second Part of the Book of Isaiah*, Brill, Leiden, 1967.

Overman, J. A. *Matthew's Gospel and Formative Judaism.* Fortress Press, Philadelphia, 1970.

Pagels, Elaine. *The Gnostic Gospels.* Random House, New York, 1979.

— *The Gnostic Paul: Gnostic Exegesis of the Pauline Letters.* Fortress Press, Philadelphia, 1976.

Patterson, Stephen J. *The Gospel of Thomas and Jesus.* Polebridge Press, Sonoma, Calif., 1993.

Pearson, B. A. ed. *The Future of Early Christianity: Essays in Honor of Helmut Koester.* Fortress Press, Minneapolis, 1991.

— "1 Thessalonians 2:13-16: A Deutero-Pauline Interpolation." HTR 64 (1971), p.79-94.

Perrin, Norman, and Dennis C. Duling. *The New Testament: An Introduction* (2nd ed.) Harcourt Brace Jovanovich, New York, 1982.

— *What Is Redaction Criticism?* (Guides to Biblical Scholarship). Fortress Press, Philadelphia, 1969.

Petersen, Norman R. *Literary Criticism for New Testament Critics.* (Guides to Biblical Scholarship). Fortress Press, Philadelphia, 1978.

Plato. *Timaeus and Critias.* Penguin Classics, 1965.

Plutarch. *Isis and Osiris. (Moralia,* vol. 5) Loeb Classical Library, 1993.

Randall, J. H. *Hellenistic Ways of Deliverance and the Making of the Christian Synthesis.* Columbia University Press, New York, 1970.

Ridderbos, Herman. *Paul and Jesus.* Presbyterian and Reformed Publishing Co., Philadelphia, 1957.

Ringgren, Helmer. *Word and Wisdom: Studies in the Hypostatization of Divine Qualities and Functions in the Ancient Near East,* 1949.

Robertson, Archibald. *Jesus: Myth or History?* (Thinker's Library No. 110). Watts, London, 1949.

Robinson, James M., ed. *The Nag Hammadi Library in English.* HarperSanFrancisco, 1990.

— and Helmut Koester. *Trajectories Through Early Christianity.* Fortress Press, Philadelphia, 1968.

Rudolph, Kurt. *Gnosis. The Nature and History of Gnosticism.* Harper & Row, San Francisco, 1984.

Sanders, E. P. *The Historical Figure of Jesus.* Allen Lane, London, 1993.

Sanders, Jack T. *The New Testament Christological Hymns.* Cambridge University Press, London, 1971.

Sandmel, Samuel. *Philo of Alexandria: An Introduction.* Oxford University Press, 1979.

Schoedel, William R. *Ignatius of Antioch.* Fortress Press, Philadelphia, 1985.

Schoeps, Hans-Joachim. *Paul: The Theology of the Apostle in the Light of Jewish Religious History.* Lutterworth, London, 1959.

— *Jewish Christianity.* Fortress Press, Philadelphia, 1964.

Scroggs, Robin. "The Earliest Christian Communities as Sectarian Movement" in *Christianity, Judaism, and other Graeco-Roman Cults,* II, ed. J. Neusner, Brill, Leiden, 1975.

Seeley, David. "Jesus' Death in Q." NTS 38 (1992) p.222-234.

Smith, D. Moody. *Johannine Christianity.* University of South Carolina Press, Columbia, SC, 1984.

Smith, Jonathan Z. *Drudgery Divine. On the Comparison of Early Christianities and the Religions of Late Antiquity.* SOAS, London, 1990.

Staniforth, Maxwell, trans. *Early Christian Writings,* Penguin Classics, 1968.

Stanton, Graham N. *A Gospel for a New People. Studies in Matthew.* Westminster John Knox Press, Louisville, Ky, 1992.

— *Gospel Truth? New Light on Jesus and the Gospels.* Harper Collins, London, 1995.

— *The Gospels and Jesus.* Oxford University Press, 1989.

Stein, Robert H. *The Synoptic Problem: An Introduction.* Baker Book House, Grand Rapids, 1984.

Sweet, John. *Revelation.* SCM Press, London, 1979.

Suetonius. *Lives of the Caesars.* Loeb Classical Library (2 vols.), 1924.

Tacitus. *Annals* and *History.* Loeb Classical Library (2 vols.), 1932.

Talbert, C. H. *The Myth of a Descending-Ascending Redeemer in Antiquity.* NTS 22 (1976), p.418-440.

— ed. *Perspectives on Luke-Acts.* T & T Clark, Edinburgh, 1978.

— ed. *New Perspectives on Luke-Acts.* Crossroad, New York, 1984.

The Septuagint with Apocrypha (Greek & English), trans. L. Brenton. Zondevan, Grand Rapids, Mich., originally published London, 1851.

The Theological Dictionary of the New Testament. G. Kittel and G. Friedrich, eds. (10 vols.) Eerdmans, Grand Rapids, 1964-1976.

Thompson, William Irwin. *The Time Falling Bodies Take to Light: Mythology, Sexuality, and the Origins of Culture.* St. Martin's Press, New York, 1981.

Ulansey, David. *The Origins of the Mithraic Mysteries.* Oxford University Press, 1989.

Vermes, Geza. *The Dead Sea Scrolls in English.* Penguin, London, 1987.

Wagner, Gunter. *Pauline Baptism and the Pagan Mysteries.* Loiver & Boyd, Edinburgh, 1967.

Watson, Francis. *Paul, Judaism and the Gentiles.* Cambridge University Press, 1986.

Wedderburn, A. J. M. "Philo's 'Heavenly Man'." Nov. Test., 1973.

Wells, G. A. *The Jesus of the Early Christians.* Pemberton, London, 1971.

— *The Historical Evidence for Jesus.* Prometheus Books, Buffalo, 1982.

— *Did Jesus Exist?* Pemberton, London, 1986.

— *Who Was Jesus? A Critique of the New Testament Record.* Open Court, La Salle, 1989.

— *The Jesus Legend.* Open Court, Chicago, 1996.

— *The Jesus Myth.* Open Court, Chicago, 1999.

Williamson, Ronald. *Jews in the Hellenistic World: Philo.* Cambridge Univ. Press, 1989.

Winston, David. *The Wisdom of Solomon.* Doubleday, Garden City, NY, 1979.

Wright, N. T. *The New Testament and the People of God.* SPCK, London, 1992.

— *Jesus and the Victory of God.* SPCK, London, 1996.

Young, Frances M. *Sacrifice and the Death of Christ.* SPCK, London, 1975.

[Bibliographies rarely include works of fiction, but here I want to recommend a unique project in historical fiction by the late American writer Vardis Fisher, known as the Testament of Man. This series of eleven novels, published from 1943 to 1958, spans two million years, from the dawn of human intelligence to the Christian Middle Ages. It follows the development of humanity's religious ideas, with particular focus, in the later novels, on Judaeo-Christian evolution. No. 8, *Jesus Came Again: A Parable*, and No. 9, *A Goat For Azazel*, address the question of Jesus and Christian origins. Fisher based his work on the best and most progressive scholarship of his day, meeting condemnation by critics and Church for his uncompromising portrayal of Jewish and Christian ideas.]

INDEX

OF SUBJECTS, AUTHORS, AND BIBLICAL PASSAGES

For biblical passages, only cases of significant mention are included.
Numerals are ignored in alphabetical listing of documents.
[n. = Note: see pages 327 to 362]

applied to, 19, n.10; teachings not attributed to, 28; baptism of missing, 58-9; named in Q?, 181, 186; baptism in Mark, 227; prophet in Mark, 230-1; miracle working in Mark, 234-8; in Acts, 273; language of, n.24; view of "genuine" Jesus unrealistic, n.28; not overly divine in Mark, n.80; Jesus' blood sacrifice, n.127

Jesus Seminar, 26, 27, 149, 294-5, n.28; defined, n.15

Jewish War(s), 47, 179, 194, 199, 205, 297-8, n.87

Jews: not responsible for Jesus' death, 15, 68-70, 263-4; dietary laws, 28; demonized, 65, 108; in empire, 200; response to Jesus, n.41

John, Gospel of (Jn.), 130-2, 269
Prologue, 90, 269, 277, 278, 280
Johannine community, 130f, 193
dependent on Synoptics, 130-2, 243-4
strata in, 131
crucifixion in, 131-2, 243
no Gethsemane, 132, 252
no Eucharist, 132
compared to Odes, 133

1 John (1 Jn.), 11, 13, 67, 269
dating, 13
strata in, 132, n.62
earlier than Gospel, 132, n.62
1:1-5 : 132-3
3:16 : 67
4:1 : 43, 307

2 John (2 Jn.), 13, 307
3 John (3 Jn.), 13
John the Baptist, 56, 58-9, 146, 155, 166-8, 171-3, 177-8, 179-80, 186-7; in Josephus, 215, n.89; in Mark, 225-7
Joseph (father of Jesus), 56, 305
Joseph of Arimathea, 68, 257

Josephus, Flavius, 198, 205-222, n.86; biography, 205; *Antiquities* 18 (Testimonium Flavianum), 206-215; placement of Testimonium, n.89; on the Q Jesus, 198, 214-15; on John the Baptist, 59, 215, n.89; *Antiquities* 20, 216-221; on the subject of Messiah, 210, 218; on the reason for fall of Jerusalem, 219-21, n.90

Judas, 65, 69, 250, 252, n.20
Judas the Galilean, 220
Jude, 58
Jude, epistle of (Jd.), 13, 58, 269
Julian the Apostate (emperor / philosopher, 332-363), 104, 313
Julius Africanus (Christian writer, c160-c240), 203
Justin Martyr (apologist, c100-c165), 208, 209, 259, 270, 276, 277, 281, 282, 284-5, n.41, n.107, n.112
Justus of Tiberias (historian, 1st c.), 204
Juvenal (Roman satirist, d. 138), 200

Kee, H. C., 315
Kelber, Werner, n.16
Kelly, J. N. D., 300, n.27
Kingdom movement (in Galilee), 4, 141-198; concept among Jews, 48; in parables, Gospel, 231-2
1 & 2 Kings
miracles of Elijah and Elisha, 236
Kleist, J., n.115
Kloppenborg, John, 147, 165, 170, n.93
Knibb, Michael, 107, 308-9
Knox, John, 269, 270, n.118
Koester, Helmut, 27, 152, 262, 299, 317, 320, 324, n.27, n.72, n.73, n.109